The Secret Circuit

The Secret Circuit

The Little-Known Court Where the Rules of the Information Age Unfold

Bruce D. Abramson

ROWMAN & LITTLEFIELD PUBLISHERS, INC.
Lanham • Boulder • New York • Toronto • Plymouth, UK

ROWMAN & LITTLEFIELD PUBLISHERS, INC.

Published in the United States of America
by Rowman & Littlefield Publishers, Inc.
A wholly owned subsidiary of The Rowman & Littlefield Publishing Group, Inc.
4501 Forbes Boulevard, Suite 200, Lanham, Maryland 20706
www.rowmanlittlefield.com

Estover Road
Plymouth PL6 7PY
United Kingdom

British Library Cataloguing in Publication Information Available

Library of Congress Cataloging-in-Publication Data

Abramson, Bruce D., 1963–
   The secret circuit : the little-known court where the rules of the
information age unfold / Bruce D. Abramson.
      p. cm.
   Includes bibliographical references and index.
   ISBN-13: 978-0-7425-5280-7 (cloth : alk. paper)
   ISBN-10: 0-7425-5280-2 (cloth : alk. paper)
   ISBN-13: 978-0-7425-5281-4 (pbk. : alk. paper)
   ISBN-10: 0-7425-5281-0 (pbk. : alk. paper)
   1. Appellate courts—United States. I. Title.
   [DNLM: 1. United States. Court of Appeals (Federal Circuit)]
   KF8751.A97 2007
   347.73'24—dc22   2007012293

Printed in the United States of America

⊗™ The paper used in this publication meets the minimum requirements of
American National Standard for Information Sciences—Permanence of Paper
for Printed Library Materials, ANSI/NISO Z39.48-1992.

To Judge Arthur J. Gajarsa—for sharing the privilege of public service.
And to Cindy, Micah, and Jamaica—for making it fun.

Contents

Contents

Preface

In the spring of 2001, I dropped a few judicial clerkship applications in the mail. A few days later, I received a call from Judge Arthur Gajarsa's chambers, over at the Federal Circuit. We scheduled an interview; we met; we hit it off; he offered me a job; I accepted. I left his chambers wondering what I had done. On the basis of a casual half-hour meeting, I had agreed to: block out a year of my life starting *twenty-five months in the future*; spend that year in a small office with four other people, at least two of whom I had never met; leave a professional environment where I enjoyed seniority and autonomy to be a low man on a short totem pole; have a real boss for the first time in my life; take a significant pay cut; and probably have to wear a tie every day. I shrugged it off. Anything for a good educational experience.

I arrived at the court in September 2003. Like anyone entering a new environment, I arrived with beliefs, views, and prior experiences that would color my year. I knew that our federal courts are oddly apolitical political institutions. No one gets appointed to the bench without a history of political involvement, and few make it without a history of partisan political involvement. Yet, we *require* our judges to check their partisan preferences at the courthouse steps. From the moment that they don their black robes, we expect them to forget their lifetimes of partisan involvement, the affinity and loyalty that they rightly feel toward the politicians responsible for their nominations, and often their justified antipathy for those who turned their confirmation hearings into lengthy, painful, and increasingly slanderous experiences.

Fortunately, we don't ask our judges to relinquish the beliefs, values, and philosophies that led them to favor one political faction over another. That distinction sat well with me. I'd lived in Washington long enough to appreciate the difference between partisanship and wonkery—and to know that I'm a very bad partisan, but quite an able wonk. Like the judges themselves, I arrived at the court with philosophical beliefs, a well-defined experience base, a concept of the court's job, and a desire to serve the public. I expected that the cases on which I would have the privilege to work would serve as illustrative, if not representative, data capable of teaching me about this unique institution's role in the emerging global information economy.

By way of full disclosure, the philosophical approach with which I arrived is a variant of classical liberalism. I believe that, by-and-large, the world will reach its greatest potential if free people: are empowered to make free, informed, meaningful decisions; enjoy or suffer the consequences of those decisions; and learn from those consequences how to make better decisions in the future. Within that broad framework, I also recognize that theories rarely suffice to capture the world's complexities. On occasion, I draw lessons from two other philosophies: socialism and conservatism.

Socialism offers two useful lessons. First, safety nets reduce some of the extreme risks that might otherwise skew decision-making; under the right circumstances, social risk insurance can expand the meaningfulness of decision-making, and thus enhance liberal societies. Second, sometimes government planners get things right. The beauty of free markets is that they are robust, not that they are clean. In a free market, experience replaces failure with success; the market mechanism is autocorrective. At times, markets seem unlikely to stabilize in an autocorrected equilibrium state rapidly enough to meet some societal need. Government officials typically forward a social plan or program to fill the gap. When their plans are flawed, the results can be disastrous, but not all plans are flawed. Some are appropriate responses to prevailing market conditions. Even such successes, however, tend to become rigid government programs with built-in constituencies incapable of keeping up with changing market conditions. The lesson for liberal market advocates is that successful planned programs must be reformed into market-oriented programs, not merely opposed or dismantled.

The critical lesson of conservatism is even more fundamental: institutions matter. In any society, conservatives are those most protective of their defining institutions. This basic conservative tendency cuts from Chinese conservatives championing the Communist Party's exclusive grip on political power through Iranian conservatives extolling the Supreme Leader and the mullacracy. The United States is fortunate that its own conservatives rally behind liberal institutions: the U.S. Constitution and the government that it created. Every institution has a predefined set of powers and of responsibilities. It also has a set of competencies. The greatest lesson that conservatism can teach anyone, regardless of philosophical orientation, is that inattention to proper institutional boundaries risks undermining society.

This philosophical posture—classical liberalism tempered by the lessons of socialism and conservatism—defined my outlook as I approached the court. As a good researcher, I noted my own biases and figured that I would reach conclusions only after I had seen some data. I settled in to see what a year as a Federal Circuit law clerk would teach me about this institution, its work, and its relationship to the general trends shaping the early information age.

As luck would have it, the education and the experience made it worthwhile. By the time the year was out, I agreed with then Chief Judge H. Robert Mayer: "This is a special court . . . because of the people who make it work. . . . The court is a congenial place to work." Mayer penned those words in 2002, for the foreword to a book celebrating the Federal Circuit's twentieth birthday. He continued: "Some have said this court is a permanent experiment. That of course is a contradiction in terms. From the perspective of one who has watched its evolution from an idea, not intuitively appealing to one of traditional bent, to maturity at twenty years and counting, I can only marvel at what has transpired."[1] Having spent a year at the court and a good deal longer contemplating its jurisprudence, I also agree with those who consider it to be a permanent experiment, oxymoronic or not. As with any good experiment though, it's not a bad idea to review interim data. *The Secret Circuit* collects and analyzes such data.

With those thoughts in mind, I would like to thank those who helped to make my year worthwhile, along with those who helped me organize my collected data and analyses into this book. I would never have had the opportunity to see the court from the inside were it not for Judge Arthur Gajarsa. His able assistant Cindy Proctor helped usher me through my year as a government employee with steady wit and cheer. My co-clerks, Jamaica Potts Szeliga and Micah Howe, provided the camaraderie, the intellectual support, and the lively banter necessary to turn a workplace into a home; several interns, Greg Dolin, John Heuton, James Wallace, Jacob Paul, and Andrew Chew, helped them with that most challenging of all tasks. Finally, all of the other folks whose time at the Federal Circuit overlapped with my own—the other judges, their law clerks, the court's legal and administrative staff, and the security personnel who greeted me every morning for a year—all helped to make this work possible.

I also had some help turning my data collection and analysis exercise into this book. My agent, Susan Schulman, helped me find Rowman &

Littlefield, where Chris Anazalone provided editorial advice and support. Several indulgent friends and family members provided feedback on my first draft: Ted Abramson, Trudy Abramson, Arthur Gajarsa, Seth Kaplan, Jamaica Szeliga, Sondra Tosky, and Amalie Weber all helped me improve the book. Needless to say, the boilerplate disclaimer applies: The views and opinions expressed herein are my own. Please do not attribute any of them to any past, present, or future employers, collaborators, colleagues, friends, relatives, lovers, or acquaintances—though on a good day, I humor myself by believing that some of the people I know agree with some of my opinions (sometimes).

Judges of the United States Court of Appeals for the Federal Circuit

CHIEF JUDGES

Howard T. Markey	1982–1990
Helen Wilson Nies	1990–1994
Glenn L. Archer Jr.	1994–1997
Haldane Robert Mayer	1997–2004
Paul R. Michel	2004–

JUDGES

Giles Sutherland Rich	1982–1999
Oscar Hirsh Davis	1982–1988
Philip Nichols Jr.	1982–1983; senior judge, 1983–1990
Phillip Benjamin Baldwin	1982–1986; senior judge, 1986–1991
Shiro Kashiwa	1982–1986
Howard T. Markey	1982–1991
Marion Tinsley Bennett	1982–1986; senior judge, 1986–1997
Jack Richard Miller	1982–1985; senior judge, 1985–1994
Daniel M. Friedman	1982–1989; senior judge, 1989–
Edward Samuel Smith	1982–1999; senior judge, 1989–2001
Helen Wilson Nies	1982–1995; senior judge, 1995–1996
Don Nelson Laramore	senior judge, 1982–1989
James Lindsay Almond Jr.	senior judge, 1982–1986
Byron G. Skelton	senior judge, 1982–2004

Wilson Cowen	senior judge, 1982–1997
Pauline Newman	1984–
Jean Galloway Bissell	1984–1990
Glenn L. Archer Jr.	1985–1997; senior judge, 1997–
Haldane Robert Mayer	1987–
Paul R. Michel	1988–
S. Jay Plager	1989–2000; senior judge, 2000–
Alan D. Lourie	1990–
Raymond C. Clevenger III	1990–2006; senior judge, 2006–
Randall R. Rader	1990–
Alvin A. Schall	1992–
William C. Bryson	1994–
Arthur J. Gajarsa	1997–
Richard Linn	2000–
Timothy B. Dyk	2000–
Sharon Prost	2001–
Kimberly Moore	2006–

Prologue

We are at the dawn of the global information age, but industrial-age infrastructures and institutions still dominate our world. We entered the twenty-first century with ingrained notions of education, society, community, business, family, government, politics, law, faith, religion, and life in general that rest upon structures developed to accommodate industrialization. Vacations, school years, suburbs, and nation-states are but a few of the concepts so basic to our existence that we can hardly imagine a world without them. Yet, none existed in anything like their current form more than a few centuries ago. All are relatively recent innovations in the long history of our species. And some may soon wither away or undergo radical transformation.

A single sentence both defines the information age and reveals how it differs from all earlier epochs: *Information is abundant, easy to collect and manipulate, and inexpensive to share.* Never before has any individual, no matter how erudite, had as ready access to as much information about as many topics as does the least connected member of the information age. We, a thinking species mired from time immemorial in a world of information scarcity, have suddenly found ourselves thrust into a world of information abundance. That simple twist changes *everything.* Every aspect of life that involves the collection, combination, or communication of information—in short, every aspect of life—must change to accommodate our new reality. Few can question the inevitability of this conclusion. The critical questions concern how things will change and how we will manage the transition.

The scope of such questions is staggering—and intimidating. How can we study such an epochal transformation? Big pictures tend to blur, small ones to induce myopia. Nevertheless, there are places where critical issues rise to the fore, institutions perched precariously upon transformational fault lines, where industrial-age sensibilities collide daily with information-age needs. From an economic perspective, three seismic regions are likely to dominate the transition: technological advancement, the role of the government as an economic actor, and international economic relations. A single little-known institution, the United States Court of Appeals for the Federal Circuit, sits atop the fault lines running through all three of those regions. An exploration of the relationship between the policy objectives of intelligent transition planning and the Federal Circuit's practical rulings can illuminate the progress of our transition.

This institutional perspective provides a rare glimpse of the transition's greatest challenges: disputes between people trying to apply the rules governing innovation and globalization as the information age transforms their environments. From the perspective of public policy, the proper resolution of these disputes lies in the overall goal of orienting the American economy in a direction appropriate for the information age. From a narrow legal perspective, the proper resolution of these disputes lies in a legal scheme deemed appropriate for an advanced industrial economy. When the two goals are in tension, they demonstrate the pain of transformation—a pain that all other aspects of life will encounter, though likely in less transparent settings.

The transition to the information age will necessarily begin with the institutions and the rules that guided us through the industrial age. As circumstances change, institutions and rules will adapt, though not necessarily evenly. At times, legacy rules will impede appropriate progress. Some players who fared particularly well under the old system will encourage us to keep these legacies in place; after all, new rules could lead to an uncertain and unsettling future. At other times, we will devise new rules to impel ourselves forward. But forward motion always risks leaving some folks behind, motivating them to fight progress, and motivating society at large to consider assisting them as they adjust to change. The wisdom that American society applies to these inherent conflicts will determine how successfully we adapt to the future. The Federal Circuit stands at the epicenter of this conflict. An analysis of its rulings will elucidate these conflicts, their resolutions, and the implications to the success of our transition.

These implications define the *raison d'être* of our inquiry. The nature of the challenge is hard to miss. Most people understand that our institutions and rules will have to keep pace with the changing world around us. Most people can see parts of the world changing and intuit that other parts will either accommodate the changes or fade into irrelevance. Most people see the growing importance of information, of technology, of innovation and invention, of international commerce, and of reinvented government. And most people *think* that they understand what our institutions are trying to accomplish in each of these arenas: to promote the innovations necessary for scientific progress; to devise trade policies that improve the economy; and to push government toward becoming an increasingly responsible—and less paternalistic—economic actor.

Are "most people" right? These goals certainly sound like the policies we espouse. Those of differing political orientations may disagree bitterly about the best ways to implement them, but who today disagrees with these goals themselves? Who does not wish to see science progress, trade improve the economy, and government behave responsibly? These policy objectives seem to be matters of consensus across the American political spectrum. They are certainly the policies that *we want to have*.

But are they the policies that we *do* have? That question is harder to answer. To determine the policies that we *do* have, we must investigate the resolutions of tough disputes, where different parties would push the law in different directions. To conduct this investigation, we must examine the rulings and opinions of the courts charged with resolving these disputes. For "most people," however, that examination poses an insurmountable hurdle. Court rulings tend to appear in arcane legalese—a situation exacerbated in the esoteric areas of law dealing with patentable technologies, trade disputes, and government economic responsibility. In these areas, the legal rulings are so specialized that Congress chose to sequester them within the chambers of a single, specialized appeals court—the Federal Circuit.

Fortunately, though specialized skills may be necessary to follow the court's highly technical jurisprudence, none are needed to grasp the import of its work. This court sits at the forefront of the information economy. Its rulings help us understand precisely what policies *we actually have* governing technological development, international trade, and government reinvention. The Federal Circuit is where the rules of the information age unfold. If you want to know how prepared we are to navigate the transition to the information age, you must examine Federal Circuit jurisprudence.

The Federal Circuit today remains a Washington rarity—nonpartisan, high impact, and low profile. We the people deserve to understand how the issues that this institution addresses reveal the challenges of transitioning to an information age, and how the court itself is shaping the emerging information economy. *The Secret Circuit* provides that understanding.

I

THE SECRET CIRCUIT

This book is about a court—the United States Court of Appeals for the Federal Circuit. This court is unique and specialized, but not quite as specialized as its reputation leads many to believe. Though perhaps best known as "the patent court," the Federal Circuit also encounters many other areas of the law. International trade and government claims law are its exclusive bailiwick; other bodies of law work their way onto the docket as well. The very existence of such a court raises many questions: Why does it exist? What does it do? What goals should we ask it to achieve? How does it further the needs of a liberal society on the cusp of the information age? How can we assess its performance? Why don't we hear more about it? And perhaps above all: Why is it such a secret?

1

✛

A Court Is Born

PRESIDENTS PARK

Lafayette Park, also known as Presidents Park, is often in the news. From presidential inaugurations to mass demonstrations, the park across Pennsylvania Avenue from the White House has appeared in far more than its fair share of news clips. But to Washingtonians, Lafayette Park is more than just a good place for a rally. It's the central square of our city, ringed by buildings housing the most coveted of government jobs. Many Washingtonians could identify not only the White House but also the stately buildings that flank it: the Treasury Department and the Eisenhower (still better known as the Old) Executive Office Building. Most could point to the tony Hay-Adams Hotel across H Street, just north of the park. And most could identify the red brick New Executive Office Building towering over the historic brownstones of Jackson Place, to the park's west. But ask about its twin along Madison Place, east of the park, and even the proudest of Washingtonians would ruffle their brows. Some might identify it as some kind of court. Few would know even that much. Upon reflection, they would likely concede that this prime piece of Washington real estate must house something both secret and influential. They would be half right: The proceedings inside this building are critical to the welfare of the American economy, but they are hardly secret; they are open to the public, though few members of the public ever venture inside.

The main entrance to this mysterious building bears three signs: "Howard T. Markey National Courts Building"; "United States Court of Federal Claims"; and "United States Court of Appeals for the Federal

3

Circuit." Mystery solved. Or is it? It seems that Washingtonians are not the only group strangely unaware of the Court of Appeals for Federal Circuit—or, for that matter, of the Court of Federal Claims, an important trial court whose work the Federal Circuit reviews. Mention "the Federal Circuit" to most *lawyers*, and they'll ask you: "Which one?" But though there are thirteen federal circuit courts of appeals, there is only one Court of Appeals for the Federal Circuit. And so, the visitor to Lafayette Park must be left to wonder how a court so obscure that its very existence baffles most lawyers managed to secure such a prime location.

Obscurity has both its reasons and its virtues. The reasons are simple. Much of the Federal Circuit's work deals with specialized technical areas of the law: patents, trade, government contracting, takings, veterans affairs, and government employment. The virtue is subtler and reflected in the court's self-image. In the words of former Chief Judge H. Robert Mayer:

> This is a special court, not only because of its broad and national jurisdiction over disparate matters, but because of the people who make it work. The jurisdiction was made broad intentionally to keep the court from becoming a narrow specialized tribunal. . . . The Court has been a relatively secret gem in the judiciary until recently. No other court permits judges to work only on matters of significance with an absolute minimum of tedium and routine.[1]

In many ways, the Federal Circuit is a model of government at its best. Its judges are deeply committed to the bodies of law that they oversee. They treat each other with civility and respect and approach their jobs without partisan rancor. They form a technocrat's court laboring to understand the facts of each case and to apply the law correctly to resolve complicated disputes without injecting undue ideological biases upon the outcome. Few observers even know which of the judges were Democrats and which were Republicans prior to joining the court, and even fewer have reason to care. While many judges on many courts strive to achieve this same ideal, few seem to succeed as consistently as do the judges of the Federal Circuit—in no small part because of the obscurity of the issues with which their court deals.

There in a nutshell lies the great mystery of the Federal Circuit. For though it may be obscure, it remains uniquely powerful. Its judges issue rulings daily, rulings that shape technology industries; that determine the rights of importers and exporters, and by extension all who compete in the global economy; that define what it means to do business with the federal government and to whom the government owes money; and that assess the rights of America's noble veterans and government workers. Its role in these areas is almost unassailable. Only the Supreme Court and Congress can review and reverse its rulings, and neither does so very often.[2] Though the Federal Circuit's oversight of the areas of patent law, trade law, and government business law is bringing increasing numbers of companies and industries under its sway, it remains relatively unknown beyond some narrow legal communities—still something of a "secret gem."

Inklings of interests are beginning to show. The Supreme Court has recently demonstrated increased attention to Federal Circuit issues, particularly though not exclusively in patent law.[3] Scholars of intellectual property (IP) law and of innovation economics, the Federal Trade Commission (FTC), and the National Academy of Sciences (NAS) have all written recently to lament the state of America's patent system at the dawn of the information age.[4] All of these observers think that the patent system has grown too strong and that it risks becoming a regulatory burden strangling scientific research and technological commercialization. All have proposed changes to the system. Perhaps most significantly, all have levied much of the blame for the system's current plight on the Federal Circuit. At least some of their criticisms, however, blame the court for decisions made elsewhere—many in the halls of Congress—and none of these critiques reach the significant portions of the Federal Circuit docket unrelated to patent law. Furthermore, all of these contemporary critics concede that Congress created the Federal Circuit in 1982 precisely to strengthen a weak patent system whose inability to motivate innovation threatened to perpetuate the economic malaise of the 1970s. And so, it might be fair to say that the growing portion of the public interested in patents now knows of the Federal Circuit, but the public understanding of its mission remains erroneously narrow.

Even those aware of the Federal Circuit tend to view its work as arcane and esoteric. They may be right. The primary legal issues with which the Federal Circuit grapples *are* arcane and esoteric. The legal community considers every one of them a narrow specialization. Most law students avoid the specialized courses that address these areas of the law, and their aversion typically follows them when they enter legal practice. Federal Circuit issues never work their way into Hollywood's courtroom dramas, and precious few make more than occasional headlines. With the possible exception of takings law, partisan splits on Federal Circuit issues are rare; few political candidates can find votes in any of them, rendering them poor material for hyperbolic stump speeches. Finally, even many of the people who work on these issues concede that they are hypertechnical, confusing, and not infrequently *boring* areas of the law.

So why should anyone care? And more to the point, why should anyone want to pursue a book-length inquiry into admittedly dry legal doctrine? The answer—as always—is that there is more to the Federal Circuit than meets the eye. This nonpartisan court, laboring in relative anonymity to resolve disputes about hypertechnical issues in arcane areas of the law, is formalizing and applying the rules that govern the American economy as it transitions from the industrial age to the global information age. Anyone interested in understanding the issues shaping the economic portions of that transformation should care about the Federal Circuit. And anyone who cares about the Federal Circuit should take the time to understand the history, the philosophy, and the mission that led to its birth. This prenatal background will lay the groundwork for answering a critical question: *Are the policies we have the policy we want?*

BEYOND THE MALAISE

How did the Federal Circuit, peculiarly situated atop the fault lines where industrial economy and information economy collide, come to occupy its powerful niche—not to mention its prestigious address? The court's position at the forefront of information economy issues is hardly coincidental.[5] It is an intentional outcome of a critical policy inquiry that President Jimmy Carter launched in 1978. The Domestic Policy Review of Industrial Innovation was a far-ranging, high-level, nonpartisan collaboration of American industry and government. Secretary of Commerce Juanita Kreps, who officially ran the review, charged its various committees with reconsidering the policies governing economics and trade, regulation, labor, the environment, industry structure, antitrust, tax, R&D, creativity, and patents. Its goal was nothing less ambitious than the salvation of the American economy.

This review can make sense only in historical context. The 1970s were not a high point in American history. More than a decade of bumbling economic management at home and inept responses to increasingly assertive competitors and enemies abroad had placed the country in a precarious state. Our leaders seemed unable to cope with the rapid changes buffeting an increasingly global economy. Though few realized it at the time, the industrial age was drawing to an end. The institutions, theories, and policy perspectives that had enabled global industrialization and impelled the United States to become the unquestioned leader of both the Free World and of the free-market world were nearing the end of their useful lives. The time had come to rethink many basic assumptions about economic policy, to recognize that tried-and-true remedies were unlikely to succeed, and to venture into uncharted policy terrain.

Carter assumed the presidency with the American economy facing its greatest challenges since the Great Depression, and the decline accelerated on his watch. The budget deficit was out of control, unemployment was high, exports were dropping, imports increasing, and inflation surging to record highs. The new word "stagflation" arose to describe this period of national malaise. Conventional economic thinking, mired in the belief that governments can rescue weak economies by increasing spending, introducing new public-sector programs, and stimulating responsive economic activity, was of little use. The proclivity to trust the government's ability to manage the economy more than the private sector's ability to generate sustained, broad-based growth—a preference that had underpinned the New Deal and all of America's subsequent economic success—was losing its luster. Many were beginning to question whether government truly deserved the people's trust, in areas far beyond the economy. The empirical evidence was overwhelming: Traditional approaches weren't working. New ideas were necessary.

His numerous and overwhelming faults notwithstanding, Carter did take a few tentative steps away from statist orthodoxy and toward a more liberal future. The questions that he posed to the committees conducting his Domestic Policy Review were among those steps. The inquiry began by observing that high-tech industries remained the only area in which American companies continued to dominate world markets, and then moved quickly to a critical question: What sorts of rules would motivate America's technology industries to expand in ways that enhance both domestic employment opportunities and global leadership?

This break with conventional economic wisdom was stark, if subtle. For perhaps the first time in fifty years, the American government sought economic salvation in the private sector. In what may have been the first official inquiry into the nature of the information economy, Carter's Domestic Policy Review left behind the preference for government action to search instead for ways to unleash America's brainpower and innate intellectual curiosity—and to commercialize the innovative fruits of that collective intellect by building better technology companies. The transition to the information age had begun.

When the dust settled, several of the Domestic Policy Review's key recommendations concerned patents—the lynchpin of American innovation policy since the Constitution empowered Congress "to promote the progress of science and useful arts, by securing for limited times to . . . inventors the exclusive right to their . . . discoveries."[6] Pauline Newman, then a private-sector representative to that committee and since 1984 a Federal Circuit judge, recalled:

> The committee worked for over a year, and made several recommendations to implement the unifying conclusion that a viable patent system was important to support technologic innovation. . . .
>
> The committee recommended a change in the judicial structure for patent litigation. It was clear that patents could never serve as reliable investment

incentives when their fate in the courts was so unpredictable, and the judicial attitude in general so hostile. We felt that most judges didn't understand the patent system and how it worked, and that this lack of understanding was accompanied by a general view that patents were bad for the nation and should be struck down. Whatever the source of this judicial viewpoint, it was clear to industry and the innovation community that it was unsound, and that research-based technology was being seriously disadvantaged— particularly in international competitiveness, but also for its effect on investment in new domestic technologies.

The costs of industrial innovation were rapidly increasing, and the industry response to increased commercial risk was a matter of simple economics. The statistics of the fate of patents in court were such that no patent could be counted on to survive litigation. Forum shopping was rampant, for some courts hadn't ever sustained a patent, and bragged about it. And the Supreme Court held that you could attack the same patent in court after court, until it finally fell.[7]

Two further complications increased the potential for controversy almost immediately. The first was easily predictable to anyone possessing even a modicum of familiarity with Washington. Every institution in American life has a built-in constituency, a group that feels certain ownership rights over a public enterprise despite recognizing the far-reaching effects of the government agency that it claims to own. In the case of judicial structure and litigation, that constituency is known as "Bench and Bar," America's judges and lawyers. No change to either court structure or the practice of litigation is likely to pass against the concerted opposition of this key constituency. The second was also predictable to anyone reading the tea leaves in 1979. The American people swept Carter from office before Congress could take any action on the committee's recommendations. Ronald Reagan arrived in Washington for his inauguration intent upon burying conventional economic thinking. The new Reagan administration adopted relatively few Carter administration programs or recommendations, particularly on matters related to the economy.

Sometimes the stars align appropriately. The few Carter proposals and programs that Reagan did endorse were precisely those that deviated from conventional "big government" thinking. Reagan administration officials did more than simply endorse the committee's recommendations to strengthen the patent system—they expanded them. Reagan ushered in a new era of economic thinking, one much better suited to the information economy than was its big-government predecessor. As a matter of governing economic philosophy, Reagan believed in unleashing individual creativity and innovation, in promoting private-sector commercialization, and in rewarding successful calculated risk-taking. His administration took the first definitive steps away from the industrial-age view of government as an economic manager to the information-age view of government as an economic facilitator.

The economic philosophy that Reagan brought to Washington in 1981 represented a decisive and necessary break with the past; President Bill Clinton's observation fifteen years later that "the era of big government is over"[8] was little more than a casual recognition of empirical reality. But between them, these two presidents laid the groundwork for an information-age economy. The Federal Circuit was among the first new institutions developed for that new economy. Because it was such an early innovation, though, it both derived from an incomplete understanding of that new economy and helped us educate ourselves as we learned more about it.

How is this little-known court shaping the economy of the information age? Our inquiry must begin by considering the needs of an information-age economy. Contemporary American economic thinking combines eighteenth-century liberalism with the hard-learned lessons of the past two centuries. Liberalism, or perhaps more accurately in the economic sphere "liberal market capitalism," is a politico-economic philosophy that emphasizes liberty and individual autonomy. Liberal ideas have appeared in philosophical tomes for quite some time, but it was not until the late eighteenth and early nineteenth centuries that they began to influence government policies in any significant manner. Adam Smith, Thomas Jefferson, James Madison, Alexander Hamilton, David Ricardo, John Stuart Mill, and others laid the groundwork for the transition from the agrarian age to the industrial age. When England and the United States adopted economic policies and government structures that these writers advocated, their economies boomed and their societies prospered.

Economies tend to change faster than societies, though, and massive social upheaval accompanied the rapid industrialization. Although the disruptions were greatest in continental European countries with weak liberal traditions and institutions, social disquietude eventually engulfed the Anglo-American world as well. Empirical evidence of the liberal program's incompleteness accumulated; as a philosophy grounded in economic theory, it had omitted much of the human dimension. In response, many nineteenth- and twentieth-century thinkers rejected liberalism outright and developed instead an affinity for social planning. In their view, a paternalistic meritocracy would allocate resources more effectively—and more fairly—than would chaotic liberal markets. As the unrest grew, these socialist ideas gained traction in one country after another, at times in the guise of benign bureaucracies and at others in the guise of authoritarian dictatorships. Liberalism retreated for more than a century.

Liberal thinkers split. Some insisted that the original program *was* complete and that, even though a return to it might disadvantage some, the period of their disadvantage would end much more quickly under liberal policies than under socialist policies. Others rejected the socialist program, but nevertheless conceded that some of its great thinkers had identified real problems in need of resolution. Perhaps the greatest tragedy in twentieth-century liberalism was the animosity that emerged between these two camps. The former generated soaring, uplifting rhetoric, but refused to acknowledge political reality and chose to wallow in oppositional ideological purity rather than to join governing coalitions. The latter injected reforms into the liberal program, some sensible, many less so. Where these pragmatic liberals were able to govern, they developed social safety nets to help people avoid the full consequences of catastrophe, and thus to temper natural risk aversion. They invested in infrastructure that freed private actors to improve the efficiency of their transactions. They developed regulations that improved markets by increasing transparency, information flow, and robust competition. Unfortunately, shorn of their natural ideological allies, these liberal reformers came to rely too heavily on the support of social planners. Their programs also incorporated destructive elements like tariffs, confiscatory taxes, wealth redistribution, price stabilization, and command-and-control regulation.

This hodgepodge of a liberal agenda, sensible reforms, and a socialist overlay defined the American economy through the middle decades of the twentieth century. Carter was savvy enough to understand that the mix was failing, but far too timid to fix it. Reagan's rhetoric reengaged many missing liberals in the business of government. They surveyed the terrain after their decades in exile, recognized that some of the reforms that they had long opposed had actually worked, and began to sensitize themselves to the political realities that constrain governments in a liberal democracy. They set out to disassemble the more mechanized aspects of economic policy without destroying the underlying infrastructure.

Clinton and his team continued the country's economic transformation. After Reagan entered office in 1981, it became clear that the economy was not a machine that technocratic planners could manage—but it remained unclear just what the economy was. Clinton discovered the answer: the economy is a network. The Clinton administration kept taxes relatively low, freed trade, assumed fiscal responsibility, turned government handouts into incentive-based programs, replaced command-and-control with market-based regulations, established joint public-private research initiatives, created an environment in which innovative entrepreneurs could flourish, and advocated universal access to information technology—and thus to information.

The program proved powerful. Under two decades of liberal market capitalism, the American economy once again boomed and American society flourished. But two critical problems remain—problems for which

Reagan and Clinton share the blame rather than the credit. First, *all* transitions are disruptive; the faster the disruption, the greater the potential for a backlash—and the greater the backlash, the greater the threat to continued prosperity and success. Reagan paid insufficient heed to the backlash at home, Clinton to the backlash abroad. The country continues to pay the price for both oversights. Second, the rigid political division that split liberals throughout the twentieth century remains intact. Reagan, Clinton, and their most vocal supporters sharpened these partisan differences rather than blunting them. As a result, America's political "conservative" movement embraces philosophies ranging from liberalism through conservatism and into authoritarianism, while its political "liberal" movement embraces philosophies ranging from liberalism through socialism and into authoritarianism. Political liberalism has become almost completely untethered from its roots in philosophical liberalism; political conservatism drifts further from its own philosophical roots with each passing year.

Philosophical liberalism is tailor-made for the information age, particularly when tempered with the practical lessons of conservatism and of socialism. Whereas industrial-age governments tried to manage their national economies as if they were machines, factories, or product lines, information-age governments must treat their economies as networks. In the information age, the government's primary role is to develop infrastructures within which free citizens can make meaningful decisions. Suitable economic policies must spread opportunity, increase choice, and/or provide the information necessary for choices to have meaning. The unplannable shape of the information economy "emerges" from the myriad actions of individual members of the economic network, members whose actions are of little consequence individually but are hugely important in the aggregate. The government's role is to enable those independent actions, sometimes by investing in infrastructure, sometimes by removing impediments, sometimes by disseminating information, and sometimes by providing incentives. Information-age governments are essentially economic standard-setters rather than plant managers. Economic policies based upon different conceptions of the information-age economy cannot succeed for long. Though much work remains even today toward realizing the liberal goals of opportunity, choice, information, and freedom, the Reagan team swept away many of the impediments to deriving an economic philosophy suited to the information age, and the Clinton team ensured that the emerging free economy would maintain a human face.

On matters pertaining directly to the Federal Circuit, the Reagan administration broke cleanly with the big government past and pointed the American economy in the right direction. Patent policy played a small though not insignificant role in this redirection, and the Federal Circuit was a central component of patent policy reform. Within this newly liberal approach, the constitutional idea that limited rights could motivate innovation struck a resonant chord. Despite the regulatory burden that a strong patent system would impose upon various aspects of scientific research and technological commercialization, the Reagan team believed that increased incentives were worth the cost. In its view, a viable patent system would motivate innovation, unleash creativity, impel technology industries forward, and increase productivity.

Between 1980 and 1984, four major legislative changes and two lines of Supreme Court rulings altered the contours of the American patent system almost beyond recognition. Inquiries into the best ways to enhance American competitiveness motivated all six changes. One inquiry considered the challenge of motivating universities to engage in the sorts of technology transfer necessary to leverage their research into marketable products. The Bayh-Dole Act allowed universities to patent inventions developed in whole or in part through federal research grants and to retain the entire commercial benefits of those patents.[9] A second inquiry assessed the relationship among branded drug companies, generic drug producers, and their federal regulator, the Food and Drug Administration (FDA). The Hatch-Waxman Act allowed the branded companies to extend their patents to reclaim some of the time lost to lengthy regulatory reviews, but eased the way for generics to experiment and develop products that they could launch as soon as those patents expired.[10] A third inquiry identified inconsistency among the appellate courts as a significant source of uncertainty hanging over the entire patent system. The Federal Courts Improvement Act created the Federal Circuit.[11] Meanwhile, the Supreme Court determined that two new classes of inventions—laboratory-synthesized microorganisms and algorithms encoded as software—were eligible for patent protection.[12] These five inquiries and their solutions all proved to be significant, and all flowed from the goals of invigorating the patent system and of liberalizing the economy. The sixth reform, motivated more by economic nationalism than by liberalism, has been inconsequential; Congress created a *sui generis* regulatory regime to protect America's semiconductor industry from Japanese competition.[13] The net effect of these reforms was remarkable. Two decades later, the country has numerous successful technology transfer programs, faster releases of generic drugs, and increased consistency in patent law—though the effect of these reforms on the semiconductor and software industries was not entirely positive.

All of these reforms flowed from the Domestic Policy Review committee's recommendations. The Reagan team arrived in Washington positively predisposed to ideas that would strengthen the moribund patent system. The new administration proved receptive to the recommendations concerning a restructured, strengthened patent system, including its judicial elements. The complication of political change proved easy to clear; the Domestic Policy Review committee's recommendations survived the transition from the Carter administration to the Reagan administration. That left "only" the Bench, Bar, and Congress in need of persuasion.

BENCH AND BAR

The sorry state of the American patent system in the late 1970s also played a role in soliciting support from the legal community. To appreciate that role, however, it is necessary to know something about the three-tiered structure of the federal courts. Trials take place on the first tier, known as "federal district courts" or "trial courts." Parties unhappy with the trial's outcome—and at least one party is *always* unhappy with the outcome— may appeal the verdict to one of the thirteen courts on the second tier, known as "federal circuit courts" or "appeals courts." Twelve of these courts, the First Circuit through the Eleventh Circuit plus the D.C. Circuit, have regional jurisdiction; the Federal Circuit is the thirteenth. Prior to the Federal Circuit's creation, the trial's location determined its appellate path—hence "regional" jurisdiction. The situation today is a bit trickier. The trial's location determines which of the circuits will hear the appeal *unless* the subject matter falls to the Federal Circuit.

This first appeal is a matter of right. Anyone unhappy with a trial's outcome may ask the appropriate appellate court to review the trial judge's work with respect to a specific error, and the appellate court *must* review that work. Parties unhappy with the appellate review may keep the process going even longer by appealing to the only court on the third tier, the Supreme Court of the United States. The Supreme Court, however, has broad discretion as to which cases it agrees to consider; it grants writs of *certiorari* (or "cert"), accepting only a tiny fraction of litigants' requests. As a result, the rulings of the second-tier circuit courts tend to determine both what the law means and how those laws apply to real litigants in real cases.

While this system may sound straightforward, it operates with a curious twist: the middle-tiered appellate courts are coequal sisters. These sisters, like many siblings, take each others' recommendations seriously, but don't always agree—and under the structure of the federal court system, they can't force uniformity upon each other. That lack of enforcement can lead to one of the most perplexing oddities in federal law—a "circuit split." When sister circuits split, behavior that is legal under federal law in some parts of the country is illegal *under the same federal law* in other parts of the country. Here's a simple example: American citizens possess inherent rights to free speech and free assembly. These rights, enshrined in the First Amendment, allow political and religious groups to advocate their positions in public places—but don't give them any necessary rights to enter private property. In the modern world, we spend increasing amounts of time in places that are neither obviously public nor obviously private—airports, for example. The operating authorities of several airports enacted rules that limited the speech and assembly rights of advocacy groups. Circuit courts had to study First Amendment law to determine whether or not it applied to airports. The Chicago-based Seventh Circuit concluded that it did; the New York-based Second Circuit that it didn't. As a result, O'Hare was a public forum in which peaceful protesters could demonstrate with impunity, while JFK was private property whose owners could limit religious advocacy within its confines.[14]

Anomalous, perhaps, but hardly earthshaking. Americans have learned to live with such circuit splits, despite recognizing that they can provide "unfair" advantages to citizens and companies in some parts of the country, particularly when they arise in areas like criminal procedure[15] or bankruptcy law.[16] The usual prescription for a circuit split is to let it simmer for a while. Eventually, the Supreme Court will marshal the insights of the various appellate judges whose rulings led to the split, resolve the conflict, and announce a uniform federal law that all judges—both trial and appellate—must follow. In the airport example, the Supreme Court eventually agreed with the Second Circuit; advocacy groups now enjoy full First Amendment rights neither in O'Hare nor in JFK.[17]

But the existence of circuit splits has long struck many people—including many members of the legal community, the Domestic Policy Review panel, and ultimately Congress—as more troubling in some areas of the law than in others. It seemed economically hazardous as well as unfair to allow different circuit courts to apply differing interpretations of both patent law and individual patents. Divergent interpretations made it impossible for patent examiners at the U.S. Patent and Trademark Office (PTO) to apply appropriate standards when determining which patents to issue, and skewed domestic commercialization attempts by labeling products and activities that were permissible in some states as infringing in others. These regional differences motivated litigants to run around the country "forum shopping" for a court likely to apply favorable interpretations of the patent laws. Yet under the general principles guiding relationships among the sister circuits, nothing prevented such an outcome.

Professor Rochelle Cooper Dreyfuss, an early and influential Federal Circuit observer and analyst, recalled that by the time Carter commissioned his Domestic Policy Review, some circuits imposed difficult burdens on patentees, or light ones on infringers. Statistics demonstrate that in the period 1945–1957, a patent was twice as likely to be held valid and infringed in the Fifth Circuit than in the Seventh Circuit, and almost four times more likely to be enforced in the Seventh Circuit than in the Second Circuit. It is no wonder that forum shopping was rampant, and that a request to transfer a patent infringement action from Texas, in the Fifth Circuit, to Illinois, in the Seventh Circuit, would be bitterly fought in both circuits and, ultimately, in the Supreme Court. Furthermore, without knowing where a patent would be litigated, it became impossible to adequately counsel technology developers or users. In such a legal environment, the promise of a patent could hardly be considered sufficient incentive to invest in research and development.[18]

And so, much as the Domestic Policy Review committee's focus on the *effects* of the American patent system in practice concluded that the country needed to reform and to strengthen it, the legal community's focus on circuit splits as a *cause* of this problem conceded that a restructuring of the patent litigation system might be in order.

The 1970s were an active era among those who favored judicial reform. In 1971, Chief Justice Warren Burger appointed Professor Paul Freund to head a committee studying ways to lighten the Supreme Court's growing workload. Burger realized that there were too many complex lawsuits arising from too many complex issues for the Supreme Court to consider all of them, and that unresolved circuit splits were becoming a growing challenge to the uniformity of federal law. The Freund Committee recommended a number of structural changes to the court system, though it notably considered and rejected the idea of specialized single-issue courts. In the style that Washington has come to know and love, the Freund Committee's primary legacy was that it motivated Congress to create another committee (or more precisely, a commission), this one headed by Senator Roman Hruska (R-NE). In 1973, the Hruska Commission report specifically considered the challenges destroying the patent system—essentially foreshadowing those that the Domestic Policy Review committee would detect several years later—but again cautioned against creating a specialized patent court. Instead, the Hruska Commission recommended a "National Court of Appeals" to serve as a sort of junior Supreme Court. Again, nothing happened.

But the seeds of judicial reform were in the air. In 1977, Attorney General Griffin Bell created a new office within the Justice Department, the Office for Improvements in the Administration of Justice (OIAJ). Bell hired Professor Daniel Meador to run OIAJ. Meador, in turn, hired Professor Charles Haworth to focus on issues concerning the appeals courts, drawing upon not only the Freund Committee and the Hruska Commission but also a 1968 American Bar Association study. OIAJ's inquiry into structural reforms of the court system thus began with input from reports commissioned by the Supreme Court, Congress, and the private Bar. According to Meador:

> We were determined to do something significant, something that was not merely tinkering, but which was also politically doable, drawing on all the ideas that had been generated over the past decade but also hoping to develop some fresh approaches.
>
> We were concerned overall with the problem of managing the large growth in appellate litigation in a way that would also enhance national uniformity in federal decisional law. Many years earlier Erwin Griswold had advanced the idea of centralizing appellate review in tax cases, pointing out the special desirability of national uniformity in tax law. Studies by the Hruska Commission had identified the patent law field as one where national uniformity was especially desirable. In pounding the streets of Washington, Haworth identified the Court of Claims as an existing special court already deciding some tax cases. He also found the Court of Customs and Patent Appeals (CCPA), with a large amount of patent jurisdiction. This tax and patent jurisdiction, however, was limited and did not extend nationwide.
>
> Somewhere along the way during the late spring of 1978, in our numerous discussions in OIAJ, the idea of extending the jurisdiction of these courts nationwide, to include review of district court decisions in tax and patent cases, came to the surface, although I cannot pinpoint the exact day or hour. Along with that idea, there emerged—again I cannot pinpoint the exact time—the idea of combining those two courts into a new appellate court. They already occupied the same building and shared many of the same facilities.[19]

An idea was born. Meador and Haworth proceeded to solicit the political support that they knew they would need to move their new court from an idea to a reality. The judges already sitting on the two courts that they hoped to merge proved amenable, if somewhat skeptical. Chief Justice Burger similarly "voiced no objection and seemed interested in the idea."[20]

Armed with this rousing lack of opposition, Meador and Haworth turned to the parts of the legal community likely to experience the most direct effects: the tax bar and the patent bar. Opposition from the tax bar was considerable and widespread. The response from the patent bar was subtler; litigators generally opposed the idea, while corporate counsel supported it. Even that partial support proved sufficient. Bell dropped the proposal's tax components out of sheer political expediency, and soon gained the support first of Senate Judiciary Committee chairman Ted Kennedy (D-MA, at the time Carter's primary opponent for the 1980 Democratic presidential nomination), then of President Carter, and then of the full Judiciary Committee.

THE HILL

By 1980, the contours of the idea that would soon become the Federal Circuit were close to complete. The merger of two existing courts—the appellate part of the Court of Claims and the Court of Customs and Patent Appeals (CCPA)—proved to be a masterstroke. According to Judge Marion T. Bennett, one of the two Court of Claims judges designated to attend all relevant congressional hearings (and subsequently a member of the Federal Circuit's founding roster):

> Congress observed that the new circuit court of appeals would not add to the number of federal courts because the two older courts would be abolished. . . . The Federal Circuit, at little or no additional expense to taxpayers, would make maximum use of facilities and experienced personnel already in place and already part of the federal judicial system. It was also congressional consensus that the new court would provide a ready forum for later legislation, expanding its jurisdiction as need arose.[21]

The strikingly similar recommendations of the Domestic Policy Review and of OIAJ hit Capitol Hill about the same time. The unified proposal of a new court, coequal with the regional circuit courts and thus subject only to Supreme Court review, charged with appeals in all patent cases *plus* the preexisting appellate dockets of the Court of Claims and the CCPA *plus* other new areas that Congress might someday feel require a single federal forum, proved to be a winner. It promised to collect all patent cases into a single forum capable of imposing uniformity and certainty upon the patent system without falling prey to the tunnel vision that overspecialization so often engenders. And the "brokered marriage" of two existing courts already housed in the same building made the matter transparent to taxpayers.[22] Congress was pleased. A House report explained that

> by combining the jurisdiction of the two existing courts along with certain limited grants of new jurisdiction, the bill creates a new intermediate appellate court markedly less specialized than either of its predecessors and provides the judges of the new court with a breadth of jurisdiction that rivals in variety that of the regional courts of appeals. The proposed new court is not a "specialized court." Its jurisdiction is not limited to one type of case, or even to two or three types of cases. Rather, it has a varied docket spanning a broad range of legal issues and types of cases. It will handle all patent appeals and some agency appeals, as well as all other matters that are now considered by the CCPA or the Court of Claims. The Court of Claims decides cases involving federal contracts, civil tax issues if the government is the defendant, Indian claims, military and civilian pay disputes, patents, inverse condemnation, and various other matters. The CCPA decides patent and customs cases from several sources, and those cases often include allegations of

defenses of "misuse, fraud, inequitable conduct, violations of the antitrust laws, breach of trade secret agreements, unfair competition, and such common law claims as unjust enrichment."[23]

A Senate report added that "the subject matter of the new court will be sufficiently mixed to prevent any special interest from dominating it."[24] With those concerns addressed, Congress finally incorporated the idea into the Federal Courts Improvement Act (FCIA).[25] In a Rose Garden ceremony on April 2, 1982, President Reagan signed the FCIA into law. Meador stood behind the president, flanked by the last chief judge of the Court of Claims, Howard T. Markey, and the last chief judge of the CCPA, Daniel M. Friedman. Six months later, on October 1, 1982, the new United States Court of Appeals for the Federal Circuit, comprised of the former judges of the two merged courts and with Markey designated chief judge, held its inaugural session in the National Courts Building that is still its home—that redbrick building on the east side of Lafayette Park now known as the Howard T. Markey National Courts Building.

That story answers many lingering questions. The Federal Circuit inherited its prestigious address from two much older courts. Its centrality to technological innovation was intentional; it stemmed from widespread agreement that a reformed patent system was critical to America's economic survival. The rest of its docket was essentially coincidental; it emerged from the desire to avoid creating either a new court or a specialized court. Its power derives from its position and from its exclusive oversight of important substantive areas of the law; its sister circuits cannot force a split, and only the Supreme Court can trump it in a dispute. Its inherent nonpartisanship and low profile are understandable; few can follow the complexities of the laws that it oversees. And its ability to shape the economy of the information age is manifest; its decisions guide the development of technology industries, trade arrangements, and the ways that citizens do business with the government.

Answers to one set of questions inevitably give rise to another set, often more challenging than those just answered. The mystery of the Federal Circuit is no exception. The court was born to move the patent system and other critical parts of our economy into the information age. How well has it done?

2

✢

Conservative Liberalism

BLACK ROBES, BLACK BOXES

Performance is often hard to measure, particularly when assessing contributions rather than stand-alone efforts. There is no doubt that the Federal Circuit's jurisprudence has led to a patent system that is stronger, more predictable, and better able to reward innovation than was the one that it found on October 1, 1982; that the court has had a palpable if lesser effect on the other areas of economic law that it oversees; or that during the court's brief lifetime, the American economy has become healthy, strong, robust, and resilient. How much credit does the Federal Circuit deserve?

Grading team projects is always tough. At best, the Federal Circuit might have been a significant contributor to America's economic recovery. At worst, it might have been a drag on a recovery that would have been even stronger without it. Performance assessment requires discriminating among the points on the spectrum that these polar extremes define to better understand the court's contribution to the overall economic picture. Discrimination, in turn, rests upon a clearer understanding of the Federal Circuit's job. It is impossible to determine how well the court (or any other institution or person, for that matter) is doing at its assigned task without understanding that task. And that inquiry, in turn, motivates an excursion into law, public policy, and the relationship between them.

Law and policy are not always friends. They often answer to different masters. In the United States, Congress is the master of policy; the courts are masters of the law. The primary reason that we elect representative

19

legislators is to ensure that they take the public's pulse on policy questions before translating policy goals into statutes; appointed judges are in no position to do so. By and large, Congress is supposed to take policy objectives as inputs and output statutory laws implementing those policies. Parties—including the government—who dispute the appropriate interpretation or application of those laws must take their disputes to the courts. With only a few rare exceptions, courts are not supposed to look back to policy statements. Instead, those who don the black robes must assume that statutes implement policy correctly, and consider only the relationship between the written law and the case-specific facts. As a result, Congress sees policy statements and general rules, while judges see general rules and their impact on specific people. Because of that helpful division of labor (in this instance, also known as the separation of powers), neither Congress nor the courts can fully appreciate the relationship between broad policy objectives and the laws that actually affect people's lives. That task falls to analysts, scholars, journalists, and other observers of law and policy.

What is "policy"? At one level, policy is an articulation of a goal, a description of what we would like to achieve. At another level, policy is an accumulation of empirical evidence, a description of what we actually do. The former level has a lot more flair. Everyone loves a good policy pronouncement. Abraham Lincoln prayed that a divided nation would "strive on to finish the work we are in, to bind up the nation's wounds, to care for him who shall have borne the battle and for his widow and his orphan, to do all which may achieve and cherish a just and lasting peace among ourselves and with all nations."[1] Franklin D. Roosevelt reminded a nation whose economic woes had shattered its self-image that confidence "thrives only on honesty, on honor, on the sacredness of obligations, on faithful protection, on unselfish performance; without them it cannot live. Restoration calls, however, not for changes in ethics alone. This Nation asks for action, and action now. Our greatest primary task is to put people to work."[2] John F. Kennedy committed America to "pay any price, bear any burden, meet any hardship, support any friend, oppose any foe, in order to assure the survival and the success of liberty."[3] Most recently, George W. Bush announced "to the peoples of the world: All who live in tyranny and hopelessness can know the United States will not ignore your oppression or excuse your oppressors. When you stand for your liberty, we will stand with you."[4] All are bold, exciting proclamations of American values and needs as expressed by our chief executives on the occasion of their inaugurations. All are beyond reasonable dispute—after all, who would *not* like to achieve a just and lasting peace, put people to work, assure the success of liberty, or stand for liberty? And all are *much* more easily said than done.

In order for a proclamation of public policy to change reality, it must pass through the messy, complicated process of becoming a law and the even messier, more complicated process of altering behavior. Congress must listen to the various interest groups trying to bend the new law to favor their own objectives, consider the implications of both the policy itself and the proposed implementing laws to residents of all 435 congressional districts and all fifty states, contemplate the interactions of new laws with existing laws (and at times with treaty obligations to other countries), exploit partisan divisions, and grandstand for the press. Eventually this process of analysis, gesticulation, coercion, and cajolery may lead to a statute capable of commanding majorities of both houses that the president is willing to sign. That statute defines "the law," though citizens often need further definition to understand precisely what it means.

That's where the federal courts get into the picture. People unable to agree about their relative legal responsibilities sue each other. Many of these disputes require a judge to interpret the statute at issue before either that judge or a jury can consider the relationship between the case's facts and the applicable law. Many also require a panel of appellate judges to review the trial judge's work. This judicial resolution of disputes on the ground furthers the drive to turn policy pronouncements into reality by differentiating between permissible and impermissible actions: The bold, simple statements tell us what American policy *should be*. Congress drafts statutes that tell us what American policy *is*. Court rulings tell us *how we should behave*.

These judicial instructions are critical. The entire purpose of articulating policy goals and enacting laws is behavior modification. Elected leaders must believe that the country—if not the world—would be better off if people behaved in ways consistent with articulated policy goals. Statutes are supposed to motivate "responsible" behavior, by either enabling or rewarding people who conform their behavior to the policy goal, and by either deterring or punishing those who behave otherwise. With a few rare exceptions, however, the courts are supposed to ignore policy goals when interpreting statutes. We *require* our judges to presume that Congress expertly captured the policy goal when it enacted the statute in question and to focus exclusively upon the statutory language.

In some Panglossian world, that presumption is true. In the real world, it often is not. This presumption of congressional fidelity to articulated policy goals is little more than a useful fiction that helps organize government by drawing clear lines between the responsibilities vested in each of the three branches. It *is not* a valid general description of public policy's journey from pronouncement to law. Judges who read this fiction closely must develop a myopic focus on statutory language set against a blurry policy background. The challenge facing those outside the court is therefore to scrutinize judicial rulings through a corrective policy lens. Only then will we be able to see whether the policies we have are motivating the behavior that we claim to want.

Unfortunately, the mere mention of public policy and the judiciary in the same sentence can raise hackles across the political spectrum. Judges who inquire about congressional fidelity to public policy are invariably labeled "activists" by those who disagree with their conclusions. Even judges who feel that their lifetime appointments insulate them from such opprobrium must nevertheless heed the Supreme Court: "The judiciary may not sit as a superlegislature to judge the wisdom or desirability of legislative policy determinations made in areas that neither affect fundamental rights nor proceed along suspect [constitutional] lines."[5]

Critics of our inquiry might therefore contend that it would be more than simply unfair to grade judges on their fidelity to broad policy goals—it would be counterproductive; high scores might well indicate poor job performance. Were assessments of judicial performance to rest upon such a grading scheme, the entire system could unravel. As Justice Felix Frankfurter cautioned,

> the vital difference between initiating policy, often involving a decided break with the past, and merely carrying out a formulated policy, indicates the relatively narrow limits within which choice is fairly open to courts and the extent to which interpreting law is inescapably making law. . . . Judges may differ as to the point at which the line should be drawn, but the only sure safeguard against crossing the line between adjudication and legislation is an alert recognition of the necessity not to cross it and instinctive, as well as trained, reluctance to do so.[6]

Instinct, training, discipline, and a sense of judicial duty are thus the only protections that our democratic institutions possess. Judges must never substitute their own policy views for those that Congress actually adopted when it wrote concrete statutory language, even when the judge's views are closer to those that Congress espoused when debating the statute than are those embodied in the statute itself. Judges must accept the policies enacted in the Constitution and—when, as in the vast majority of cases, the Constitution is silent—those enacted by statute.

It is thus critical that we not grade judges and courts on their fidelity to public policy. It is equally critical, however, that we recognize the courts as part of a complex system that implements public policy through a body of laws. We can then grade the overall system by asking a straightforward, though extraordinarily complicated, question: *How well do our laws reflect the policy objectives that we espouse?* Our inquiry will assess systemic performance across the narrow swath of policies and laws that fill the Federal Circuit's docket.

Though such a performance assessment may be atypical in a legal setting, it is hardly unusual. It is a hallmark of the information sciences, a variant of "black-box testing." In engineering terms, a tester who is unaware of a device's inner workings may regard that device as a black box. Black-box testing can have two objectives: either to learn how the box works or to determine whether or not the box is working correctly. An engineer facing the first challenge will assemble a set of test inputs, observe the outputs, and reason backward to infer the box's inner workings. An engineer facing the second challenge will start with an idea of what the box is supposed to do, assemble a set of test inputs that should lead to known outputs, run the input set through the box, and compare the box's outputs with the correct answers.

We face a variant of the second challenge—though a variant that most engineers would consider hopelessly informal. From our perspective, policy pronouncements are inputs. Judicial rulings consistent with those pronouncements provide the "right" answers, or the desired set of outputs. Actual judicial rulings are the system's actual outputs. And the entire system that moved from bold policy pronouncement through legislative agreement and adopted statute to judicial ruling defines the black box that we are testing.

Edsger Dijkstra, one of the pioneers of software design and analysis, recognized both the strengths and the weaknesses of black-box testing.

> When faced with a mechanism . . . one can ask oneself "How can I convince myself of its being correct?" As long as we regard the mechanism as a black box, the only thing we can do is subject it to all possible inputs and check whether it produces the correct outputs. But for the kind of mechanisms we are considering this is absolutely out of the question. . . . The first moral of the story is that program testing can be used very effectively to show the presence of bugs but never to show their absence. But as long as we regard the mechanism as a black box, testing is the only thing we can do. The conclusion is that we cannot afford to regard the mechanism as a black box, i.e., we have to take its internal structure into account. One studies its internal structure and on account of this analysis one convinces oneself that if such and such cases work "all others must work as well."[7]

Dijkstra's admonition applies to legal systems as comfortably as to software systems. Black-box testing of the system that converts policies to statutes to rulings can help isolate some of the places it has gone astray. It cannot confirm that the system will always work, even if the tests fail to uncover any problems.

Professor Lawrence Lessig famously proclaimed: "Code is Law."[8] That insight tells only half of the story, for *law is code* as well. A legal system outputting rulings inconsistent with advertised policies is as disturbing as a critical software system outputting miscalculations. Most people recognize that if their software is making mistakes, the sooner they catch the errors, the better; they engage in informal black-box testing and try to peek inside the box to learn the truth. In the same vein, if the American legal system is not ruling in ways likely to strengthen our economic position as we enter the information age, the sooner we catch the errors, the better. We had best engage in some informal black-box tests and peeking inside ourselves.

INSIDE THE BOX

The Federal Circuit lives inside a serially coupled black box. In the legislative component, Congress writes statutes that allegedly implement our policy objectives with respect to patents, trade, government business, and the other areas on the Federal Circuit's docket. In the judicial component, judges affix specific meanings to ambiguous words and apply those words to specific, real-world facts. A peek inside the judicial box is critical to appreciating its workings.[9]

In any lawsuit, the litigants must make three presentations: They must describe the facts as they see them, the law as they believe it to be, and the way they think the law applies to the facts.[10] Litigants present their arguments first to a trial judge in a first-tier federal district court. At times, the trial judge concludes that the law is so clear that *no reasonable* recounting of the facts could possibly allow the party who was mistaken about the law to prevail. In those cases, the facts are pretty much irrelevant; once the judge has ruled on the law, the case is over. The party whose view of the law prevailed wins her case on "summary judgment."

Other cases are more interesting. The trial judge is still in charge of resolving the legal disputes, but victory for either side remains possible even after the law is settled; the facts will determine the outcome. Parties suing each other, however, rarely agree on all of the relevant facts. Invariably, they need some disinterested "trier of fact" to hear both of their stories and decide whom to believe. Sometimes the trial judge also serves as trier of fact, in a "bench trial." At other times, the parties turn to a jury to resolve their factual disputes. When that happens, the trial judge explains the law to the jury. The trial is then a staged show, in which the litigants present their conflicting factual stories to the jury. Each one argues that if the jury will only accept his version, the application of the law to those facts will mandate his victory. The trier of fact eventually announces its resolution of the factual dispute and the outcome of the lawsuit.

With the trial thus concluded, the appeals can begin. An appeal is not a second bite at the apple; it is a request for three appellate judges to review the work of the single trial judge and to correct potentially outcome-determinative errors. The appellate process is a critical aspect of our civil justice system. It guarantees to anyone who enters a federal court at least four judges to consider the accuracy of her claim (assuming that the party in question is wealthy enough to afford the substantial legal fees that almost all meaningful lawsuits incur). Without appellate oversight, trial judges would reign supreme. The appellate system guarantees that a panel of three coequal judges, distanced from the specifics and personalities that may have induced biases at trial, protect the integrity of the system. Review by an appellate panel holds the trial judge in check, the judges on the panel hold each other in check, and the system minimizes any proclivity toward abuse, corruption, or negligence that might otherwise arise among the members of an institution as powerful as the federal judiciary. The review also provides a useful error-checking mechanism and represents a serious government effort to build judicial institutions capable of dispensing accurate, consistent, dispassionate rulings—if not of dispensing justice.

An appeal is therefore more than simply a complaint about the trial's outcome. It is an assertion that something significant went wrong at the trial. Appellants (i.e., those who appeal the judgment) write briefs explaining where they believe an error occurred, why they believe it is erroneous, how the appellate court should correct it, and how the correction of that error would lead to a more favorable judgment. They then append a small selection of documents, trial transcripts, and exhibits to support their assertions. Appellees (i.e., those who support the judgment and are consequently appealed against) counter the appellants' brief with a brief of their own and append selected supporting material. Both sides send their briefs to the clerk of court (not to be confused with the law clerks who assist the judges), an administrative officer of the appellate court. Each month, the clerk of court draws judges at random from the court's roster to assemble several panels of three and then assigns cases at random to the panels. The three judges assigned to the case review the parties' submissions and hold a brief oral argument in which each side presents its case. The panel then deliberates the parties' claims, votes on the case's outcome, and assigns one of the judges voting with the majority the task of explaining the court's decision in writing. The other two members of the panel may, at their individual discretion, contribute concurring opinions (if they agree with the outcome, but not the reasoning) or dissenting opinions (if they disagree with the outcome). The court publishes these judicial opinions to educate the public (or at least its lawyers) and to guide both the behavior and the legal arguments of parties who face situations similar to those at issue in the decided case.

What sorts of arguments qualify as claims that "something significant went wrong at the trial"? As at trial, litigants may assert errors in one of three basic areas: the facts, the law, and the application of the law to the facts. Appeals based upon the facts are tough to sustain, and they rarely win. Appellate courts assume that a trier of fact who lived in the courtroom, immersed itself in the case's details, heard live testimony, and saw the entire trial record rather than just selected excerpts, emerged better positioned to weigh the evidence, draw conclusions, and divine the truth than a detached, disinterested panel. Under most circumstances, appellate courts will overturn factual findings only if they are entirely inconsistent with the evidence. If a "reasonable" jury (or judge) *might* have reached the trial court's factual findings, the appellate court will affirm those findings—and thus the ruling against the appellant. The prospects of winning an appeal based upon a claim that the trial court misapplied the law to the facts, without also disputing the trial court's rulings on the law, are similarly slim. Most appellants therefore try to convince the appellate judges that the trial judge was mistaken about the law.

"The law," however, can be tricky to pin down. There is no single source of "the law," and frequently no easy place to look it up. The very structure of the federal system creates a crazy quilt of laws that only those armed with a scorecard—or a legal training—can follow. It begins with a body of "common law," rules that judges began to craft in England long before the Revolutionary War. This "Anglo-American tradition" of common law defines the bedrock legal principles guiding all judicial decisions at all levels—unless and until the legislative branch decides to either enshrine them or overturn them by statute. The resulting body of codified law starts with the Constitution, a living document that the judiciary must constantly interpret and apply to new and previously unforeseen circumstances. The Supreme Court is the ultimate arbiter of the Constitution's meaning, and both Congress and all other courts are bound to follow it. Supreme Court interpretations of the Constitution tell us what "the law" is. Following closely on the heels of constitutional law is statutory law, the collection of statutes that Congress drafts within the confines of its rather broad constitutional latitude, and that the president then signs "into law." The official compilation of these statutes, the United States Code (U.S.C.), is a voluminous document currently divided into fifty thematic "titles," each consisting of numerous chapters and sections. The U.S.C. is a work under constant revision; every new law changes part of its text, complicating the task of ascertaining "the law" even further.

The first time a controversy arises concerning a new statute, the parties disputing its meaning arrive in federal court, each intent upon convincing the trial judge that his interpretation is correct. That first trial judge must apply a "statutory construction" toolkit to interpret the statute's language. But though that judge's interpretation resolves the dispute between those first two parties, it does not qualify as "the law" as far as anyone else is concerned. If two other parties bring a dispute over the same statute to a different judge, that second judge is free to interpret it differently—the first trial judge's ruling may carry a certain amount of "persuasive" authority, but it does not "bind" any other trial judges. The crazy quilting bee has begun.

The party who lost the trial in front of that first judge has a pretty clear basis for his appeal. He can simply claim that the trial judge misinterpreted this new statute. Once again, the trial judge's written explanation of her interpretation may persuade the appellate judges to agree with her, but appellate judges are not particularly deferential to the legal rulings of "lower courts." They see statutory interpretation as one of their primary jobs. A randomly assigned three-judge panel from the circuit court overseeing that first trial applies the same canons of statutory construction as did the trial judge and issues its own interpretation of the statute. Their ruling is sort of "the law." It binds all trial judges holding trials under the watchful gaze of *that same circuit*. It also binds all future panels drawn from that same circuit court. The only way that the circuit court can undo that first panel's ruling is to hold an *en banc* session, in which the entire court (or at the very least, a much larger panel) reviews and reverses the judgment of those first three randomly assigned judges.

This first appellate ruling does not bind judges conducting trials appealable to other circuits, not to mention the other circuit courts themselves. The crazy quilt grows. When other circuits disagree with that first one, the circuits split—leading to the problem in patent law that first motivated the Federal Circuit. Of course, in addition to solving the patent-law circuit split problem, the Federal Circuit also threw a curious twist into the determination of which circuit court rulings bind which trial judges. Prior to the advent of the Federal Circuit, the twelve regional circuits oversaw all trials originating in their regions; today, trial judges are bound by "the law" of their regional circuit courts in all matters *except* those that the Federal Circuit oversees, in which case Federal Circuit law binds them.

Circuit splits are relatively rare. Most of the time, the circuits agree about the meaning of a statute, and that agreed meaning becomes "the law." But not always. The Supreme Court remains the ultimate arbiter of "the law," and the only court authorized to resolve circuit splits. When the Supreme Court chooses to hear a case that involves a disputed statute— an option that it exercises on less than 1 percent of circuit court cases—it is not bound by any of the circuit courts' rulings, *even if all of the circuit courts agreed about the statute's meaning*. In statutory law, as in Constitutional law, the Supreme Court has final say as to what "the law" is.

To make matters even more interesting, because *every* session of the Supreme Court is an *en banc* session, the Supreme Court can always over-rule its own previous decisions. It can interpret a statute one way on Monday, the opposite way on Tuesday, and then switch back to its original interpretation on Wednesday. Were the Supreme Court to act in such a capricious manner, however, no one would ever have any idea what "the law" is. America would become a lawless society, adrift in an unstable legal environment in which planning and investment are impossible. The only defense against this possibility lies in *stare decisis*, literally "to stand by things decided" but practically understood as a "doctrine of precedent." Precedent is perhaps the single most important self-constraint on the Supreme Court. Ignoring *stare decisis* could undermine the primary source of the Court's power—public confidence. According to Justice Sandra Day O'Connor:

> There is . . . a point beyond which frequent overruling would overtax the country's belief in the Court's good faith. Despite the variety of reasons that may inform and justify a decision to overrule, we cannot forget that such a decision is usually perceived (and perceived correctly) as, at the least, a statement that a prior decision was wrong. There is a limit to the amount of error that can plausibly be imputed to prior Courts. If that limit should be exceeded, disturbance of prior rulings would be taken as evidence that justifiable reexamination of principle had given way to drives for particular results in the short term. The legitimacy of the Court would fade with the frequency of its vacillation.[11]

This deference to precedent, coupled with the en banc requirement to overturn a circuit court ruling, stabilizes the legal system without strangling it. It allows the law to adapt and to evolve without losing its essential form. It also makes it possible for those with a suitable legal training to discern "the law."

But just because the Supreme Court is "the law's" final stop within the judiciary doesn't mean that the Supreme Court has the final say. There is, in fact, one institution authorized to upend the Supreme Court's interpretation of a statute. That body is Congress. If Congress disagrees with the state of "the law" after a Supreme Court ruling (or at any other time, for that matter), Congress is free to change the statutory language. The entire process can then repeat itself from scratch, starting with a new "first" trial judge. Meanwhile, if Congress chooses *not* to act, the courts tend to assume that they got "the law" right. In this context, congressional silence implies assent—strengthening the courts' deference to its own precedent even further.

This tortuous path toward determining "the law" has served the country well. The Supreme Court's ability to trump Congress on constitutional matters while Congress trumps the Supreme Court on statutory matters is among the system's more important checks and balances. The myriad persuasive opinions generated along the way to a definitive legal interpretation help air differing opinions and arguments, and ensure that the ultimate decision rests upon informed debate. Above all, the ability to overturn past judgments as circumstances change or as understanding expands keeps the system alive. After all, though a living society needs a living legal system, life requires only enough flexibility to adapt. Societies that interpret their laws too rigidly draw inward, wither, and die. Those that let their legal codes become amorphous slide into chaos and anarchy. Optimal organic growth arises through the proper admixture of interpretive flexibility and deference to precedent.

THE SMALL PICTURE

So much for the judicial box's inner workings. In the big-picture sense, the box's purpose is easy enough to discern: The Federal Circuit is supposed to issue rulings that help the American economy succeed in the information age without imposing unbearable transition costs. Smaller pictures can add mind-numbing levels of detail, but they don't really change the image. Congress doesn't simply wave its hands, create a court, and tell the judges to go take care of patents, trade, and government business. Instead, Congress enacts a statute prescribing precisely which sorts of cases work their way onto the Federal Circuit's docket:

> The United States Court of Appeals for the Federal Circuit shall have exclusive jurisdiction—
>
> (1) of an appeal from a final decision of a district court . . . if the jurisdiction of that court was based, in whole or in part, on [the Patent Act] . . . ;
> (2) of an appeal from a final decision of a district court . . . if the jurisdiction of that court was based, in whole or in part, on [the Little Tucker Act, which allows district courts to hear small monetary claims against the federal government] . . . ;
> (3) of an appeal from a final decision of the United States Court of Federal Claims;
> (4) of an appeal from a decision of . . . the Board of Patent Appeals and Interferences of the United States Patent and Trademark Office . . . ;
> (5) of an appeal from a final decision of the United States Court of International Trade;
> (6) to review the final determinations of the United States International Trade Commission relating to unfair practices in import trade . . . ;
> (7) to review, by appeal on questions of law only, findings of the Secretary of Commerce under . . . the Harmonized Tariff Schedule of the United States [i.e., customs classifications] . . . ;
> (8) of an appeal under . . . the Plant Variety Protection Act;

(9) of an appeal from a final order or final decision of the Merit Systems
Protection Board . . . ;

(10) of an appeal from a final decision of an agency board of contract appeals . . . ;

(11) of an appeal under section 211 of the Economic Stabilization Act of
1970 . . . ;

(12) of an appeal under section 5 of the Emergency Petroleum Allocation Act
of 1973 . . . ;

(13) of an appeal under section 506(c) of the Natural Gas Policy Act of
1978 . . . ;

(14) of an appeal under section 523 of the Energy Policy and Conservation
Act. [12]

Even this detailed statutory list is incomplete—demonstrating once again just how hard it is to look up "the law." The Federal Circuit also pops up in statutes describing the authority of other tribunals. For example, neatly tucked into the statutes discussing veterans benefits lurks the benefit of judicial review: "After a decision of the United States Court of Appeals for Veterans Claims is entered in a case, any party to the case may obtain a review of the decision. . . . The Court of Appeals for the Federal Circuit shall decide all relevant questions of law, including interpreting constitutional and statutory provisions."[13] Nothing in the Federal Circuit's "own" jurisdictional statute even hints at its role in veterans law.

Nevertheless, the extent to which the small picture mirrors the big picture is clear: The Federal Circuit is the sole court authorized to review cases dealing with patents (whether they begin in district court or at the PTO); monetary claims against the federal government (whether they begin in district court, the Court of Federal Claims, or an agency board of contract appeals); and trade (whether they begin in the Court of International Trade, the International Trade Commission, or the Customs Service). This subject matter defines the bulk of the Federal Circuit's docket and represents the court's primary areas of responsibility. Its other areas of authority are either narrow legal checks for outrageous behavior in selected administrative tribunals or holdovers from specialized legislation, largely defunct but still on the books, that can no longer support its own specialized tribunal—burdens that the Federal Circuit bears simply because it is the only appellate court with nationwide jurisdiction.

Nationwide jurisdiction also places these bodies of law inside a particularly opaque black box; it eliminates many of the common sources of questions and challenges. Judge Randall Rader has noted the

distinct institutional difference between the United States Court of Appeals for the Federal Circuit and the other twelve circuits. Whenever a Federal Circuit panel makes an error interpreting the patent code, every district court in the nation, and even every later Federal Circuit panel, is obliged to follow and perpetuate the error. Even the Supreme Court has difficulty identifying errors for correction because this court's national jurisdiction requires universal application of a mistake.[14]

That "institutional difference" is hardly restricted to patents; it creates parallel challenges in each area of Federal Circuit jurisdiction. The downside of nationwide uniformity is a lack of collegial scrutiny. Sometimes circuit splits are *good*, particularly if the first three-judge panel to consider a law got it wrong. The societal need for external inquiries and analysis is therefore likely *greater* in the areas of exclusive Federal Circuit jurisdiction than it is in the other areas of the law. And yet, because these areas of the law are so complex and esoteric, public scrutiny beyond the confines of the legal community is rare.

That need for public scrutiny suggests testing two serially connected black boxes. In the first box, Congress translates input policy prescriptions into statutory outputs. Those outputs, in turn, serve as the inputs to the second box, where the Federal Circuit interprets them, combines them, applies them to case-specific facts, and outputs legal opinions. How well is this coupled system working? If we detect some faults, can we trace them to their source—or in nonengineering terms, can we tell whether Congress or the courts deserves primary blame for laws that deviate from our public policy goals?

This query leads to another critical component of black-box testing, "test sequence design." A test sequence is nothing more than the set of inputs used to test the box, such as the set of policies that we—the voting public—*think* we told Congress to embody in the laws that the Federal Circuit interprets. At an intuitive level, these policy goals are not hard to outline. Patents are supposed to motivate innovation. Trade is supposed to strengthen the American economy. When the government acts as a business, it should behave as an ethical business.

Each of these policy goals also has unstated downsides that complicate our desire to cast them as simple test sequences. Patents elevate prices to consumers and may actually deter some innovation. Trade can displace workers and businesses. Parties to a contract, and employers and employees, often differ about the ethics of their relationships. These downsides explain in part why so many of the statutes that Congress drafts are so complicated. Congress must try to achieve these policy goals without imposing unacceptable costs on the less fortunate members of society as the world undergoes its transition from industrial age to information age. High transition costs will engender a backlash—and in the areas of law on the Federal Circuit's docket, the backlash is likely to carry serious political clout. The tension between overall policy goals and that expected backlash defines the challenge of transition planning. It is not enough for Congress and the courts to craft laws appropriate to an information-age economy. They must also craft laws that help the citizenry navigate the transition successfully.

THE NETWORKED ECONOMY

A meaningful economic policy for the information age must begin with the age's defining feature: *Information is abundant, easy to collect and manipulate, and inexpensive to share.* Information, however, is meaningless in a vacuum; information that is not communicated, shared, combined with other information, or used, might as well not exist. Communication thus requires connectivity, and connectivity places a premium on infrastructure—both physical and virtual. Physical infrastructures such as wires or satellite links enable people to stream electrons or photons toward each other. Virtual infrastructures, also known as "standards" or "protocols," allow people to arrange those electrons into decipherable sequences that convey meaning—and to decipher the sequences that they receive from others.

Anyone seeking to learn a new way to communicate must first ensure physical connectivity and then select a communication protocol. Because the most popular protocols create the greatest number of new communication opportunities, they attract the greatest numbers of new students—in turn becoming even more popular. This "virtuous cycle" of growth is the defining feature of an economic network.[15] Though none of the Court's parents knew it when they set the Federal Circuit in motion, their new judicial overseers of technology, innovation, trade, and government would soon become gatekeepers to some of the world's most important networks.

Any economic policy likely to succeed in such a networked economy must recognize that networks create two new sources of power. First, network interconnectivity allows empowered individuals to bypass traditional middlemen. Information abundance allows willing buyers and sellers to find each other easily, to negotiate directly, and to trade without paying traditional intermediaries to conduct the transaction. Second, network protocols confer enormous power upon their owners—particularly if an owner possesses monopoly control of a secret protocol key. A monopoly protocol owner is capable of assuming the privileged position of first-among-equals on the network and extracting tribute from the rest of the network. From the perspective of the network's members, some privilege for the owner is acceptable—even desirable. If ownership conferred no benefits, few would venture to design or to maintain new protocols.

Extreme privilege, however, is unacceptable. Once network membership becomes indispensable, the owner is capable of blackmail most vile. Public policies appropriate to an age of networked economies must therefore foster individual empowerment while restraining the network owner's ability to exploit the network's other members. These two new sources of power thus redistribute power throughout the economy: individuals get stronger, middlemen get weaker, and protocol monopolists reign supreme. People who work for those weakened middlemen often get caught in the crunch.

The battle lines of the early information age are thus drawn, as are the policy prescriptions. The primary goal of public policy must be to harness empowered individuals to achieve the maximum good. Individual empowerment, if allowed to flourish with relatively few constraints, will move the economy toward the "competitive ideal" of modern microeconomic price theory: large numbers of well-informed buyers and sellers, individually too small to affect the market, will negotiate individually and freely so that the "invisible hand" allocates society's resources optimally. The secondary goal of public policy must be to ensure that suitable infrastructures exist, but that no single owner can use them exploitatively. Developing unencumbered infrastructures requires a balanced combination of government investment in public goods, incentives including but not restricted to those embodied in intellectual property law, and enforcement of the antitrust laws. The tertiary goal of public policy must be to prevent disintermediated middlemen from impeding socially beneficial progress. Such predictable challenges to the commonweal arise whenever technology impels reform; it is an inherent property of transitions that those who fared well under the status quo will fight against change. The quaternary goal of public policy must be to help those that progress displaces adjust to the new environment and remain productive contributors to the economy. Without such adjustment programs, social upheaval and political opposition risk undermining the policies that serve the first three goals.

These goals outline a sound economic policy for the information age. Technology will continue to inform the citizenry. Informed citizens will seek to leverage that information in the pursuit of happiness. Free markets will provide the most effective mechanisms for allocating scarce resources among those happiness-seeking citizens. In short, the key to any viable economic policy in the information age is the simultaneous nurturing of competitive markets and meaningful opportunities for the citizenry. Debates over the best means to this end will arise, but an age of informed, empowered individuals must also be an age of free, competitive markets. The four policy goals all serve this end; they ensure that broadly available competitive markets will emerge and persist. Success in the information age will accrue to the countries and the societies that most successfully spread opportunity, increase choice, and provide people with the information necessary for their choices to have meaning. The laws governing the patent and trade systems will be central to implementing such economic policies.

CENTRAL THESIS

How well do current laws correspond to these asserted policy goals? The key to understanding policy pronouncements is to focus on the values that guide them. In the United States today, that focus hinges upon two misunderstood philosophies, liberalism and conservatism. The differences between *political* liberals and conservatives in contemporary America are hard to miss, but the philosophical genesis of these differences is subtler.

Philosophical conservatives believe that American institutions made the country great. Part of the brilliance of the American constitutional system is that its separation of powers and its checks and balances allowed numerous competing institutions to develop, each vibrant in its own way, each powerful in its own sphere, and each required—at some ultimate level—to justify itself to the people. Attempts to erode the boundaries between institutional spheres of power, or to remove ultimate oversight from the people, threaten the vitality of these grand institutions and represent an existential threat to our national future. Philosophical liberalism begins with the individual—not the institution. This focus leads to both analyses and conclusions that differ from those arising from a more conservative bent, and "[not] until the ordinances of law and of opinion are so framed as to give full scope to all individuality not positively noxious, and to restrain all that is noxious, will the two classes of sympathies ever be entirely reconciled."[16]

Philosophical conservatives approach their analyses of policy reforms and legal changes by considering the ways that they will shuffle authority among institutions. Where the proposals will lead to a significant reordering of institutional power or authority, conservatives will unite in opposition; where the institutional effect is negligible, different conservatives may take different views. Philosophical liberals approach their analyses of policy reforms and legal changes by considering the ways that they will affect individual rights, liberties, and opportunities. Where the proposals promise to expand opportunities, liberals will unite in favor. Where the proposals promise to contract opportunities, liberals will unite in opposition. And where the proposals will either expand some opportunities at the expense of others or promise to have little effect on the individual, different liberals may take different views.

In short, conservatives believe that our institutions have made us great and that robust institutions provide the best guarantee of our liberty and our prosperity. Liberals believe that our liberty is the source of both our prosperity and our institutions' greatness. Both perspectives are critical to understanding the Federal Circuit's role in the American economy during the current transitional era; the underlying challenge is to determine the role of a specific institution within a liberal economy.

The relationship between individual liberties and the Federal Circuit docket may appear tenuous. This court rarely if ever encounters issues tied to free speech, religious expression, criminal procedure, abortion, discrimination, gun ownership, sexual orientation, or civil rights—the issues that most Americans associate most readily with individual rights.[17] At a slightly deeper level, however, the bodies of law on the Federal Circuit docket play critical roles in shaping the economy: Are people free to profit from their own creative genius? Are they free to read patents without being accused of infringing them intentionally? Are patents true "property rights" due the same respect as real property and personal property? Are they mere impediments to the free market that prohibit businesses from providing consumers with the best available products at the lowest possible prices? Or are patents regulatory mechanisms designed to overcome a perceived market failure (i.e., an insufficient supply of new innovation) by creating a market in innovation rights? Are people free to trade with whomever they wish? Is it ever appropriate to force traders to internalize environmental, labor, intellectual property, or other moral costs or concerns into the prices that they negotiate? When, if ever, is it appropriate to adopt trade provisions that serve narrow interests to the detriment of the broad public? Does society owe some form of adjustment assistance to displaced workers and businesses who lose so that the public at large can enjoy the benefits of free trade? Can people trust the government to stand by its obligations? Precisely where is the line between government *qua* government and government as economic agent, and should it matter?

All of these questions are critical to determining the sort of economy we want and to recognizing the sort of economy that we have. The Federal Circuit's institutional perspective as the court given primary oversight responsibility for the laws shaping the innovation, trade, and government business sectors provides a unique window on the economic policies unfolding as we enter the information age. A liberal look through that window will tell us how well we are implementing the free-market capitalism that information-age economic networks require—and thus give us a glimpse of our own prospects for continued prosperity and success. A conservative look through that same window will reveal how well the court observes the institutional boundaries that constrain its authority, and where those constraints are impeding proper economic policy development.

The central thesis of this book is that the liberal policy perspectives that helped motivate the Federal Circuit will also lead to a successful information-age economy, subject to a conservative respect for institutional competencies and boundaries. The liberal policy pronouncements are simple. On patents: *Promote innovation!* On trade: *Strengthen the American economy and make Americans richer!* And when it comes to government business: *Adhere to the highest standards of ethical business behavior!* The conservative constraints dictate where and when it is appropriate for the court to affect policy—and where the court may comment on policy but do nothing to implement it. They also highlight relative institutional competencies: Congress is the right place to debate rules; the courts are the right places to see how those rules guide behavior.

In the final analysis, though it is neither possible nor wise to ignore the broader political and social contexts within which laws unfold, the Federal Circuit is a court of law and the matters on its docket all involve fact-intensive disputes between specific parties. Where is there room to consider policy? Many of those trekking·to Lafayette Park serve as surrogates for other similarly situated parties. This surrogacy justifies the task that occupies most of an appellate judge's time—writing opinions that explain the law and the reasoning underlying the court's rulings. Institutional rules circumscribe the tools, perspectives, and biases that judges may bring to this task, but they do not preclude either the judges themselves or the extrajudicial observers of their work from commenting on the relationships among philosophy, policy, law, behavior, and the parties bringing their suits to appellate courts. The imposition of Federal Circuit rulings on specific individuals defines a black-box output; it is the result of an intricate process that started with a test sequence of policy inputs and worked its way into statutory language long before arriving in Lafayette Park. The relationship between the initial policy inputs and those judicial outputs returns us to the critical question from which we embarked upon our detour through history, philosophy, and methodology: *Are the policies we have the policies we want?*

II

THE PATENT COURT

Though the Federal Circuit is more than *just* the "patent court," it is indeed the patent court. The court's founders assigned it several tasks, but its central mission was clear: Strengthen the patent system. Inject enough stability and certainty into the patent law for investors to see patents as reliable tools of business strategy. But that was a quarter-century ago. How well has the court done? Is today's patent system reliable enough to be useful? Are there still lingering problems—and if so, where? What happens at the cutting edge of innovation, where standard legal principles seem to make little sense? If the court has achieved its original objective, what should it do now? And perhaps above all: Do today's patent laws truly motivate innovation in line with the constitutional goal of "promoting the progress of science and the useful arts"?

3

✝

From Pilgrims to Progress

GENESIS

In September 1620, a band of intrepid Pilgrims set sail from England seeking the freedom to practice their faith. Though Virginia bound, they landed instead in what is now Massachusetts. Every American schoolchild knows that much (or at least they did back when I went to school). Few children—and likely no more than a few adults—know that this improper landing presented the Pilgrims with a serious problem of patent law. Before leaving England, the Pilgrims had secured a patent to colonize Virginia. That patent outlined their rights and responsibilities vis-à-vis the English Crown. Their northerly landing placed them in a quandary; they had no authority to settle that far north. Their decision to do so literally exceeded their patent grant—a problem in any patent system. Fortunately, they were soon able to resolve this difficulty by obtaining a new patent, the Pierce Patent of 1621, allowing them to settle in Plymouth Bay.

That's pretty much where patent law started. Throughout medieval times, European kings and queens issued numerous "letters patent," open letters granting the bearer some royal privilege and informing all readers that the Crown stood behind the grant. In the fifteenth century, the practice truly came into its own. Global trade, innovation, and entrepreneurship began to revolutionize stodgy businesses like agriculture, textiles, and shipping. Western Europe entered a period of explosive economic growth. The combination of closed command economies, new commercial opportunities, and an altered competitive environment, put the kings commanding those economies in a powerful position. Opportunities for

39

patronage and corruption abounded. Europe's kings issued letters patent granting monopolies on trade routes, domestic businesses, and various other economic activities—typically, for the right price. The Venetians realized that there might be money in licenses that allowed inventors to use their new inventions. Though this idea conflicted with the more common monopoly licenses that allowed incumbents to squelch new and threatening inventions, other European sovereigns were willing to add this arrow to their patronage quivers. After all, a sale is a sale.

In sixteenth-century England, where the Anglo-American legal tradition was gestating, Queen Elizabeth I's patents granted monopolies on the manufacture and sale of soap, alum, leather, salt, glass, knives, sailcloth, sulfur, starch, iron, paper, and other commodities. But even patronage has its limits; the good queen refused to patent Sir John Harrington's "water closet" on the grounds of propriety. In 1603, her successor James I— perhaps better known for the eponymous translation of the Bible that he commissioned than as an originator of Anglo-American patent law— ascended the throne and accelerated the practice.[1]

Needless to say, this system of royal monopolies was rife with corruption, bad for commercial development, and horrendous for English consumers, workers, inventors, and entrepreneurs. Resentment built, and the judiciary started to complain about the system's inherent inequity. In 1610, King James bowed to the pressure. He revoked all previous patents, declaring "monopolies are things contrary to our laws," with the sole exception of "projects of new invention."[2] His declaration changed the world of patents. Letters patent remained useful diplomatic tools; after all, a king might want to write an open letter for reasons unrelated to monopoly (e.g., letting some Pilgrims colonize Plymouth Bay). An important subset of these letters rewarded projects of new invention. Over time, this new-invention subset assumed increasingly distinct characteristics and became a distinct government grant, rarely confused with a diplomatic communiqué.

Before James's reign ended, Parliament had done him one better. The Statute of Monopolies of 1624 enshrined both the ban on monopolies and the innovation exception. Section VI of the statute specified:

> Provided also and be it declared and enacted that any declaration before mentioned shall not extend to any letters patent and grants of privilege for the term of fourteen years or under, hereafter to be made, of the sole working or making of any manner of new manufacturers within this realm, to the true and first inventor and inventors of such manufacturers which others at the time of making such letters patent and grants shall not use, so as also they be not contrary to the law or mischievous to the State, by raising prices of commodities at home, or hurt of trade, or generally inconvenient.[3]

In contemporary parlance, the Statute of Monopolies established some basic properties for the letters patent belonging to this new subset: They are time-limited grants to an inventor for a specific invention, subject to several provisos protecting the public interest.

Roughly 165 years later, the framers of the U.S. Constitution followed suit. They empowered Congress "to promote the progress of science and useful arts, by securing for limited times to authors and inventors the exclusive right to their respective writings and discoveries."[4] American patents (and copyrights) exist today solely because the framers chose to empower Congress to motivate progress by reserving exclusive rights to inventors (and authors), and because Congress chose to exercise that power. The very first Congress passed the Patent Act of 1790, incorporating the basic notion of a time-limited grant to an inventor for a specific invention into the fledgling body of federal statutory law.

The marriage of patents to invention is thus older than our republic. Other countries and cultures have tried to divorce the two or to cheapen their relationship for a spell, but American law has never wavered. Switzerland, for example, operated without a patent system from 1850 to 1907, and the Dutch did likewise from 1869 to 1912.[5] More recently, India doubted that its British patent-law bequest could meet the needs of a developing country. In 1970, India reworked its patent system to motivate domestic industrialization and employment rather than innovation.[6] Though this experiment led to some interesting results (notably the development of some of the world's largest manufacturers of generic drugs), India abandoned it under duress when the World Trade Organization's (WTO) Agreement on Trade-Related Aspects of Intellectual Property Rights (TRIPS) essentially globalized the patent-invention marriage that the Anglo-American tradition had long recognized and thus likely ended all such experimentation for quite some time. What therefore King James has joined together, let not man put asunder.

Joined or asunder, the relationship between patents and innovation has had its rocky moments—even within unwavering American law. Thomas Jefferson was an early champion of the patent system, its enabling constitutional provision, and the 1790 Patent Act. Congress overhauled that early system with the Patent Act of 1836. The system grew, flourished, gained definition, and developed new rules and formalisms throughout the nineteenth century; the Patent Office also began to assume the bureaucratic form that remains familiar today. Throughout the twentieth century, however, public opinion about patents oscillated wildly. As a leading casebook explains:

> By the 1920s and 1930s, a number of people began to believe that large companies with patent portfolios were a little *too* powerful. Spurred in part by a

series of anticompetitive acts by large companies whose patents dominated an industry, courts became less willing to enforce patent rights and more willing to punish patentees for exceeding the scope of their patent grant. The pendulum swung back towards patentability in the 1940s. As the nation threw all available resources into the war effort, the armed forces called on engineers and scientists to perfect a vast array of new technologies in short order. Companies during this era had neither the time nor the ability to try to exclude their competitors: government-directed industrial development and "mandatory cooperation" replaced exclusionary acts. By the time the war was over, there was a consensus in Congress in favor of a strong patent system. In fact the 1952 Patent Act, the first major revision of the patent code since the nineteenth century, marked a return to the principles of that century in many respects.

The patent system by general consensus reached a low-water mark during the 1960s, in the wake of this period of strong protection. The patent office issued patents rather freely, without particularly rigorous examination in many circumstances. On the other hand, it was difficult to get a patent upheld in many federal circuit courts, and the circuits diverged widely both as to doctrine and basic attitudes toward patents. As a consequence, industry downplayed the significance of patents. In 1982 Congress passed the Federal Courts Improvement Act, creating the new Court of Appeals for the Federal Circuit.[7]

. . . and that's where we came in. The industrial age was ending. The American economy was in trouble. Industrial innovation was its only bright spot, the only hope for salvation. America seemed poised to lose even that edge, as Japanese and German firms moved into positions of world leadership. The country knew that it needed some radical changes. It turned to the patent system as a promising source of those changes.

REGULATING IDEAS

Anyone turning toward the patent system should arrive with one burning question: What's a patent? Professor Suzanne Scotchmer, a prominent innovation economist, cut right to the chase in her "Primer for Non-lawyers on IP":

A patent gives its owner the right to sue for infringement if anyone tries to make, use, sell, offer, import, or offer to import the invention into the country issuing the patent. It thus grants a legal monopoly. In addition to infringement, there is also a concept of contributory infringement. This lets patent holders sue to stop third parties from knowingly selling inputs that are "especially adapted" for use in patented combinations or processes. Patents are the gold standard of IP protection. With other forms of protection, if a third party duplicates the protected innovation independently, he or she can use it. The absence of this independent-invention defense makes patent law uniquely powerful.[8]

This brief explanation is extraordinarily insightful. At its heart, a patent is little more than the right to file a lawsuit. But a lawsuit about *what*? Just what does a patentee "own"? And what's so bad about "infringement"? How can independent invention *not* be a defense? Can it really be against the law for, say, a guy in San Diego to think up a new idea, cobble together a gizmo prototype in his garage, and build a business around it, just because a woman in New Jersey, whom he's never met and of whose work he was totally unaware, came up with the same (or even a similar) idea a few weeks earlier and filed a set of secret papers with the PTO?

Yes. That not only can be the law, it *is* the law. And the stakes behind these patent lawsuits—and all lawsuits involving intellectual property—are enormous. But to appreciate that enormity, it is necessary to take a step even further backward to understand the role of patents within the broader realm of IP rights that Scotchmer mentioned. American law recognizes four major (and several minor) types of "intellectual property," or more accurately "rights in ideas": patents, copyrights, trademarks, and trade secrets. Each of these categories serves a different goal, and each is subject to its own body of complex laws.

These varying "rights in ideas" define a regulatory regime for information—and thus a critical component of the information-age economy. They interact in a sophisticated way to motivate various types of information collection, innovation, commercialization, and dissemination. Trade secret law encourages businesses to develop proprietary databases, strategies, customer lists, recipes, and various other innovations important for maintaining a competitive edge, but of minimal scientific or technological interest to the broad public (though trade secret law also protects those who choose to maintain as secrets innovations that society would prefer to see disclosed in patents). Patent law encourages innovation directed toward practical inventions, as well as the enhancement of public knowledge by making it commercially safe (and often advantageous) for an innovator to reveal her new discovery's inner workings. Copyright law traditionally promoted the literary and artistic expressions that enhance culture, but the information age has given it a new role and embroiled it in new controversies; as the scope of copyrighted digital expression has grown from software to music and beyond, it has strained the traditional boundaries of copyright law.[9] Trademark law is perhaps the oldest known form of consumer protection; it protects a producer's ability to place its recognizable "signature" on its products, thereby providing consumers with valuable reputational information.

Because each of these bodies of law serves a different goal, each one incorporates a different set of trade-offs. The information age makes these trade-offs stark. Each body of IP law strives to increase either the abundance or the meaning of information (to the public's benefit) by recognizing and enforcing a private party's decision to restrict the free flow of that information (to the public's detriment). This characterization immediately places cost-benefit analysis at the center of any consideration of IP policy, and frames any discussion about the alignment or misalignment of IP policy and IP law. As Professor William Landes and Judge Richard Posner commented, "Today it is acknowledged that analysis and evaluation of IP law are appropriately conducted within an economic framework that seeks to align that law with the dictates of economic efficiency."[10] We therefore approach the black box of patents with a straightforward test question: Do the various doctrines of patent law create more value by increasing the quantity and quality of public information than they cost by impeding information flows?

The technical nature of this query masks a deeper question buried just beneath its surface. Are IP regimes—specifically the patent laws—truly "property" regimes, or are they more correctly viewed as "regulatory" regimes? The differences between these two views are profound, and their implications to law and policy are potentially revolutionary.

Private property enhances social value because people tend to exert their greatest efforts, and invest their greatest resources, to improve the things that they own. The liberal gospel preaches that by parceling the world and its items among individual owners, society will maximize the likelihood that individuals will improve a piece of the world. When someone finds something with no evident owner, or with an owner who gave the item up as lost (e.g., a shipwreck), the law often crafts rules allowing the finder to claim ownership; such rules motivate people to recover and improve dormant items. The same logic applies to intellectual goods, and in particular to patentable ideas. Society wants people to devise new ideas, to turn those ideas into useful products, and to share both with the public at large.

So perhaps we should view patents as mechanisms that motivate "idea hunters" to find unrecognized ideas, to claim ownership of those ideas, and to improve them; in return, we require them to "register" their ideas publicly so that all can marvel at their discoveries and improvements. Viewed in this way, patents seem little different from deeds, titles, and other documents supporting an individual's ownership right—and her right to sue anyone who "infringes" or "trespasses" upon that right. We should refrain from asking too many questions about whether patentees are using their property "responsibly," much as we typically refrain from asking too many such questions about other property owners.

Then again, we live in a basically free-market economy. In the absence of some specific regulation to the contrary, people can exchange whatever resources they want upon any terms to which both contracting parties agree. This free-market default is the basis of liberal market capitalism, and all regulations with economic components interfere with this default structure. Good regulations interfere only minimally in return for making new transactions possible, economically viable, or meaningful. Bad regulations simply elevate some legislator's priorities over those of the market. But *all* regulations necessarily rest upon an underlying belief that market forces alone cannot meet some socially beneficial goal.

So perhaps we should view patents as regulations that impede the free exchange of ideas and new inventions to promote the socially beneficial goal of idea creation. Viewed in this way, patent law appears little different from other regulatory codes, and "infringement" is more akin to a regulatory violation than to a trespass. We needn't be quite so tolerant of people in technical regulatory compliance whose behavior nevertheless works to serious public detriment—and we might want to be quite tolerant of those whose behavior is beneficial, though technically noncompliant. The range of antisocial acts that can lead the government to retract a regulatory grant is much larger than the range of actions justifying a government confiscation of property.

It's hard to differentiate between these perspectives because both seem justifiable. Case law often compares patents to deeds and titles, describes patentees who stay within the scope of their patents as property owners, and views patentees who exceed the scope of their patents as attempting to exercise ownership over someone else's property. Instances in which the courts, including the Federal Circuit and the Supreme Court, are supposed to consider the *effects* of a patentee's behavior on either commercial development or scientific knowledge are few and far between. These characteristics of the patent system support the patent-as-property view. At the same time, the basic structure of patent law differs markedly from that of traditional property law. Congress issues detailed rules about what patentees can and cannot do with their patents, and the PTO—a regulatory agency—augments that complex statute with an even more detailed set of regulations.

Had Congress been clear in treating patents as a regulatory system—an unlikely occurrence given that patents predated the regulatory state by a century and a half—the division of labor in patent law would look quite different than it does today and might even match the relative strengths of the participating institutions. Congress is an excellent place to craft general rules, but a poor place to consider the many different effects those rules can have. Regulatory agencies may have a greater eye for detail, but their rule-making procedures are no better attuned to individual effects.

Courts are excellent places to see different effects unfold and, in particular, to catch aberrant effects flowing from otherwise sound rules. A judiciary empowered to correct those few cases—as courts are in some legal arenas outside the IP umbrella—can leave the generally beneficial rule intact while policing its misapplications. Judicial opinions can also provide Congress with useful feedback about the frequency of such "exceptions," or instances of actual effects deviating from intended policies. That is not, however, the system that Congress put in place. The existing patent system is a hybrid: a regulatory regime that creates property-conferring rights and responsibilities similar to, yet distinct from, other sorts of property.

A TIME FOR REFORM?

Is it time to consider reforming the patent system? The results of our black-box tests will inform the answer. The early 1980s ushered in a new era of patent law, but the American economy has changed significantly since then. Perhaps it is time to reform the patent laws yet again. Perhaps it is even time to consider overhauling the Patent Act itself, as Congress did in 1836 and 1952, but not in the early 1980s.

If our black-box tests conclude that such revolutionary reform is necessary, Congress may face a new hurdle. India was not alone in relinquishing her rights to IP experimentation to the WTO. By writing a 1990s conception of IP law into a key international treaty, Western trade negotiators tied Congress's hands as well. TRIPS limits experimentation with alternative concepts, structures, and rules of IP—including patents. The gains in this bargain were enormous; respect for IP around the globe, though still far below what some patentees and copyright holders might want, has never been higher. But no one considered its full costs. If an early 1990s understanding of IP is basically appropriate for economies at all stages of development as they enter the information age, the cost is minimal. If not, who knows how much damage TRIPS may have wrought. Our inquiry is unlikely to resolve this dilemma, but it may frame some questions for consideration throughout the global trading community.

Patents and copyrights (and to a lesser extent, trademarks and trade secrets) are central to global trade and development in the information age. About the time that trade negotiators from the developed world were enshrining their own understanding of these rights in ideas into international law, technology writer Fred Warshofsky warned of looming patent wars:

> In the war for global economic dominance, the fiercest battles today are over
> IP. Where nations once fought for control of trade routes and raw materials,

they now fight for exclusive rights to ideas, innovations, and inventions. The battlefields in this bloodless war are the world's courts, where billions of dollars are won and lost each year through patent litigation. Beyond licensing fees and individual companies' rights to manufacture specific products, what is at stake is the ultimate control of key high-tech industries such as biotechnology, electronics, and communications. . . .

In the final analysis, IP is quite simply handmaiden to the profit motive that drives the economic engine we know as capitalism. In the competition for world markets, it is the nation that innovates best and has the means to both encourage and protect those innovations that will provide the jobs and highest standard of living for its citizens.[11]

Warshofsky reported on some early skirmishes in these wars, and some of them even made front-page headlines. But America soon diverted its attention to other wars, some related, some not. We watched the birth of the commercial Internet, the rise and fall of the dotcoms, the Y2K non-apocalypse, the mapping of the human genome, the conflation of stem cell research with abortion, the growth of global trade and the response of antiglobal anarchists, the fall of the Twin Towers, and the acknowledgment of Islamic terrorism.

The grossly misnamed "global war on terror" in particular struck many observers as countering the claims of the patent wars' centrality. They argued that the 1990s focus on technology and economics had blinded us to the threats brewing in the world's darkest caves. Some of this criticism was undoubtedly warranted; we got so excited about progress and growth that we paid insufficient attention to a backlash that we should have known was inevitable. But many of these same observers, stung by this oft-internalized self-criticism, responded by pushing too far in the opposite direction. They began to ignore the global technology trends that had seemed so important through the summer of 2001, and focused almost entirely on the assorted violent anarchic or totalitarian antiliberal hatemongers who dominate the Arab/Islamic world. But distance provides perspective. As the years since the terror attacks of September 11, 2001, mount, increasing numbers of people are waking to realize that globalization, technology, and terror are *all* defining characteristics of this transitional era. In large part, the shape that the information age will assume depends upon the way that we understand these trends, respond to them, and integrate our responses into a coherent whole.

New York Times foreign affairs columnist Tom Friedman, a keen observer of the global technology trends of the 1990s, reported that his own reawakening led him to conclude that "the world is flat":

It's not only the software writers and computer geeks who get empowered to collaborate on work in the flat world. It's also al-Qaeda and other terrorist networks. The playing field is not being leveled only in ways that draw in and superempower a whole new group of innovators. It's being leveled in a way that draws in and superempowers a whole new group of angry, frustrated, and humiliated men and women. . . . [My] recognition that the world was flat was unnerving because I realized that this flattening had been taking place while I was sleeping, and I had missed it. I wasn't really, sleeping, but I was otherwise engaged . . . traveling in the Arab and Muslim worlds.[12]

Friedman reports that he "lost the trail of globalization" for two-and-a-half years after 9/11. He returned to it only in February 2004, on a visit to Bangalore, India's answer to Silicon Valley, where he resumed his role as a war correspondent in the patent (or more accurately, the technology) wars; his columns and his subsequent book once again began to reflect the issues of Warshofsky's *Patent Wars* and my own *Digital Phoenix*. His frontline reporting noted the growth of research and development capabilities in India, China, and Russia, and predicted "the globalization of innovation and an end to the old model of a single American or European multinational handling all the elements of the development product cycle from its own resources."[13] He continued:

We in the U.S. are the lucky beneficiaries of centuries of economic experimentation, and we are the experiment that has worked. . . . The quality of American IP protection . . . further enhances and encourages people to come up with new ideas. In a flat world, there is a great incentive to develop a new product or process, because it can achieve global scale in a flash. But if you are the person who comes up with that new idea, you want your IP protected. No country respects and protects IP better than America . . . and as a result, a lot of innovators want to come here to work and lodge their IP.[14]

Warshofsky's patent wars will play a significant role in determining the winners and losers on Friedman's flat world, a world in which abundant information flows quickly to those who will use it most efficiently. If we ignore the increase in global intellectual competition; if we neglect life-long education, constant retraining, and labor mobility; if we shut out talented immigrants and fail to maximize the potential within our own people; if we do not adapt our laws and our institutions to meet the needs of the information age; if we do not recognize that a world of abundant, inexpensive, freely flowing information can change everything but our fundamental values—then we risk losing our advantaged position as first among equals. Our lead at the moment is so great that many Americans cannot imagine it disappearing, but if history is any guide, by the time a genuine competitor becomes visible, both our decline and its ascent will be too far along to reverse. America must marshal its intellectual capital to keep its economy strong, its companies creative, its people educated, its workers employed, its consumers informed, and its values intact.

The prospects for victory depend, in large part, on the extent to which we are the most efficient users of information. Efficiency as information originators and users hinges on the propriety of the systems that regulate information—in short, the IP systems. "Creation and discovery are mysterious processes," Scotchmer wrote to introduce her study of innovation, "but whatever else is required, economists are reasonably certain that incentives matter."[15] The study of patent law is the study of those incentives. We all think that we know what Congress was trying to do when it passed the Patent Act. The question that we must ask is what Congress actually did. Are the policies that we have the policies that we want? There is no better place to look for answers than the Federal Circuit—a court created, after all, to better align the American patent system with the needs of a changing postindustrial economy.

THE GAME BEGINS

When it comes to patent law, the policy pronouncement is right in the Constitution: *Promote Progress!* The Constitution also provides Congress with a helpful tip: provide inventors with time-limited exclusive rights. Congress was under no obligation to exercise this constitutional power, but it apparently felt—with some justification—that the English patent system had developed quite nicely since the days of James I, that it did a reasonable job of promoting progress, and that despite its interference with the natural market in ideas, there was something inherently fair about helping inventors profit from their inventions. Congress began the arduous task of translating a vague policy prescription into a concrete statute.

That statute—the Patent Act, or Title 35 of the United States Code—is now in its third incarnation. Its basic contours are simple: Suppose you invent something that you think warrants a patent. You write a description of your invention and file a patent application with the Patent and Trademark Office, a part of the Department of Commerce. The PTO assigns an examiner to consider your application—typically someone who knows something about both the general subject matter of your invention and the state of the art in your field. That examiner, a government employee, now represents the public. The public gave her definite instructions about what sorts of inventions it was willing to "buy" through the patent system: only products or processes that are new, useful, and "nonobvious" (i.e., more than trivial improvements to the "prior art"). The two of you then engage in a bit of a negotiation known as "patent prosecution."

Because you undoubtedly hired an excellent patent lawyer to help you negotiate the best deal, you probably went in asking for far too much. "My invention," you initially claimed, "revolutionizes the entire field, and therefore entitles me to a patent covering virtually every related innovation likely to arise within the foreseeable future." The examiner is a bit skeptical. You retreat. The examiner asks more questions. You retreat further. Eventually, you agree about the patent's terms. You enshrine this agreement in a "specification" document containing two major parts: a list of "claims" detailing precisely what you own, and a "written description" explaining your invention clearly enough for someone of ordinary skill in the relevant discipline (or "art") to replicate it (and incorporating a number of other technical requirements). When you have agreed with the examiner on this document's contents and its wording, the deal is sealed. The PTO issues your patent. It then files all of your correspondence with the examiner in a public document called your "prosecution history" or "file wrapper." The public "sold" you your claims; you "paid" with your written description.

Congratulations, you're a patentee. You may or may not choose to "practice" your patent by selling the product that it claims, but you *will* write letters to other people or companies who work in your field, show them your patent, and threaten to sue them if they practice your patent without your authorization. Of course, your first letter may take a friendlier tone and offer to license your invention—particularly if you've not chosen to make your money by selling the patented product yourself. But though the tone may differ, a letter offering a license is precisely a letter threatening to sue those who refuse your proffered terms. So you negotiate a couple of license deals and file a couple of lawsuits. Now you're not only a patentee, you're also a plaintiff in a patent suit. Some defendants may crumble immediately; they will either take your license terms or stop doing whatever it is that you contend infringes your patent. Others will do neither. They will march into court right behind you and insist, first, that the PTO erred when it issued your patent and, second, that even if you deserved your patent, their accused product or process doesn't infringe. One or both of you will insist upon a trial by jury as the Seventh Amendment allows you to do.

Welcome to your first "vanilla" patent suit. Though your suit involves no special complications—such as allegations of fraud, nasty counterclaims, or attempts to hang some third party's liability on the defendant—it is still a complex, expensive bit of litigation. At a bare minimum, the district court is going to have to consider three sets of issues: What did you buy in your claims section? Did you really deserve the patent, or did the PTO err in issuing it? And does the defendant's accused product (or process) infringe? In legal lingo, these issues are called "claim construction," "validity," and "infringement," respectively. The game begins.

METAPHYSICS

Welcome to court. Several issues are on the table, but claim construction comes first. In fact, claim construction *must* come first, because until the court knows what the patent means, there's no reasonable way to consider either validity or infringement. Most patent lawsuits begin with disagreements about the precise meaning of at least some words in the claims. The court must begin by determining what those disputed words mean. This exercise is trickier than it sounds.

Why? Well, before a court can think about construing disputed terms in any particular patent, it has to nail down the rules. Where should the court look to resolve linguistic disputes? For that matter, who should do the looking—the judge or the jury? The answer to this latter, seemingly straightforward, question leads straight into metaphysics: What is a patent? Is it a technical document that one skilled artisan wrote for another, or is it a legal document that lawyers wrote for other lawyers? Should technical witnesses testify about words' meanings in their narrow fields of specialization, or should the court just look them up in a standard dictionary? Is claim construction a factual question or a legal question?

Litigation and metaphysics are not comfortable bedfellows. Patent scholars may devote their time and energy to the metaphysical aspects of these questions, but litigants, practicing lawyers, and judges need concrete answers. Hundreds of thousands of active patents, billions of dollars, and the respective roles of judges and juries all hang in the balance.

If claim construction is a factual question about the meaning of a technical document, the obvious resolution would be for the court to hire a technically trained "special master," well versed in the relevant technology and beholden to neither party, and assign that expert the task of disambiguating disputed terms. Unfortunately—at least for present purposes—that's not the way the American civil justice system works. In a jury trial, the jury is the sole "trier of fact." Certainly, if both parties agree to let the judge appoint a technical expert and to drop all terminological disputes in favor of the expert's construction, no one would object. But such agreements are rare, and though trial judges may try to cajole parties into one, even such cajolery succeeds only rarely. No, in a jury trial the parties present all disputed facts to the jury, present evidence supporting their interpretation of the facts, and then let the jury resolve all factual disputes. Unless the jury reaches a conclusion that is entirely inconsistent with the evidence, neither the trial judge nor an appellate court will re-open its factual findings.

In short, if the claims section of a patent is a technical document and disputes over the meaning of its words are factual disputes, only the jury can decide what they mean. But jurors are rarely expert in either the technology underlying a patent or the legal niceties involved in patent drafting. No one, regardless of his training, has ever read his first patent and found it comfortable and familiar. Patents are quite simply unique documents, similar in some ways to technical articles and similar in others to legal documents, but also quite different from both. The idea that an untrained jury could resolve disputes over specific technical terms embedded in a patent is a "legal fiction" at best. If we want juries to construe claims, we're just going to have to pretend that they know what they're doing.

Such a pretense, however, is not strictly necessary. We could go the other way and insist instead that a patent is nothing more than a legal document, like a contract or a deed, that lawyers write for other lawyers to read. If that's the case, judges shouldn't really need technical testimony or expert help. Federal judges are all qualified attorneys, more than capable of differentiating between the arguments that the parties' equally capable attorneys put forward. And if they fail, appellate courts—in this case, the Federal Circuit—need show them no deference. Appellate courts review legal questions *de novo*, or from scratch, and claim construction appears to be *precisely* the sort of issue that motivated Congress to create the Federal Circuit. Though trial judges who encounter patents infrequently may be unfamiliar with the nuances of patent language and patent law, Federal Circuit judges have no such excuse. Not only are they immersed in those nuances, they *wrote* them. If we can't trust the Federal Circuit to impose uniformity on claim construction, whom can we trust?

This approach, namely classifying patents as legal documents so that courts can resolve disputed terms as matters of law, seems to make a lot more sense. Except for one tiny little item: *It's absurd!* Patents exist to promote progress. Motivating innovation is an important part of that promotion, but it's only part. If motivation were the only goal, patent-ees could keep their inventions secret rather than buying their claims by explaining their inventions in terms comprehensible to their colleagues and competitors. How in the world can the law then turn around and insist that patents are not technical documents? Either inventors write them so that other inventors can understand them or lawyers write them so that other lawyers can understand them. Which is it? Patent *policy* seems to imply that patents are technical documents. But patent *law* suggests that there is no meaningful way to resolve linguistic disputes unless patents are legal documents.

Congress was silent on this question; the Patent Act doesn't provide any useful insights. That leaves the matter to the courts. For 205 years, the courts rose to the challenge by keeping the issue open. Sometimes judges construed claims as a matter of law, and sometimes juries construed them as findings of fact. Sometimes appellate courts were highly deferential, and sometimes they weren't. And then one day in 1995, more than two centuries after Congress passed its first Patent Act, the Federal Circuit decided to force the issue with an unsolicited *en banc* session—a session whose tale ushers us into the main tent of patent law, where claim construction, validity, and infringement crowd out all else.

4

✚

The Main Tent

SAGA OF A DRY CLEANER

Herbert Markman was a pioneer in the field of dry cleaning, the possessor of a patented technology for tracking "inventory" in a dry-cleaning establishment. His patent, like all patents, contained two parts. Its written description taught the public how to implement an inventory-tracking system. Its claims section specified what the public gave Markman in return for the written description. Like most patentees, Markman had claimed a number of variations on his basic theme of a computerized inventory control. Each claim specified a slightly different setup involving an input device, a data processing device "including memory operable to record [inventory] information and means to maintain an inventory total," a dot matrix printer, and a scanner capable of reading bar codes. The system, operating as a whole, must be able to "detect and localize spurious additions to inventory as well as spurious deletions therefrom."[1]

In other words, the bargain that the Patent and Trademark Office—acting on behalf of the public—had struck with Markman was simple. For the life of his patent, no member of the public could use any of the claimed setups without Markman's permission—but Markman could not prevent members of the public from using related but unclaimed devices or setups.

One day, Markman noticed that Althon Enterprises, the owner of two dry-cleaning establishments, was using Westview Instruments' DATAMARK and DATASCAN devices. Markman sued both Westview (for *making* and *selling* an infringing device) and Althon (for *using* an infringing device). Westview's machines combined a data processor, a printer, and a scanner to track dry-cleaning invoices and receipts.

Markman requested and received a jury trial. Three witnesses testified on Markman's behalf, the first two to explain the claim language to the jury and the third to convince the jury that Westview's devices infringed the patent: The first witness was Markman himself, testifying that he knew what his patent and its claims meant. The other two were a patent lawyer to testify about the way that a trained patent expert would read the claims, and an expert on bar code technology to explain Westview's devices to the jury. All of this testimony, of course, makes sense only if claim construction is a factual question that juries decide.

Westview took a different approach. It called only a single witness, its president, who explained to the judge and the jury how his company's devices worked. In particular, he pointed out that the devices tracked only invoices and receipts, not clothing. As he saw it, a dry cleaner's "inventory" is clothing; a tracking device incapable of tracking clothing may be many things, but it cannot be an infringing inventory-tracking system. Though this testimony makes sense whether claim construction is factual or legal, Westview's next move did not. Westview asked the judge to rule, *as a matter of law*, that its products could not infringe Markman's patent.

The trial judge, Marvin Katz, probably should have decided whether the question was factual or legal, but since this case occurred in the pre-1995 muddle, he decided not to decide. He told the jury to "determine the meaning of the claims using the relevant patent documents including the specifications, the drawings and the file histories. . . . Also relevant are other considerations that show how the terms of a claim would normally be understood by those of ordinary skill in the art." He further told the jury "to compare the claims with the Westview device to determine if it infringes."[2] In other words, Katz decided to treat all of the relevant questions as factual and to let the jury, as trier of fact, decide them. The jury did, and concluded that Westview's devices infringed some but not all of Markman's claims.

So far so good—except for the denouement. Having told the jury—and the parties—to treat patents as technical documents and claim construction as a factual question, Katz *then* turned around and announced that claim construction is a matter of law, for the judge alone to decide. He adopted Westview's view of the patent, announced that as a matter of law, the DATAMARK and DATASCAN could not infringe, and ruled for Westview. Not surprisingly, Markman appealed.[3] According to Markman, Judge Katz was just wrong when he announced that claim construction was a legal question; claim construction is, he asserted, a factual question, and factual questions in jury trials belong to the jury.

The Federal Circuit took the unusual step of bypassing a three-judge panel and agreeing to hear the case *en banc*. Why? Because, as Chief Judge Glenn Archer explained,

> The opinions of this court have contained some inconsistent statements as to whether and to what extent claim construction is a legal or factual issue, or a mixed issue. . . . At its inception, the Federal Circuit held that claim construction was a matter of law. Our first opinion deciding a question of claim construction, [decided July 15, 1983] said so explicitly. . . . The first Federal Circuit case to deviate from this precedent and state that claim construction may have underlying factual inquiries that must be submitted to a jury was [decided on April 27, 1984]. . . . Notwithstanding the apparent inconsistencies in our opinions, the Supreme Court has repeatedly held that the construction of a patent claim is a matter of law exclusively for the court. . . . We therefore settle inconsistencies in our precedent and hold that in a case tried to a jury, the court has the power and obligation to construe as a matter of law the meaning of language used in the patent claim.[4]

Though Archer stated this inconsistency in rather matter-of-fact terms, it was quite an admission of failure. Numerous committees and commissions had spent almost fifteen years debating the wisdom of a single court for patent appeals. Finally, after both the Carter and Reagan administrations signed onto the deal, Congress passed an enabling statute and told the Federal Circuit to clean up patent law. The court held its first session in October 1982. Seven and a half months later, it announced unambiguously that claim construction is a legal question—implying that jury input is inappropriate and that judges must resolve linguistic disputes themselves. Nine and a half months after that, it announced unambiguously that claim construction is a factual question—implying that a ruling from the bench is inappropriate and that juries must resolve all linguistic disputes. According to Archer, that second ruling contradicted explicit and consistent instructions from the Supreme Court. Yet, he conceded that for more than a decade, the Federal Circuit had generated numerous decisions following each of these contradictory unambiguous announcements, thoroughly confusing patentees, accused infringers, and district court judges. In his view, thirteen years after its birth and eleven years after sowing (or at the very least perpetuating) confusion about this basic metaphysical question of patent law, the Federal Circuit was finally going to do the job that Congress had assigned it.

Archer announced a ruling providing clear instructions to anyone—litigant, lawyer, judge, or juror—involved in patent litigation. A patent is a legal document that lawyers write for other lawyers to read. If litigants disagree about the meaning of a word in a claim, the trial judge must

resolve this legal dispute *before* the trial. Juries must never hear erroneous
interpretations of a patent—any more than they should hear erroneous interpretations of a contract, a law, or the Constitution. After all, "it is emphatically the province and duty of the judicial department to say what
the law is."[5] Juries exist as finders of fact. Who cares what a jury thinks
about the law?

How should we feel about this conclusion as a matter of policy? Archer
had some views about that, as well.

> There is much wisdom to the rule that the construction of a patent should be
> a legal matter for a court. A patent is a government grant of rights to the pat-
> entee. By this grant, the patentee owns the rights for a limited time to exclude
> others from making, using, or selling the invention as claimed. Infringement
> of the patentee's right to exclude carries with it the potential for serious con-
> sequences: The infringer may be enjoined and required to pay increased
> damages, costs and attorney fees. . . . To treat the nature of the patented in-
> vention as a matter of fact, to be inquired of and determined by a jury, would
> at once deprive the inventor of the opportunity to obtain a permanent and
> universal definition of his rights under the patent, and in each case of in-
> fringement it would subject him to the danger of false interpretation, from
> the consequences of which he could not escape. By confiding this duty to the
> court, however, its decision as to the nature of the patented invention be-
> comes reviewable to the same extent as any other legal question.[6]

Archer focused on the meaning of a patent *in litigation*. When people
get involved in a lawsuit, all sorts of documents assume a strange new
status as "evidence." In different sorts of trials, evidence can include
contracts, invoices, newspaper and magazine articles, handwritten
notes, and so on. There are some pretty clear rules about evidence.
Those categorized as "legal documents" have legally fixed meanings.
All others have factual meanings that might be subject to differing interpretations. As a result, if litigants dispute the meaning of a contract,
the judge will resolve the dispute as a matter of law. If they dispute the
implication of a newspaper article or a love letter, the jury will resolve
the dispute as a question of fact. Which is a patent more like? Archer is
almost certainly correct in answering "contract." A patent *is* a legal document, in many ways a bill of sale between the government and an inventor; the inventor owns the claims and the public the underlying
knowledge as explained in the written description.

So far, so good. A patent is a legal document, its meaning is a legal issue, and legally trained judges must resolve disputes about that meaning as a matter of law. But Archer also provided another explanation.
"Further," he argued,

it is only fair (and statutorily required) that competitors be able to ascertain to a reasonable degree the scope of the patentee's right to exclude. They may understand what is the scope of the patent owner's rights by obtaining the patent and prosecution history—the undisputed public record—and applying established rules of construction to the language of the patent claim in the context of the patent. Moreover, competitors should be able to rest assured, if infringement litigation occurs, that a judge, trained in the law, will similarly analyze the text of the patent and its associated public record and apply the established rules of construction, and in that way arrive at the true and consistent scope of the patent owner's rights to be given legal effect.[7]

This second argument is hardly compelling; if anything, it negates the point that Archer was trying to make. The patentee's "competitors" reading the patent to gain the knowledge that the government secured on their behalf are technologists, not lawyers. They want to keep up with the state of the art of their fields and incorporate it into their products. Is it fair to insist that every scientist who reads a patent must also consult an attorney to see how a legal eye might view this technical document? If so, what does that say about the patent system and the "little guy"? What protection does the tinkerer in his garage have? And just how large do our corporate patent-law departments have to be, anyway? The whole purpose of the patent system was supposed to be to promote progress. How can requiring a legal interpretation of these important new technical documents possibly promote progress?

Archer, who wrote on behalf of an eight-judge majority, didn't answer any of these questions. Two of his colleagues saw the problems quite clearly and disagreed with him quite vehemently. Judge Newman was the calmer of the two, noting simply that "patent infringement is a factual question."

Its resolution often requires finding the factual meaning and scope of the terms of scientific art and technology and usage by which the patentee described and claimed the invention. These findings usually require testamentary and documentary evidence and occasionally experiments or demonstrations, as illustrated in many of our previous decisions that are now overruled. Deciding the meaning of the words used in the patent is often dispositive of the question of infringement. Thus in the case at bar the infringement controversy is decided by finding the meaning and scope of the term "inventory" in Markman's patent, in light of the accused Westview system: if "inventory" is limited to clothing, the patent is not infringed; if "inventory" includes invoices, it is. The majority holds that this is a matter of law, devoid of any factual component; and subject to de novo appellate determination. The jury is eliminated, and new and uncertain procedures are imposed on trial judges. . . . The court creates a litigation system that is unique to patent cases, unworkable, and ultimately unjust.[8]

Judge Mayer was less restrained. In his view, the Federal Circuit had been doing its job all along. Just because a patent is a legal document hardly means that its interpretation is devoid of factual inquiries. The seeming contradictions that Archer had cited were more apparent than real. District courts had been holding trials under the current Patent Act since 1952 and under the Federal Circuit's supposedly contradictory guidance for more than a decade. Somehow, despite the confusion, they had all muddled through their caseloads and decided which issues belonged to them and which belonged to the jury. Now, in one fell swoop, the Federal Circuit was ejecting juries from an important category of civil lawsuits—an affront to, if not a violation of, the Seventh Amendment.[9] Mayer complained:

> All these pages and all these words cannot camouflage what the court well knows: to decide what the claims mean is nearly always to decide the case. But today's action is of a piece with a broader bid afoot to essentially banish juries from patent cases altogether. If it succeeds juries will be relegated, in those few cases where they have any presence at all, to rubber stamps. . . .
> There is simply no reason to believe that judges are any more qualified than juries to resolve the complex technical issues often present in patent cases. Indeed, the effect of this case is to make of the judicial process a charade, for notwithstanding any trial level activity, this court will do pretty much what it wants under its de novo retrial. We have consistently stressed that the same rules apply to patent cases as apply to all other civil disputes. The court subverts this principle and the demands of the Seventh Amendment by the ruse of reclassifying factual questions as legal ones.[10]

Mayer's passion was to no avail. He was unable to convince even one of his Federal Circuit colleagues to join his opinion, and he fared no better when the Supreme Court entered the fray. There, Justice David Souter, rarely considered one of the Court's originalists, echoed Archer's words in a rigid and surprisingly originalist opinion for a unanimous court. As he saw things, the Seventh Amendment guaranteed jury trials only for the sorts of disputes that existed when the framers wrote it. Because both patents and infringement suits existed in the eighteenth century, patentees and accused infringers possess the constitutional right to demand a jury trial. Because eighteenth-century patents lacked formal claims sections, however, the Seventh Amendment couldn't apply to claim construction. That left contemporary courts free to do pretty much whatever they wanted.

> As a matter of the sound administration of justice . . . judges, not juries, are the better suited to find the acquired meaning of patent terms. The construction of written instruments is one of those things that judges often do and are

likely to do better than jurors unburdened by training in exegesis. Patent construction in particular is a special occupation, requiring, like all others, special training and practice. The judge, from his training and discipline, is more likely to give a proper interpretation to such instruments than a jury; and he is, therefore, more likely to be right, in performing such a duty, than a jury can be expected to be.[11]

Souter, like Archer, elevated a patent's status as a legal document above its status as a technical document, all in the name of "the sound administration of justice."

Does his ruling really improve the administration of justice? Or does it open more questions than it resolves? A leading casebook that went to press shortly after the Supreme Court's ruling (and thus before much if any empirical evidence of its effect existed), saw at least one set of further issues that the Federal Circuit would now have to address:

> On the practical side, *Markman* raises a number of potentially challenging issues for the patent system. Most importantly, it threatens to change a number of routine practices in patent cases. For example, patent cases are usually appealed only after a full trial. The trial will very often include a claim interpretation issues but will of course also cover a host of other issues. *Markman* raises the threat that a full trial on many subordinate issues may become moot depending on how the Federal Circuit interprets a claim. For example, if the claim is interpreted as excluding all of the accused infringer's products, there is no need to consider defenses. . . . Indeed, to assure that time and money are not spent on pointless issues, the parties in patent cases may well seek to obtain a trial court's legal interpretation of claims and then ask the trial court to certify that finding for interlocutory appeal to the Federal Circuit.[12]

This prediction was half right. Many litigants and trial judges are eager to gain early input from the Federal Circuit. No one wants to go through a full-blown trial for nothing, only to have an appeals court overturn an early legal ruling and make everyone—litigants and trial judges—do it all over again. As a result, numerous trial judges have held pretrial claim construction "Markman hearings" and then asked the Federal Circuit to review their work.

The Federal Circuit has been adamant in its refusal to help. One of the basic rules of the appellate system is that litigants can appeal only "final judgments." Intermediate rulings, even important ones, are subject to "interlocutory" appeal only under extraordinary circumstances. There are mechanisms, however, that let district court judges reach out for appellate help. A trial judge who reaches a particularly critical ruling may "certify" that ruling for an appeal. The appeals court may then review the ruling, consider the judge's reasoning, and decide to help out—but it is under no obligation to do so. Appellate courts retain sole discretion over which certified questions they accept. When it comes to claim construction, many trial judges have sought the Federal Circuit's input. The Federal Circuit has rarely, if ever, acceded to such a request. This refusal has caused great consternation among litigants and trial judges alike. Parties, judges, and jurors pour valuable time, effort, and money into a trial, the losing party appeals, and the Federal Circuit issues a ruling overturning the claim construction from the Markman hearing. And such an overruling is hardly a rare event; few today doubt that the court's refusal to review constructions between Markman hearings and trials has led to an enormous waste of both public and private resources.

The Federal Circuit's ruling in *Markman* thus leads to at least one clear failure of public policy—an inefficient allocation of litigation resources. But it hardly stops there. Policy failures abound in this brave new world of purely legal claim construction.

DANCE OF THE DICTIONARIES

Few trial judges seem to know precisely what set of legal tools they're supposed to use to construe these legal instruments called patents. And believe it or not, the point of greatest confusion long involved the role of *dictionaries*. Now, there's no way for anyone to understand that particular problem without a bit of background. So let's back up to that great skill that Judge Archer and Justice Souter attributed to our judiciary: the ability to review linguistic disputes in light of "the evidence."

Judges group evidence into a series of concentric circles, and work their way outward until they have resolved the disputes over claim terms. They begin with "intrinsic" evidence, or items that relate specifically to the document (here, a patent) that they are analyzing. Suppose, for example, that Markman had written a definition of "inventory" into his patent. He could have chosen any definition, either a narrow one recognizing that a dry cleaner's inventory usually includes only dirty clothing, or a broad one explaining that for the purposes of his patent, the term "inventory" also includes invoices, receipts, and cash on hand. Had he chosen that route, the dispute would have been over before it started. Regardless of any standard understanding of dry-cleaning inventory, the patent itself would have told anyone reading it—dry cleaner, patent lawyer, or judge—what the term meant in the claim. But *Markman* included no definition in the patent itself. Under such circumstances, judges turn to other "intrinsic" evidence, such as the prosecution history.

If ambiguity remains after the judge has reviewed all of the intrinsic evidence, he must turn to "extrinsic" evidence, or generally available reference materials that might explain the patent's terms. That's where things get confusing. What constitutes usable extrinsic evidence? How should a judge choose between two extrinsic sources that compound the ambiguity rather than clarify it? These are the sorts of questions that only the Federal Circuit can answer. Federal Circuit panels must review the various approaches that district court judges take, critique them, and craft a "claim construction toolkit" telling trial judges how to conduct valid *Markman* hearings.

Unfortunately, the Federal Circuit's two most significant attempts to build this toolkit pointed in subtly different directions, directions different enough to compound the confusion and to lead once again to arguably conflicting lines of cases. Judge Paul Michel provided the first useful post-*Markman* guidelines:

> In determining the proper construction of a claim, the court has numerous sources that it may properly utilize for guidance. . . . The court should look first to the intrinsic evidence of record, . . . [as] the most significant source of the legally operative meaning of disputed claim language. In most situations, an analysis of the intrinsic evidence alone will resolve any ambiguity in a disputed claim term. In such circumstances, it is improper to rely on extrinsic evidence. . . . Extrinsic evidence is that evidence which is external to the patent and file history, such as expert testimony, inventor testimony, dictionaries, and technical treatises and articles. . . . Judges are free to consult such resources at any time in order to better understand the underlying technology and may also rely on dictionary definitions when construing claim terms, so long as the dictionary definition does not contradict any definition found in or ascertained by a reading of the patent documents.[13]

A few years later, Judge Richard Linn offered expanded—and confusingly different through probably not contradictory—advice:

> Dictionaries, encyclopedias and treatises are particularly useful resources to assist the court in determining the ordinary and customary meanings of claim terms. . . . Such references are unbiased reflections of common understanding. . . . Indeed, these materials may be the most meaningful sources of information to aid judges in better understanding both the technology and the terminology used by those skilled in the art to describe the technology. . . . It is entirely proper for both trial and appellate judges to consult these materials at any stage of a litigation, regardless of whether they have been offered by a party in evidence or not. Thus, categorizing them as "extrinsic evidence" or even a "special form of extrinsic evidence" is misplaced and does not inform the analysis.[14]

Most readers would look at these two sets of instructions and ask, "So what?" To anyone without a legal training, judges Michel and Linn seem to be in broad agreement: If the patent is explicit about the meaning of its words, the inquiry is over. Otherwise, dictionaries and other forms of extrinsic evidence are useful ways to determine what the words would mean to most readers—and thus to affix a concrete legal meaning to the disputed terms. But to the legally trained eye, the difference between these two toolkits is glaring. Michel noted that judges, like most other people, occasionally look up words in a dictionary. Linn launched into a panegyric of the genre. He elevated dictionaries to some rarified state above either intrinsic or extrinsic evidence. Where does that leave them? He didn't tell us. More to the point, though, this seemingly minor dispute led to two distinct schools of thought on the Federal Circuit about the role of dictionaries in claim construction—schools distinct enough to convince the court to revisit the matter *en banc* some ten years after supposedly laying the matter to rest—not to mention ten years after the Supreme Court's own *Markman* decision took the big claim construction question out of the Federal Circuit's hands and announced that claim construction was a legal matter unless and until either Congress or the Supreme Court declares otherwise.

How distinct were these schools? Professors Polk Wagner and Lee Petherbridge conducted an empirical study of Federal Circuit rulings on claim construction after *Markman*.[15] They reached a startling conclusion: different Federal Circuit judges favored different methodologies. In particular, they identified two distinct approaches to claim construction; Wagner and Petherbridge called the first "procedural" and the second "holistic." The procedural approach, as they described it,

> starts with a general presumption in favor of the ordinarily understood meaning of claim language, typically drawn from a relevant—often technical—dictionary, reference works, or common usage. . . . Any suggested alteration from the ordinary meaning must be accompanied by significant proof that such an alteration is required under the circumstances.[16]

The holistic method, on the other hand,

> adopts a distinctly more free-form approach, seeking the correct meaning according to the particular circumstances presented. . . . The holistic approach is significantly more relaxed than the procedural method in moving away from the abstracted "ordinary meaning" of a term in favor of a more localized understanding.[17]

Not surprisingly given these characterizations, they were strong advocates of proceduralism.

Their analysis of the differences, however, was almost certainly more striking than their ultimate recommendations. For as they described it, three of the court's judges—Dyk, Clevenger, and Linn—were strong and consistent proceduralists, employing Linn's claim construction toolkit and relying heavily on dictionaries to provide an abstract notion of "common meaning." Three other judges—Lourie, Bryson, and Newman—were strong and consistent holists, employing Michel's claim construction toolkit, focusing closely on the specifics (and often the peculiarities) of the intrinsic evidence, and using dictionaries only as necessary. The court's remaining judges, including Michel himself, fell somewhere in the middle; they were considerably more deferential to the intrinsic evidence than were the proceduralists, but more likely to cite favorably to dictionary definitions than were the holists.

Once again, this debate may not sound like much, but when there's as much riding on an outcome as there often is in a patent case, seemingly subtle distinctions in claim construction methodology can have enormous effects. According to Wagner and Petherbridge, the court's claim construction methodology from 1996 through 2002 hinged upon the makeup of the panel hearing a case. Though they did not say so explicitly, their analysis implied that the proceduralist and holistic methodologies led to different outcomes often enough to cause problems and to promulgate uncertainty. If that implication were true, the Clerk of Court's roulette wheel may have determined many outcomes when he assigned cases to panels. Litigants, who have little or no advance warning of the makeup of their panel, could not possibly prepare accordingly.[18] Damning criticism indeed for a court chartered specifically to impose predictability upon the patent law.

Wagner and Petherbridge saw an easy solution—one that they contended was already in the making. They recommended "that the court recognize the importance of methodology and move to standardize the procedural methodological approach—the evidence suggests that the procedural approach is inherently more consistent than holistic analyses."[19]

Their opinion notwithstanding, the procedural approach had more than its share of problems. Consider what happened to Novartis, a major pharmaceutical company, shortly after Wagner and Petherbridge's article appeared in print.[20] One of Novartis's patents described a way to administer cyclosporin—a drug that reduces the risk of a patient's body rejecting a transplanted organ—as a "hydrosol." What is a hydrosol? According to Novartis, any time cyclosporin dissolves in water, it forms a hydrosol—even if it doesn't dissolve until it's inside the patient's stomach. So Novartis sued Eon Labs for selling capsules in which the cyclosporin is dissolved in ethanol; when a patient ingests the capsule, the ethanol frees the cyclosporin, which then combines with stomach water to form a hydrosol. Eon predictably disagreed, arguing that Novartis's patent covered only hydrosols formed outside the body. Arguments of this sort are quite common among pharmaceutical companies and rarely lead to anything more interesting than a vanilla patent suit. Which of these interpretations is correct? To a layman, Eon's argument probably sounds more reasonable. But no one writes patents for laymen. Depending on where you stand on the fact/law divide, the intended audience for Novartis's patent was either pharmacologists, patent lawyers and judges, or both. One member of one of those audiences, Judge Joseph Farnan, who happened to preside at the trial, agreed with Eon's construction, resolved the linguistic dispute at the *Markman* hearing, and granted a summary judgment in Eon's favor.

Novartis appealed to the Federal Circuit. The clerk of court spun his wheel, and the case landed in front of judges Clevenger, Dyk, and Prost. With two of the court's strong proceduralists on the panel, Wagner and Petherbridge would have had little doubt as to how the analysis would proceed. The court would look to a dictionary for the plain, commonly understood, meaning of "hydrosol," and then turn to the intrinsic evidence to see if anything necessarily contradicted that dictionary definition. Clevenger and Dyk would both be on board, and Prost—one of the court's swing methodologists—could either join them or dissent. But that's not quite what happened. Dyk did pursue a proceduralist analysis that led him to agree with the district court. Prost joined him to form a panel majority affirming Eon's victory. But Judge Raymond Clevenger dissented in a manner that revealed not only a stark division within the proceduralist camp but also an inherent limitation of the methodology:

> The majority starts with its dictionaries in hand, and goes first, as makes sense, to the word "hydrosol." It uses *Webster's Third New International Dictionary* to learn that "hydrosol" means "a sol in which the liquid is water." Other dictionaries could be used to arrive at the same definition. . . .
>
> [The majority] pursues the search in the dictionary, relying on *Webster's Third New International Dictionary* (2002). There, it finds as a definition for "sol" the following: a "dispersion of solid particles in a liquid colloidal solution." For the majority, this definition from this particular chosen dictionary is crucial, for it permits the court to move to a further degree of separation away from the word "hydrosol" to investigate the meaning of "solution." Had the majority used the *Merriam Webster Medical Dictionary* (2003) definition of "sol," it would have been deprived of the opportunity to pursue the meaning of "solution," because the more pertinent medical dictionary defines "sol" simply as "a fluid colloidal system; especially: one in which the dispersion medium is a liquid." The pursuit of the meaning of "solution" is also blocked if one had turned to *Webster's Ninth New Collegiate Dictionary* (1984) which defines "sol" as "a fluid colloidal system; esp: one in which the continuous phase is a liquid." . . .

Having found a need to define "solution"—remember, the need is in order to know the meaning of "hydrosol"—the majority again relies on its dictionary in the next degree of separation to produce two meanings for "solution." One meaning, "a liquid containing a dissolved substance" is deemed by the majority, correctly, to be broad enough to relate back to "hydrosol" without imposing any restrictions on the manufacturing site of the hydrosol. The other meaning, however, is pay dirt for the majority. That second definition of "solution" is "a liquid and usu. aqueous medicinal preparation with the solid ingredients soluble." . . . In the next degree of separation, the majority embraces the term "medicinal preparation," and forthwith abandons *Webster's* in favor of *The Oxford English Dictionary* 548–49 (2d ed. 1989), to plumb the depths of the meaning of the word "medicine." (The reader should not forget that the word we are trying to define is "hydrosol," not "medicine.") . . .

At the end of the long search in various dictionaries, the majority concludes that "hydrosol" is ambiguous because of "multiple possible" conflicting dictionary definitions. I am at a loss to understand why this dictionary search creates such an ambiguity. . . . "Hydrosol" simply means "a sol in which the liquid is water."[21]

Clevenger concluded that "dictionaries are fine tools to assist in the exercise of claim interpretation, for sure, but in this case the majority has simply overworked the dictionaries to a point of error."[22] The dance of the dictionaries had gone too far even for one of the court's proceduralists. The court realized that it had reached a critical juncture. It needed to reconcile the differing implications of Michel's and Linn's toolkits. It needed to decide just how central dictionaries were to the analysis deemed so inherently legal that judges had to conduct it before even impaneling a jury. And it needed to do so quickly.

BAFFLING

As luck would have it, about the same time that Novartis and Eon were slugging it out over "hydrosol," a man named Edward Phillips sued the AWH Corporation for infringing his patented invention of vandal-resistant building modules. The key word in this dispute was "baffle."[23] Once again the Clerk of Court spun his wheel, and once again it fell upon Judge Dyk. This time, however, he found himself sitting with judges Newman and Lourie, two of the court's strongest holists. To no one's surprise, these two holists formed the court's majority. Lourie looked at both the intrinsic evidence and a dictionary. He concluded that though *Webster's* defines *baffle* as "something for deflecting, checking, or otherwise regulating flow," Phillips himself had defined the term somewhat

more specifically in his patent. Dyk dissented, arguing that the dictionary definition should have prevailed.

Phillips, like most losing parties, asked the court to reconsider its decision *en banc*. The court saw this dispute over a single word governing a
patent in an easily understandable area of technology as a golden opportunity to clean up its claim construction jurisprudence. It agreed to hear
the case, framed the specific questions that it wanted Phillips and AWH to
address, and invited all interested parties to submit answers in the form
of amicus briefs. The court's questions addressed the relative roles of technical and general-purpose dictionaries, the best ways to reconcile conflicts
between dictionaries, the proper role for dictionaries among judges who
turn first to intrinsic evidence, the proper way to view the relationship between the proceduralist and holistic methods, and a few related technical
legal points. By and large though, it was clear that the proceduralists had
stacked the deck. The majority of the questions, and the way the court
phrased them, elevated dictionaries to a hallowed position and requested
feedback primarily to determine just *how* sacred these books are.[24]

Only two judges even took the time to call their colleagues to task about
the biased nature of the questions. "For the sake of completeness," Judge
Rader would have at least balanced the inquiry by adding a complementary line of questions. He would have asked about the relative merits of
an "algorithmic" approach that imposed uniformity upon claim construction and an approach that selected patent-appropriate tools from a
claim construction toolkit (i.e., Wagner and Petherbridge's holistic approach).[25] Mayer (at that time, Chief Judge) went back to the heart of the
matter: "Nearly a decade of confusion has resulted from the fiction that
claim construction is a matter of law, when it is obvious that it depends
on underlying factual determinations which, like all factual questions if
disputed, are the province of the trial court, reviewable on appeal for clear
error. To pretend otherwise inspires cynicism."[26]

Once again, we seemed to be verging upon a major failure of public policy. Ambiguous patents serve no one. They motivate insufficient innovation, complicate the diffusion of knowledge, chill competitive entry, engender needless litigation, frustrate trial judges, and aggravate appellate
judges. Yet after more than a decade of concerted effort, claim construction jurisprudence had devolved to the level at which an appellate court
had to ask the patent bar how to best use dictionaries. Could that possibly be what Justice Souter had in mind when he agreed that judges were
better equipped than jurors to engage in the complex evidentiary task of
claim construction?

When the dust finally settled on Phillips' case in mid-2005, Judge
William Bryson—one of the court's strong holists—managed to corral
most of his colleagues behind his rousing support of the status quo. With

all three of the court's strong proceduralists in tow, Bryson explained that what the court had said in *Markman* "bears restating, for the basic principles of claim construction outlined there are still applicable, and we reaffirm them today. We have also previously considered the use of dictionaries in claim construction. What we have said in that regard requires clarification."[27] He then rejected the proceduralist school that had grown out of Judge Linn's instruction set in favor of Judge Michel's more holistic approach:

> There is no magic formula or catechism for conducting claim construction. Nor is the court barred from considering any particular sources or required to analyze sources in any specific sequence, as long as those sources are not used to contradict claim meaning that is unambiguous in light of the intrinsic evidence. For example, a judge who encounters a claim term while reading a patent might consult a general purpose or specialized dictionary to begin to understand the meaning of the term, before reviewing the remainder of the patent to determine how the patentee has used the term. The sequence of steps used by the judge in consulting various sources is not important; what matters is for the court to attach the appropriate weight to be assigned to those sources in light of the statutes and policies that inform patent law.[28]

He concluded that this preferred holistic approach had not attempted "to provide a rigid algorithm for claim construction, but simply attempted to explain why, in general, certain types of evidence are more valuable than others."[29]

Having scored this resounding victory for holism over proceduralism, Bryson next applied the newly affirmed tool set to the dispute over the meaning of "baffle," only to agree with the definition that had previously emerged from Dyk's proceduralism rather than from the panel's holism. Not surprisingly, judges Lourie and Newman—the two holists who had formed the panel majority—dissented on that part. "It was clear as mud, but it covered de ground, and confusion made me head go 'round."[30]

Over in the blogosphere, Professor Wagner, who had urged the court to affirm proceduralism not only in his journal articles but also in an amicus brief, shared his initial thoughts about the court's decision with the world in a posting titled "The New Rule Is There Are No Rules":

> As patent lawyers will quickly recognize, the "no rules" approach means that the Federal Circuit decision on claim construction is the only one that matters. Because the court did not constrain itself in any way, each claim construction dispute it receives will be analyzed in markedly different ways, based on the "context" of the particular case. In this way, *Phillips* is somewhat shocking in its transparent power allocation to the Federal Circuit: because only that court knows what particular mixture of information, its weighting, the use of inferences, and the like will be "appropriate" in each case, nobody else—the PTO,

lower courts, competitors, or even patentees themselves—can be anywhere near reasonably confident in their own claim construction. Want a claim construction? That will cost you three years and several million dollars.[31]

Wagner also forecast increased litigation and decreased precision in patents as likely consequences of this new no-rule environment. His forecast is probably correct, though for reasons unrelated to the proceduralism/ holism debate. Once again, it was Judge Mayer (with Judge Newman's backing), who said what most needed to be said:

> While this court may persist in the delusion that claim construction is a purely legal determination, unaffected by underlying facts, it is plainly not the case. . . . If we persist in deciding the subsidiary factual components of claim construction without deference, there is no reason why litigants should be required to parade their evidence before the district courts or for district courts to waste time and resources evaluating such evidence. It is excessive to require parties, who have already been forced to concentrate their energies and resources on persuading the trial judge that their account of the facts is the correct one, to persuade three more judges at the appellate level. If the proceedings before the district court are merely a tryout on the road, as they are under our current regimen, it is wasteful to require such proceedings at all. Instead, all patent cases could be filed in this court; we would determine whether claim construction is necessary, and, if so, the meaning of the claims. Those few cases in which claim construction is not dispositive can be remanded to the district court for trial. In this way, we would at least eliminate the time and expense of the charade currently played out before the district court.[32]

Even Mayer's plea for a return to the days in which triers of fact played the primary role in claim construction leaves two major issues unresolved: the Supreme Court's intervention and the "no rules" environment that Wagner identified. To at least most observers, the Supreme Court's *Markman* opinion appeared to lock claim construction into the legal realm unless and until the Supreme Court or Congress chooses to move it back to the realm of the factual. Mayer finessed this point by disagreeing with that conventional wisdom. As he sees it, "the Supreme Court did not suggest in affirming *Markman* that claim construction is a purely legal question. It held only that, as a policy matter, the judge, as opposed to the jury, should determine the meaning of a patent claim."[33] In other words, Justice Souter's proclamation that the Seventh Amendment guaranteed jury trials only where they existed in 1789 frees the courts to assign all claim constructions to judges whether the determination is legal or factual. If this finessing is correct, the first problem disappears. The second problem is fundamental. The lack of certainty plaguing the patent system is a function of Wagner's "no rules" environment; shifting the primary responsibility for applying those no rules from the Federal Circuit to either a trial judge or a jury seems unlikely to fix the underlying problem.

In fact, the underlying problem persists. Soon after the Federal Circuit issued its newly clarified rules for claim construction, two drug companies, Amgen and Aventis, arrived in Lafayette Park. Amgen had convinced a district court to adopt the claim construction that it preferred. On appeal, the panel split two-to-one in favor of Aventis.[34] Amgen petitioned for an *en banc* rehearing. The denial of that petition was hardly surprising—barely worthy of notice by anyone other than Amgen, Aventis, their lawyers, and their shareholders—particularly given the court's efforts on claim construction less than eighteen months earlier. What raised eyebrows, however, was that most of the court's judges felt the need to comment on this denial. Four of them—Michel, Newman, Rader, and Moore—would have taken the opportunity to try yet again to improve the rules (or as Wagner noted, the "no rules") for claim construction. Three more—Gajarsa, Linn, and Dyk—agreed that such an improvement was warranted, but preferred to defer consideration of the matter to another day.

Curiously, while Mayer said nothing at all, others grabbed the baton to champion his cause. Chief Judge Michel lamented the court's mid-1990s adoption of

> the premise that claim construction is always a purely legal exercise, devoid of factual content. We have likened claim construction to statutory construction. I believe that this analogy is open to serious question. In interpreting statutes, a judge, whether trial or appellate, essentially asks himself/herself, "What does the disputed term mean to me, the judge, as an artisan in the law?" With claim construction, on the other hand, the judge is supposed to inquire, essentially, "How would the average artisan in the relevant field of technology understand the disputed claim terms in the context of the rest of the patent, the prosecution history, and the prior art?". . . Perhaps we should routinely give at least some deference to the trial court, given its greater knowledge of the facts. Or, perhaps other adjustments to our current practice should be considered.[35]

Judge Newman added: "It is time to reopen the question and to rethink, *en banc*, the optimum approach to accuracy, consistency, and predictability in the resolution of patent disputes, with due attention to judicial structure, litigants' needs, and the national interest in invention and innovation."[36] Indeed it is.

WORD POLICY

Is the problem endemic? Obviously, it is impossible to remove *all* ambiguity; language is a finite-precision instrument. But perhaps there are ways to minimize it. Perhaps there is a set of tools or rules that will minimize ambiguity so that people can invest their time, effort, and capital reasonably certain of the patent-law consequences that lie ahead.

Perhaps the courts have had such a hard time developing such a toolkit because they have always approached the challenge from the perspective of law, rather than from the perspective of policy. The legal perspective on claim construction begins with a debate over the nature of a patent—is it a legal document or a technical document?—and then slides inexorably into discussions of evidentiary analysis. We've already seen where that approach leads.

A policy perspective begins with a very different set of questions. Rather than asking what a patent *is*, it asks what a patent *does*. A patent promotes progress in two ways: First, it motivates invention by granting the inventor exclusive rights in the claims—rights that we hope the inventor will exploit in part by commercializing his innovation as a new product. Second, it advances public knowledge by explaining the invention in the written description. These two parts of the patent specification also provide "public notice" of the claims' scope. A skilled artisan—the group from which both competitors and infringers are likely to spring—reading the patent should emerge with a reasonable understanding of what the patentee possesses and what remains in the public domain. The key claim construction challenge from a policy perspective is thus how to ensure that the public has reasonably accurate notice of the claims' scope: What is the most effective way to guarantee that skilled artisans reading a patent will understand which of their activities will infringe and which will not?

The Federal Circuit encountered a similar challenge early in its history. Yujiro Yamamoto, inventor of a voice-activated dictation device, was embroiled in patent litigation against Dictaphone when the PTO decided to reexamine his patent. Though the PTO reexamines relatively few patents, such proceedings are hardly rare. They usually occur because either the inventor discovered a flaw in his claim that would cost him an infringement suit or, as in Yamamoto's case, because some competitor who had had no opportunity to participate in the initial negotiation between the inventor and the PTO convinces the PTO that the patent may have issued in error. In a reexamination proceeding, the examiner reopens the prosecution history and engages in new rounds of correspondence with the inventor. Once again, this correspondence becomes a public document if and when the patent "reissues."

In Yamamoto's case, as in most cases, the trial and the reexamination pushed in opposite directions. In court, Yamamoto contended that his patent was broad enough to include Dictaphone's products. At the PTO, the examiner contended that an interpretation as broad as the one that Yamamoto forwarded in court would combine his own invention with many preexisting inventions. Because valid patents can't include preexisting inventions, the PTO forced Yamamoto either to adopt a narrower

construction and risk losing his lawsuit or to insist upon the broad construction and risk losing his patent. Yamamoto refused to budge, and the
PTO canceled the patent.

Yamamoto appealed the PTO's decision to the Federal Circuit. He argued—accurately—that courts like to protect patents. When a trial judge
sees two reasonable claim constructions, a broad one that would render
the patent invalid and a narrow one that would maintain its validity, the
judge is required to adopt the narrow definition—allowing the patentee
to keep her patent despite possibly losing her infringement case (a general
rule that has earned the Federal Circuit a reputation for favoring valid,
weak patents).[37] Yamamoto wanted the PTO to apply the narrower construction without any of his own written input and reissue the patent so
that he could then propose the broader construction to the trial judge,
who likely lacked the examiner's training and might not invalidate the
broader patent.

At the Federal Circuit, Judge Phillip Baldwin not only shot him down
but actually took the time to explain the public policy rationale behind
applying different rules in reexamination proceedings and infringement
trials:

> The PTO broadly interprets claims during examination of a patent applica-
> tion since the applicant may amend his claims to obtain protection commen-
> surate with his actual contribution to the art. This approach serves the pub-
> lic interest by reducing the possibility that claims, finally allowed, will be
> given broader scope than is justified. Applicants' interests are not impaired
> since they are not foreclosed from obtaining appropriate coverage for their
> invention with express claim language. . . . When an application is pending
> in the PTO, the applicant has the ability to correct errors in claim language
> and adjust the scope of claim protection as needed.[38]

In Yamamoto's case, the PTO did exactly what it was supposed to do: it
interpreted his claims broadly and invalidated his patent. The Federal
Circuit adopted the entirely sensible rule that inventors who do not avail
themselves of the opportunity to narrow their claims to exclude prior art
do not deserve patents. It also implicitly adopted the even more sensible
rule that no one should be able to get a patent by convincing the PTO that
it covers only a small set of inventions, only to turn around later and try
to convince a trial judge that the patent covers a much broader range of
products. After all, what sort of notice would such an expandable patent
give to competitors? And could such blatant double-dealing possibly contribute to progress, knowledge, or science?

The Federal Circuit's resolution of Yamamoto's disputes with the PTO
and with Dictaphone made all kinds of sense. Its ruling clearly served the
public interest. But did it go far enough? Consider flipping the public

interest argument. The examiner has given all potentially ambiguous terms their broadest reasonable interpretation. The inventor has incorporated explicit narrowing terms where necessary. The examiner okays the new language and the PTO issues the patent. Some unsuspecting member of the public, blessed with but ordinary skill in the relevant art, comes along and reads it. She may or may not notice potential ambiguities, but being a competent reader, she assigns reasonable definitions to at least enough of the patent's words to understand its teachings. As a potential competitor, she also pays particularly close attention to the claim language to ensure that she does not infringe. She does not, however, have the opportunity to discuss the language with either the patentee or the examiner. What sorts of interpretations might she apply to potentially ambiguous terms? Presumably, if she is reading the patent in good faith and exerting reasonable efforts to avoid infringement, she will interpret all claim language "reasonably." Sound policy requires rules that encourage her to do what we want her to do: learn the disclosed science, incorporate it into her own knowledge of the state of the art of her field, and if possible, develop competing, noninfringing products. The best way to motivate that behavior is to bind her only to the *narrowest* reasonable interpretation of potentially ambiguous terms.

But wait! Wouldn't that reduce the inventor's motivation? Perhaps somewhat. After all, a patent is a bargain between the inventor and the public. Anything that decreases the price the public pays also decreases the price the inventor receives. But the imposition of a "narrowest reasonable interpretation" requirement does more than that: It places the burden of clarity on the shoulders of the party best able to bear it. Patentees are free to draft any language that they desire. If a patentee chooses words with multiple reasonable definitions, it is the patentee's responsibility to make sure that readers know which one he intended. Before the patent issues, the PTO works to ensure that an inventor can't claim things that existed prior to his invention. After the patent issues, district court judges must ensure that the public doesn't relinquish anything that the inventor may have failed to request.

So anything goes? Any accused infringer who enters a courtroom asserting an interpretation necessarily wins? Not at all. That's where we remember that we're in a court of law, not a policy seminar. The accused infringer will undoubtedly arrive armed with an interpretation that removes his product from the patent's scope. The court must then answer a key question: *Is his interpretation reasonable?* Courts answer questions about reasonableness all the time. In fact, juries answer questions about reasonable behavior all the time. Defendants who trot out single obscure sources favoring offbeat interpretations are unlikely to prevail very often. We can finally agree with Judge Mayer about the factual nature of the interpretive task. And we can restore patents to their proper roles as technical documents rather than as legal ones.

Is this approach too radical? Perhaps. It's certainly not along any glide path foreseeable from recent Federal Circuit jurisprudence. It completely upends the *Markman* ruling and represents a significant change in patent law—the very sort of occurrence that Congress founded the Federal Circuit to avoid. It is, at heart, an argument grounded in the economics of transaction costs rather than in the legal tradition of patent law. Such arguments are common in the "law and economics" school of legal analysis and draw heavily upon the work of Ronald Coase, winner of the 1991 Nobel Prize in economics:

> [With zero transaction costs,] the allocation of resources remains the same whatever the legal position. . . . With positive transaction costs, the law plays a crucial role in determining how resources are used. But it does more than this. With zero transaction costs . . . contractual arrangements will be made to modify the rights and duties of the parties so as to make it in their interest to undertake those actions which maximize [value]. With positive transaction costs, some or all of these contractual arrangements become too costly to carry out. The incentives to take some of the actions which would have maximized [value] disappear. What incentives will be lacking depend on what the law is.[39]

Ambiguity in a patent creates transaction costs. It generates uncertainty among members of the public, makes inadvertent infringement more likely, and allows a patentee to file infringement suits even when he knows full well that the accused device falls outside the scope of the invention that he patented. Ambiguity can also allow intentional infringers to escape liability. Ambiguous claim language therefore creates two types of publicly detrimental transaction costs: tangible litigation expenses, and less-tangible improper pricing that arises from wrongly deterred products and from undeterred infringing products. The public as a whole loses, while some patentees and some infringers gain.

Alas, nothing comes free. Disambiguation imposes its own set of transaction costs. Someone must bear the cost of ensuring that every word in every patent is clear enough for competitors who behave reasonably and in good faith to avoid infringing inadvertently. The law can assign this burden in one of two places. Either the inventor and the PTO can bear the cost during examination or litigants and the court system can bear the cost during infringement trials. Though the latter assignment avoids some costs on the majority of patents that never arise in litigation, it also increases the costs of many important products—those relatively few patentable inventions that give rise to commercial competition and infringement suits. The current system assigns most of the costs to litigants and courts. A "narrowest reasonable interpretation" standard would assign the bulk of the cost to inventors, and in particular to those few inventors who believe that their inventions are important enough to warrant the added expense of careful disambiguation. Overall costs would almost certainly decline, and many intangible transaction costs of inappropriate pricing would evaporate. Progress would be promoted and the public interest advanced. Claim construction jurisprudence could finally make sense. Alas, none of these benefits seem likely to emerge, because there is no indication that a "narrowest reasonable interpretation" rule is even under consideration.

All told, claim construction poses a cautionary tale. The Federal Circuit identified it—correctly—as a source of uncertainty impeding the smooth flow of the patent system. In keeping with its charge, it tried to remove this uncertainty by concentrating the task in judicial hands, rather than in the hands of untrained and often unpredictable juries. A decade after the effort began, reports of rampant uncertainty and reversals of district court rulings persist. Trial judges know that they lack the tools to derive confident constructions, and repeatedly beg the Federal Circuit for help. The Federal Circuit refuses virtually all such pleas. Federal Circuit judges try to explain the procedure, but even subtle differences among their explanations can cause more confusion than they resolve. The court's recent attempt to clean up its claim construction jurisprudence yielded little that was new. But Judge Mayer's lonely voice of dissent has it right. Contemporary claim construction jurisprudence creates confusion and motivates expensive litigation. It is not moving toward a predictable, reliable patent system—the basic characteristics of any system truly capable of promoting progress. The Federal Circuit may be trying, but effort alone is not enough. *Markman* was a failure. *Phillips* seems unlikely to be an improvement. The policy we have is not the policy we want.

So, how did the black box of words known as "claim construction" perform in our informal tests? Its record is mixed, but hardly positive. Though some critics may contend that the current environment is devoid of rules, such criticism appears unduly harsh. Most observers concede that, as confusing and as unpredictable as claim construction may be today, it is nevertheless less confusing and more predictable than it used to be. While *Markman* and its progeny have yet to formalize the claim construers' toolkit, they have at least consolidated the task within the Federal Circuit, whose judges—despite their alleged panel-dependence—are nevertheless more predictable than the much larger pools of trial judges and potential jurors. To the extent that progress has been made toward certainty and consistency over the past twenty-five years, the Federal Circuit deserves the lion's share of the credit. The lion's share of the credit for a poor grade, however, is hardly praiseworthy.

When it comes to assigning blame for the current muddle, Congress, the Supreme Court, the Federal Circuit, and the PTO all seem to be working together. The Supreme Court removed the law/fact dispute from the Federal Circuit's hands; even if Judge Mayer could persuade a majority of his colleagues to revisit the issue, it's not clear that the Federal Circuit possesses the authority to do so. The PTO could improve matters by insisting upon greater specificity before granting patents, or by encouraging examiners to ask patentees to define more terms in the correspondence that will become the prosecution history. Congress could clean things up quite neatly by incorporating a "broadest reasonable meaning during prosecution, narrowest reasonable meaning during litigation" directly into the Patent Act. Unless and until that happens, though, the Federal Circuit alone possesses the ability to make the best of a messy situation. The Federal Circuit could single-handedly reduce the costs of patent litigation by accepting interlocutory appeals immediately after *Markman* hearings. The linguistic certainty that such appeals would afford would likely induce many more disputes to settle before trial and increase the number of trial verdicts upheld upon final appeal. Why the court refuses to do so remains something of a mystery.

No, indeed, the policy we have is not the policy we want. And though few—even within the patent bar—consider claim construction to be a sexy topic, all concede that it is central. For as Judge Mayer reminded us, "to decide what the claims mean is nearly always to decide the case."[40] We the people deserve better.

CENTER STAGE

Test scores aren't everything, particularly when the black box in question is only a small component in a much larger, more complex box. Claim construction may be inside the main tent, but it's hardly the main attraction. There are two issues, and only two issues, on center stage: validity and infringement. In any patent trial, "validity" raises the legal question: Did the patentee really deserve the claim at issue? If so, "infringement" then raises the factual question: Does the accused product violate the limited rights that Congress granted the patentee? Everything else in patent law is either subsidiary or auxiliary to these twin concerns; subsidiary analyses feed into either validity or infringement, and auxiliary concerns apply them to special cases, but when the dust settles, only validity and infringement remain. When Judge Mayer says that construing a claim decides a case, what he really means is that disambiguating the claim's words renders validity and infringement analysis easy—or at the very least, easier.

Even when they're easy, though, validity and infringement can still pose challenging questions. Validity is a multifaceted legal issue. A patentee must meet numerous technical requirements to gain a patent. At trial, an accused infringer attempting to prove invalidity can dredge up assertions that the patentee violated one or more of these technical requirements and that the PTO erred in issuing the patent. Although the standard of proof is rather high, it's hardly insurmountable. The courts invalidate many patents for technical violations. From a policy perspective, different technical rules have different effects. Some make U.S. patents easier to obtain than are foreign patents, and some make them harder to get. Some seem to make life easier for large corporations, some for individual tinkerers. Congress built some into the Patent Act, and others are PTO regulations. Some make more sense in certain industries than in others. Not surprisingly, a perpetual reform buzz surrounds these technical requirements—and at times, technical reforms do change the system.

While technical grounds can be critical in any given lawsuit and can easily result in multimillion-dollar decisions, they neither cut to the core of the patent system nor make for stimulating reading. The truly interesting validity questions arise when the challenge is on substantive grounds. Litigants forwarding substantive validity challenges argue that the PTO incorrectly issued a patent and claim the invention was ineligible for patenting. Ineligibility, in turn, arises for one of three major reasons:

1. The invention in question may fall into a category of "unpatentable subject matter" for which Congress never decided to grant patents.
2. It may have been "obvious" at the time that the patentee applied for the patent.
3. It may not be sufficiently "novel" because other inventions available at the time of the patent application may have "anticipated" it.[41]

Over the years, the courts have crafted numerous rules to help trial judges and patent examiners give meaning to these requirements for patentability. When it comes to patentable subject matter, the Supreme Court explained that "Congress intended statutory subject matter to include anything under the sun that is made by man. This is not to suggest that [patentable subject matter] has no limits or that it embraces every discovery. The laws of nature, physical phenomena, and abstract ideas have been held not patentable."[42]

Over the years, the courts have interpreted this rule quite broadly. In 1980, a General Electric engineer tried to patent a synthetic bacterium capable of digesting crude oil. The PTO rejected his application, claiming that microorganisms are "products" of nature and that living things are not patentable subject matter. The Supreme Court disagreed.[43] From that day forward, inventors could patent life forms—as long as they were laboratory-synthesized life forms. Debates continue to rage about just how broadly this edict should extend. Should the PTO grant patents on genes? Clones? Fetal tissue? Ethical and moral concerns enter many of these debates, but the general rule continues to hold: assume patentability unless Congress announces otherwise.

The Supreme Court also rejected another of the PTO's long-standing limitations on patentability as far back as 1972, when it announced that, at least in principle, algorithms could be patented—as long as they were applied algorithms and not abstract algorithms.[44] The Court did not, however, find an algorithm that actually qualified for a patent until 1981, when it encountered an algorithm applied to curing synthetic rubber,[45] and it remained pretty hard to get a software patent until 1994. That year, the Federal Circuit determined that the PTO had been too stingy in awarding software patents—largely because it had been summarily rejecting patent applications that applied algorithms to other algorithms.[46] The trickle of software patents gave way to a stream. Four years later, the Federal Circuit returned to open the floodgates; it ruled that "business methods" applying algorithms to specific problems in, say, finance also qualified for patent protection.[47]

This ruling led to a torrent of questionable business method patents, perhaps hitting a high point when Amazon.com convinced a trial judge that it deserved to keep its patent on one-click shopping.[48] At that point, both the Federal Circuit and the PTO recognized that things might have gone too far. The Federal Circuit overturned the trial judge,[49] and the PTO reportedly began to reflect on whether the standards for business method patents had become too permissive. This sort of activity is unfortunately all too common in the law: a high-profile case reveals poor underlying practices, courts and regulatory agencies mitigate the damage in that specific case and declare the matter fixed, and people and businesses are left picking up the pieces. In this particular instance, Barnesandnoble.com had to change its shopping software in the middle of the 1999 holiday season, while Amazon's "ephemeral" patent interfered with Internet retail development for fourteen critical months.

For better or for worse, then (and many would say for worse), the American patent system is coming quite close to achieving the Supreme Court's ideal of being open to "anything under the sun that is made by man." But the Supreme Court has been a lot less definitive in its announcements about obviousness and anticipation than it was about subject matter; it left those matters to the circuit courts. Back in the old era, different regional circuits confused patent examiners, trial judges, patentees, and accused infringers alike by crafting rules that differed by region. One of the Federal Circuit's primary early assignments was the development of a single, uniform set of rules for determining obviousness and anticipation. Though it has done so, not everyone approves of the court's rules; some patent scholars contend that they lead to poor patent policy and misallocated resources.[50] So much for the black box of validity.

Infringement is an intensely factual question—with one proviso. In an infringement analysis, the trier of fact—typically a jury—must compare the accused product with the patented invention. If the jury finds even a single significant aspect of the claim that is not present in the product, it must find the patent not infringed. And therein lies the proviso: What constitutes a "significant difference" between a patent claim and a physical product?

The Federal Circuit has crafted rules to guide these infringement analysis comparisons. The first part involves an inquiry into "literal infringement": Does the patent describe the precise product accused of infringing? If so, the answer is easy. If not, however, the jury must ask whether the product is "equivalent" to the claim—and that opens a whole new can of worms. From 1995 to 2003, the Federal Circuit and the Supreme Court engaged in an unusual back-and-forth exchange hammering out the precise contours of the "doctrine of equivalents."[51]

At the risk of oversimplification, the Federal Circuit inherited a rather broad doctrine of equivalents from some decades-old Supreme Court precedents.[52] As a conceptual matter, some such doctrine of equivalents is critical to the functioning of the patent system. If any deviation from the claim language, no matter how trivial, were sufficient to render a product noninfringing, few patents would have any value. Conversely, if any similarity to a claim, no matter how trivial, infringed, the first patent in a field would possess immense value—and innovation in that field would come to a screeching halt. The doctrine of equivalents represents an attempt to find the appropriate middle ground; some, but not all, types of similarity render a product "equivalent" to the claim, and thus infringing.

By the mid-1990s, the Federal Circuit realized that patentees were abusing this broad doctrine and claiming that all sorts of tangentially related products were "equivalent" to their claimed inventions. The court responded by attempting to narrow the notion of equivalence considerably—and thereby to improve the predictability of the patent system.[53] The Supreme Court pushed back.[54] The Federal Circuit tried again.[55] The Supreme Court pushed back again.[56] When the dust finally settled, the courts agreed to narrow equivalence somewhat—though not necessarily enough to make competitors confident that the products they launch intending not to infringe do not, in fact, infringe.[57] In the world of black-box tests, the Federal Circuit gets an A for effort, but the Supreme Court's performance brought the combined score down to a B.

Setting aside policy considerations and focusing on litigation, the notion of infringement by equivalents marks the last important component of a skeletal vanilla infringement suit. The trial judge begins with a confusing venture into the meaning of words. The parties then argue about the patent's validity, often on technical grounds (e.g., the patentee missed a filing deadline) and sometimes on substantive grounds (e.g., the claimed invention was obvious at the time). The jury then compares the accused product to the patent's claims and renders a verdict. Then the appeal begins. This process also provides the key to the "dirty little secret" about why judges spend so much time construing claims when all that really matters is validity and infringement. And truth to tell, it's not really that much of a secret. Judge Baldwin let the cat out of the bag when he was talking to Yamamoto, and Judge Mayer belled that cat so that all could hear it. Courts spend so much time construing claims because they need to determine whether the patents at issue are valid or not, and if they are, whether the accused product infringes them.

The dire state of the patent system in the 1970s arose from the absence of a uniform set of standards for judging either validity or infringement. Back then, the PTO trained its examiners to apply one set of standards to determine validity. The PTO then issued patents that numerous tribunals reviewed. Appeals from PTO decisions went to the Court of Customs and Patent Appeals, one of the Federal Circuit's predecessor courts, where a somewhat different set of validity standards prevailed. Patents that either the PTO or the CCPA deemed valid then issued and worked their way into commerce. When a patentee thought that she detected infringement, she filed suit in federal district court. Each trial judge was subject to the rules of his regional circuit court, and each circuit court had its own partial set of rules for determining validity and infringement. So the trial judge did his best, the circuit court reviewed his work, and a haphazard web of rules emerged. For the most part, it was impossible for anyone reading a patent to know whether or not a court would find it valid, and whether or not a court would determine that a similar product infringed, without knowing *where* a potential trial might occur.

This sort of uncertainty is disastrous in a business environment. The patent system, like any other regulatory regime, alters the returns that people and corporations expect to receive from their investments. Individuals need to know whether invention is a worthwhile pursuit—and even further, whether patenting an invention is worth the added time and effort. Businesses need to know whether or not to invest in research and development, and if so, how to allocate their investment among competing fields of inquiry. Businesses also need to know whether a new product under consideration is a legal entry into a competitive environment or an infringement of some patentee's rights. An uncertain regulatory scheme is the worst of all possible worlds; it is much more likely to deter than to motivate the desired behavior. Though an uncertain patent system may occasionally redound to the public's benefit by "tricking" some hapless innovator into placing his invention into the public domain, the net effect of such chicanery is unquestionably negative. The primary assignment that Congress handed the Federal Circuit in 1982 was the imposition of enough consistency and certainty upon the patent system to turn patents into useful tools for business strategy. How well has it done?

OPTIMALITY

The key to evaluating the Federal Circuit's overall performance is thus determining whether or not today's patent system is more predictable than the one that the court inherited; predictability allows intelligent planning and resource allocation. Before conducting that assessment, though, it is important to consider whether today's patent system motivates *optimal* resource allocation from the perspective of society as a whole. The basic notion of "societal optimality" flows from some standard economic definitions: The societal *value* of an intellectual property regime is the net difference between the costs that society bears to develop and to run the regime and the benefits that society accrues by establishing the regime. The societally *optimal* regime maximizes societal value.

A series of illustrations may make the matter a bit more concrete.[58]

In the mythical realm of Zip, the legislature enacted zero IP laws.[59] In Zip, some folks innovate for the sake of innovation (i.e., they enjoy the intellectual stimulation inherent in innovation), while others innovate to address their own personal needs. Still other Zippers innovate to avail themselves of market factors like the first-mover advantage or the rewards available for teaching and training. These inherent motives for innovation ensure that, even though Zip confers no special rights on its innovators, it is not a society devoid of innovation.[60] The innovations generated in Zip thus define a *base level* of innovation. Because any society could gain access to these base-level intellectual goods without awarding any private rights, the rights granted to private innovators in these goods constitute pure costs that are not strictly necessary. Zip is thus a risk-averse society that refuses to regulate the flow of ideas in any way. Zip's public does not invest in innovation directly, but remains willing to free-ride on the investments of private innovators. With no investments and likely positive returns, Zip-like regimes confer positive (or at least nonnegative) values on societies that adopt them. These values are unlikely to be very large; societies willing to incur some risks by absorbing some costs should be able to generate greater positive returns.

Next stop is Wip, whose congress enacted weak IP laws, including its patent law. Wip's residents therefore absorb some additional costs right out of the box; they reward base-level innovators for tasks that they would have undertaken even in Zip. Wip is thus worse off than Zip—unless the rights being offered motivate Wippers to divert private resources toward further successful innovation. Successful diversions generate new, useful ideas above the base-level innovations, granting Wip's public restricted benefits to both the base-level innovations of Zip and the second-level innovations that exist in Wip but not Zip. In exchange, Wip's public must cede the difference in utility between unrestricted and restricted use of the base-level innovations. If the value of restricted use of the second-level innovations exceeds the reduced value of the base-level innovations, Wip will achieve a higher return in net societal value than will Zip. Otherwise, Zip is better off and Wip's decision was a mistake.

If Wip is better off than Zip, the parliamentary decision in Sip to award strong IP rights might do even better. Once again, the incremental increase in the *private* value (i.e., the value that Sip's rights confer on private parties that Wip's do not) motivates at least some additional potential innovators to develop third-level innovations. Sip's public accrues a net societal benefit equal to the amount that the newly restricted rights on the three levels of innovation exceed the less-restricted rights on the first two levels of innovation.

This pattern of costs and benefits continues as the conceptually incremental process of strengthening private IP rights progresses—to a point. Early in the strengthening process, increased rights are likely to provide added incentives that spur additional innovation. Eventually, however, the rights may become so expansive that they block innovation. New entrants may become discouraged when virtually anything they discover infringes a right that has already been granted. Thus, societies that grant increasingly strong rights may gain increasingly restricted use of a growing pool of innovations—or they may deter future innovation and find themselves with increasingly restricted use of a *dwindling* innovation pool. As each strengthening proposal is considered, society must ask itself whether the pool is likely to grow or to contract, and if it is expected to grow, whether the increased restrictions across the larger pool are likely to result in a net gain or a net loss. Proposals that promise a net gain should be adopted; those that promise either a net loss or a smaller pool of innovations should be rejected. When no available proposals promise to yield a net benefit, the regime in place is societally optimal.[61]

A government that finds this elusive (some might say mythical) optimum has no reason to absorb the further costs implicit in granting increasingly restrictive IP rights. A society whose regime does so is overregulating innovation. Those that see available net benefits in increasing IP rights but fail to do so are underregulating innovation. Those that adopt all proposals that promise a net positive return—and *only* proposals that promise a net positive return—are regulating innovation optimally.

The parable of the Zippers, the Wippers, and the Sippers serves as a reminder that the black box of the patent system operates in two stages. Primary responsibility for determining the system's contours and overall strength belongs to Congress; the courts matter only at the margins. Primary responsibility for ensuring the system's coherence and consistency belongs to the courts—specifically, to the Federal Circuit. And that reminder leads back to the critical question about the Federal Circuit's performance: Has it increased the coherence, the consistency, and the predictability of the patent system?

PERFORMANCE

Few of the court's many observers ask this question explicitly; most combine inquiries into the court's consistency with inquiries into the correctness of contemporary patent policy, placing the burden upon their readers to tease the two issues apart. Some commentators, however, do manage to separate the two. In a recent important example, a 2004 National Academy of Sciences report on the patent system and its propriety in the early twenty-first century criticized many of the Federal Circuit's approaches to determining patent strength, but nevertheless conceded that

> both students of and practitioners before the court are in general agreement that the 1982 centralization of patent appeals in the Federal Circuit has been a vast improvement over adjudication in the circuit courts of appeals. It reduced forum shopping, focused attention and thought on neglected issues of patent law, produced innovations at the trial court level, and in general yielded greater consistency.[62]

That general agreement has prevailed throughout the court's brief lifetime. Professor Rochelle Cooper Dreyfuss was probably the first to study the Federal Circuit's effectiveness seriously. She reviewed every single patent opinion from the court's first five years, publishing her findings in 1989. Her assessment?

> Precision, as used here, means the extent to which the law produces horizontal equity. The best measure of precision would be to see whether two courts deciding the same case reach the same result. Before the [Federal Circuit], this was actually possible since patents sometimes were challenged in

more than one forum. However, with the establishment of the new court, repetitive litigation has diminished. A feel for precision, though, may be obtained in another manner—by looking at the way that the [Federal Circuit] formulates legal principles. Bright line rules, objective criteria, and minimal exceptions may not make for accurate adjudication (the "right" result in every case), but they create a body of law that is easier to apply uniformly and to predict with certainty. The decisions of the [Federal Circuit] to date demonstrate that the court has taken seriously the duty to make the law precise, and has made strides in that direction. . . . The [Federal Circuit's] jurisprudence reveals that the court has begun to make patent law more accurate, precise, and coherent.[63]

Fifteen years later, she updated her study and reached essentially the same conclusion, though not without noting that many, particularly in the academic community, disagree with her:

Those who study the patent portion of the [Federal Circuit's] docket, or practice patent law before the court, have seen both the benefits and detriments of specialization emerge during the court's two decades of existence. Practitioners appear to be in general agreement that centralizing patent appeals in a single court is a vast improvement over regional adjudication. Although there were suspicions of a pro-patentee bias in the court's early years, these have largely abated. . . . At the same time, however, some practitioners and many academics have voiced concern about the court's methodology and jurisprudence. It has been said that the court has been slow to look at the ramifications of its decisions [on the PTO,] the lower courts, and the consumers of its law; that it has been less interested than other courts in considering the academic literature or incorporating the lessons of social science research into its decisionmaking; and that it has veered in other ways from standard judicial practice.[64]

Dreyfuss also addressed the question of consistency directly, reaching the surprising conclusion that the Federal Circuit maintains an "appropriate" level of intentional inconsistency in the patent law, just to let new issues percolate a while before locking them down.

To develop good case law, it is helpful for judges to have an opportunity to see how different approaches operate in practice and to debate with their colleagues about which approach works best. If the Federal Circuit is to obtain these advantages in the specialty portion of its docket, then the debate would largely be among the panels of the court, rather than with the regional circuits. Accordingly, some level of inconsistency in outcomes should be tolerated: the issue is how much is appropriate. Some critics think that there is currently too much. Thus, the Federal Circuit has been criticized for construing the same patent differently in successive cases.[65]

Professor Dreyfuss believes that the Federal Circuit has been effective at imposing coherence and consistency upon the patent system, and that where its opinions appear inconsistent, it is probably just trying to recreate the "percolation" effect that allows circuit splits to inform the Supreme Court. She recognizes, however, that others may reasonably believe otherwise.

Perhaps the most surprising element of Dreyfuss's updated analysis was her assertion that the court's early pro-patent reputation has abated. That abatement might well be news to some of the Federal Circuit's most strident contemporary critics. Professors Adam Jaffe and Josh Lerner, for example, wrote a 200-page book, *Innovation and Its Discontents*, which they subtitled *How Our Broken Patent System Is Endangering Innovation and Progress, and What to Do about It*. They lay the lion's share of the blame for breaking the patent system squarely on the Federal Circuit's doorstep—and precisely for its pro-patent stance.

> Legal commentators—whether sympathetic to the court's rulings or not—collectively agree that the primary direction of the [Federal Circuit's] changes has been in the direction of strengthening patent-holders' rights. As we have emphasized, patents serve an important social function, and some recalibration in the direction of stronger patent protection was probably due given the long twentieth century decline. But . . . the strengthening of patent rights has now gone beyond recalibration to reach troubling proportions.[66]

In many ways, Lerner and Jaffe are more typical of Federal Circuit observers than is Dreyfuss. Dreyfuss correctly separated the Federal Circuit's work on enhancing *systemic strength* by imposing coherence, consistency, precision, and discipline from the congressional role in drafting the rules of *patent strength* inherent in the system's basic contours. Most commentators repeat Lerner and Jaffe's mistake by blurring the two. If the patent system grants patentees too many rights in exchange for too little, the primary fault lies with Congress (or possibly with the PTO). If patentees and potential patent applicants are uncertain as to what rights Congress has granted them, the primary fault lies with the courts. As a result, a perverse implication of the Federal Circuit's harshest critics is that the court is doing its job well.

Professor Glynn Lunney provided one such backhanded compliment. He described a "quiet revolution in patent law" in which Federal Circuit revisions of two key legal doctrines, the nonobviousness requirement and the doctrine of equivalents, has led to an economy overrun with valid, narrow patents—patents that hold up in court but lose infringement suits. These doctrines are central to the patent system, and no assessment of the system is possible without understanding what they are and where they came from. Fortunately, though they can, have, and do lead to complex, detailed legal reasoning, they also embody simple, commonsense ideas. Congress built nonobviousness into the Patent Act; patents are unavailable for inventions that any ordinarily skilled artisan could have cobbled together given the state of the art. What that requirement means, however, is a matter for the courts to decide. And the courts themselves crafted the doctrine of equivalents, which as noted is a toolkit helping judges determine when an accused product is "close enough" to infringe a patent. As Lunney describes it:

> Before 1982, courts . . . ensured that patents were rarely valid, but if valid, broadly enforced. However, since 1982, the nature of patent protection has gradually changed. . . . Intended, at least by some of its supporters, to rescue patents from a judiciary often suspicious, if not overtly hostile, towards patents, the Federal Circuit has taken its role as defender of the patent system seriously. . . . Under the Federal Circuit we have moved from patents that were rarely valid, but if valid broadly enforced, towards patents that are routinely valid, but narrowly enforced. . . . The statistics suggest a shift from rarely valid, but broadly enforced towards routinely valid, but narrowly enforced, patents since 1982. . . . At a purely subjective level, the single resolution most representative of the Federal Circuit era was a ruling, as a matter of law, that the patent was valid, but not infringed.[67]

Lunney is not happy with the Federal Circuit, though it's not clear why he blames the courts, rather than Congress, for a trend that he dislikes. He concedes that Congress created the Federal Circuit to "defend" the patent system—and that the Federal Circuit has responded by presuming that the PTO generally issues valid patents (an explicit instruction that Congress built into the Patent Act),[68] but that in doing so, it sold the patentee only those products she genuinely claimed. That certainly sounds like a reasonable defense of the system. From the perspective of all who agree with Lunney's assessment of the Federal Circuit's approach to validity and infringement analysis, the court seems to be performing well at its assigned task; blame for deviations of that task's results from a desired public policy belongs on Capitol Hill, not in Lafayette Park.

A second line of criticism hits closer to home. Ever since *Markman*, when the court ejected juries from claim construction and gave the job to trial judges, those trial judges have been screaming for guidance. That guidance has been grudging and less than crystalline. In 2004, the Case Western Reserve Law School hosted a symposium on the past, present, and future of the Federal Circuit. Its speakers included a panel of three trial judges—Kathleen O'Malley, Patti Saris, and Ronald Whyte—and the Federal Circuit's Judge Paul Michel. No one pulled any punches. Judge O'Malley opened with a sentiment that her colleagues shared: "Sometimes we think that the only thing that really is predictable in this area of the law is that we district judges will likely get it wrong, or at least that the Federal Circuit will say that we got it wrong."[69] From her vantage point, it appeared that the Federal Circuit had never told trial judges:

> when you construe claims, what tools you use to construe the claims, what you should and should not consider, how you go about determining the ordinary meaning of words in this context, what weight to give various aspects of the intrinsic/extrinsic evidence, whether any presumptions apply, whether you should consider the allegedly infringing product when you are doing your analysis, or whether, and to what extent, the [Federal Circuit] might consider any kind of immediate appeal from a claim construction decision. . . . Some clues have been given by the [Federal Circuit], and district judges have struggled mightily to answer these and other questions in the almost ten-year period since 1995.[70]

Judge Michel's defense was less than compelling. Rather than addressing the problem directly, he chose instead to explain why things were not quite as dire as Judge O'Malley (and the many commentators who agree with her) made things seem:

> One question . . . is why the reversal rate is so high for patent cases. I do not know what the reversal rate is. The last figure I looked at for reversal of district court patent cases, on all issues, was thirty-two percent. My feeling is the reversal rate for claim construction alone has to be less than that figure. . . . I doubt these figures signal a crisis or that the system is terribly sick. Consequently, we must keep this issue in perspective. It concerns me greatly to learn that district judges sometimes feel demoralized. . . . We do not analyze a claim construction from scratch—not only should we not, we really cannot. . . . I read the district judge's opinion on the claim construction to find out what his interpretation was and how the judge got there. If it is convincing and is not contradicted by something that is clearly stated in the claims, specification, prosecution history, or other such sources, I am highly inclined to affirm.[71]

This debate returns us yet again to claim construction, an activity that dominates the time and attention of anyone litigating a specific patent, but that nevertheless remains a sideshow when assessing the patent system as a whole. The differences between Judges O'Malley and Michel combine with the critiques of Professors Jaffe, Lerner, and Lunney and with Professor Dreyfuss's more favorable observations to provide an interesting picture of the two-stage black box that is our patent system.

Congress has translated the basic policy prescription of innovation motivation into a powerful patent grant. The system is structured to promote both innovation and disclosure through patenting. Congress created the

Federal Circuit in part to ensure that potential innovators would appreciate the merits of the patent system and participate in it willingly. The Federal Circuit ran with that task and attempted to address three key questions: First, what do the words in a patent mean—and how can courts resolve disputes about a patent's meaning? Second, did the patented invention really belong in the patent system? Third, is a product accused of infringement close enough to the patent claims to qualify as infringing? These questions lead, respectively, to considerations of claim construction, the nonobviousness requirement, and the doctrine of equivalents. By general consensus, the Federal Circuit has crafted rules that clarify answers to the latter two questions but continues to struggle with the first. As a result, patent litigation now hinges almost entirely upon linguistic disputes; once the claims have been construed, the courts are likely to find the claimed inventions patentable and narrow—leading to Lunney's observation that the single most common outcome in patent litigation is a finding that a valid patent was not infringed.

The poor grade on claim construction notwithstanding, the Federal Circuit has performed well at its primary assignment. It injected significant certainty into the patent system and turned patents into real motivators of innovation. As Judge Michel noted at the Case Western symposium, however, simply crafting coherent rules is insufficient. "We owe the bar, the district courts, the Patent Office, and anybody else interested, coherent explanations of why we ruled the way we did. We must do this for several reasons: credibility of the courts, development of law, clarification of the law, and predictive power." He added, "With this in mind, in the end, we have tremendous potential to make course corrections."[72]

Those course corrections proceed apace, as do the court's explanations of its rulings. Nowhere is either more evident than in cases lying at the cutting edge of technology—technologies whose very contours confound the assumptions that have long underpinned the law of patents, and that call some of the system's most basic assumptions into question. One such technology pushed every judge who touched it to wonder how to navigate uncharted waters without introducing course "corrections" likely to cause more long-term harm than good. The technology in question was *ice-nine*.

5

✛

From Cutting Edge
to Front Page

ICE-NINE

In 1963, Kurt Vonnegut released his beguiling *Cat's Cradle*. Lest his tale of global cataclysm cause a panic, Vonnegut placed an unusual disclaimer on the book's copyright page: "Nothing in this book is true."[1] Buried inside the text itself lies a more cryptic warning: "All of the true things I am about to tell you are shameless lies."[2] Vonnegut then proceeded to tell some shameless lies that the Federal Circuit would one day discover were true things.

As Vonnegut told his tale, it all began with Marines sick of wallowing in mud. They wanted something small, something that would allow them to transport their heavy equipment and machinery through swamps and streams without becoming mired in the muck. They went to the renowned Dr. Felix Hoenikker, who explained a theory that might be able to help:

"There are several ways in which certain liquids can crystallize—can freeze—several ways in which their atoms can stack and lock in an orderly, rigid way. . . . So it is with the atoms in crystals, too; and two different crystals of the same substance can have quite different physical properties."

He told me about a factory that had been growing big crystals of ethelyne diamine tartrate. The crystals were useful in certain manufacturing operations, he said. But one day the factory discovered that the crystals it was growing no longer had the properties desired. The atoms had begun to stack and lock—to freeze—in different fashion. The liquid that was crystallizing hadn't changed, but the crystals it was forming were, as far as industrial applications went, pure junk.

How this had come about was a mystery. The theoretical villain, however, was . . . "a seed," . . . a tiny grain of undesired crystal pattern. The seed, which had come from God-only-knows-where, taught the atoms the novel way in which to stack and lock, to crystallize, to freeze.

"Now think about cannonballs on a courthouse lawn or about oranges in a crate again," he suggested. And he helped me to see that the pattern of the bottom layers of cannonballs or of oranges determined how each subsequent layer would stack and lock. "The bottom layer is the seed of how every cannonball or every orange that comes after is going to behave, even to an infinite number of cannonballs or oranges."[3]

The conversation then shifted back to Marines mired in mud. Hoenikker's insight was that there might also be different configurations of the water molecule—configurations whose melting point exceeded 32 degrees Fahrenheit. The key to these progressively higher melting points was increased stability; the more stable the configuration, the higher the melting point. Furthermore, these water variants would educate each other, so that a single seed of a relatively stable configuration would "convert" its less stable brethren to its own form immediately upon contact. The ninth such configuration, *ice-nine*, would have a melting point high enough to help the Marines; were they able to seed a swamp with *ice-nine*, the water would solidify, "and the United States Marines would rise from the swamp and march on!"[4] *Cat's Cradle* told the tale of *ice-nine* unleashed upon an unsuspecting world, with consequences sufficiently severe to warrant Vonnegut's disclaimer about his novel's veracity.

Forty years later, *ice-nine* worked its way onto the Federal Circuit's docket, where it turned out that Vonnegut had been mistaken. For though his tale of *ice-nine* may have been a shameless lie, it nevertheless contained the seed of a true thing. And when that seed came into contact with patent law, it set in motion a chain reaction whose consequences may reverberate for years to come. The seed was known not as *ice-nine* but as paroxetine.[5] And paroxetine, though not as central to human life (or to Marines mired in mud) as is water, is nevertheless quite valuable. For paroxetine, you see, is the active ingredient in the antidepressant Paxil. And when the rights to make and sell valuable chemicals are in dispute, the Federal Circuit's involvement is all but inevitable.

The true thing known as paroxetine made its first appearance in Denmark in the 1970s, when scientists at Ferrosan synthesized a new class of chemical compounds, some of which possessed antidepressant properties. Paroxetine was among those compounds. So Ferrosan did what companies do. It applied for, and on February 8, 1977, received, U.S. Patent number 4,007,196 (known in the trade as "the '196 Patent"). In 1980, Ferrosan licensed its patent to the larger Beecham Group. Several mergers later, the Beecham Group became part of GlaxoSmithKline (GSK), one of the world's largest pharmaceutical companies.[6]

GSK (though Beecham was not yet part of GSK when most of these events unfolded) began to experiment with its newly licensed chemicals in 1981. Paroxetine, though chemically powerful, was rather hard to use: it formed a chalky powder that reacted poorly when it came into contact with moisture. That difficulty complicated GSK's efforts to commercialize this valuable chemical. GSK's attempts to improve paroxetine's handling properties led to some interesting scientific inquiries and discoveries.

On May 29, 1985, a GSK scientist named Alan Curzons penned his "Paroxetine Polymorphism" memo. Curzons had identified the paroxetine equivalents of *ice-one* and *ice-two*. Paroxetine *an*hydrate, the old powdery form that behaved poorly when it met water, was no longer alone on this Earth. Paroxetine *hemi*hydrate, which integrated water molecules directly into the paroxetine's molecular structure, had joined it. And the hemihydrate was much more stable than the anhydrate; it was much easier to handle even when wet.

These two molecular structures of the same chemical qualified them as "polymorphs,"[7] much as coal and diamond are carbon polymorphs and Vonnegut's nine hypothetical ices are water polymorphs (or at least they would be, were they true things). But the paroxetine polymorphs have more in common with the various ices than they do with coal and diamond because, like cannonballs on a lawn or oranges in a crate, they educate each other when they meet. Specifically, when a paroxetine hemihydrate seed encounters paroxetine anhydrate, it "teaches" the anhydrate how to absorb nearby moisture and join it in hemihydrous stability. In the presence of a hemihydrous seed, paroxetine anhydrate became a "disappearing polymorph."

Curzons's discovery of this new stable form made his bosses at GSK quite happy; its superior handling properties finally let them launch a commercial product. It also, however, provided another significant step toward the patent challenge that would perplex the federal judiciary almost two decades later. GSK applied for a British patent on Curzons's discovery on October 25, 1985, and for an American patent almost exactly one year later, on October 23, 1986. On January 26, 1988, the U.S. PTO issued Patent number 4,721,723 ("the '723 Patent"), recognizing GSK's claimed ownership of Curzons's new invention: "Crystalline paroxetine hydrochloride hemihydrate."

For a variety of technical legal reasons rooted in the Hatch-Waxman Act of 1984—an offshoot of our late-1970s inquiry into ways to enhance our industrial competitiveness that established special rules for commercially viable drug patents—the '196 Patent reserved GSK's exclusive right to *any form* of paroxetine until 1998.[8] When that right lapsed, generic drug companies intent upon selling low-priced antidepressants that were equivalent (or technically, "bio-equivalent") to Paxil swooped down. These companies, led by Apotex, announced that they would work entirely with the off-patent paroxetine anhydrate and leave GSK's still-patented paroxetine hemihydrate untouched.

But Apotex and its generic brethren had a problem. Paxil's widespread distribution had already seeded the atmosphere with hemihydrate molecules, and any contact between even a single hemihydrate seed and a pile of paroxetine anhydrate taught at least some of the anhydrate how to convert itself into hemihydrate. No matter how hard Apotex might try to manufacture and sell pure anhydrate, chances were overwhelming that a hemihydrate seed would wander by and convert some of its anhydrate into hemihydrate. The end product that Apotex made and sold would therefore inevitably combine paroxetine anhydrate—now in the public domain—with GSK's patented hemihydrate. And it violates the patent laws to make or to sell even a little bit of someone else's patented product without authorization. GSK was in no mood to authorize Apotex to manufacture low-priced Paxil equivalents. Instead, GSK sued Apotex for infringement and asked the federal courts to block Apotex's generic product from the market.

So much for the fun part. Now we've got to do some hard work. Few cases present as stark a contrast between simple policy pronouncements and legal nuance. From a policy perspective, the outcome should be clear: Apotex should win. Certainly, GSK deserved compensation for its scientific breakthroughs, and policy considerations dictate compensation significant enough to motivate further research investments. That's precisely why the patent laws preserved GSK's exclusivity on paroxetine anhydrate from 1977 through 1998 and its exclusivity on the superior hemihydrate polymorph through at least 2006. But public policy also dictates that we open "old" innovations to the broad public, so that competitive forces can drive prices downward and benefit consumers. In this case, Apotex's best efforts to market a pure off-patent paroxetine anhydrate product fail through no fault of its own. A judgment in favor of GSK would effectively pull a valuable product out of the competitive market and restore it to the consumer-unfriendly monopoly market—seemingly without justification. But the patent laws are more than simply policy statements. After all, in 1998 we were in the midst of rewarding GSK for its hemihydrate breakthrough. A judgment in favor of Apotex would cheapen the '723 Patent and thus reduce GSK's incentive to continue investing in pharmaceutical research—again, seemingly without justification.

DEPRESSED

This *ice-nine* quandary perplexed every member of the federal judiciary to touch it, first at the trial level and then at the Federal Circuit. As Judge Arthur Gajarsa would frame the problem much later in the game:

> Paroxetine hemihydrate is presumably a synthetic compound, created by humans in a laboratory, never before existing in nature, that is nevertheless capable of "reproducing" itself through a natural process. This crystalline compound raises a question similar to one that might arise when considering the invention of a fertile plant or a genetically engineered organism, capable of reproduction, released into the wild. Consider, for example, what might happen if the wind blew fertile, genetically modified blue corn protected by a patent, from the field of a single farmer into neighboring cornfields. The harvest from those fields would soon contain at least some patented blue corn mixed in with the traditional public domain yellow corn—thereby infringing the patent. The wind would continue to blow, and the patented crops would spread throughout the continent, thereby turning most (if not all) North American corn farmers into unintentional, yet inevitable, infringers. The implication—that the patent owner would be entitled to collect royalties from every farmer whose cornfields contained even a few patented blue stalks—cannot possibly be correct. The underlying question that engaged the district court, and that led it to develop numerous alternative holdings, is *why* this implication is incorrect.[9]

Why, indeed. The district court's "numerous alternative holdings" provided several possible answers. Judge Gajarsa added one of his own to the mix. But neither his opinion nor those of the two trial judges—Kocoras and Posner—defines the law, for the other two judges on the Federal Circuit panel offered yet another explanation. As a matter of law, Judge Rader, with whom Judge Bryson joined to form a majority of the appellate panel, got the final word. As an analytic excursion to the cutting edges of patent law, however, each proposed solution has something to offer.

GSK and Apotex first faced off in front of Judge Charles Kocoras, an experienced trial judge in the Northern District of Illinois. Kocoras presided over a number of pretrial motions, in which parties argue that they should win on summary judgment and not have to incur the expense and bother of a full-blown trial. The standard for summary judgment is straightforward. The judge assumes that the party requesting the judgment is wrong about *every* disputed fact and then determines whether, as a matter of law, that "moving party" must win anyway. But this victory need not decide the case; in fact, it often does not. Litigants typically move for summary judgments on individual legal questions.

In this case, as in most cases, many of these pretrial points were fairly technical, and though some *sounded* like factual disputes, they all eventually came down to legal debates. Kocoras issued two basic rulings. First, Ferrosan's discovery of paroxetine anhydrate did not contain hemihydrate in a way that had made its discovery inevitable; in legal terms, the anhydrate did not "inherently anticipate" the hemihydrate.[10] Second, GSK's clinical studies designed to learn whether or not paroxetine hemihydrate was useful as an antidepressant were experimental; in legal terms, they did not trigger the "public use" bar, starting a one-year clock beyond which GSK would lose its right to apply for a patent.[11] Though these rulings did not decide the case, they would have had he ruled the other way. The PTO does not grant patents on inherently anticipated inventions, because there is no particular reason to reward the "discoverer" of something whose discovery was inevitable. And had the clinical trials *not* qualified as experimental, GSK would have missed its filing deadline. Under either circumstance, the court would have invalidated the '723 Patent, and GSK would have lost.

Judge Kocoras also started a critical discussion that he never quite finished. Precisely what was it that GSK possessed under the '723 Patent? Was it every single crystal of paroxetine hemihydrate? If so, what sorts of tests would the court have to conduct to determine whether or not a specific batch of Apotex's product infringed? Would this test change as scientific instrumentation improved? These questions cut to the heart of the dispute—and as Kocoras noted, most of them needed a full-blown trial, replete with a review of all evidence and the testimony of experts—before the court could answer them.

Before that trial could occur, a new judge took over. Judge Richard Posner, one of the nation's most respected jurists and legal theorists, assumed the helm. This assignment was unusual because Posner *is not* a trial judge. Posner is a member of the Seventh Circuit Court of Appeals, the appellate court that normally reviews trials from the Northern District of Illinois; he sat as a trial judge "by designation," or special appointment. The Seventh Circuit had not seen a patent appeal since the Federal Circuit's birth in 1982. As a result, patents were among the few areas of contemporary law—and in particular, among the few areas of contemporary law central to a liberal, information-age market economy—that Posner had not influenced. People began to take notice. Even those not enticed by *ice-nine* were curious about Posner's view of patents.

Posner did not disappoint. He conducted a bench trial lasting two and a half weeks, listened to numerous experts, digested all of the evidence, and issued a detailed, complex opinion elucidating numerous alternative theories leading to a ruling for Apotex. Perhaps the best way to understand these various theories and the paths that they take to reach that same endpoint is to annotate Posner's own summary.

[*Posner's actual ruling:*] [The '723 Patent claims] crystalline paroxetine hydrochloride hemihydrate in any commercially significant quantity, and so construed the claim is valid against the various attacks on it made by Apotex but clearly will not be infringed by Apotex's anhydrate product. [*GSK keeps its patent, but Apotex wins the case.*]

[*Alternative #1:*] I hold that if [the patent] is construed to claim single crystals of crystalline paroxetine hydrochloride hemihydrate, it is infringed, but that if the claim were so construed it would be invalid because of indefiniteness. [*GSK loses its patent, and thus the case.*]

[*Alternative #2:*] If [the patent] is construed to claim crystalline paroxetine hydrochloride hemihydrate in amounts detectable by means that existed when the patent was applied for or issued, I find that [GSK] has failed to prove by a preponderance of the evidence that Apotex's product will infringe [the patent]. [*GSK keeps its patent, but Apotex wins the case.*]

[*Alternative #3:*] I reach the same conclusion (though with less confidence) if [the patent] is construed to claim crystalline paroxetine hydrochloride hemihydrate in amounts detectable by any means. So construed, the claim might fail for indefiniteness, but I do not reach that question. [*GSK probably loses its patent, and thus the case.*]

[*Alternative #4:*] If contrary to the above, [the patent] is valid and will be infringed either by a single crystal of hemihydrate or by a barely detectable amount of it, Apotex has a complete affirmative defense that [GSK] is the cause of the infringement. [*GSK keeps the patent and proves that it should win, but Apotex's defense trumps GSK's argument.*]

[*Alternative #5:*] If [the patent] is valid and will be infringed and Apotex has no defense to liability, I hold that [GSK] nevertheless is entitled to no relief: neither an injunction against Apotex's making its anhydrate product nor an order based on the Hatch-Waxman Act delaying Apotex's sale of its anhydrate product until [the '723 Patent] expires. The grant of injunctive relief, whether under the patent statute or under the Hatch-Waxman Act, would be contrary to the principles of equity. [*GSK keeps the patent and proves that it should win the case, but the court will refuse to enforce the patent because to do so under these circumstances would be inequitable.*]

... For these reasons I am instructing the clerk of the district court to enter a final judgment for the defendants, dismissing [GSK]'s suit with prejudice.[12]

Anyone familiar with patent law could tell you that this opinion covers a stunning range of legal issues. Anyone familiar with legal writing could tell you that this opinion presents an unusual array of alternatives. And anyone at all could tell you that this opinion is confusing. The Federal Circuit panel had its work cut out for it. Just what was Judge Posner saying? Was he right?

Posner's ruling hinged on two sets of issues: claim construction (or what the patent's four words actually mean) and equity (or fairness). Most of the other issues fall into place given those two issues. On the matter of claim construction, Posner noted that GSK itself had had a hard time saying exactly what it thought the patent claimed, though it did eventually announce that it owned every single crystal of paroxetine hemihydrate in existence. Posner rejected that interpretation because it would have made accidental or incidental infringement widespread: "If a worker in a chocolate factory popped a Paxil into his mouth and as a result the factory became seeded with hemihydrate crystals, and the seeds found their way into chocolate that was then sold, the sale would infringe."[13] But Posner knew that such a ruling would be little more than an impermissible interjection of his own policy concerns into patent law, so he took another route to rejecting the "single crystal" theory. He concluded that his chocolatier's difficulty in assessing whether or not a stray paroxetine hemiydrate crystal had attached itself to his confections meant that GSK had failed to provide said chocolatier with suitable notice of what the patent claimed. Such a lack of suitable notice renders a patent invalid for "indefiniteness," a fatal legal flaw.

> For remember that inadvertency is not a defense to infringement; there is no defense of independent creation. The primary purpose of this requirement of definiteness in claims is to provide clear warning to others as to what constitutes infringement of the patent, because a zone of uncertainty which enterprise and experimentation may enter only at the risk of infringement claims would discourage invention only a little less than unequivocal foreclosure of the field.[14]

Posner thus concluded that if GSK "won" by convincing him of the single-crystal theory, it would immediately lose its patent and the case would be over.

But he didn't rule that way. Instead, he did GSK a "favor" by attaching a different meaning to the patent—a meaning that would cost GSK its suit against Apotex but that would allow it to retain its valuable patent on paroxetine hemihydrate. He noted that the only reason that GSK ever got the '723 Patent was that the hemihydrate possessed useful commercial properties that the anhydrate lacked—and therefore interpreted "crystalline paroxetine hydrochloride hemihydrate" to mean "crystalline paroxetine hydrochloride hemihydrate, excluding hemihydrate produced by involuntary conversion of a proportion of an anhydrous mixture so small as to lack any commercial significance."[15]

Posner's legal support for this conclusion was rather thin. He noted that the Federal Circuit, whose patent law rulings bound his own in this case, had instructed trial judges that "general descriptive terms will ordinarily be given their full meaning."[16] So Posner italicized the word "ordinarily" and explained that "this is the rare case in which the qualification that I have italicized comes into its own."[17]

Posner knew that his claim construction had little chance of making it through the Federal Circuit untouched. He knew that the standard rules of claim construction still lay in that italicized word "ordinarily." What if the Federal Circuit disagreed with him and concluded that this case was quite ordinary after all? If that should happen, Posner insisted that Apotex should *still* win, as a matter of simple equity. After all, GSK was responsible for seeding the atmosphere; molecules spun off GSK's own Paxil were the seeds creating the problem. It seemed entirely unfair to let GSK keep Apotex's product off the market because GSK itself had released a chemical into Apotex's plant that made it inevitable for Apotex to infringe.[18]

GSK had lost six ways from Sunday—once under each of Posner's six theories. Either it lost its patent (and its suit), it lost its suit (but kept its patent), or it kept the patent and proved its point but could not ask a court to enforce its victory because to do so would be inequitable. So it was no surprise that GSK appealed. What might be a bit more surprising is that Apotex *also* appealed, arguing that just in case the Federal Circuit disagreed with everything that Posner had said, it should also disagree with Kocoras and rule that GSK had missed one of its technical filing deadlines.

By the time that the matter hit the Federal Circuit docket, confusion reigned supreme. The patent bar had watched Posner's gyrations intently and wondered what the Federal Circuit would do. Public policy certainly seemed to favor Apotex, but it was painfully hard to find a way to get the law to go along. If it had been easy, Kocoras and Posner would have taken the easy route. But when two gifted jurists see only complexity, chances are pretty good that the case is complex. *Ice-nine* eventually destroyed the world. It caused all moisture to crystallize, turned the oceans rigid, and slowly snuffed out all life. Would paroxetine hemihydrate do the same for patent law?

ANTIDEPRESSED

Posner's claim construction persuaded no one at the Federal Circuit. Though it is hard to argue with his assertions that paroxetine is no ordinary invention and that the dispute that it engendered is no ordinary dispute, it is not hard to find fault with his conclusion that that '723 Patent is no ordinary patent. From a vanilla patent dispute perspective, this one is *easy.* The '723 Patent is quite clear; it names the substance that GSK invented. There is no ambiguity in its language, and no real factual dispute about its implication. GSK's '723 Patent claims every single crystal of paroxetine hemihydrate, and Apotex's products will inevitably contain at least trace amounts of hemihydrate. All three judges on the Federal Circuit panel reached this conclusion.

So . . . end of story? Did GSK prevail on its infringement claim? Did the Federal Circuit block Apotex's low-priced generic competitor to Paxil from the market?

No. It did not.

Like Posner, the Federal Circuit judges kept the analysis going. Unlike Posner, who concluded that if the Federal Circuit reached this point it should consider equity, the panel's members looked elsewhere. Judge Rader found a technicality that resolved the case without addressing the tough issues. Judge Gajarsa argued that the apparent complexity in this matter arose because everyone involved had overlooked a basic principle of patent law—a principle so fundamental that few people ever give it a second thought. Judge Bryson cast the deciding vote without additional comment—in favor of Rader's view.

Rader followed Apotex's lead. He not only disagreed with Posner but also disagreed with Kocoras. One of Apotex's early arguments had been that GSK had missed a critical filing deadline for the '723 Patent. Under U.S. law, an inventor has one year from the date that he first reveals his invention to the public to file for a patent; failure to file on time precludes its ever being patented. Rader cited Federal Circuit precedent: "Public use . . . includes any use of the claimed invention by a person other than the inventor who is under no limitation, restriction or obligation of secrecy to the inventor."[19]

But there's a catch. There's an exception to this "public use" rule known as "experimental use."[20] "Experimental use negates public use; when proved, it may show that particular acts, even if apparently public in a colloquial sense, do not constitute a public use"[21] of the sort that starts the one-year clock running. GSK had run clinical trials more than a year before filing for its U.S. patent on paroxetine hemihydrate. Were these clinical trials "experimental"? Kocoras had concluded that they were. But Rader wondered just what it was that they were testing. "In [GSK's] own words, the purpose of the clinical trials was 'to establish that [paroxetine hemihydrate] actually worked (and was safe) as an antidepressant.'"[22] Rader then turned to the law governing the relationship between experimentation and public use. "The determinative inquiry," he wrote, "is whether [GSK] tested the invention of the asserted claim. Testing or experimentation performed with respect to non-claimed features of the device does not show that the invention was the subject of experimentation."[23]

To Rader, this last point made all the difference in the world: If the tests were truly "public," then the only sorts of experimentation that would stop the clock from running would be experiments that related *directly* to the features at issue—in this case, the very existence of paroxetine hemihydrate.

> Clinical trials designed to establish the efficacy and safety of the compound as an antidepressant for FDA approval are not experimental uses of the claimed invention. In other words, the claim covers the compound regardless of its use as an antidepressant. The antidepressant properties of the compound are simply not claimed features. Consequently, the clinical tests, which measured the efficacy and safety of the compound as an antidepressant, did not involve the claimed features of the invention. The 1985 clinical tests, therefore, do not qualify as an experimental use. . . . A patentee should understand that testing the properties, uses, and commercial significance of a compound claimed solely in structural terms may start the clock . . . for filing a claim that is not limited by any property, commercially significant amount, or other use of the compound. Because these clinical trials tested only the safety and efficacy of PHC hemihydrate as an antidepressant, those trials were not an experimental use of the invention.[24]

Rader certainly seemed to have found a clean solution to a tough problem: just tell GSK that it lost its patent on a technicality. In many ways, Rader's logic was similar to Posner's decision to declare this case extraordinary. They both employed a legal trick known as "distinguishing a case on its facts." Judges who employ this trick realize that for some very special reason, the case in front of them *must* come out one way. They are concerned, however, lest their ruling create a precedent that persuades—or even worse, binds—future courts facing cases that are somehow similar but lack the special feature that impelled them to rule the way that they did. They then take the case in front of them and try to describe it in terms that are so unusual that no other judge could ever see another case as basically similar. A judge who succeeds in isolating a single case from greater legal trends and precedents has bought himself *a lot* of extra maneuvering room. Posner used it to ignore the ordinary canons of claim construction. Rader used it to insist that we never need address the truly challenging questions because of a technical glitch in GSK's patent filing.

But Rader's approach was problematic. He conceded, for example, that other parts of the '723 Patent also claimed related inventions, such as *the use* of paroxetine hemihydrate to treat depression, and that GSK's clinical trials *did* test that claim. The implication left the entire pharmaceutical industry in a bind. Suppose that you discover a new chemical compound that you believe possesses valuable clinical properties. You would like to file a patent application that claims both the compound itself and its use as a medication. This situation is hardly unusual, and pharmaceutical companies have long done pretty much what GSK did here—they start their clinical trials, assume that their "public use" clock is not running, and apply for a patent when convinced that their discovery is worth patenting. Though Rader may have tried to distinguish this case on the facts, many members of the patent bar—and their clients in the pharmaceutical industry—were afraid that he hadn't. They were afraid that Rader had just announced a new rule that would cost them many of their valuable patents. Did the Federal Circuit really want to inject such massive uncertainty into the pharmaceutical industry? Did the law really say what Rader implied it said? Had everyone been mistaken all along? Did this new view of clinical testing serve either law or policy?

Judge Gajarsa was the first to note these problems when he explained why he rejected the reasoning of the panel majority despite agreeing with its ruling in favor of Apotex. As he saw it, Kocoras, rather than Rader, had applied Federal Circuit precedent correctly to conclude that GSK's public trials *had not* started the clock running and *did not* invalidate the '723 Patent on technical grounds. Rader had explained that GSK may have needed these tests to see if paroxetine hemihydrate worked, but it didn't need them to develop the invention in question (i.e., a single crystal of paroxetine hemihydrate). Gajarsa noted that the Federal Circuit had never required this sort of connection before—and cited numerous examples in technologies unrelated to pharmaceuticals. He saw "no principled grounds on which to distinguish this case from our precedent" and accused his colleagues in the majority of "trying to reach an ultimate conclusion of invalidity while avoiding the road less traveled."[25]

He himself took that less traveled road. It led him back to the most basic issue in all of patent law, an issue so basic that it literally qualifies as "Patents 101" (or technically, Section 101 of the Patent Act): the division of all potential discoveries into those that are patentable and those that are unpatentable.

The asserted breadth of [the '723 Patent] makes sense only under the erroneous belief that patents may protect products spread and reproduced by natural processes, directly contradicting our well established understanding of the limits imposed by Section 101. Given current scientific trends, such a belief could easily lead to misdirected research investments, to inappropriately issued patents, and to a widespread in terrorem effect crippling entire industries whose artisans learn that even their best efforts to respect patent rights may not save them from liability as inadvertent, inevitable infringers. . . . Though the majority's approach . . . defuses these negative consequences with respect to paroxetine, it does so at the cost of creating unfortunate precedent that will complicate future considerations of the experimental use doctrine. It also fails to address the central anomaly that [Judge Posner] identified. . . . We should announce, as a court, that the patent law does not sanction the concept of inevitable infringement—lest someone mistakenly believe that it does.[26]

In many ways, Gajarsa's approach was similar to one of the alternatives that Posner had advocated, should the Federal Circuit find itself precisely where it found itself—with a valid patent claiming every single hemihydrate crystal and a generic manufacturer whose product would "inevitably" infringe. But whereas Posner saw no salvation in patent law and thus turned to the weaker concept of equity, Gajarsa argued that a proper reading of patent law would lead to the right conclusion. According to Gajarsa, the keys to this case lay in two concepts so basic to patent law that few professionals revisit them: Section 101 and public notice.

Section 101 describes the very broad range of inventions suitable for patenting: "Whoever invents or discovers any new and useful process, machine, manufacture, or composition of matter, or any new and useful improvement thereof, may obtain a patent therefore."[27] According to the Supreme Court, Section 101 may let inventors patent *most* inventions, but it certainly doesn't let them patent *all* inventions. "In choosing such expansive terms as 'manufacture' and 'composition of matter,' modified by the comprehensive 'any,' Congress plainly contemplated that the patent laws would be given wide scope." That wide scope nevertheless excludes laws of nature, natural phenomena, and abstract ideas. "Such discoveries are manifestations of . . . nature, free to all men and reserved exclusively to none."[28]

Public notice is the very reason that we have patents altogether—to convince inventors to share their knowledge by notifying the public of their inventions and discoveries. The Federal Circuit had recently explained that "the essence of public notice" lies in patent language sufficiently clear for readers with ordinary skill in the art to "discern which matter is disclosed and discussed in the written description, and to recognize which matter has been claimed." This sort of clarity "tells the public which products or processes would infringe the patent and which would not."[29] But the Supreme Court had emphasized the centrality of public notice long ago, in a pair of opinions dating back to the mid-nineteenth century:

Whoever discovers that a certain useful result will be produced, in any art, machine, manufacture, or composition of matter, by the use of certain means, is entitled to a patent for it; provided he specifies the means he uses in a manner so full and exact, that any one skilled in the science to which it appertains, can, by using the means he specifies, without any addition to, or subtraction from them, produce precisely the result he describes. And if this cannot be done by the means he describes, the patent is void. And if it can be done, then the patent confers on him the exclusive right to use the means he specifies to produce the result or effect he describes, and nothing more.[30]

Accurate description of the invention is required by law, for several important purposes: 1. That the government may know what is granted, and what will become public property when the term of the monopoly expires. 2. That licensed persons desiring to practise the invention may know during the term how to make, construct, and use the invention. 3. That other inventors may know what part of the field of invention is unoccupied.[31]

As Gajarsa saw it, the facts here "highlight the unique challenge that the infringement analysis of the '723 Patent poses: infringing matter has an unusual tendency to 'appear' even where it is unwanted. Such a spontaneous appearance of a patented product vitiates the public notice function of patents. . . . When the claimed product can be 'made' via the spontaneous conversion of a noninfringing product into an infringing one, adequate notice is impossible—even if the claimed product was initially synthesized in a laboratory."[32] He continued:

Paroxetine hemihydrate forces us, for the first time, to confront the requirement that "a patentee specify in a manner so full and exact, that any one skilled in the science to which it appertains, can, by [avoiding] the means he specifies," avoid producing the claimed product. Otherwise, there will be no way for "other inventors [to] know what part of the field of invention is unoccupied." Effective notice is impossible if a natural physical process can convert a noninfringing product into an infringing one. . . .

Were we to . . . hold Apotex liable as an infringer, . . . we would effectively remove a valuable public-domain antidepressant, paroxetine anhydrate, from the market, and likely motivate potential inventors of superior grades of paroxetine to refocus their efforts elsewhere. This result is inconsistent with patent policy and—more importantly for the purposes of this court—it is incompatible with patent law. We would be holding valid a patent incapable of serving its important public notice function. . . . But the failure of notice is a consequence of its invalidity, not the source of it. We must consider whether or not the '723 patent covers only patentable subject matter.[33]

Not surprisingly, Gajarsa concluded that it doesn't. The '723 Patent, as he explained it, combined patentable paroxetine hemihydrate—the stuff synthesized in a lab through human effort—and unpatentable paroxetine hemihydrate—the stuff that appears spontaneously without human intervention. He compared the situation to one that scientists encounter when they discover how to synthesize, in bulk, chemicals that appear naturally in the human body in only small amounts. Obviously, these inventors cannot claim all molecules of the chemical—that would turn all humans into infringers. On the other hand, they should be able to claim *something* for their efforts—and for their contributions to medical science.

The solution that the Federal Circuit has endorsed is to let these folks patent all "non-natural" or "non-human" instances of the chemical.[34] But GSK never protected itself. It claimed to own *all* paroxetine hemihydrate, including the crystals that appeared spontaneously in Apotex's labs.

Gajarsa's opinion discussed policy issues—always gutsy in judicial circles—and reached back into concepts so fundamental that few other than law students taking their first patent course ever discuss them. But it cut directly to the chase. *The policy we want is the policy we have.* Patent policy could *never* sanction inevitable infringement. Patent law prohibits inevitable infringement. GSK sued Apotex as an inevitable infringer. "Despite the complexity of the issue, the analysis is straightforward."[35] GSK claimed too much, loses its patent, and Apotex wins. Simple, straightforward, and persuasive—though not where it counted. While Gajarsa's views swayed all three members of the panel considering the paroxetine patents at the District Court of the Hague[36] (the sole tribunal that Dutch law authorizes to hear patent disputes) and earned some good press from the parts of the farm lobby that admired his blue-corn hypothetical,[37] he was unable to persuade either of his panel colleagues to join him.

ANTIDEPRESSED REDUX

Gajarsa's critique of the experimental use analysis resonated widely. Many of the folks involved in pharmaceutical testing shared his belief that Rader's opinion—and as the majority opinion, a binding bit of Federal Circuit law—would wreak havoc upon both existing patents and industry practice. More to the point though, GSK asked the Federal Circuit to reconsider the matter *en banc*, a request that, as everyone knows, the court ordinarily denies. But as Posner noted, this case was hardly ordinary. Though the *en banc* court didn't give GSK what it wanted, it did give it something: it gave the case back to the same three-judge panel and asked the judges to vacate the experimental-use ruling and try again.

Gajarsa remained unable to convince either of his colleagues. This time, Rader fell back upon the "inherent anticipation" theory that Kocoras had explicitly considered and rejected.[38] Gajarsa repeated his concurrence, contending that his colleagues once again reached the right conclusion for the wrong reason, although without explicitly commenting on that reason. This time, however, he didn't have to—another judge did it for him. When a circuit court agrees to reconsider a case *en banc*, even if it ultimately decides (as it did here) to ship it back to the panel with additional instructions, every member of the court gets to weigh in on the matter. Only Judge Newman availed herself of the opportunity. She objected to the new panel majority opinion in terms suggesting that it may be no better than the one that it supplanted.

> The panel now holds that a product that existed in trace amounts, although unknown and undetected and unisolated, is "inherently anticipated" and barred from the patent system after it is discovered. The patentability of antibiotics, hormones, antibodies, and myriad other previously unknown or unisolated products would be called into question by this new ruling, giving rise to uncertainty as to existing patents, as well as negation of searches for the beneficial components of existing materials. The breadth of the panel's theory of inherent anticipation contravenes long-established precedent.[39]

What's more, inherent anticipation knocks out the safeguards for future pharmaceutical companies that Judge Gajarsa envisioned. Had the problem been that GSK's claim was so broad that it swept unpatentable matter into a claim with patentable matter, future inventors could fix the problem simply by claiming "synthetic," or "non-naturally occurring," instances of their discoveries. If paroxetine hemihydrate was inherent in its anhydrous polymorph, no one can ever patent *any* of it. And the situation gets worse. Under the vacated experimental use ruling, GSK retained its patent on paroxetine hemihydrate used as an antidepressant, even though it lost its patent on the chemical itself. Under an inherent anticipation theory, it's hard to see why using this new paroxetine polymorph to achieve what science already knew the old polymorph would achieve wouldn't also be anticipated. In other words, by "winning" its petition for a rehearing *en banc*, GSK likely lost additional portions of its patent.

GSK may take some small solace in a passage that Gajarsa added when his colleagues progressed from experimental use to inherent anticipation.

> Many of the "absurd consequences" that [Judge Posner] foresaw are, in fact, absurd, and would ill-serve the public were they the law. The proper place for resolutions of such conflicts between patent law and patent policy, however, is Congress, not the courts. For the most part, though, such absurdities are likely to lie not in the law itself, but rather in misapplications of the law.[40]

The Federal Circuit had ruled. GSK lost yet again, this time because of inherent anticipation. Such is the law, and it binds all future patentees who find themselves in similar situations. Will Judge Newman's dire warnings about the future of our pharmaceutical industry come to pass?

"I opened my eyes—and all the sea was *ice-nine*. The moist green earth was a blue-white pearl."[41] I could not help but wonder. *Ice-nine*, blue corn, paroxetine. The playthings of genius in imperfect hands. Are they true things, or shameless lies? Do their apparent absurdities lie in the law itself, or do they rest within the hands of those who would misapply it? Vonnegut stretched our minds to consider but a few implications of disappearing polymorphs—the threat to nature should a new polymorph run amok. The '723 Patent stretched our minds to consider another—the legal implications of a polymorph that appears in trace amounts. Gajarsa's blue corn dares us to contemplate a middle ground—the legal aspects of an invention that changes nature, not in a fundamental way but in a manner significant enough to spread the inventor's imprimatur far and wide. The information age may throw all of these challenges in our paths. Patent specialists will dwell on the last two, but their resolution will reverberate far beyond the patent bar. When we decide whether we will give such inventors the windfall control that GSK sought, or take from them what GSK lost, we will also decide which sorts of research we wish to motivate and which we prefer to deter. Our decision will truly shape the economy of the information age. How does the policy we want relate to the policy we have? Some black boxes are more opaque than others.

BYE BYE BLACKBERRY

Life at the cutting edge of anything can be exhilarating, but the air can get a bit rarefied. No matter how compelling it may be to blur the lines between patent law and science fiction, disappearing polymorphs seem unlikely to assume center stage—even in the information age. The real action (in the patent world, at least) is likely to lie where it always has: in the run-of-the-mill vanilla patent suit, the kind that plaintiffs file every day, the kind that involve little more than claim construction, validity, and infringement, the kind that judges and juries know how to resolve (more or less), and the kind that occupies the bulk of the Federal Circuit's docket. The overwhelming majority of these cases generate little comment, even among members of the patent bar. Every now and then, though, one leaps beyond all familiar boundaries and lands smack on the front pages—where readers who spend little time thinking about patents suddenly get a glimpse of the patent system in action. What they see rarely pleases them.

One such matter engaged public interest throughout most of 2005. *Fortune* magazine spoke for large parts of the American public when it pondered:

> What would Osama bin Laden give to be able to knock out every BlackBerry in America and achieve an instant, sweeping disruption of commerce? The good news is he can't do it. The weird and disconcerting news is that a company called NTP can and, unless it's paid off, probably will sometime before Christmas. NTP has this remarkable power because it is nearing victory in its

four-year-old patent litigation with Research in Motion (RIM), the maker of the BlackBerry. RIM faces the real likelihood of a court-ordered BlackBerry blackout (government devices would be exempted) unless it agrees to pay essentially whatever sum NTP names, which some analysts think will approach ten figures.[42]

Fortune was wrong on at least one minor point—RIM made it through Christmas without paying NTP a red cent—which led *Forbes* to caution: "Sorry, BlackBerry addicts. Despite what you may have heard, the strange and sickening saga of *NTP v. Research In Motion* isn't over just yet."[43]

Were these popular magazines issuing sound warnings to their readers in the business world, or were they just crying wolf? Was NTP really poised to impose "an instant, sweeping disruption of commerce?" Was the matter of *NTP v. RIM* really a "strange and sickening saga" capable of generating "weird and disconcerting news"? Or was this matter little more than a run-of-the-mill patent suit to which the popular press and its readers happened to pay attention?

The answers require a bit of background and a disclaimer. First, the disclaimer. This case wasn't entirely vanilla. RIM is a Canadian company operating an integrated North American network for its subscribers. Patents, and other forms of intellectual property, are strictly territorial. Because U.S. patent rights end at the nation's borders, activities in Canada cannot infringe U.S. patent rights. RIM's product is a sophisticated communications network with some components in American subscribers' hands and some centralized components on Canadian soil. RIM claimed that even if the courts concluded that NTP deserved to win on the vanilla issues of claim construction, validity, and *substantive* infringement, the Canadian components of its operation should ensure that it could not be liable for *territorial* infringement. At one point in the game, the Canadian government even took the unusual step of intervening on RIM's behalf. All, however, to no avail. Though RIM's appeals to territoriality did raise some interesting issues in international patent law and did exempt it from liability on a few of NTP's infringement claims, they did not suffice to change the basic complexion of this case: NTP claimed that RIM's Black-Berry infringed its valid U.S. patents; RIM disagreed about the patents' meaning, their validity, and their relationship to the BlackBerry.

Now for the background. Everyone knows RIM and its ubiquitous BlackBerry, the handheld device that millions of people use to check their e-mail while away from their desks. But who—or what—is NTP, a heretofore unknown entity that respectable members of the business press casually liken to a butcher whose mass-murdering admirers seek to destroy Western civilization? Most sources, striving for a bit more objectivity, describe NTP as simply a company that an inventor, Thomas Campana, and a patent lawyer, Donald Stout, founded in 1992 to protect Campana's patents. Who, in turn, was Campana? According to a downright gushing obituary on the *America Daily* website:

> Born in the working class neighbourhood of Marquette Park, Chicago and the son of a milkman, young Thomas grew up indifferent to money. His drive and ambition sent him to university where he earned an engineering degree from the University of Illinois. Tinkering in his basement in below freezing weather became his namesake, and neighbours would often drop by during his long hours innovating to help and work with Thomas.
>
> Today, the late Thomas Campana Jr. is known for inventing the "push email" service found in wireless devices such as the BlackBerry (by Research in Motion). . . . But this was not his first foray into the technology world. . . . In 1971, he founded ESA, an early technology company dedicated to building and supplying paging equipment. . . . Thomas is considered an "American Success Story" and re-affirms our belief in the American Dream. From humble roots to great success is often considered a hallmark of the American Dream and Thomas epitomizes this in his dedication to technology.
>
> Thomas Campana Jr. died at the age of 57 (in June 2004) from esophageal cancer linked to his chain smoking addiction. . . . He will be remembered fondly by family and business associates and carries with him the legacy of a great forward thinker and entrepreneur. The stuff legends are made of.[44]

Hardly the profile of a bin Laden wannabe. It seems that there might have been more to this dispute than the folks at *Fortune* and *Forbes* let on.

The dispute itself, like all patent cases, began with inventions and patents—in this case, a series of patents that the PTO granted to Campana and his colleagues between 1991 and 1999. Each of these patents contained numerous claims, and together they carved out a broad swath of terrain surrounding the integration of e-mail systems and wireless communication networks. Campana assigned all of these patents to NTP. Like many small inventors, Campana lacked the ability to commercialize his innovations on his own, and for whatever reason, he either chose not to or was unable to find the investors or corporate partners necessary to do so. Instead, he accepted the simplest bargain that the patent system offers to inventors: he "sold" his innovations to the public by explaining them in the patents' written description and "bought" exclusive rights to the claimed innovations.

Campana was hardly the only one thinking about the synergies between the Internet and wireless telephony. By the late 1990s, several commercial attempts to marry the two had launched and failed. In 1999, RIM launched the BlackBerry. The world had its first commercially successful e-mail relay system that tied the mail servers people used in their offices and on the Internet to a wireless network. People joined the BlackBerry network in droves. RIM's profits grew by orders of magnitude. NTP began to wonder whether its patents entitled it to part of RIM's profit stream.

On November 13, 2001, NTP sued RIM for infringing more than forty claims drawn from five of its patents.[45] NTP filed its suit in the Eastern District of Virginia, a trial court known both for its aptitude at handling patent cases (it is, after all, the district housing the PTO) and for its speedy trials (earning it the nickname "the rocket docket"). RIM countered with a number of arguments about claim construction, validity, infringement, and, as noted, territoriality.

The case fell to Chief Judge James Spencer, who demonstrated that his court deserved its reputation for speed. On August 14, 2002—nine months after NTP filed its suit and, though sufficient for an entire human to gestate, a mere blink of the eye in the normally glacial pace of patent litigation—Spencer issued his first critical rulings on various matters of law. His *Markman* ruling construed thirty-one disputed claim terms, mostly in NTP's favor. He accepted a few of RIM's arguments, but not many. In fact, he granted NTP summary judgment that RIM had infringed four of its claims, explaining that no reasonable trier of fact could fail to see that RIM's BlackBerries infringed the claims (the standard required for summary judgment). He did, however, recognize that the relationship between some of the claims and the BlackBerries was less clear, even after he had resolved the linguistic disputes over claim construction. He also understood that reasonable people could differ in their determinations about just how much money RIM owed to NTP. Because those determinations were all disputed questions of fact, he held a full-blown jury trial and let the jury decide them.

Roughly three months later, on November 21, 2002, the jury decided. It found for NTP on all claims. It also decided that the "reasonable royalty" rate at which RIM should have been able to license NTP's patents was 5.7 percent, and that RIM therefore owed NTP $23 million. But that was hardly the end of the bad news for RIM and its increasingly addicted customer base. On August 5, 2003, Spencer cleaned up all of the parties' posttrial motions and entered his final judgment in favor of NTP. By the time the dust settled, RIM owed NTP just under $54 million. Spencer also issued an injunction: from that day forward, RIM could not continue its infringing behavior unless and until it negotiated a license from NTP. In other words, Spencer threatened to shut down the nation's BlackBerries. He did, however, give America's BlackBerry users a brief reprieve: he stayed his injunction pending appeal.

To this point, if anyone beyond the patent world was paying attention, it didn't show. Consumers continued to buy BlackBerries without demanding a discount—seemingly oblivious to the possibility that if the injunction went into effect, they might be left holding a chunk of worthless plastic molded around some inoperative electronic components. Wall Street treated RIM stock pretty much the same way that it treated other tech stocks; its performance throughout 2002 showed a bit more volatility than the NASDAQ indices, but conformed to the same basic pattern. None of the court's critical ruling dates seemed to stand out as disconti-nuities in investor thinking about RIM's prospects. But RIM reportedly stepped up its efforts to find ways to "work around" NTP's patents so that it could keep its network going without infringing them—a standard part of the patent game, and one that seemed to mollify any consumers or investors who might otherwise have been concerned.

RIM also did more on the legal front than just appeal the judgment. RIM petitioned the PTO to reexamine all of NTP's relevant patents—a proce-dure that the PTO had already begun at its own discretion. RIM hoped that NTP would fare no better in these reexaminations than Yamamoto had during his patent dispute with Dictaphone roughly twenty years earlier, but NTP was hardly despondent. Many reexaminations lead to reissued patents, sometimes in precisely the same form as the originals, sometimes in slightly revised forms, but frequently in ways that strengthen their va-lidity claims and do little to let infringers off the hook. Besides, reexami-nations are time consuming, and NTP already had a jury verdict in its pocket concluding that RIM had infringed many of the claims in many of its patents. All NTP had to do was to hang onto *some* of these infringed claims, and its position would remain pretty much unaltered: it could shut RIM down or insist upon significant royalty payments.

STAY—JUST A LITTLE BIT LONGER

The reexamination notwithstanding, RIM's appeal put the matter on the Federal Circuit's docket. The assignment wheel landed on Judges Michel, Schall, and Linn. On December 14, 2004, Judge Linn issued a unanimous opinion: Judge Spencer had construed thirty of the thirty-one disputed claim terms correctly and had been right about everything else. Though that conclusion meant that NTP had retained enough of its victories to cause serious trouble for RIM and its customers, it also meant that Spencer had a bit more work to do. He had to determine whether the term that he had misconstrued had been prejudicial enough to affect the dam-age assessment; if it had, he would have to reduce the jury's award.

Having dealt RIM this body blow, however, Judge Linn summarized his ruling in the kind of language with which lawyers—and only lawyers—are familiar: "we affirm-in-part, vacate-in-part, and remand for further proceedings."[46] Wall Street was confused. RIM's stock, which had opened the day at $90.18, shot up to $103.56 minutes after the court made its ruling public. Traders were tripping over themselves to celebrate RIM's great victory by investing in its unblemished future. Then they turned the page. RIM's stock drifted lower—precipitously. The exchanges halted trading in RIM shares for several hours. By the time the day was out, RIM closed at $82.18. The import of this ruling continued to sink in. By late January, RIM had dipped as low as $64.01—losing more than a quarter of its value in a period when NASDAQ dropped by less than 8 percent. The trickle of articles became a stream. Reports of concerned members of Congress began to surface. Were we really going to let a patent dispute destroy our precious national communications infrastructure? Would we once again have to cope with only primitive twentieth-century technologies? Could we let the patent system—designed, after all to promote progress, rather than to retard it—bring our efficient twenty-first-century businesses and government agencies to a screeching halt? Could we be on the cusp of our first true communications crisis of the information age?

These were the questions that engaged the public. No one much cared about the nuances of patent law. No one much cared about what the patents said, what the words meant, or what we the public had chosen to give Thomas Campana in exchange for his willingness to teach us his innovative techniques. No, what people cared about was the idea that some ruling from the federal courts might interfere with their precious BlackBerries—yet another instance of a power-hungry judiciary oblivious to the needs of America's real-world citizens. All eyes turned back to Judge Spencer—whom folks hoped would demonstrate the good sense to dissolve his injunction—and toward the PTO, where America joined RIM in urging a speedy reexamination leading to the cancellation of all of NTP's patents.

The PTO seemed to be obliging, though on its own timetable and at its own pace. One after another, the PTO's reexaminations led to preliminary rejections of NTP's claims. The courts, which started earlier and seemed to be moving faster, maintained a significant lead. Those accustomed to patent litigation could see the writing on the wall. Reexaminations take time. Preliminary rejections are just that: preliminary. Patentees whose claims fall to preliminary rejections can negotiate with the examiner. When negotiations fail, the rejections become "final" only with respect to the examiner. Patentees can appeal such rejections to the PTO's internal Board of Patent Appeals, and then to the Federal Circuit and then (at least in principle) to the Supreme Court. Patent cancellations only truly become "final" at the end of this potentially lengthy appeals process.

The prospects for all of NTP's claims falling before the injunction took effect were slim. And once the injunction took effect, the nation's Black-

Berry addicts would have to go cold turkey—even if the PTO subsequently concluded that they should not have had to do so. The only hope was that Spencer would stay the injunction pending the resolution of the reexamination—something he had said repeatedly that he would not do. Nevertheless, RIM seemed determined to try to run out the clock.

RIM did catch a few breaks. Like most losing parties, RIM asked the Federal Circuit to reconsider the panel decision, preferably by taking the matter *en banc*. The court agreed to have the panel reconsider it—but only with respect to the territoriality question. That kept the suit in play for a few more months and gave the PTO a bit more time to reexamine the patents and RIM a bit more time to rally a sympathetic press to its cause. Though RIM's stock did recover, it never quite made it back to where it had been immediately prior to the Federal Circuit ruling. When Judge Linn reissued his opinion on August 2, 2005, it contained an expanded discussion of the international issues, but changed little of relevance to the bottom line.

Wall Street barely took notice of the new opinion; it seemed to have already priced RIM's loss into its estimate of the company's value. RIM tried its hand again, and again asked the court to reconsider. At that point, virtually any observer of the Federal Circuit (or of any federal court, for that matter) would have recognized this request as a mere dilatory tactic; there was no chance that the Federal Circuit would reconsider the matter yet again in any way that would absolve RIM of its liability. Apparently though, no one on Wall Street conferred with a Federal Circuit observer, because when the court rejected RIM's motion on October 7, 2005, RIM's stock fell by more than 10 percent and the exchanges again halted trading in both the United States and Canada. That's when *Forbes* and *Fortune* started writing about this "strange and sickening saga" generating "weird and disconcerting news." The Christmas deadline that *Fortune* had foreseen came and went. Posturing and media coverage continued into the new year. RIM announced a software work-around that would allow it to continue providing uninterrupted service even if the injunction held, but took no steps to launch its new noninfringing version. Finally, on March 6, 2006, RIM and NTP agreed upon a $612.5 million licensing deal, nearly $400 million less than the ten-figure settlement of which *Fortune* had warned. Wall Street rewarded RIM with an immediate stock bump of almost 15 percent.

The strange and sickening saga had ended without the apocalyptic meltdown of the national communications system. RIM paid NTP some money; Campana's widow, Stout, and a number of their colleagues and attorneys became quite wealthy; RIM may have considered higher price points for its BlackBerries in light of its increased costs; and life went on without a blip for millions of BlackBerry users. Some people found new causes: *America Daily* found a great American hero in Thomas Campana; and James Balsillie, RIM's chairman and co-CEO became a champion of patent reform:

> "RIM's case is a prime example of why patent reform is critical," Mr. Balsillie told the House of Representatives subcommittee on the courts, the Internet and IP. . . . Quoting from a *Newsweek* article, Mr. Balsillie compared RIM's treatment by the court with "a judge in a murder case pondering execution while ignoring DNA evidence that exonerates the accused." . . . He said RIM was virtually held up for ransom by NTP, while its business suffered and it faced a possible shutdown of the popular BlackBerry e-mail system across the United States.[47]

The truly weird and disconcerting news continues to unfold. Wall Street's overreaction to the Federal Circuit's denial of RIM's second petition for reconsideration—a completely predictable nonevent if ever there was one—hints where it lies. *Fortune*'s disturbing implication that a band of inventors and lawyers attempting to enforce their patent rights are unwitting dupes of al Qaeda provides a second hint. The numerous commentators urging congressional intervention to save their precious handheld communicators—and the announced exemption of government BlackBerry users from the effects of an injunction—provides a third.[48] As any observer of the Federal Circuit could tell you, the only really interesting issues in this case were those related to territoriality and international law. The technology at issue was hardly *ice-nine*, the claim construction flowed smoothly from rules that the trial judge understood and applied correctly, the jury reached reasonable though hardly unassailable conclusions about all matters relevant to validity and infringement, and the damage calculations emerged plausibly from standard economic models of reasonable royalties. *NTP v. RIM* was a run-of-the-mill patent case with particularly high stakes. The truly weird and disconcerting news is that the myriad observers who ventured into the world of patent litigation to watch this case arrived with no context and will likely leave believing that it represented something unusual.

Regular observers of patent litigation know better. As George Wheeler, a Chicago-based IP lawyer, wrote for the *National Law Journal*:

> A variety of factors suggest that NTP's patents are much stronger than many people believed. First, RIM had steadfastly maintained for years that NTP's patents were invalid, and had repeatedly requested that the U.S. Patent and Trademark Office (PTO) re-examine their validity. Despite all of those efforts, NTP's patents have held strong. . . . Second, NTP's patents were shown to be much stronger than many observers believed because RIM was reluctant to implement its announced work-around option. . . . RIM's choice to settle in-

stead of distributing its work-around software suggests that its new software either was inferior to its current technology or was still likely to infringe upon NTP's patents. Thus, one should be skeptical about RIM's assertion that NTP is a mere "patent troll," asserting supposedly dubious patents to extract a nuisance settlement. NTP used the patent system as it was intended to be used-to reward the first inventor of a worthwhile development and also encourage more development by that inventor and others.[49]

All of which leaves us with a particularly perplexing question: What does this dispute teach us about the big black box of the patent system? Does it get high grades for rewarding the tinkering genius of Thomas Campana or low grades for extorting money from commercially important RIM and its many dedicated customers? And regardless of whether the score is high or low, does it contain any lessons that teach us ways that we might be able to do better? Now that we've seen patent law in action—from the courtrooms to the front pages—do we leave better informed about the relationship between the policies we want and the policies we have?

6

✛

Innovation Regulation

BEWARE THE TROLLS

"What was will be, and what was done will be done, and there's nothing new under the sun."[1] Perhaps the weirdest, most disconcerting thing about the BlackBerry's brush with oblivion is the sense of déjà vu that the tale conveyed. Long-time observers of the patent world might recall an epic battle between Polaroid and Kodak that started in 1976, drove Kodak out of the instant photography business in 1986, and cost Kodak's customers and shareholders almost a billion dollars—nearly half in interest that accrued while the case was working its way through the courts.[2] Expensive litigation, questionable patents, overlapping procedures, prohibitive legal fees, threatened injunctions, and cries of extortion have long been parts of the game. The public stakes are usually low enough to interest few outside the courtroom, but the size of the stakes can't change the nature of the game. And patent litigation is a game without cheap tables. As the National Academy of Sciences reports:

> From the point of view of the inventor or firm applying for a patent, it is estimated that the average corporate U.S. patent prosecution now costs the applicant $10,000–$30,000 in fees. Legal counsel represents the vast majority of that amount, as fees paid to the USPTO are low and have been fairly stable since 1990. The costs at least to large entities of most elements of U.S. patent prosecution have been increasing at an annual rate of 10–17 percent, according to a survey of corporate and private practitioners conducted biannually by the American IP Law Association (AIPLA). These figures should be interpreted cautiously, as they represent only two sets of observations over a few

years and derive from a nonrandom survey of attorneys. Corporate managers and attorneys agree that the costs of conflicts over patents have also increased rapidly. The median cost to each party of proceeding through a patent infringement suit to a verdict at trial is at least $500,000 where the stakes are relatively modest. Where more than $25 million is at risk in a patent suit, the median litigation cost is $4 million for each party, according to the AIPLA survey results.[3]

Good companies pay extortionate settlements to avoid the costs, risks, and distractions of litigation. Worthy inventors get ruined trying to enforce the rights that the government granted them in exchange for their valuable contributions to our collective knowledge. Neither occurrence is even remotely rare.

Some people beyond the normal IP-watchers are starting to notice. What they're finding is troubling, but it's nowhere near as one-sided as the BlackBerry's maker contends. After all, RIM was hardly the first company to feel abused by a "competitor holding patents" but not manufacturing products. Peter Detkin, Intel's then litigation chief, coined the term "patent troll" as far back as 2001 to describe these new villains of the business world. Yet it was during 2006 that they truly leaped into the public imagination. In addition to the end of the BlackBerry battle, 2006 was also the year of the (first?) congressional troll hearings and the year that the Supreme Court resolved a dispute pitting technologist eBay against troll MercExchange. During the run-up to oral argument in that case, the *Wall Street Journal* took the opportunity to caution its readers that the trolls might be getting a bad rap.

> For one thing, most U.S. research universities fit Mr. Detkin's definition. . . .
> A look at friend-of-the-court briefs filed in the eBay case shows that troll-bashers, while riding high on the current fears of BlackBerry addicts, remain a minority in the world of business. Filing briefs supporting eBay are Yahoo, Microsoft, Intel, Oracle and—no surprise here—BlackBerry maker Research in Motion. Weighing in on the "troll" side are all the brand-name pharmaceutical companies, the entire biotechnology industry, as well as General Electric, 3M, Procter & Gamble and DuPont. At a time when the U.S. advantage in global trade is its IP, weakening patent protection, these companies all argue, would be a big mistake.[4]

Excellent framing notwithstanding, the *Journal* still oversimplified the matter by insisting that the problem "isn't companies that don't commercialize their own patents. Rather, it is bad patents. . . . A good first step would be to beef up the patent agency. This is one form of regulation that, if practiced properly, is clearly good for the economy, not bad for it."[5] For good measure, the *Journal* also recommended allowing opponents of new patents to weigh in earlier.

As uncharacteristic as it may be for the *Wall Street Journal* to advocate either increased regulatory budgets or expanded regulatory authority, neither of its suggestions is particularly novel. In fact, they were two of the Federal Trade Commission's ten recommendations in its 2003 report on the relationship between competition policy and intellectual property.[6] A quick review of the entire FTC list explains why the *Journal*'s "bad patents" formulation is an oversimplification. Two recommendations involved expanding the role of economic analyses, market effects, and context sensitivity in patent litigation. Two recommendations would make it easier for the Patent and Trademark Office to deny patents and for accused infringers to subsequently win validity cases—one by tightening the meaning of "obvious" and the other by reducing the standard of proof necessary to invalidate a patent. Another two recommendations also served the interests of accused infringers by preserving some notion of "prior user" rights and by making it harder for a patentee to prove that an infringer's behavior was willful (and thus subject to enhanced damages). One recommendation was to speed up the publication of patent applications. The final multipronged recommendation was to modify certain PTO rules and to help the PTO implement its own strategic plan.[7]

The FTC's laundry list leads to some interesting observations. Most if not all of its recommendations would make life harder for patent applicants and patentees and easier for accused and adjudicated infringers. This unidirectionality led to the widespread perception that the FTC report was "anti-patent," or at the very least that it believed that our patent system has become too strong. This perception, along with some of the report's actual language, fed the forces critical of the Federal Circuit and, to a lesser extent, of the PTO. But another quick perusal of the FTC's recommendations yields a surprising result: Five of the ten begin with the phrase "Enact legislation to . . . ," and one of the remaining five recommends increasing the PTO's budget. Six of the FTC's ten primary instructions for fixing the patent system thus fall to Congress. Yet, few of the patent system's vocal critics allocate more than a small fraction of their venom to Congress; most of it seems directed toward the "pro-patent" Federal Circuit, with the remainder reserved for the "bad patent" PTO.

Congressional responsibility, of course, can hardly counter the claims that the Federal Circuit is pro-patent or that the PTO issues bad patents. It is hardly a secret that Congress founded the Federal Circuit to strengthen the patent system, making a pro-patent bias almost a prerequisite for doing its job. And by all accounts, the PTO is underfunded, understaffed, and particularly unprepared for the flood of software and business method applications that began to arrive about a decade ago; applications to join the Patent Bar favor traditional scientific or engineering training over training in computer science, mathematics, statistics, economics, business, or finance.[8] What the recognition of congressional responsibility can do, however, is emphasize the extent to which "pro-patent" and "bad patent" are mere epithets masking some deep and complex issues. Here are some of the other questions that we ought to be asking:

Is the tension over patent trolls pitting companies in the software and electronics sectors against companies in the pharmaceutical and basic industries a coincidence? Or does it derive from the very different roles that patents play in their industries? If so, is it really appropriate to try to motivate innovation in both sets of industries under a common set of rules? Doesn't such a "unitary" patent system guarantee overprotection in some areas and underprotection in others?

Should the stakes matter? When the courts—or the PTO, for that matter—look at patents embroiled in litigation, should they ever consider the effects of their rulings? Or should they insist that a patent is a patent, that it says what it says and claims what it claims, and that patentees can do whatever the law permits them to do without regard for its effects?

Should patentees really possess the exclusionary rights necessary to threaten to shut down a competitor? Should these rights give way to a "compulsory license," whereby anyone willing to pay "reasonable and non-discriminatory" (RAND) royalties could use the patented invention? If so, who would set the royalty rates and enforce collection? Would compulsory licenses suffice to promote progress, or would potential innovators choose not to innovate without the guarantee of exclusivity? Would innovators in different industries answer these questions differently?

Is procedure driving substance? Are there specific procedural rules that increase expense, decrease certainty, prolong litigation, or promote extortion? If so, who put these rules in place, and who has the power to change them? Would increased funding and better training make matters better? Should such training focus on PTO examiners, trial judges, or both?

What role has the Federal Circuit played in shaping the patent system? How much credit does it deserve for the system's strengths? How much blame does it deserve for the system's weaknesses? Does it have the authority to correct systemic flaws? If not, who does?

These are the questions that will inform our remaining black-box tests of both the overall patent system and the Federal Circuit's contributions to that system.

EVERYONE'S A CRITIC

Critics of the patent system tend to be particularly harsh on the Federal Circuit. They often look at Federal Circuit rulings that appear to run counter to public policy and blame the court for ruling as it did. Of course, "the public interest" is often in the minds of the beholder. Critics from industry understandably focus on the effects that these rulings have on their own business models and bottom lines. The scholarly critics that our universities employ, though subject to their own biases, agendas, and pet theories, nevertheless arrive with broader perspectives. Professors Adam Jaffe and Josh Lerner studied the patent system from the perspective of economics. That vantage point provided them with certain benefits that a court lacks, because the economic view of patents is *precisely* the policy perspective—it stems from the cost-benefit analysis that drove the mythical legislatures of Zip, Wip, and Sip.[9]

Jaffe and Lerner commend the Federal Circuit for its role in helping to strengthen the system when it was mired in the underproductive suboptimality of the 1970s, but believe that the pendulum has swung too far in the opposite direction; in their view, the system is now dangerously overprotective—and just as suboptimal as it used to be. They articulate four specific areas in which they believe that the primary fault for today's suboptimal, overprotective patent system lies with the Federal Circuit:

> The [Federal Circuit] has enhanced the ability of patent-holders to gain substantial damages. . . . [and] injunctive relief. . . . The court [has] enabled patentees to shut down a rival's business (through a preliminary injunction) even before a patent was proven valid. . . .
> The past several decades have seen an expansion of the number of areas where patent protection extends. . . . [The Federal Circuit] has played an important role in expanding the scope of what can be protected. . . .
> One of the critical tests as to whether an invention is patentable relates to whether it is "obvious." . . . Numerous observers . . . have noted that the [Federal Circuit] has shown a willingness to see patents as non-obvious, even when there appears to be abundant prior art. . . .
> A fourth dramatic change that has occurred on the [Federal Circuit]'s watch is an increasing reliance on juries in patent trials. . . . It might be thought that the increased reliance on juries is not disturbing. . . . But there does seem to be a discernable pattern: juries are much more sympathetic to patent-holders than judges.[10]

Jaffe and Lerner presented ample empirical support for their claims about these four significant changes. They showed that, since 1980, penalties for infringement have stiffened, the scope of patentable invention has grown, the threshold for obviousness has dropped, and the prevalence of juries for the factual components of patent disputes has grown. None of these points are matters of serious dispute. But even assuming that their net effect is negative—a point that *is* disputed—the question remains: Is the Federal Circuit to blame? The Federal Circuit's job is to implement the policy we have. If Congress made poor policy calls and the Federal Circuit implemented them correctly, is it fair to blame the court for the failure of policy?

Their first major criticism involves penalties. The Federal Circuit has tried to promulgate a consistent set of rules about the penalties for infringement—and as Jaffe and Lerner noted, most of these rules lead to fairly stiff penalties. Prior to 1982, different courts punished infringers differently. Some ordered infringers to pay damages plus interest; others awarded damages in nominal dollars, without interest. Some insisted that the appropriate measure of damages was the "reasonable royalty" that the patentee would have received had the parties negotiated a fair license; others awarded patentees the full and often larger amount of profits that they may have lost because of the infringing activity. Most importantly, some but not most pre-1982 Federal Circuit courts enjoined future infringement, and a subset of those courts also granted preliminary injunctions.[11] The Federal Circuit established injunctions, both final and preliminary, as the preferred way to avoid ongoing infringement.

Is this criticism of the court warranted? It's hard to see top business economists like Jaffe and Lerner arguing either with the goal of promoting consistency and predictability in litigation or with the insistence that losing defendants pay their debts in real dollars (i.e., including interest) rather than in nominal dollars. In that respect, the Federal Circuit unquestionably moved in the correct direction as a matter of economics—and thus of policy. The debate pitting reasonable royalty calculations against lost profits is a matter of taste. Lost profits are the standard measure of damages in most commercial litigation, and numerous commentators have shown that they are consistent with sound economic policies—though only if they are calculated reasonably, and lost-profit calculations in patent cases are often much more complex and controversial than are similar calculations in disputes involving a breach of contract or a business tort. Poor economic modeling can destroy any element of fairness, consistency, or predictability that lost-profit analyses are supposed to convey.

Jaffe and Lerner's preference for reasonable royalties and their distaste for injunctive relief stem from their understanding of patent *policy*. One of the critical unanswered questions about patents remains whether they are true property rights, regulatory grants, or some combination of the two. Those who focus on intellectual property policy often conclude that patents are regulatory grants. If the system's only goal is to motivate innovation, a steady stream of license fees should suffice. Negotiated royalties, court-ordered reasonable royalties for past infringement, and prospective royalties rather than injunctive relief for future infringement should all serve the policy's goal. Those who focus on IP *law* often conclude that patents are a form of property. Congress has granted patentees the right to exclude others from making, using, or selling their patented innovations—and the right to exclude is the quintessential property right. Judicial opinions have long compared a patent's enumerated claims to the "metes and bounds" of a real estate deed and infringement to trespassing.

Shortly before the Federal Circuit's third birthday, Judge Giles Rich— the primary architect of the 1952 Patent Act and probably the twentieth century's most influential voice on patents—made it clear what policy he believed Congress adopted:

> In [an infringement] case, we hold that a preliminary injunction preserves the status quo if it prevents future trespasses but does not undertake to assess the pecuniary or other consequences of past trespasses. . . . [The] arguments that infringement and related damages are fully compensable in money downplay the nature of the statutory right to exclude others from making, using, or selling the patented invention throughout the United States. . . . If monetary relief were the sole relief afforded by the patent statute then injunctions would be unnecessary and infringers could become compulsory licensees for as long as the litigation lasts.[12]

Rich's language suggests that, at the very least, the patent policy we have incorporates many elements common to property law and uncommon to regulatory law.

Where does that leave us? Jaffe and Lerner made a compelling argument that the widespread use of injunctions is inconsistent with the policy we want. Judge Rich made a compelling argument that Congress structured the Patent Act in a manner more consistent with a property regime than with a standard regulatory regime, and thus that injunctions are an important part of the policy we have. Taken together, the black box housing the overall patent system seems to fail this test: the policy we have is not the policy we want. The Federal Circuit, whose job is to craft rules that implement the policy that Congress chose rather than to align law with policy, seems to have performed well; the penalties in place for patent infringement are both internally consistent and broadly consistent with those that we apply to invasions of property.

Nevertheless, the Federal Circuit still deserves to get dinged in the grading for failing to use one of its most powerful tools: the bully pulpit. When the court encountered controversial injunction cases, it should have used dicta to highlight the problem. Instead, it went the other way. In 2005, after Jaffe and Lerner's data were already matters of public discussion, Judge Bryson reiterated Rich's preference for injunctions on behalf of a unanimous panel:

> Because the right to exclude recognized in a patent is but the essence of the concept of property, the general rule is that a permanent injunction will issue once infringement and validity have been adjudged. To be sure, courts have

in rare instances exercised their discretion to deny injunctive relief in order to protect the public interest. Thus, we have stated that a court may decline to enter an injunction when a patentee's failure to practice the patented invention frustrates an important public need for the invention, such as the need to use an invention to protect public health.[13]

The Supreme Court intervened and—in a unanimous opinion—reversed the Federal Circuit.[14] The new rule gives trial judges discretion to grant or deny preliminary injunctions as dictated by the broad concerns of equity. It's far too soon to tell whether or not this new rule will have much practical effect. Many trial judges may adhere to the patent-as-property view and thus grant injunctions in all but extraordinary circumstances. Then again, its effect could be profound if many trial judges adopt the patent-as-regulation view and deny numerous motions for injunctive relief. Only time will tell how significant this change is and how far it will go toward addressing the policy failure that Jaffe and Lerner identified.

In terms of black-box scores, the Federal Circuit loses points for trying to push the law in a direction counter to the policy we want, but this Supreme Court intervention improved systemic performance. This intervention did not, however, resolve the underlying conflict between the two views of patents, nor did it urge Congress to embrace the patent-as-regulation characterization consistent with the policy we want. By failing to use its own very loud bully pulpit while removing a serious impetus for congressional reconsideration of the issue, the Supreme Court's ruling in the right direction might make matters worse in the long run.

Jaffe and Lerner's second major criticism concerned the expanding scope of patentable subject matter. That expansion, as noted, arose when the Supreme Court's grudging recognition that some class of algorithms might be patentable morphed, over the space of two decades, into a much-criticized Federal Circuit ruling that "business methods" are patentable algorithms. Judge Rich derived the patentability of business methods from the statutory pronouncement: "Whoever invents or discovers any new and useful process, machine, manufacture, or composition of matter, or any new and useful improvement thereof, may obtain a patent therefor, subject to the conditions and requirements of this title."[15] From there, he reasoned:

The Supreme Court has identified three categories of subject matter that are unpatentable, namely "laws of nature, natural phenomena, and abstract ideas." Of particular relevance to this case, the Court has held that mathematical algorithms are not patentable subject matter to the extent that they are merely abstract ideas . . . constituting disembodied concepts or truths that are not "useful." From a practical standpoint, this means that to be patentable an algorithm must be applied in a "useful" way. [We have previously] held that data, transformed by a machine through a series of mathematical calculations to produce a smooth waveform display on a rasterizer monitor, constituted a practical application of an abstract idea (a mathematical algorithm, formula, or calculation), because it produced "a useful, concrete and tangible result"—the smooth waveform. . . . Today, we hold that the transformation of data, representing discrete dollar amounts, by a machine through a series of mathematical calculations into a final share price, constitutes a practical application of a mathematical algorithm, formula, or calculation, because it produces "a useful, concrete and tangible result"—a final share price momentarily fixed for recording and reporting purposes and even accepted and relied upon by regulatory authorities and in subsequent trades.[16]

It's easy to disagree with Rich's conclusion, but it's hard to fault his logic. If, as the Supreme Court taught, Congress really wanted to extend the Patent Act to cover any innovation under the sun, why shouldn't it cover data transformations useful to business? Once again, Congress seems to be the culprit. The systemic black box fails, but the Federal Circuit performed well—though if there were ever a place for a court to chastise Congress about the negative policy implications of statutory language, this was it. While there may be substantive and scientific merit to rewarding business innovators willing to document and to teach the public their new and useful methods, the patent system grants them rights much broader than mere rewards. Business method patentees seeking to gain commercial advantage may enjoin their competitors from employing useful business methods. This outcome may be part of the policy we have, but it's hard to see how it fits into the policy we want.

Jaffe and Lerner's third complaint—about nonobviousness—raises a number of complex issues. It is therefore worthwhile to consider their complaint about juries first. That complaint is easy to address. The Federal Circuit's declaration that claim construction is a legal question—and therefore unfit for jury deliberation—was but a part of the drive to disentangle factual questions from legal questions in an intensely fact-specific area of the law. Once the court declared which components of a patent suit are legal and which are factual, there was no good reason to deny litigants their Seventh Amendment right to a jury trial. Or rather, there was only one good reason to do so—juries are notoriously flaky. That objection, however, is a general one. It has little to do with either patents or the Federal Circuit. Many people believe that jury trials are always a mistake—particularly in complex, fact-intensive civil disputes. There is no particular reason to believe that juries are either more or less reliable in patent cases than they are in other complex areas of the law, such as antitrust or securities. But none of that much matters. Though it may be a policy mistake, the Constitution is clear: American courts have a preference for jury trials. The Constitution tells us the policy we have, and the Federal Circuit's preference for jury trials implements that policy effectively. To the extent that Jaffe and Lerner see a specific criticism of the patent system in the flakiness of juries, they seem to be off base.

Their critique of the Federal Circuit's obviousness jurisprudence, on the other hand, is quite damning. On this matter, Congress issued simple instructions: don't grant patents on "obvious" innovations. That certainly sounds like the policy we want. If the policy we have is implementing this instruction poorly, blame must fall squarely on the Federal Circuit—the court charged with drawing the line between the obvious and the nonobvious. Are Jaffe and Lerner correct? Has the Federal Circuit drawn the line in the wrong place? They're hardly alone in arguing that it has. Professor Glynn Lunney also complained that the Federal Circuit has allowed far too many inventors to keep patents on their obvious inventions—and to compensate, construed those patents so narrowly that they had no commercial value.[17] Such compensation, however, is hardly complete; a valid, narrow patent can still cost litigants a fortune in legal fees.

POLICY LEVERS

Lunney was not the only legal scholar echoing Jaffe and Lerner's critique of the Federal Circuit's obviousness jurisprudence. Professors Dan Burk and Mark Lemley contend that the Federal Circuit's standards for obviousness differ depending on where you look. In a pair of controversial articles, they argue that the Federal Circuit has applied opposing standards to biotechnology patents and software patents—and yet a variety of other standards to other industries:

> Fundamental shifts in technology and in the economic landscape are rapidly making the current system of IP rights unworkable and ineffective. Designed more than 100 years ago to meet the simpler needs of an industrial era, it is an undifferentiated, one-size-fits-all system. . . . With very few exceptions, the statute does not distinguish between different technologies in setting and applying legal standards. . . . In theory, then, we have a unified patent system that provides technology-neutral protection to all kinds of technologies. . . .
>
> [But] patent law is becoming technology-specific. The legal rules applied to biotechnology cases bear less and less resemblance to those applied in software cases. While there may be good policy reasons to treat the two industries differently, the current legal rules . . . do not reflect optimal patent policy in either biotechnology or software.[18]

[T]here is no reason to believe that these differences in the law represent a reasoned response to industry differences. The [Federal Circuit] has generally not acknowledged that it is designing industry-specific patent policy. . . . At least in the industries of biotechnology and software, however, the Federal Circuit has gotten the policy precisely backwards, perhaps because it is not making industry-specific patent policy intentionally.[19]

Burk and Lemley contend that the Federal Circuit treats different patents differently. They see these differences beginning with the question of obviousness and extending to the various "written description" requirements—the rules governing whether or not patentees disclosed their inventions in specific enough detail to teach them to the public. The written description requirements are as central to validity analyses as is obviousness. Much as an invention that the courts rule obvious is shorn of its patent protection, so too a patentee whose written description is insufficiently educational is deemed to have "shortchanged" the public during prosecution; since the public does not truly possess the underlying knowledge, the patentee cannot retain her patent. According to Burk and Lemley, the Federal Circuit has done far worse than simply encouraging inventors to patent meaningless, obvious advances—it has injected inconsistency into the standards for patenting and applied those inconsistent standards in a manner that is consistently incorrect!

It is hard to imagine a more damning criticism. As the old saying goes, even a stopped clock is right twice a day. Almost any consistent standard would produce the right result sometimes. In Burk and Lemley's view, the Federal Circuit has devised a system that is always wrong. Yet their overall verdict is far from negative. The biggest problem that they see lies not in the court's use of industry-specific standards, but rather in its reluctance to admit that it is shaping industry-specific standards. Were the court to proclaim this drive boldly and loudly, the technologists and patent specialists steeped in the various industries could help them, and patent law could develop the context-sensitivity needed to better align the policy we have with the policy we want.

Burk and Lemley contend that the Patent Act is a relatively flexible statute, in which statutory language leaves a great deal of room for judicial "tailoring" to ensure that the laws make sense as applied.

Such tailoring activity necessarily vests a fair degree of discretion in the judiciary in order to adapt the general statute to the particular circumstance. The discussion of patent tailoring thus partakes to some extent in the long-running debate over the comparative merits of rules versus standards. Within this debate, "rules" have been characterized as bright-line and definite decisional criteria. Rules are cheap to administer because they are simple and straightforward, but due to their inflexibility they may lead to costly outcomes if they fit a given situation poorly. Standards, by contrast, are characterized as flexible case-by-case decisional criteria that can take situational variance into account. But standards are typically and intentionally stated indeterminately. As a result, they offer little guidance to expected behavior and so may impose costs associated with this uncertainty. Standards typically imbue courts or decisionmakers with greater discretion than would a rigid decisional rule, and so standards are favored where greater discretion is needed.[20]

They conclude that "the need to allow courts flexibility to accommodate different technologies within the general framework of patent law militates in favor of a standards-based patent statute."[21] But they then go one controversial step further: they contend that we already have a suitably flexible standards-based patent system.

Their argument about what we need is compelling. One of the reasons that the Federal Circuit has drawn so much fire is that it applies a uniform set of rules to industries with different capital needs, commercialization timetables, underlying scientific complexity, and business structures. The chances that these rules would make sense for more than a small fraction of modern industries is slim. The entire concept of a unitary patent system seems destined to fail most black-box tests of interest in the information age. The policies that we have will, at best, be the policies that we want only in selected industries.

What share of the blame for this shortcoming does the Federal Circuit bear? The answer depends in part upon the extent to which Burk and Lemley are correct about the nature of the Patent Act. As they see it, Congress got things right when it enacted a flexible Patent Act that empowered the judiciary to consider the numerous context-sensitive policy implications of its rulings. The Federal Circuit responded poorly, by crafting rigid rules instead of flexible standards, thereby prohibiting judges and juries from tailoring their rulings to fit the specific needs of the specific industries and parties represented in their courtrooms. Burk and Lemley identify a sizable set of "policy levers," or broad statutory prescriptions, that the Federal Circuit could have crafted into flexible guidelines allowing trial judges to cater to the varying needs of different directions for different industries. They argue that the Federal Circuit already has congressional authority to generate a patent system replete with context-sensitive guidelines, but that it has failed to avail itself of this authority. They also argue against trying to persuade Congress to make this potential explicit, because raising the specter of industry-specific guidelines in front of Congress risks falling prey to what economists call "rent seeking," policy analysts call "capture," and laymen call "special-interest lobbying":

Both public choice theory and practical experience warn that each new amendment to the patent statute represents an opportunity for counterproductive special interest lobbying. Technology-specific patent legislation will encourage rent-seeking by those who stand to benefit from favorable legislation. Patent law has some balance today in part because different industries have different interests, making it difficult for one interest group to push through changes to the statute. Industry-specific legislation is much more vulnerable to industry capture.[22]

Stripped to its simplest form, they argue that the drafting and application of a law that applies to a single industry will generate a great deal of interest within that industry—and relatively little elsewhere. As a result, all inputs into the legislative process will come from an industry intent upon bending the legislation to serve its own interests. Broader laws can draw inputs from a much broader spectrum; this phenomenon is evident in the arrays of large corporations taking opposing sides in the patent troll fight, or in the battles over digital music downloads pitting the heavy-weights of Hollywood against the masters of the Silicon Valley. Whereas industries often capture their regulators, the PTO's broader charter has so far kept it relatively safe. Burk and Lemley contend that we are better off with a unitary but flexible patent system than we would be with numerous categories of industry-specific IP rights.[23]

They then contend that the Patent Act is already flexible enough to accommodate such a system. This contention leads them to determine that the biggest problem facing patent law is the Federal Circuit's refusal to use all of the tools that Congress gave it to shape policy:

> The growing complexity of innovation and the patent system itself poses the greatest challenge to patent policy in the history of the Republic. The patent statute has sufficient flexibility to meet the needs of all new and existing technologies, but only if it is applied with sensitivity to the industry-specific nature of innovation.
>
> It makes sense to take economic policy and industry-specific variation into account explicitly in applying general patent rules to specific cases. . . . Patent law gives the courts substantial freedom to do this by means of flexible legal standards we call "policy levers" [which] implicitly or explicitly permit the courts to take account of different types of innovation in different industries.
>
> Unfortunately, while the patent statute leaves ample room for courts to consider the needs of particular industries, the Federal Circuit has proven somewhat reluctant to embrace its role in setting patent policy. Not only has it proven unwilling to pay much attention to the empirical evidence about innovation, but it has also taken a number of steps toward eliminating the flexible standards of the patent common law in favor of bright-line rules.[24]

If they are correct that the Federal Circuit has made poor use of the policy levers that Congress handed it, they are also correct in laying much of the systemic blame on the court's doorstep.

But are they correct? Professor Polk Wagner argues that even the technology-specific differences that Burk and Lemley identified are insufficient to suggest that Congress authorized the Federal Circuit to establish industry-specific laws:

> That distinctions in treatment will exist between various technologies is both expected and unremarkable; rather than leveraging these differences for policy effect, the goal should be to embrace the flexibility while retaining the essential strengths of the unified patent system. Submerged in the Burk and Lemley analysis is an important conceptual distinction between two types of technological-specificity: micro-specificity, which applies the variable legal rules to specific technological circumstances; and macro-specificity, which countenances distinct legal rules across different technologies, and relatively more similar application within related technologies. . . . Micro-exceptionalism is a more accurate description of the current patent law—as well as a normatively justifiable position. . . . But this, I suggest, does not itself make the case that the doctrine is macro-specific. . . . Indeed, a transaction-cost-focused analysis would suggest that it is Burk and Lemley, rather than the Federal Circuit, that have it "exactly backwards."[25]

According to Wagner, the Patent Act is flexible enough to allow a bit of tinkering around the edges, but not nearly flexible enough to generate the sort of industry or technology specificity that Burk and Lemley advocate. Furthermore, Wagner thinks that this lack of flexibility is a good thing; he does not favor what he calls a "macro-flexible" system.

While many observers of the patent system agree with Burk and Lemley, at least as many agree with Wagner. And then there are those of us who fall somewhere in between: I agree with Wagner about the patent system we have, but with Burk and Lemley about the patent system we want. In my view, there is no mechanism in the Patent Act capable of tailoring biotech patents to promote optimal innovation in biotechnology and software patents to promote optimal innovation in software. Court rulings about any patent in a unitary system bind all patents in that system; fine biotech tailoring risks destabilizing software, and vice versa. If we're ever lucky enough to discover that patent law is promoting optimal innovation in two industries, we should consider ourselves just that: lucky. The rigid statutory system we have is not the flexible system we want (at least in my view—Burk, Lemley, and Wagner apparently all disagree with me).

A pending oddity illustrates the extent to which patent-heavy industries all share a single fate. The notion of "distinguishing a case on the facts" that judges Posner and Rader tried to use to help them rule for Apotex in the paroxetine case without confusing subsequent litigants is only the court's second-best trick for achieving this goal. The best trick is known as the "nonprecedential" or "unpublished" opinion. In many areas of the law—including patent litigation—appellate courts can issue rulings that bind only the parties in front of them. Such opinions are not really part of "the law"; they do not bind subsequent trial judges or panels even of the same circuit. The Federal Circuit issues many such unpublished opinions (though technically, they are all published in the unofficial *Federal Appendix*). Most of them resolve a dispute, bind the litigants, and are of no further consequence. In an unusual move, however, the Supreme Court granted certiorari to review a nonprecedential Federal Circuit opinion in 2006.[26]

The dispute in question concerned Teleflex's patent on an adjustable automobile pedal assembly. Teleflex alleged that KSR infringed; KSR countered that the patent was obvious, and therefore invalid. Judge Lawrence Zatkoff agreed with KSR and granted summary judgment in its favor. On appeal, in an unpublished opinion on behalf of a unanimous panel, Judge Alvin Schall reversed Judge Zatkoff, explaining that he had misapplied the test for determining whether or not the combination of several ideas within the prior art rendered a patent invalid for obviousness. "When obviousness is based on the teachings of multiple prior art references, the movant must also establish some 'suggestion, teaching, or motivation' that would have led a person of ordinary skill in the art to combine the relevant prior art teachings in the manner claimed."[27]

Rather than simply heading back to Judge Zatkoff's courtroom for a trial, KSR appealed to a higher authority. The Supreme Court granted certiorari to reconcile the Federal Circuit's "suggestion test" with the Supreme Court's own obviousness jurisprudence. Numerous amici jumped on board, including many from the software industry, where advocates believed that the "suggestion test" would render even trivial software advances patentable and work to the detriment of scientific and technological progress. The message here is clear—and fairly standard. Any tests that the courts apply to determining obviousness in pedal assemblies also apply to software, pharmaceuticals, biotech, and every other industry.

Beyond that basic message, the grant of certiorari in *KSR* appears to have had an interesting ripple effect across numerous aspects of the debate over obviousness. Some observers believe that the Federal Circuit used the window between the grant of certiorari and oral argument to "clean up" its obviousness jurisprudence. An exchange between Justice Antonin Scalia and Teleflex's counsel, Thomas Goldstein, reflected this perception:

MR. GOLDSTEIN: [The Federal Circuit] has had decades to look at [the test for obviousness] to try and elaborate a standard. . . .

JUSTICE SCALIA: And in the last year or so, after we granted cert in this case after these decades of thinking about it, it suddenly decides to polish it up.

MR. GOLDSTEIN: Justice Scalia, if you actually believe that, then you just don't believe the judges in the Federal Circuit because in each of these opinions they say quite explicitly we are not changing it.[28]

Justice Scalia was hardly alone; Professor Lemley evidently shared his belief. Early in the proceedings, Lemley joined an amicus brief asserting that "the Federal Circuit's incorrect interpretation of the obviousness standard, as applied in this case, provides incentives for seeking rights on obvious extensions of existing technologies."[29] By the time that the Supreme Court heard oral argument, however, he had shifted his position and joined an amicus brief taking the opposite view.[30] The blogosphere was aflutter: "What happened? Lemley says that after he filed his June certiorari petition, the U.S. Court of Appeals for the Federal Circuit issued three decisions that made him change his mind. 'If the Federal Circuit had issued those decisions two years ago, I would not have supported KSR's petition for cert,' he says."[31] With that, Lemley availed himself of a prerogative that legal scholars possess but practicing lawyers do not: he flipped his position in light of changing evidence.

This recent step in a direction that Lemley considers positive notwithstanding, there is no reason to believe that he has retreated from the position that he and Burk put forward: The Federal Circuit underuses the policy levers that Congress granted it. Though that point remains hard to dispute, even rigorous use of those levers is unlikely to achieve the structural reforms that the patent system needs. The Patent Act in its current incarnation does not approach the level of flexibility that an information-age economy requires. It incorporates no specific mechanisms for differentiating among industries—as the industry amici in *KSR* implicitly acknowledge. The Patent Act that we have is not the Patent Act that we want, and only Congress can fix it.

Should the Federal Circuit follow Burk and Lemley's advice anyway? After all, why not try to solve the problems with our patent system by influencing the Federal Circuit, the institution most likely to effect positive change? Why risk the sorts of industry capture and economically disastrous rent seeking to which congressional action is prone?

Any good conservative could answer those questions: Because the barriers between institutions matter. They matter a lot. The Constitution gave *Congress* the power to promote progress. Congress responded with a complex statute that awarded the courts little authority over context-sensitive issues. Congress has been rather clear. Patent law is what the Patent Act says it is, and the Patent Act leaves little room for differentiating among patentees. As long as Congress maintains that legal framework, the criticisms hurled at the Federal Circuit about the basic structure of patent law are misplaced. The Federal Circuit has done a reasonable job devising consistent standards for obviousness—as well as other critical issues related to patent validity and infringement. The policy levers at its disposal might allow the court to do better in the future than it has done in the past, but they cannot allow it to do *well*. Congress must empower the PTO and the judiciary to consider context when promoting progress. Anything else risks either incoherence or economic decline—or both.

REFORMATION

Professors Jaffe, Lerner, Lunney, Burk, and Lemley cite significant challenges facing the patent system—challenges suggesting that the patent system we have is not the patent system we want. When it comes to testing the systemic black box, we should grade the Federal Circuit only on its own part. We gave it a poor grade on claim construction because of its own rulings on claim construction—rulings that the Supreme Court may have locked in place, but that Congress did not compel. We gave it a good grade on improving certainty and predictability because there, too, the results flowed from the court's own efforts. On the bigger issues, though, the Federal Circuit is not the key player. The key player is Congress.

As a matter of sound public policy, Congress should extricate itself from a role that it is ill equipped to play. IP law *should be* context sensitive. Congress should pare down the Patent Act and give the courts greater explicit authority to consider the context and the policy consequences underlying many patent disputes; it should replace the current dense Patent Act with a smaller statement of principles (perhaps along the lines of the much shorter antitrust statutes). Congress should authorize at least several variants of IP rights to motivate appropriate innovation in industries with different investment, risk, and return profiles.[32] Some, if not all, of these rights should specify guidelines for compulsory licensing, thereby removing the prospects for further threats like the BlackBerry shutdown. And Congress should revisit the many procedural rules that seem to be having pernicious substantive effects—because whether they started with Congress, the PTO, the Federal Circuit, or the Supreme Court, Congress has the power to fix them. When the dust finally settles over all of these reforms, Congress should leave us with a set of industry-appropriate IP rights, each easier to understand, prosecute, and litigate than existing patents, and a judiciary empowered to consider the context, the effects, and the policy implications of its rulings. In short, we should stop pretending that patents are property and treat them like what they truly are—licenses or regulatory grants that attempt to motivate more innovation than the free market would generate if left only to its own devices.

Is any of this realistic? Is there any hope of Congress pushing through such a radical reform of the IP system? And is it even possible, given the way the United States locked itself—along with the rest of the world—into the TRIPS agreement enshrining advanced industrial-age notions of patents and copyrights for all time? It's hard to say. Radical reform always appears unlikely until it happens. But reform efforts are already under way.

On the Hill, the folks with clear constitutional authority are starting to get interested in patent reform. In June 2005, Representative Lamar Smith (R-TX), with bipartisan backing, proposed what would have been the most sweeping reform to the Patent Act since 1952. In addition to a number of significant procedural improvements,[33] Smith proposed to add teeth to a recent failed reform. For decades, commentators and competitors had complained about the unfairness of letting patent applicants negotiate secretly with the government and emerge with patents that courts must presume are valid. In the late 1990s, Congress introduced a procedure that would let "interested parties" participate in a PTO proceeding contesting the patent. That procedure proved to be too specialized, too narrow, and too cumbersome to use; few parties availed themselves of the opportunity. Smith proposed to streamline and reinvigorate these procedures so that people might actually use them. Of perhaps the greatest significance, though, Smith also proposed to address Jaffe and Lerner's concerns about remedies by reducing the scope of damage calculations and by making it harder for patentees to gain injunctive relief. Dennis Crouch, a Chicago-based patent lawyer and active blogger, memorably described the Smith Act as containing "something to offend almost every interest."[34]

Property rights advocate Jim DeLong, for one, viewed Smith's procedural proposals favorably, but took some offense at the proposed move away from injunctions:

> The techies want the power of eminent domain, the right to take property and then have a court determine just compensation. This would not be as novel as it sounds, and again the 19th century is illustrative. Many network-type industries have been granted eminent domain powers by state legislatures, especially those that were building rights-of-way, where the last parcel problem can be acute. Their first line of defense is often a ringing affirmation of the sanctity of property rights, sometimes in language that would do credit to a 19th century Robber Baron. Comparative equities should have nothing to do with it because patents are property and property is *sacred*. . . .
> The IP owners have some *realpolitik* policy arguments that are better, though.
> . . . The IP owners will win this injunction issue, as they should, given the lack of empirical support for the proposition a real problem exists. . . . But it

raises interesting questions, and it will not go away. The techies may come to the next battle better armed.[35]

DeLong was part right and part wrong. The Smith Act did not become law in 2005, so the legislative status of injunctions remains unchanged. Less than a year after penning his prediction that the IP owners would win the injunction issue, however, DeLong had to watch the Supreme Court dissolve patentee MercExchange's injunction against techie eBay.

The Supreme Court's decision to grant certiorari on the question of injunctions had set the peanut gallery aflutter. Some commentators urged the Court to squelch the use of injunctions in patent cases altogether. Others hoped for a ringing endorsement of the Federal Circuit's insistence upon inunctions in all but the most extraordinary cases. The *Wall Street Journal*'s Holman Jenkins saw history as suggesting "that things go best when patent rights are strong, but not too strong," and encouraged the Court to intervene, if for no reason other than to dampen congressional enthusiasm for undertaking the job that the Constitution gave it.

> From the looks of it, innovation is just fine in America even with the nuisance of patent litigation. We boldly suggest that a certain background hum of litigation is even a healthy sign: It shows progress and competition aren't being hampered by, ahem, undue regard for patent rights. . . . What's the lesson here for "patent reform"? . . . The Supreme Court has an opportunity to right this balance in the eBay case, and should—by rolling back the presumption of an automatic injunction. . . . If the Supreme Court uses this invitation to tweak the system back in a more serviceable direction, Congress could chuck the idea of legislating, always an invitation to make matters worse.[36]

Jenkins's analysis also hinted at the root of the problem: "Patents are a kind of property not merely protected by government but created by public policy."[37] He did not, however, take that anomaly to its logical conclusion to ask the critical underlying question: Is "property created by public policy" entitled to the same strong forms of protection as is other property—or only to the weaker protections that we afford to other regulatory expectations created by public policy?

The Supreme Court didn't answer that question, either. Far from offering clarification, the Court's brief opinion and its two briefer concurrences fanned the flames of confusion. The Court replaced the Federal Circuit's "general preference" for injunctive relief in patent cases with the standard balancing test that district courts use to determine the propriety of injunctive relief in most areas of the law. That moved patent law one step away from property law, where injunctions *are* generally preferred, and toward more standard commercial and regulatory settings, where injunctions are rare. Nevertheless, Justice Clarence Thomas, writing for the Court, noted that the Patent Act

> declares that "patents shall have the attributes of personal property," including "the right to exclude others from making, using, offering for sale, or selling the invention." . . . But the creation of a right is distinct from the provision of remedies for violations of that right. Indeed, the Patent Act itself indicates that patents shall have the attributes of personal property "subject to the provisions of this title."[38]

According to Thomas, just because the Patent Act *says* that patents are property doesn't mean that we have to treat them like property. That "clarification" may help determine how much discretion trial judges retain in deciding when to grant patent injunctions, but it doesn't inform the ultimate inquiry. It's hardly news that patents possess some but not all attributes of property; transferable licenses or permits *also* possess some attributes of property, despite not being property in the strictest sense of the concept. All regulatory grants deserve respect, and all transferable grants are "kind of like" property. The question remains whether they are *merely* "kind of like" property or they are *actually* property.

Chief Justice John Roberts weighed in with a reminder that the very nature of the patent right suggests that patent law shares property law's preference for injunctions because of "the difficulty of protecting a right to *exclude* through monetary remedies that allow an infringer to *use* an invention against the patentee's wishes."[39] Nevertheless, he agreed that a "general rule" favoring patent injunctions went too far—once again evading the central analytic question.

Justice Anthony Kennedy truly muddied the waters. He took this opportunity to rail against patent trolls and business method patents as inconsistent with patent policy, but fell far short of providing useful insights into his view of patent law:

> An industry has developed in which firms use patents not as a basis for producing and selling goods but, instead, primarily for obtaining licensing fees. For these firms, an injunction, and the potentially serious sanctions arising from its violation, can be employed as a bargaining tool to charge exorbitant fees to companies that seek to buy licenses to practice the patent. When the patented invention is but a small component of the product the companies seek to produce and the threat of an injunction is employed simply for undue leverage in negotiations, legal damages may well be sufficient to compensate for the infringement and an injunction may not serve the public interest. In addition injunctive relief may have different consequences for the burgeoning number of patents over business methods, which were not of much economic and legal significance in earlier times.[40]

In this central paragraph of a brief concurring opinion, Justice Kennedy (with justices Stevens, Souter, and Breyer along for the ride) undermined everything we thought we knew about patents. He attacked the unitary system by differentiating between business method patents and other patents. He expressed contempt for an entire class of patentees who choose to use their government grants as the basis for negotiations— ordinarily an entirely appropriate use of property. He criticized price gouging despite congressional silence on the matter. And he explicitly told the lower courts to consider the public interest and the effects of their rulings on the commercial marketplace.

Was Kennedy serious about all of these changes to patent practice? If so, this paragraph suggests that at least four members of the Court are prepared for a radical overhaul of patent law. If we take Kennedy at his word, the judiciary maintains broad discretion over a huge number of issues— not just injunctions. Which patents warrant the property-like treatment of injunctive relief, and which become forms of compulsory licenses? According to Kennedy, the judiciary must decide based upon context and effects. Should the judiciary employ the full set of Burk and Lemley's policy levers to interpret various statutory requirements differently for patents granted to different industries? Following Kennedy's logic, absolutely. After all, if the unitary nature of the patent system collapses in the determination of remedies, there's no obvious reason to retain it elsewhere. Should the courts look at the effects of a patentee's actions on the commercial marketplace when determining whether or not the Patent Act condones her behavior? Kennedy states explicitly that they should. Should the judiciary intrude into negotiations over patent licenses between two private parties to determine whether one of them is behaving unreasonably? Again, Kennedy says that it should. And finally, are factors like the identity and the productivity of a patentee relevant to determining whether his behavior is appropriate under the patent laws? Kennedy certainly seems to think so.

The implications of this brief paragraph are overwhelming. Is Kennedy echoing Burk and Lemley's contention that the apparently detailed, complicated Patent Act is really a flexible bit of law encouraging the judiciary to inject policy concerns into its rulings? He certainly appears to be— though a departure from contemporary thinking about patent law that radical deserves more than a paragraph rife with interesting implications in a brief concurrence.

I remain unconvinced. I continue to believe that a sparse statutory structure in which Congress drafted general rules and charged the judiciary explicitly with considering context and effects would move our patent system closer to the policy we want. I also continue to believe, however, that our present statutory system precludes that interpretation. I simply cannot square the direct implications of Kennedy's concurrence with the Patent Act of 1952, as currently amended. In fact, I even have a hard time squaring Thomas's opinion for the Court with a statutory structure more consistent with the patent-as-property theory than with the patent-as-regulation theory—though I remain pleased to see the Court moving in the right policy direction wherever even a bit of wiggle room remains. In the final analysis, it seems unlikely that the Supreme Court will soon resolve the patent-as-property vs. patent-as-regulation debate.

Congress seemed no more interested in resolving it than was the Court. The proposed-but-not-enacted Smith Act of 2005, like the Supreme Court's ruling for eBay, might have taken a step away from standard property principles, but it never really addressed the question. With this philosophical divide and numerous other issues capable of offending almost every interest lurking in the background, it is no surprise that Smith's proposed Act did not work its way into law. But it did put patent reform on the legislative agenda. If history is any guide, it will stay there for quite a while before leading to a newly reformed Patent Act.

A PATENT ACT FOR THE INFORMATION AGE

What reforms might such a Patent Act incorporate? In keeping with my central thesis that the liberal policy perspectives that helped motivate the Federal Circuit will also lead to a successful information-age economy, a Patent Act for the information age would retain the greatest strength of the present system—its harnessing of market mechanisms—while dampening the aspects of the present system that lead to abuses detrimental to public policy.

Such a reform might authorize the PTO to flesh out clearer guidelines for patentability that differ by industry. It might incorporate workable administrative procedures for third parties to contest pending patent applications and granted patents without incurring the expense of full-blown litigation. It might clean up some of the procedural rules that complicate and lengthen patent litigation. It might introduce mechanisms for reducing the number of deadweight patents that do little other than cloud commerce—say, a significant annual maintenance fee that motivates patentees to relinquish their hold on patents that they have not yet learned to commercialize. It might replace exclusivity with some sort of compulsory license, or perhaps inject a "practice it, license it, or lose it" requirement into the patent law. It might contain explicit provisions allowing courts to order compulsory licenses under appropriate circumstances if the exclusivity provisions remained intact. It might encourage the judiciary to consider the effects of a patentee's action on commercial markets and the public interest when determining the legality of patentee behavior. It might enhance judicial discretion in crafting remedies. Above all, it might explicitly incorporate the flexibility that Burk, Lemley, and maybe even Justice Kennedy already see lurking beneath the surface.

Most of these changes represent a drift away from the patent-as-property view and toward the patent-as-regulation view. In a liberal market economy, regulations serve a single purpose: they deliver a socially important good that the free market cannot deliver on its own. Both economic theory and empirical experience suggest that without a system regulating and rewarding new ideas, innovations, and inventions, investors would put their time and money elsewhere. The stream of innovative new products to which we have grown accustomed would slow to a trickle. The consequent innovation shortfall would hurt us all; innovative new products generate "positive externalities," or benefits that society at large enjoys. Innovators unable to recoup their investments are unlikely to become such public benefactors.

A regulatory system that guarantees innovators an opportunity to generate a suitable return (which is not the same as a guarantee of a suitable return) provides a way around this quandary. "Partial appropriability" allows innovators to internalize some benefits that would otherwise be externalities. These rights thus allow innovators to appropriate some—but never all—of the benefits that their innovations generate. Professor William Baumol has demonstrated the centrality of partial appropriability not only to the IP laws but also to the smooth functioning of market economies themselves.[41] Stated succinctly, a total absence of appropriability would provide innovators will little incentive to orient their activities in socially productive directions. Full appropriability would leave society with minimal reason to care whether innovators generated productivity increases, because only the innovators themselves would benefit. Only various schemes of partial appropriability allow the public at large to enjoy significant positive externalities while simultaneously motivating innovators to channel their energies in directions likely to enhance overall welfare. Liberal market economies *need* appropriate IP regulations.

Appropriate IP regulations must harness market mechanisms. The patent system has long embraced this approach. A patent-as-regulation view does not mean that the long-standing system of marketable "innovation rights" should give way to a bureaucracy administering a system of compulsory licenses—or even worse, to the sorts of command-and-control approaches that long defined the regulatory state. The best regulations have always been those that create systems of tradable permits and then encourage grantees to participate in robust secondary markets. An explicitly regulatory patent system would fall within this tradition. Patents would still be "like property" and would still exhibit many "attributes of personal property." The agencies administering them and the courts adjudicating disputes about their use, however, would gain flexibility. The agencies (and Congress) would be freer to tailor rights and responsibilities to different industries, taking into account matters like capital investment, risk, time to return, and complexity of commercial products. The courts would be freer to consider the effects of patentee behavior on the public at large and less locked into a framework in which behavior permitted to one patentee in one industry under one set of circumstances is necessarily permitted to all patentees in all industries under all sets of circumstances.

A system of compulsory licenses in which patentees are free to specify "reasonable and non-discriminatory" (RAND) terms and courts adjudicate disputes about reasonableness or discrimination would meet these criteria. Other restructured patent systems might, as well. Such a radical restructuring of IP law is far from becoming a reality, but it should be on the table as a subject of public and scholarly debate, as we continue moving into the information age.

In an era of information abundance, inexpensive information exchange, and numerous amorphous networks, public policy must empower individuals. Liberty and autonomy are the keys to success. Opportunity, information, and choice are paramount. In a patent context, increased choice translates into patent rights strong enough to reward genuine creativity, motivate innovation, and improve product diversity, but not strong enough to impede legitimate experimentation and competitive activity. Meaningful information flows when we require patentees to educate the public about their inventions as the price of their patents. Patents also spread opportunities subtly, by reducing the barriers that would otherwise negate investments in innovation—the free-riding that complicates an innovator's drive to recoup his initial investment and to turn a profit commensurate with his risks.

These reforms all relate to systemic patent law—the big black box within which the Federal Circuit must operate. Many of them would require a renegotiation of TRIPS as well as a revision of American law, and none of them appear imminent. Then again, radical reforms always appear to be long shots until they actually happen. The stirrings have begun. We're better off than we were twenty-five years ago, but the policy that we have is still not the one that we want. The Federal Circuit is doing well at the primary task that Congress assigned it, but the patent system itself is in need of an overhaul. Congress did a good job when it rethought the American patent system in the early 1980s. The time has come for it to rethink the system yet again—and in so doing, hand the Federal Circuit a revised assignment. The myriad challenges of the information age demand no less.

III

+

NOT JUST THE PATENT COURT

The Federal Circuit is more than just "the patent court." It also "owns" appeals from two important special courts: the Court of International Trade and the Court of Federal Claims. As the appellate authority whose rulings bind these court's trial judges, the Federal Circuit plays a critical role in international trade and in claims for remuneration from the federal government. Federal Circuit oversight of several other agencies and tribunals involved in trade and in federal financial obligations further expands its role in these legal arenas. Those who ignore these critical parts of Federal Circuit jurisdiction do so at their own peril. What policies and rules define these esoteric bodies of law? How does the Federal Circuit's role in these laws expand its view of the emerging global information age? And perhaps above all, how do these laws contribute to the shape of the information economy?

7

✛

Are We Poor Enough Yet?

ADVANTAGE

The Statute of Monopolies that Parliament foisted upon King James in 1624 was but one step in the long, hard slog toward a liberal economy. The monopolies that it banned—the royal grants to favored manufacturers—were but a small part of an economic theory known as "mercantilism." Gold (or technically, capital) was the key to a good mercantilist's heart, and every good mercantilist knew that the way to collect gold was to sell more stuff than you buy. How did they do it? At the risk of oversimplification, they combined three time-tested tricks: tariffs (import taxes), war, and patronage. The formula was simple. First, erect high tariffs on imports, so that any foreigner who chooses to sell something to your citizenry arrives with a built-in cost disadvantage. Second, go conquer other territories so that your manufacturers can export their goods without having to pay any bothersome tariffs. Third, offer a small number of expensive domestic production licenses. Voila! Domestic manufacturers sell at high prices at home, protected from foreign competition by high tariffs, and at high prices in your colonies, where they enjoy an effective monopoly. Increased sales generate domestic jobs, and employed workers generate taxable economic activity. Tariffs, license fees, and taxes transfer funds to the royal coffers. Everyone lives happily ever after.

Everyone, that is, except maybe consumers. And maybe foreigners whose cost structures are so much lower than those of your domestic producers that they could undersell them, even given transportation costs, were it not for the tariffs. And maybe some of your own producers, whose hopes of becoming exporters are dashed by other countries' retaliatory tariffs. And maybe entrepreneurs, who might benefit from having inexpensive inputs imported to help them reduce their own costs. And maybe innovators who might drive incumbent producers to improve their methods to better compete with efficient foreigners. And maybe the next generation of students, whose education might have benefited from the need to train them to become innovators and entrepreneurs. And just possibly the royal coffers themselves, where increased prosperity might have generated higher revenues. And, of course, colonials—but then again, who really cares about colonials? But other than those potentially disgruntled losers, pretty much everyone lives happily ever after under mercantilism.

In 1776, when a bunch of overtaxed, underrepresented colonials on our side of the Atlantic were distracting the king, Scottish economist Adam Smith explained the folly of mercantilism to George III and anyone else who cared to listen:

> What is prudence in the conduct of every private family can scarce be folly in that of a great kingdom. If a foreign country can supply us with a commodity cheaper than we ourselves can make it, better buy it of them with some part of the produce of our own industry, employed in a way in which we have some advantage. The general industry of the country . . . will not thereby be diminished . . . but only left to find out the way in which it can be employed with the greatest advantage. It is certainly not employed to the greatest advantage when it is thus directed toward an object which it can buy cheaper than it can make.[1]

Smith explained how mercantilist rules forcing Britons and British companies to buy expensive domestic products rather than less expensive imports diminished the country's overall wealth. He thus developed a theory of "absolute advantage": every item should be produced wherever production is most efficient. Nations should then trade—freed of tariffs or other barriers—to receive the mix of products that their people need.

Absolute advantage was a neat theory, and Smith was clearly correct that trade barriers forcing Great Britain's manufacturers to pay more than necessary for their inputs were making the country poorer rather than richer, but he didn't follow the logic of his own argument to its ultimate conclusion. Forty years later, Englishman David Ricardo finished Smith's work:

> Under a system of perfectly free commerce, each country naturally devotes its capital and labour to such employments as are most beneficial to each. This pursuit of individual advantage is admirably connected with the universal good of the whole. By stimulating industry, by regarding ingenuity, and by using most efficaciously the peculiar powers bestowed by nature, it

distributes labour most effectively and most economically: while, by increasing the general mass of productions, it diffuses general benefit, and binds together by one common tie of interest and intercourse, the universal society of nations throughout the civilized world.[2]

That intimate connection between individual advantage and universal good represents the fundamental moral underpinning of liberal market capitalism and explains why liberal societies are so much better at improving their citizens' living standards than are societies where other philosophies govern: While most philosophical approaches to economic development attempt to subvert our natural inclinations, liberalism attempts to harness them. Though Ricardo and his fellow nineteenth-century liberals recognized this moral principle, they also recognized the need for concrete illustrations of practical economics. Ricardo thus presented one of the most famous examples in all of economics: He explained why the French and Portuguese made wine, the Americans and Poles grew corn, and England specialized in manufactured goods:

If Portugal had no commercial connexion with other countries, instead of employing a great part of her capital and industry in the production of wines, with which she purchases for her own use the cloth and hardware of other countries, she would be obliged to devote a part of that capital to the manufacture of those commodities, which she would thus obtain probably inferior in quality as well as quantity.

The quantity of wine which she shall give in exchange for the cloth of England, is not determined by the respective quantities of labour devoted to the production of each, as it would be, if both commodities were manufactured in England, or both in Portugal.

England may be so circumstanced, that to produce the cloth may require the labour of 100 men for one year; and if she attempted to make the wine, it might require the labour of 120 men for the same time. England would therefore find it her interest to import wine, and to purchase it by the exportation of cloth.

To produce the wine in Portugal, might require only the labour of 80 men for one year, and to produce the cloth in the same country, might require the labour of 90 men for the same time. It would therefore be advantageous for her to export wine in exchange for cloth. This exchange might even take place, notwithstanding that the commodity imported by Portugal could be produced there with less labour than in England. Though she could make the cloth with the labour of 90 men, she would import it from a country where it required the labour of 100 men to produce it, because it would be advantageous to her rather to employ her capital in the production of wine, for which she would obtain more cloth from England, than she could produce by diverting a portion of her capital from the cultivation of vines to the manufacture of cloth. Thus England would give the produce of the labour of 100 men, for the produce of the labour of 80.[3]

With that example, Ricardo illustrated the principle of "comparative advantage." Comparative advantage works because resources are finite. It makes sense for every country to apply its finite resources in ways that will help it build the greatest surplus—a surplus that it can then draw down by trading for its other needs. Tariffs and other trade barriers interfere with this scheme by raising the effective price for efficient foreign production above the price for domestic production, thereby motivating domestic consumers to pay enough for the local good to motivate a misallocation of resources. Countries will only allocate resources in accordance with their comparative advantage if those distortive barriers disappear.

Comparative advantage is about as close as you can get to a provable "truth" in the social sciences. In an oft-repeated (and oft-embellished) exchange, the mathematician Stanislaw Ulam challenged Nobel laureate economist Paul Samuelson to "name one proposition in all of the social sciences which is both true and non-trivial." It reportedly took Samuelson several years to reply: comparative advantage. "That it is logically true need not be argued before a mathematician; that it is not trivial is attested to by the thousands of important and intelligent men who have never been able to grasp the doctrine for themselves, or to believe it after it was explained to them."[4] The disbelief persists to this day; the World Trade Organization (WTO) concedes that comparative advantage—the theory underlying most of its organizational tenets and justifying its existence as the world body overseeing international trade—"is one of the most misunderstood ideas in economics, and is often wrongly assumed to mean an absolute advantage compared with other countries."[5]

> What did David Ricardo mean when he coined the term comparative advantage? According to the principle of comparative advantage, the gains from trade follow from allowing an economy to specialize. . . . A country does not have to be best at anything to gain from trade. The gains follow from specializing in those activities which, at world prices, the country is relatively better at, even though it may not have an absolute advantage in them. Because it is relative advantage that matters, it is meaningless to say a country has a comparative advantage in nothing.[6]

Given that seeming convergence of mathematics, economics, and common sense, one thing about our trade policy should be clear: The policy we *want* is the one that best positions the United States to specialize, and so to avail ourselves of our own comparative advantage.

What would such a policy entail? The answer sits subtly in the middle of the WTO's clarification: "at world prices." Comparative advantage rests upon the notion of *free* exchange. If a Brazilian company can turn Brazilian sugar into ethanol, ship it to the United States, and still sell it for less than corn-based ethanol produced domestically, Americans should welcome the contribution to the nation's energy supply. Instead, a 54¢-per-gallon tariff prevents Americans from buying Brazilian ethanol "at world prices." Why would the American government do such a thing? For a reason familiar to eighteenth-century mercantilists: to protect domestic producers from more efficient international competitors. Producers frequently lobby Congress for various forms of such protection, and Congress often grants it. World prices prevail only in the absence of distortive trade barriers.

This observation impels Americans to ask three compelling questions: How can we get our own government to stop distorting trade? How can we get other countries to stop distorting trade? And how should our laws respond if others refuse to cooperate? These questions frame virtually all of trade law and policy—and dominate the Federal Circuit's trade docket.

BACKLASH

Economic theory, as important as it may be, is not the only guide to public policy. In a democratic system, politics is important—as, unfortunately, is populism. Domestic producers are hardly the only ones who complain about global competition. Their workers often also get into the act. Consider the fate of England's poor vintners back in Ricardo's time. Were England to buy all of its wine from Portugal, England's vintners would have to choose between moving to Portugal, finding some other line of work, or remaining unemployed. Workers facing such choices often create a fourth option—they lobby for regulations that protect their jobs by reducing foreign competition. When domestic producers and workers combine, they can form a formidable lobby. Professors Burk and Lemley warned of the power of such lobbies when contemplating patent reform, but the phenomenon is widespread; it is particularly strong in matters of trade, where domestic voters square off against non-voting foreigners.[7]

James Buchanan and Gordon Tullock, the founders of public choice theory, asked: "Can the pursuit of individual self-interest be turned to good account in politics as well as in economics?"[8] They demonstrated that it can, and that interest groups competing for influence can explain large parts of a country's public policy terrain—particularly when the articulated policy favoring the broad public is not the actual policy adopted. According to public choice theory, barriers to free trade represent elevations of interest-group politics seeking to protect their positions above the general welfare. Interest-group lobbying is thus the most straightforward explanation for the trade barriers that persist to this day.

Not everyone sees protectionist pressures that way. Some agree with
Nobel laureate and former World Bank chief economist Joseph Stiglitz that

> the theory of trade liberalization . . . only promises that the country as a
> whole will benefit. Theory predicts that there will be losers. . . . If liberaliza-
> tion is not managed well, the majority of citizens may be worse off—and see
> no reason to support it. It is not a matter of special interests opposing liber-
> alization, but of citizens correctly perceiving the world as it is. But this is not
> the world as it has to be. Trade liberalization can, when done fairly, when ac-
> companied by the right measures and the right policies, help development.
> . . . [T]he most successful developing countries in the world have achieved
> their success through trade—through exports. The question is: can the bene-
> fits that they enjoy be sustained, and be brought to all of the peoples of the
> world? I believe they can be; but if that is to be the case, trade liberalization
> will have to be managed in a way very different from that of the past.[9]

Stiglitz and those who share his concerns often rally around the flag of
"fair trade." After all, who opposes fairness? The answer depends upon
whose notion of fairness prevails—and there, Stiglitz seems to be the odd
man out. Most "fair traders" are simply protectionists hiding behind a variety of benign-sounding social objectives. According to several advocacy
groups using the collective acronym FINE, for example:

> Fair trade is a trading partnership, based on dialogue, transparency and re-
> spect, which seeks greater equity in international trade. It contributes to sus-
> tainable development by offering better trading conditions to, and securing
> the rights of, marginalized producers and workers—especially in the South.
> Fair Trade organizations (backed by consumers) are engaged actively in sup-
> porting producers, awareness raising and in campaigning for changes in the
> rules and practice of conventional international trade.[10]

While such groups often champion important objectives like the provision of consumer information about the labor and environmental practices of foreign producers, they also tend to oppose extending the benefits
of free trade to developing countries that fail to mandate their preferred
labor and environmental standards (and in some cases, intellectual property regimes). For the most part, these groups try to complicate treaties
and reduce trade flows to poor countries rather than to eliminate the barriers in rich countries that already suppress trade between the developed
and the developing worlds. This posture has the unfortunate consequence
of locking in poverty; many fair traders essentially campaign for the right
of the world's poor to remain impoverished.

Not all fair traders favor such policies. Stiglitz himself defines "fairness" in a way that would have made Smith and Ricardo proud: "What,
then, should one mean by fair trade? There is a natural benchmark: the

trade regime that would emerge if all subsidies and trade restrictions were eliminated. The world, of course, is nowhere near such a regime."[11]

Why is the world nowhere near such a regime? The political answer of public choice theory and FINE's equity arguments provide significant insights: Truly free trade *would* hurt some politically powerful interests and *would* induce poorer countries to sacrifice labor and environmental standards that richer workers and citizens enjoy in order to increase their domestic employment opportunities. These outcomes make many people unhappy and motivate them to lobby for rules that protect incumbents in the wealthy world, and that force workers in poorer regions to trade broad employment opportunities for higher labor standards for the few employed fortunates. Neither of these notions of "fairness" promotes movement toward Stiglitz's "natural benchmark" of truly free trade.

But the true problem runs deeper, as does the linguistic confusion. According to John Jackson, one of the foremost contemporary theorists of international trade law and a staunch advocate of free trade, "the basic liberal trade philosophy is constantly reiterated by government and private persons, even in the context of justification for departing from it!"[12] Those justifications for departure are pervasive:

> The objective of "national security" is frequently recognized as justifying a departure from liberal trade policies. . . . A second but related argument, is that a nation needs to avoid being too dependent on other nations (or even on the world economy). . . . More subtle is the possibility that a national consensus could explicitly opt for a choice of policies that would not maximize wealth . . . but would give preference to other noneconomic goals. . . . The "infant industry" argument proposes the use of import barriers to enable a new or young industry to become established and viable. . . . And in a democratic nation, national leaders will be observably influenced in their trade-policy decisions by the desire to get elected or reelected. . . . Business leaders and labor leaders can also be seen to have similar tendencies.[13]

Jackson demonstrates that although all of these seemingly plausible reasons for deviating from free trade require truly exceptional circumstances to justify the deviation, their proponents seem to find myriad circumstances to which they apply. Why? The last of Jackson's enumerated "noneconomic goals" returns us to public choice theory for the answer. Protectionist measures often receive massive political acclaim from palliated workers afraid of change, while evoking few protests from consumers, to whom the higher prices are invisible. What politician could resist?

A subtler and more interesting question is whether politicians *should* resist. Perhaps Stiglitz's call for new approaches to managing trade liberalization requires an occasional concession to protectionism—both to stave off destructive populist forces and to accommodate the rare occasion when even sound economics advocates a temporary trade barrier. After all, though economic theory predicts that distortions will correct themselves "eventually," some eventualities arrive rather slowly. Perhaps the policy we *really* want would allow politicians to effect such emergency measures.

Trade law in most countries includes two such categories of political mechanisms: "Countervailing" measures allow importing countries to undo "unfair" policies that exporting countries adopt to favor their own producers. "Safeguards" allow importing countries to nurture domestic industries caught unaware by sudden competition from abroad. Taken together, these measures can provide a political safety valve to protect against the worst tendencies of hard-core protectionists, remove the distortive ripples of unfair foreign laws, and enable smooth transitions in industrial development and employment.

At least, these worthy goals describe what countervailing and safeguard measures can achieve *in theory*. What do they achieve in practice? Michael Finger and Julio Nogués recently coordinated a World Bank study of the role that such measures played in seven Latin American countries. All of these countries incorporated such "defensive" countervailing and safeguard mechanisms as they liberalized their trade regimes. All liberalized successfully despite rather checkered histories—and all became richer for the experience.

> [T]he seven countries . . . had passed through several cycles of protection and openness. . . . Creating trade defense mechanisms was often part of the bargain to gain industry acceptance of liberalization. . . . From the perspective of maintaining the momentum of liberalization, these mechanisms, once in place, should serve as a means to accommodate and isolate pressures that might otherwise grow into large-scale threat; they should allow the possibility of one step back to preserve two steps forward. In each country, trade liberalization did generate substantial increases of imports, hence the need for mechanisms to manage these pressures. Thus, maintaining an economically sensible trade policy was, in significant part, a matter of managing pressures for exceptions—for protection for a particular industry—so that the exceptions remained exceptions and the decision process reinforced, rather than undermined, the political liberalization.[14]

Trade economist Seth Kaplan commented: "These case studies answer the often-neglected question—do these laws encourage trade liberalization in a world of second-best solutions? Surprising to many, the answer is yes—but only if administered impartially and based on sound economic foundations."[15]

This dynamic is the key to trade law and trade policy: As a general rule, free trade is good economics and bad politics, while protectionism is bad economics and good politics. Exceptions are rare; economists claiming to have identified such an exception must clear a high hurdle to be convincing. But a high hurdle is hardly an insurmountable one—particularly given the ways in which today's world differs from the day that Ricardo could claim that

> the difference . . . between a single country and many, is easily accounted for, by considering the difficulty with which capital moves from one country to another, to seek a more profitable employment. . . . If capital freely flowed toward those countries where it could be most profitably employed; there could be no difference in the rate of profit. . . . Experience, however, shows that the fancied or real insecurity of capital . . . together with the natural disinclination which every man has to quit the country of his birth and connections, and intrust himself, with all his habits fixed, to a strange government and new laws, check the emigration of capital. These feelings, which I should be sorry to see weakened, induce most men of property to be satisfied with a low rate of profits in their own country, rather than seek a more advantageous employment for their wealth in foreign nations.[16]

Ricardo's sorrow notwithstanding, the past few decades have witnessed tremendous growth in the harmonization of international commercial laws and the flow of capital across borders. At least one of the assumptions underlying Ricardo's derivation of comparative advantage seems to be weakening. Nothing suggests that the theory itself is in any danger, but the weakening of an assumption does suggest that exceptions might be more common than they once were.

The situation may thus be murkier than it first appeared to be. The trade policy we *want* still eliminates barriers, allows goods to flow freely across international borders, reduces prices throughout the U.S. economy, and consequently enriches the citizenry. If we adopt such a policy, we can reinvest our savings as we see fit, likely retaining most at the individual level but using at least part of the bounty to compensate and assist displaced workers or producers. That reinvestment might prove as politically powerful as is the push for distortive barriers—if our political leaders are bold enough to try it and patient enough to explain it to the citizenry. Is such a policy still possible in a world of populist political pressures and international capital flows? Or must we retrench to focus on Kaplan's "world of second best solutions"? In that world, political safety valves, occasional distortions, and defensive political mechanisms may all serve the cause of liberalization, as Finger and Nogués demonstrate they did in Latin America.

These are the questions that confront Congress when it chooses to regulate trade. How has Congress answered them? Title 19, the part of the U.S. Code dealing with trade, provides the formal answer, but its turgid prose is almost indecipherable. The meaningful data lie in the proceedings of regulatory agencies and courts, where the resolution of disputes over the trade laws reveal the policies that we have and lay them bare to stand beside the policies we want. The Federal Circuit's trade docket can thus provide valuable insights into the nature of contemporary American trade regulation.

ORGANIZATION

These trade regulations themselves flow from two streams: domestic law and international obligations. The two are intimately related; international treaties provide the framework on which domestic law hangs. The existence of a comprehensive framework for international trade is a relatively recent phenomenon. In the years immediately following World War II, many of the world's leaders recognized the need for new institutions capable of regulating relations between nations—and between the citizens of different nations. They started to think about formalizing and institutionalizing many of the customs that had come to serve the purpose of regulating international relations. Though many treaties, structures, and organizations existed before the late 1940s, the post–World War II attempts were by far the most ambitious and the most comprehensive that the "international community" had ever attempted. World leaders tried to create institutions capable of addressing two distinct sets of concerns: "public" international law (i.e., the rules governing international security, diplomacy, and war) and "private" international law (i.e., the rules governing international economic relations). History has shown that their attempts to institutionalize public law were a total and abject failure. Their attempts to institutionalize private law, while not without some problems, were largely successful.

From an institutional perspective, the San Francisco Conference of 1945 founded the United Nations as the central forum for maintaining international security. The Bretton Woods Conference of 1944 established the International Monetary Fund (IMF) to stabilize the global financial system and the International Bank of Reconstruction and Development (IBRD)—which has since grown to become the World Bank Group—to provide the funding and assistance necessary for the reconstruction of Europe and Japan, with a secondary charge of assisting development in Asia, Africa, and Latin America. The third organization conceived at Bretton Woods, the International Trade Organization, was stillborn. In its stead, a group of twenty-three nations reached a noninstitutionalized General Agreement on Tariffs and Trade (GATT). Discussions about tariffs and trade continued, GATT signatories conducted several rounds of negotiations, more nations joined, and the agreement expanded. At the end of the Uruguay Round of the GATT that had begun in 1986, representatives of 124 countries and the European Union's forerunner signed the Marrakesh Declaration of April 15, 1994, establishing the World Trade Organization (WTO). Eight and a half months later, on January 1, 1995, the WTO was born as the central institutional arbiter of international trade disputes.

The GATT, the WTO, and their adjunct and affiliated agreements have played important and mostly positive roles in shaping the global trading system. They have also played a critical role in improving the trade laws of many individual countries, including the United States. Under normal circumstances, national governments chafe at the thought of relinquishing even a modicum of their sovereign discretion and power. Citizens, particularly citizens of liberal democracies, like to believe that their elected officials will implement policies suitable to their nations and times. After all, the policies that *we* want may not be the policies that *other countries* want. Why should their preferences bind us? At times, there is no good answer to such questions. At others, however, there is. Trade is one such exception—in no small part because comparative advantage shows how, if all countries follow the right policies, all countries can win simultaneously. Unfortunately, the inherent conflict between good trade economics and good trade politics suggests that politicians will often trip over each other to see who can best placate the widest array of clamoring interest groups. This cycle of stumbling politicians will inevitably lead to staggering trade barriers.[17] The GATT and the WTO throw politicians a lifeline that allows them to withstand domestic pressure groups in favor of good economics by removing many of the most egregious practices of past trade policies from their political quivers.

Political leaders in WTO member states agreed to bind their hands in several key ways. They agreed to two rules of nondiscrimination: "national treatment" and "most favored nation" (MFN). The national treatment obligation prohibits political leaders from discriminating against imports once they are in the country legally; internal laws must afford the same treatment to goods produced internally and to imports. The MFN obligation requires member states to grant all WTO members the best deal that they offer to anyone. Political leaders further agreed to eliminate all "nontariff barriers," to replace them with tariffs, and then to reduce the tariffs. Under traditional trade policies, ingenious politicians around the globe had devised numerous ways to raise the price of imports without an explicit tariff; WTO rules prohibit all such practices, although it is not always easy to detect or to catalog the practices prohibited. The idea underlying this prohibition was to turn all implicit barriers into explicit tariffs, where sunshine would disinfect them into oblivion. Through these three principles, the GATT and the WTO set out to liberalize global trade, to eliminate barriers to the flows of goods and services across national borders, and to encourage the economic specialization that would lead each country to pursue its own comparative advantage—with the consequent enrichment of people around the globe. With international law thus binding their hands, many political leaders have found it easier to withstand the entreaties of interest groups seeking to elevate their own parochial concerns above those of the public at large.

So much for international trade obligations. What of national trade laws? What role do they play? Their role, unfortunately, is largely negative. National trade laws unshackle politicians and interest groups. They allow legislators and executives to exploit intentional gaps and unintentional loopholes in WTO rules, to thwart the goals of free trade, to erect trade barriers, to discriminate against imports, and to make goods more expensive for domestic consumers and for domestic producers reliant on low-priced inputs from abroad. They allow interest groups to exploit the defensive safety valves necessary to address exceptional situations in circumstances that are far from exceptional. Of course, even these negatives have their merits; as Finger and Nogués noted, these political safety valves can do what safety valves are supposed to do—allow populists to blow off steam without exploding the drive toward liberalization.

Policing those safety valves, unfortunately, is the Federal Circuit's primary job in trade law. U.S. trade regulation has its own institutional homes: the Commerce Department's International Trade Agency (ITA); the Department of Homeland Security's Customs and Border Protection Service; and the International Trade Commission (ITC), an independent agency. It also has a specialized Court of International Trade in New York that hears disputes with these institutions' findings. And appeals from both the ITC and the Court of International Trade go to—you guessed it— the Federal Circuit.

COMEDY

To Americans returning home after a stint abroad or to foreigners visiting the United States, filling out a customs form and gaining clearance from the Customs Service is a pro forma denouement to a long international flight. To importers hoping to sell their goods in the United States, on the other hand, the Customs Service can pose a significant hurdle, for it is the agency charged with enforcing the Harmonized Tariff Schedule of the United States (HTSUS). The HTSUS is a very lengthy attempt to categorize, as the Supreme Court said in another context, "anything under the sun made by man," as well as most things not made by man. Any importer wishing to bring any object into the United States must work with the Customs Service to determine the specific category (or subcategory or sub-subcategory) to which the item belongs. Then, subject to a few exceptions and rules, the two must look up the tariff rate appropriate for that category and determine the applicable tax. When the importer pays the tax, Customs clears him to bring his wares into the country—where they are then subject to national treatment per WTO rules.

As long and as comprehensive as the HTSUS might be, it is still not comprehensive enough to classify all objects without generating an occasional dispute. Many products defy obvious classification. In almost all such cases, the importer concludes that the appropriate classification is the one with the lowest applicable tariff, while Customs often concludes that the appropriate classification is the one with the highest applicable tariff. The importer and the Customs agent bring their dispute to a board internal to the Customs Service, then to the Court of International Trade, and then to the Federal Circuit. Many of these disputes come as close to comic relief as is possible within the federal judiciary—or at least, they would were they not such clear illustrations of a serious rift between the policy we want and the policy we have.

Take, for example, the humble Euro Clip, a picture frame that Structural Industries sought to import into the United States. Euro Clips consist of three components: a Masonite wood board as backing, a flat glass cover, and a set of four metal clips. People wishing to use Euro Clips simply slide a picture between the board and the glass, and secure all three in place with the clips. Here's the question that kept Structural Industries, Customs, the Court of International Trade, and the Federal Circuit occupied for almost six years: What is a Euro Clip?

The obvious answer, of course, is a picture frame. A Euro Clip, however, cannot possibly be a picture frame because the two HTSUS categories for picture frames (one for those made of wood and one for those made of metal) both require an actual *frame*, the component that the Euro Clip eschewed in favor of clips. So the one thing that is certain is that this picture frame is *not* a picture frame—and in fact, both the Court of International Trade and the Federal Circuit gave this possibility short shrift as a thought barely worthy of mention.

If not a picture frame, then, what is a Euro Clip? The answer is clear: It is a "composite good consisting of different materials or made up of different components." How does the HTSUS classify such composite goods? According to its General Rules of Interpretation: it applies the "essential character" test to classify them "as if they consisted of the material or component which gives them their essential character." Which leaves us with but further more question: What gives the Euro Clip its essential character? Three answers are possible: the wooden backing, the glass front-plate, or the metal clips. Structural Industries thought that the wood was essential, rendering the Euro Clip an "other article of wood," and co-incidentally yielding a lower tariff rate than would either of the other candidate classifications. Customs, oddly enough, found the glass essential, and sought to classify the Euro Clip as "glassware of a kind used for table, kitchen, toilet, office, indoor decoration or similar purposes," thereby landing it in the candidate classification with the highest tariff rate. Both agreed that the metal clips were not essential—after all, an essential characteristic with the middle tariff rate would be silly. What was not silly was their debate as to whether this picture frame that is not a picture frame is "essentially" a glass ashtray or a wooden tchochke.

What's the answer? At the Court of International Trade, Chief Judge Carman granted summary judgment in favor of the Customs Service's conclusion that the Euro Clip is essentially glassware.[18] At the Federal Circuit, judges Gajarsa, Linn, and Dyk all agreed that more evidence was necessary before this momentous decision was possible.[19] On remand, Chief Judge Carman held a full-blown evidentiary hearing and concluded, first, that the wood backing provided the Euro Clip's essential character—without the wooden backing, the picture, the glass, and the clips would all fall down—and, second, that the Euro Clip *was* a frame after all.[20]

That ruling followed closely on the heels of the Federal Circuit's related inquiry into glassware, concluding that the Pomeroy Collection's lamps were subject to a 5.2 percent tariff rate as "glassware of a kind used for indoor decoration," rather than being eligible for duty-free entry as "other articles of glass."[21] In recent years, the Federal Circuit has resolved numerous such momentous disputes, concluding, for example, that Häagen-Dazs dessert bars are predominantly frozen ice milk intermixed with yogurt rather than sorbet;[22] that Certs Powerful Mints are a preparation for oral or dental hygiene rather than a food preparation not elsewhere specified or included;[23] that ice-hockey pants are hockey equipment rather than sports clothing;[24] and that, even though cheap earrings and lapel pins with Halloween and Christmas themes are indeed festive articles, they are more properly classified as imitation jewelry.[25] All of these rulings were unanimous. The Federal Circuit panel split, however, when it came to classifying Halloween costumes: The importer, Judge Wallach at the Court of International Trade, and Judge Bryson in dissent all believed that that they, unlike the holiday-themed lapel pins and earrings, are most appropriately classified as festive articles, while judges Gajarsa and Newman deferred to Customs' persuasive argument that these costumes were, in fact, wearing apparel.[26]

All of which seems mildly amusing until you begin to think about the significant public and private resources invested in fighting these battles—all so that the U.S. government can force American consumers to pay higher prices than are strictly necessary. The only nice thing about any of these cases is that customs classification battles occasionally provide a decent forum for hashing out the finer points of administrative law. Small consolation for bad laws. Is the policy we have the policy we want? The question is hardly even worth asking.

TRAGEDY

Customs classifications cases persist because the WTO's rules don't bind the political hands on the tariff schedule. In fact, one of the perverse outcomes of the WTO's rules is that they actually *encourage* such cases by foreclosing nontariff barriers. That leaves tariffs as the only (or at the very least, the best) WTO-compliant mechanism for politicians seeking to protect their constituents by discriminating against foreigners—not to mention a good way to levy taxes that voters won't see. And if customs classification cases were truly the last vestige of a restrained trade system that the WTO was working to phase out of existence, they would be a small price to pay. Unfortunately, although the WTO may be taking the world on a glide path toward freer trade, customs classification cases are hardly the last vestige of protectionism; as Finger and Nogués noted, countervailing measures and safeguards both remain viable options under WTO rules.

Safeguards are relatively rare. Every now and then, a global industry falls into a state of such disequilibrium that efficient producers in one country simply cannot compete with their less efficient producers elsewhere. In such cases, government action to buy a bit of breathing room while the domestic industry restructures *might* be justifiable; WTO rules allow member countries to impose tariffs even though everyone in the world just wanted to play "fairly."

Countervailing measures arise when at least someone is being "unfair." Under WTO rules, when a country determines that one of its trading partners has engaged in unfair trade practices to give its exporters an unfair advantage, the targeted country may impose remedial duties to "countervail" the unfairness and to restore a level playing field upon which its domestic producers can compete fairly with the previously advantaged importers. As a result, Americans are constantly vigilant for importers whose prices are unfairly low.

Federal law includes to two such punitive measures: countervailing duties and antidumping. The former is rather straightforward: Suppose that the U.S. trade agencies conclude that some foreign government subsidized some of its producers, so that they can now come to the United States and underbid our own domestic producers in our own home market. WTO

rules allow members to assign a "countervailing duty" on those producers equal to the amount of their subsidy. As a result, their goods arrive in
U.S. markets with no unfair cost advantage vis-à-vis their domestic competitors. The motivation for a government to subsidize its producers is
easy to discern—it is a vestige of mercantilist thinking in which exports
are good and imports bad. Whether the United States should work to
counter this thinking is another question entirely; after all, low-priced imports do have their merits, particularly if you're an American consumer.

Dumping is a bit more complex: A good is "dumped" in the United
States if an importer offers to sell it at "less than fair value," defined as
anything below either its price in the manufacturer's home market or its
cost of production. When the members of a domestic industry feel that an
importer is victimizing them by dumping, they ask the federal government to investigate. The government solicits detailed proprietary information about costs, customers and/or sources, revenues, profitability,
and so forth from both the domestic and foreign producers. In many
cases, there are either gaps in the data or characteristics of foreign markets
that make it difficult to compare prices and costs to those in the American
market. When that happens, the government applies a complicated set of
rules to extrapolate reasonable data from the "facts available" (formerly
known as the "best information available"). With the data thus collected
or otherwise invented, the government publishes its findings and issues a
ruling. If the ruling concludes that the importer has seized an unfair advantage by dumping and that the domestic industry has suffered a "material injury" because of this dumping, the ruling also includes a duty
rate. From that point forward, the importer in question—and often all importers from its home country—will have to pay the antidumping penalty
on top of all other applicable tariffs.

The world's first antidumping laws began protecting Canadian industries in 1904. The United States got into the act a decade later. American
antidumping laws first appeared in the Revenue Act of 1916, a law best
known as the first significant increase to the three-year-old federal income
tax. Why then? In the late nineteenth and early twentieth centuries, Germany had a closed, protected, cartelized economy—and a global specialization in selected chemical and metal industries. In some of these industries, production was not very flexible; a manufacturer could either
operate a plant at full blast or turn it off entirely. Suppose that demand in
Germany called for one and a half plants' worth of production (at the in-
flated price that Germany's trade barriers allowed German producers to
charge German consumers). A German producer with two plants could
either shutter the second plant and forgo sales—risking the introduction
of foreign competition and a voice lobbying for reduced tariffs—or run
the second plant and produce a surplus. But what if inventorying that

surplus was expensive? Then the producer would probably choose to sell it immediately. If the German producer sold its surplus in Germany, its prices and profits would plummet. If the sales went abroad, the producer could continue to reap high profits in the protected German market while collecting lower competitive profits on the surplus abroad. With the profits in Germany subsidizing its sales abroad, the German producers would arrive in an export market—say, the United States—with an unfair advantage vis-à-vis domestic producers. With the Great War raging in Europe and fears of Germany running high, Congress enacted its first antidumping law to stave off that possibility.

The specificity of the conditions necessary to warrant such fears should suggest immediately that even if dumping is possible in theory, it rarely occurs in practice—and it certainly doesn't occur often enough to warrant letting remedial actions interfere with the benefits of free trade. Nevertheless, Congress has chosen to let it reduce the benefits of free trade in numerous industries.

How does the Federal Circuit get into this bleak little game? The investigations themselves are split between the ITA and the ITC. The ITA, an agency within the Department of Commerce, and the ITC, an independent commission, each bear responsibility for certain determinations relevant to the ultimate finding—which the ITC issues. These inquiries are highly technical. They start with *sui generis* definitions of terms like *product, market, domestic, majority, cost, price, facts available,* and numerous others. As in many technical bodies of law, the trade law definitions of these terms are similar but not identical to their colloquial meanings— or to their meanings in other legal settings. Complex and highly specialized accounting, financial, and economic analyses lead to conclusions about "fair value," "dumping margins," and "material injury." Both the domestic producers petitioning for protection and the importers accused of dumping typically hire expert economists to help present their cases. At times, political leaders express an "interest" in the proceedings. A recent hearing over a dispute between American and Canadian cattlemen, for example, reportedly drew 10 of our 100 senators to the ITC hearings—undoubtedly because they all developed a sudden interest in the arcana of trade economics. When the ITC finally reaches its conclusion, the losing party may appeal to the Court of International Trade, and from there to the Federal Circuit.

By the time an antidumping or countervailing duty case reaches the Federal Circuit, the issues will have transcended the merely technical and worked their way into the hypertechnical. Federal Circuit review of an antidumping or a countervailing duty case typically hinges on either the finer points of administrative law or on some nuance in the ways that the ITA and the ITC conducted their investigations. Nevertheless, a quick

review of Federal Circuit antidumping and countervailing duty jurisprudence reveals a cross-section of America's weakest (or greediest) industries. During calendar year 2005 alone, for example, the Federal Circuit
ruled in cases pertaining to petitions filed by the domestic producers of
cold-rolled steel,[27] hot-rolled steel,[28] uranium enrichment services,[29] polyethylene,[30] dynamic random access memory,[31] TV sets,[32] towels,[33] honey,[34]
candles,[35] and mushrooms.[36]

The obvious question is: So what? After all, if foreign governments either
overtly subsidized their producers or created the conditions that promote
dumping, why *shouldn't* the United States protect its own producers by
countering this unfair behavior? Finger and Nogués answered that question in the Latin American context, but their assessment applies equally
well to the United States: "From an economics perspective, WTO rules on
safeguards and antidumping are too generous with respect to separating
either good interventions from bad or fewer interventions from more. Although antidumping, in theory, is about interventions that make economic
sense, in reality WTO guidelines allow restrictions that amount to ordinary
protection."[37] Too many countries misuse defensive countervailing loopholes that might be justifiable under unusual economic situations as WTO-
compliant political safety valves. The United States is among them.

The same holds true with respect to safeguards. By putting remedial
mechanisms in place and giving them an institutional home, U.S. law
encourages every industry facing disappointing profits to seek a solution
by casting blame abroad. The vast majority of industries who seek protection from foreign competition simply want to enhance their profits indefinitely without undertaking the hard work of restructuring. Laws that
permit—and even encourage—such behavior damage the American
economy. They hit consumers and producers reliant on imported inputs
immediately, they promote inefficiency among the protected producers,
and they misallocate skills among workers. They are detrimental to national economic health in both the short and the long terms.

Much of this damage is immeasurable, particularly the long-term damage. Nevertheless, it is possible to put a price tag on certain categories of
short-term damage. In the mid-1990s, U.S. Trade Representative Mickey
Kantor asked the ITC to estimate the effects of the "unfair trade practices"
that antidumping and countervailing duties are supposed to counteract—
and of those duties themselves. ITC staffers built a simulation model to
consider what would have happened to the American economy in the absence of all 239 antidumping and countervailing duties in place in 1991.
They concluded that the economy would have grown by $1.59 billion (approximately 0.03 percent of gross domestic product).[38]

Their conclusion leads to two interesting observations. The first, and
more obvious, is that the data demonstrate what theory predicted: trade

barriers decrease overall national welfare. The second is subtler: countervailing trade measures defused at least some populist pressures for a cost of only 0.03 percent of GDP. Does this sort of deal serve the public interest? Not surprisingly, the ITC report neither asked nor answered this question. Few politicians like to admit that they are mere political palliatives. They prefer to see the agencies they serve as instruments of positive public policies. In the ITC's case, those policies address the distributional effects of trade. Vice Chair Janet Nuzum and Commissioner David Rohr explained:

> By focusing on the aggregate economy-wide effects, this study . . . does not recognize or take into account certain distributional effects within the United States of unfair trade practices. The real world effects of unfair trade practices affect not hypothetical households, but real firms and real workers, with particular skill levels, who work in particular geographic areas of the country. The opportunities for those firms and workers to engage in other productive pursuits in the absence of trade remedies are a function of the state of the economy in their region, their mobility, and the transferability of their skills. . . . This study . . . does not analyze the disproportionate distributional effects that unfairly traded imports or their remedies may have had on certain parts of the United States, or certain types of workers. It also does not examine the real costs of reallocating resources over time based on the particular circumstances facing those firms and workers affected by the unfair trade.
>
> It must be remembered that the purpose of the antidumping and countervailing duty laws is not to protect consumers, but rather to protect producers. Inevitably, some cost is associated with this purpose. However, unlike the antitrust laws, which are designed to protect consumer interests, the function of [these trade] laws is, indeed, to protect firms and workers engaged in production activities in the United States. So it should not come as a surprise that the economic benefits of the remedies accrue to producers and the economic costs accrue to consumers. The United States Government, through legislation, has made a conscious policy choice to provide these trade remedies in recognition of the reality that free and open trade does not yet exist worldwide.[39]

Are Nuzum and Rohr right? Do these distributional problems really justify countervailing measures even in the absence of exceptional economic conditions? We last asked these questions in the context of nineteenth-century England's poor vintners, where we suggested that the most appropriate response to such dislocation was to help displaced workers and businesses adjust rather than to impose trade barriers that trap them in a comfortable past. Good public policies should look to the future, rather than to the past. Distributional effects thus seem to provide a weaker justification for countervailing measures than does public choice theory.

Meanwhile over at the Federal Trade Commission (FTC), where protecting consumers is official job number one, Morris Morkre and Ken Kelly studied every antidumping and countervailing duty case decided between 1980 and 1988 for which they could collect adequate data—179 in all—and assessed the damage that foreign competition had caused the petitioning domestic industry. They found three clear cases of significant injury, eighteen cases where domestic industry revenues dropped by 10 percent or more, and fifty cases where revenues dropped by more than 5 percent, despite widespread fears in the 1980s and early 1990s that unfair foreign competition was destroying the American industrial terrain. They wondered:

> Why are our results so at variance with popular perceptions? First of all, these perceptions often are not based upon systematic evidence. Second, our methodology is designed to isolate the effects of unfairly traded imports from the effects of other influences on the domestic industry. Firms that compete with unfairly traded imports may be experiencing difficulties independent of import competition. . . . [Our results] should not be construed to suggest that domestic industries are never, or almost never, injured by dumped or subsidized imports. . . . The relevant question is not whether there is any injury, rather it is how much injury is suffered.[40]

From a policy standpoint, though, the key questions are the follow-ups to the one that Morkre and Kelly posed: Are the injuries significant enough and widespread enough to warrant a remedy that risks doing more harm than good? Or does the remedy buy enough political breathing room inexpensively enough to be worthwhile?

These are the questions that Congress must contemplate when converting policy prescriptions about trade into actual trade laws, and to a lesser extent that the ITC must consider when conducting its detailed inquiries. According to a general principle of administrative law, when Congress gives an independent agency primary oversight over an area of law, that agency's decisions are final as long as they are "reasonable." The primary role for the federal courts is to determine whether or not the agencies are behaving reasonably. In one recent case, for example, two Russian companies considered it unreasonable for the ITC to have concluded that the U.S. silicon industry was "materially injured by reason of silicon metal imports from Russia that were sold at less than fair market value," when comparable low-priced silicon was available from numerous other sources. As they saw it, even if the United States imposed antidumping duties on Russian imports, the American industry would still not recover. They appealed to the Court of International Trade and, when they lost there, to the Federal Circuit. Judges Dyk and Gajarsa agreed with them; Judge Archer did not. As Dyk explained it:

The sole point of contention in this appeal is whether the [ITC] established that the injury to the domestic industry was "by reason of" the subject imports. . . . [T]he "by reason of" requirement mandates a showing of causal—not merely temporal—connection between the [goods sold at less than fair value] and the material injury. . . . Causation is not shown if the subject imports contributed only minimally or tangentially to the material harm. The [ITC], like other federal agencies, must examine the relevant data and articulate a satisfactory explanation for its action. . . . Normally, an agency rule would be arbitrary and capricious if the agency . . . entirely fails to consider an important aspect of the problem. Where commodity products are at issue and fairly traded, price competitive, non-subject imports are in the market, the [ITC] must explain why the elimination of subject imports would benefit the domestic industry instead of resulting in the non-subject imports' replacement of the subject imports' market share without any beneficial impact on domestic producers.[41]

Dyk thus reminded the ITC that it had to conduct careful economic analyses that considered all aspects of the problem that it was trying to fix—and of the proposed fixes that it was considering. Failure to do so rendered its conclusions inherently unreasonable.

Could the court do more? The answer is almost certainly yes—but not a lot more. Admonitions of the type that Dyk issued to the ITC in the silicon case are few and far between. Of potentially greater significance, however, was his notion that the ITC had to consider all important aspects of a problem. The implications of such a requirement transcend merely thinking about import substitution. They verge on Finger and Nogués's recommendation to

mandate identification of the impact on users and consumers as well as the impact on competing domestic producers. The policy process would ask: Who in the domestic economy would benefit from the proposed import restrictions, and who would lose? By how much? The technicalities would be simple: recognize domestic users and consumers as interested parties, and require that the investigation determine the effect on them of the proposed restriction in parallel with its determination of injury from trade to the protection seeker. The effect of the restriction on users would be measured in the same dimensions as injury—for example, jobs lost because of higher costs and lower profits—the standard metric of effect. . . . Even in those instances in which the decision is to restrict imports, the process would bring forward the reasoning behind the liberalization, the benefits from openness. . . . Beyond making economic sense, such a process would be politically balanced. It takes into account the effect of trade on all interests in the country: those that benefit from liberalization and those who are burdened.[42]

This recommendation forms the flipside of Nuzum and Rohr's "distributional" defense of countervailing measures by addressing the importance of distribution to a liberal trade system. It ensures that everyone can see the winners and losers of each proposed trade deal, and advocates deviating from free-trade principles only where it makes economic sense to do so. While it would increase the costs of running an ITC investigation, it might also reduce the amount that we have to spend buying off populist political pressure. It is excellent advice. If taken, it would bring the policies we have closer to the policies we want. Congress would achieve a higher score in its own component of the black box of trade policy. In the meantime, public choice theory remains the best way to explain most of the trade policies we have—narrow interest groups wanted them, lobbied for them, and got them. Federal Circuit observers can only marvel at their handiwork. All that the Federal Circuit can do in its own part of the black box is to insist that the ITC pay reasonable attention to all economic effects of the barriers that it is considering.

FARCE

Though the Federal Circuit's role in trade policy is largely that of an observer, the view from its trade docket reveals many things. Among the most salient are the gyrations of shackled politicians chafing beneath WTO obligations—or at the very least, the effects those gyrations have on selected American industries. Such gyrations emanate from a dirty little secret about legislation. Under the Constitution, *any* bill that both houses of Congress pass and the president signs becomes law, even if it is clearly unconstitutional. In theory, for example, congressional passage plus a presidential signature on bills that declared a specific religion illegal, prohibited all gun ownership among private citizens, or shut down all independent newspapers would immediately become the law of the land— and would stay the law of the land unless and until the Supreme Court declared them unconstitutional. That declaration of a law's unconstitutionality would strip them of all legal force. During the window between the president's signature and the Court's declaration, however, they would be just as valid as every other law. Fortunately, American legislators and presidents tend to be too responsible to enact laws that are overtly unconstitutional—though they're not beyond testing the boundaries of constitutional provisions that they dislike or that lead to policies that they consider unfortunate or inconvenient.

When it comes to mere international obligations, however, politics can overwhelm responsibility. Some political leaders are perfectly happy to enact policies that violate WTO obligations, reasoning that they're not really violations until the WTO labels them as such. The political salience of countering WTO free-trade rules with blatant protectionism has tempted leaders from both political parties and has eroded the bipartisan consensus on free trade that prevailed in the 1990s. The most detrimental effect of these actions lies beyond the realm of measurable economics. Each politically inspired deviation from the principles of free trade—including those that comply with WTO rules and that address truly exceptional economic circumstances—erodes America's standing as a free-trading nation. Every political success in the United States emboldens protectionists abroad, retards the spread of free trade, complicates the world's movement toward a system of global comparative advantage, and consequently mires parts of the developing world in poverty for a bit longer than is strictly necessary.

Consider the fallout from the victory of Senator Robert Byrd (D-WV) in the wee hours of October 28, 2000. Byrd found a way to transfer money from American consumers to selected corporate interests. While such a congressional achievement is hardly a rarity, the panache with which Byrd circumvented standard procedures earned the Continued Dumping and Subsidy Offset Act of 2000 a nickname: "the Byrd Amendment."[43] The idea behind the Byrd Amendment was simple. Although antidumping and countervailing duties raise import prices, they do not deter all targeted imports. Importers continue to bring their goods to U.S. shores, pay both the standard tariff rates and these "remedial" duties, bring them into the country, and sell them to American consumers. Their payments create a pool of money that Customs collects. What happens to that money? Until late 2000, it went into the general fund, from which Congress builds the nation's budget. But Byrd had a better idea. He believed that Customs should divert those funds to the pockets of the domestic producers who had petitioned successfully for the antidumping and countervailing duties that built that money pile.

The idea itself was hardly a brilliant insight; various members of Congress had introduced similar bills many times over the years. Each time, a debate ensued. Opponents complained, first, that such a bill would create a perverse incentive that encouraged American companies to waste their time and effort filing trade petitions rather than improving their efficiency and, second, that it would violate WTO (or earlier, GATT) rules prohibiting subsidies.[44] On every previous occasion, these objections swayed Congress, and the bill failed. Byrd concluded—both perceptively and correctly—that the problem lay in letting Congress deliberate and debate the idea. Late one night, while Congress was locked in its annual rush to pass the appropriations bills necessary to fund the government, Byrd and his aides acted. They attached the amendment to an entirely unrelated, already long and complex agriculture appropriations bill. The bill passed when Congress chose to fund agriculture for the year—and the Byrd Amendment along with it. President Bill Clinton signed the bill under duress, reasoning that a bad trade provision was a small price to pay for an agriculture appropriations bill, and asked Congress to repeal the Byrd Amendment. Somehow, the Republican Congress managed to withstand the entreaties of the lame-duck Democratic president. The Byrd Amendment became law.[45]

Over the next four years, selected corporate interests shared a windfall in excess of $1 billion in unearned Byrd Amendment revenues—again, a pittance if theses funds did nothing other than defuse populist political pressures. Few laws or policies, however, achieve only such narrow political goals. While the lucky American winners were busy accumulating their bounty, the rest of the world seethed. The Byrd Amendment hurt the credibility of the U.S. Trade Representative, complicated trade negotiations, and earned opprobrium from America's trading partners, liberal market advocates, and U.S. companies that relied upon imports as inputs into their own products. It likely cost the United States far in excess of $1 billion in increased advocacy costs and loss of goodwill. Of likely greater significance though, the WTO labeled it an unfair trade practice.

Many might reply to such a labeling by paraphrasing Stalin: How many divisions does the WTO have? The answer is, even fewer than the Pope, who after all does have his Swiss Guards. The WTO has no direct enforcement capabilities. In fact, this sophisticated institutional guardian of the global trading system can defend its rules using only a schoolyard ploy: it can offer the tough kids a free shot. When the WTO rules against a country, it gives that country a window within which to change its laws. If the country losing refuses, the WTO lets the countries that had complained about the offending practice enact retaliatory and discriminatory barriers without violating WTO rules. In 2004, a second WTO arbitration panel announced that eight complaining countries could erect $150 million per year in such barriers discriminating against imported U.S. goods. The European Union, Canada, Mexico, and Japan all introduced retaliatory tariffs in 2005.[46] The *Economist* summarized the matter rather cleanly:

> The Byrd Amendment . . . is one of the most outrageous weapons in America's trade-protection arsenal. . . . [It] offers American firms a cash incentive to clamour for protection. . . . It is a pity that, while America's lawmakers squeal about the importance of fair rules for global trade, they are reluctant to accept the WTO as a judge of what is fair and what is not.[47]

Still and all, a law is a law. Beginning in 2001, the ITC compiled an annual list of qualifying producers, sent the list to Customs, and Customs released the funds. Domestic producers who felt slighted could file suit in the Court of International Trade and then appeal to the Federal Circuit. Most eligible domestic producers of most products navigated these new procedures happily and successfully, but some of America's candle makers found the Byrd Amendment definitions and procedures complex and confusing.

The Candle Corporation of America (CCA) was the first to arrive at Lafayette Park seeking Byrd Amendment funds. But CCA had a problem. In 1985, when America's candle makers had first filed their antidumping petition, CCA was busily importing the allegedly dumped candles from China. As a result, CCA chose not to support the petition that threatened to strangle its business. That import business wasn't quite as robust a few years later, with antidumping penalties eroding its profits. Perhaps because of this profit erosion or perhaps for unrelated reasons, CCA acquired two domestic candle makers, Lenox and Cape Cod, both of whom *had* participated in the original petition. In 2001, CCA claimed that it was a domestic producer affected by dumping and lined up, hat in hand, awaiting Senator Byrd's largesse. Alas, the ITC disagreed, concluded that CCA was not an "affected domestic producer," and sent it home without unearned disbursals. The Court of International Trade agreed with the ITC.

The question thus came to the Federal Circuit: Is CCA an affected domestic producer? Judge Dyk found CCA's claim hard to swallow. As he read the Byrd Amendment, its statutory language may not have answered the question, but its "purpose" did. The Byrd Amendment was about motivating domestic producers to file petitions. If a company could oppose a petition yet still reap Byrd's rewards merely by acquiring a small supportive competitor, where was the incentive? He thus agreed with Customs that Congress had demonstrated a clear intent "to prevent a company, business or person who opposed an antidumping or countervailing duty investigation from obtaining benefits under" the Byrd Amendment.[48] Judge Gajarsa wondered how either Customs or the court could determine the congressional intent behind an amendment snuck onto an unrelated appropriations bill in the wee hours of the morning.[49] Judge Michel agreed with Dyk. CCA is not an affected domestic producer.

Candle maker confusion continued when the Cathedral Candle Company and the A.I. Root Company awoke to discover that the ITC had left them off its list of eligible recipients, even though they *had* supported the original petition. The reason for this omission was simple: Their support in 1985 had been confidential. The ITC continued to respect that confidentiality many years later when it assembled its list of companies that qualified for 2001 and 2002 Byrd Amendment funds. When Customs disbursed the money, Cathedral and Root received none. They eventually complained, but the ITC concluded that they had had ample notice of the eligibility list before Customs disbursed the funds, and that if they felt slighted, they should have complained while the money was still around. The Court of International Trade agreed with Customs. The candle makers appealed to the Federal Circuit, where the assignment wheel fell once again on Judge Dyk, this time pairing him with judges Bryson and Lourie. Once again, opinion split. This time Judge Dyk found the statutory language both clear and dispositive: Because the statute imposed no time limit for filing, Customs and the ITC had overstepped their proper bounds when they imposed one. Judges Bryson and Lourie disagreed. They thought that Customs and the ITC had interpreted the statute reasonably and that the court's job was thus to defer to these reasonable agency interpretations. Neither Cathedral nor Root could reclaim the past Byrd Amendment funds to which they might otherwise have been entitled.[50]

The Federal Circuit's rulings against those three candle makers were no small matter; the candle industry was one of the Byrd Amendment's three big winners. It, along with the ball bearing and steel industries, took home almost half of the roughly $1 billion distributed during the Byrd Amendment's first four years. According to *Forbes*:

> Steel producers have been the big winners under Byrd. In 2004, the government paid $58 million to producers of pure steel products and another $80 million to those that produce steel-containing items, namely bearings. Timken alone garnered $52.7 million from suits against imports from 11 countries, including China, Japan, Mexico, Italy and Argentina, according to U.S. Customs data. The second-largest Byrd check last year went to—of all things—candle maker Lancaster Colony. The $26.2 million lump sum contributed 35% of Lancaster's operating cash flow for the last quarter of 2004. Producers of pencils, pineapples, pasta and polyester staple fiber received millions in Byrd money as well.[51]

Forbes also noted that "opposition to Byrd is growing louder. The Bush administration has called for repeal." In the final analysis, it was congressional self-interest rather than presidential opposition that undid the Byrd Amendment. Under the Deficit Reduction Act of 2005, Congress decided that it would rather keep the money collected under the antidumping and countervailing duties itself—and maybe even use it to reduce the budget deficit.[52] To avoid doing anything that might disrupt the free-money expectations of American petitioners, though, Congress made the repeal effective as of September 30, 2007. According to *Forbes*, that repeal should qualify as "one item on the Bush agenda that could actually win friends abroad."[53]

REPUTATION

The Bush trade team certainly needed some friends abroad, because the president himself had shot them in the foot some years earlier. George W.

Bush, never one to be outdone by a Democrat, managed to back a trade measure that engendered even more anger than did the Byrd Amendment—though in the President's defense, solid economic analysis supported *his* measure. In Bush's case, the opportunity arose when the domestic steel producers claimed to have fallen into one of those unusual sets of economic circumstances in which the global industry was so out of whack that even efficient companies risked ruin, and asked the government to impose the sort of safeguards that WTO rules permit in just such circumstances.

The steel industry pointed to a combination of intense competition from abroad and bad legacy policies in the United States as the sources of their woes. The intense competition arose when the financial crises of the late 1990s led to a screeching halt in Asian construction and a consequent glut of steel on the world market. The bad legacy policies were crushing even operationally efficient American producers beneath obligations to pensioners and others with whom they had once contracted. The American steel producers brought their concerns to the ITC, where the staff conducted and commissioned careful economic analyses that simulated the likely effects of the requested tariffs on the steel industry, on various other affected groups within the U.S. economy, and on the economy as a whole. Having thus conducted precisely the sort of broad-based analyses that Finger and Nogués advocate, the staff concluded that protection was warranted: The global market was in disequilibrium, the requested tariffs could allow the domestic industry to restructure, and the broad welfare effects would be minimal to positive.

When the ITC's recommendation reached the President, he noticed that in addition to the staff's conclusion that steel tariffs would help the American economy, the petitioning companies were clustered in electorally competitive states. This combination of factors proved compelling. Bush picked the lock on the WTO's shackles and imposed a three-year program of tariffs on most foreign steel products, with some rates as high as 30 percent. With that, he angered steel producers and free traders around the world—even though the ITC's economic conclusions appear to have been correct and several American steel companies did restructure successfully under their umbrella and emerge as stronger competitors in the global steel market.

Even before they completed that restructuring, America's steelmakers were grateful for the breathing room. They were not, however, too bashful to ask the federal government to grant them *even more* protection from foreign competition. As Judge Bryson told the story, "Section 201 of the Trade Act of 1974 authorizes the President to take appropriate action to protect domestic industries from substantial injury due to increased quantities of imports,"[54] which Bush did in March 2002. Meanwhile, in September 2001, several domestic steel producers had petitioned for antidumping and countervailing duties on cold-rolled steel.

> The [ITC]'s responsibility . . . is to determine if a domestic industry is materially injured or threatened with material injury by reason of imports. . . . [The ITC] found that the . . . President's remedy fundamentally altered the U.S. market for many steel products, including cold-rolled steel[;] . . . that imports of those products declined sharply and that domestic prices increased significantly in the period after the imposition of the Section 201 tariffs[;] . . . that, according to purchasers, the reduction in imports due to the Section 201 tariffs had led to higher prices, supply shortages, and some broken or renegotiated contracts[;] . . . [and that] the domestic cold-rolled steel products industry is neither materially injured nor threatened with material injury by reason of subject imports.[55]

Not surprisingly, the ITC refused to impose antidumping or countervailing duties. The Court of International Trade agreed with that conclusion.

Even the president's largesse is not without its downsides. Rather than receiving the potentially long-term protection of an antidumping duty and its consequent benefit of Byrd Amendment funds, the beleaguered American steel industry had to settle for Section 201 tariffs that were never expected to last more than three years. They didn't last even that long; Bush lifted the steel tariffs in December 2003. *Forbes* described this action "as a victory for free trade and for international law . . . but only a half victory. International law [got] a bit of a boost when the U.S. decided to comply. But it's only a half victory as the idea of law is that people will obey them first of all, not just after they get caught."[56]

In July 2005, eighteen months after the U.S. repealed the Section 201 tariffs on steel, a unanimous Federal Circuit panel affirmed the Court of International Trade's decision rejecting the petitioning steel producers' request for antidumping protection.[57] The temporary tariffs had improved the standing of domestic producers so much that they couldn't convince *anyone* that they were suffering a material injury in 2002. The steel producers must still be wondering whether they won or lost on the deal, although they do appear to have used the restructuring window wisely and to have emerged more competitive than they would be had Bush not imposed the tariffs. As to America's credibility in trade negotiations, little doubt remains. Policies like the Byrd Amendment and the Bush steel tariffs only complicate the job of American trade negotiators claiming to champion the cause of free trade—even when their economic effects are minimal or positive.

8

✛

Looking Forward

TOWARD EFFECTIVE ADJUSTMENT

As tempting as it is to deride artificial barriers to free trade as mere political opportunism, it's important to recall that political opportunism exists for a reason: *voters!* If protectionism were nothing more than corporate welfare, it would carry a political price. It doesn't. In the early twenty-first century, many Democrats and a fair number of Republicans actually boast of their protectionist credentials, as do politicians around the globe. Why? The answer lies in the elusive notion of "fairness."

International free trade is capitalism on steroids. The lower the trade barriers, the easier it is for foreign companies to compete with domestic companies. The greater the competition, the more intense the pressure on domestic companies to improve their efficiency. Intense pressure produces both greater successes and greater failures. The successes improve living standards for their customers and strengthen the American economy. The failures lay off workers and eventually shutter their operations. The political calculus is simple: Free trade eliminates specific jobs, and comparative advantage eliminates entire categories of jobs. Protectionist politicians invariably present themselves as defenders of jobs and of workers. In a contest between a candidate promising to protect *your* job, requiring *your* skill set *today*, and one promising to create *more* jobs, requiring *as-yet-to-be-determined* skill sets *soon*, the politically salient choice is clear. Once again, the general rule prevails: free trade is good economics and bad politics, while protectionism is bad economics and good politics.

Anyone even remotely interested in both international trade and basic human decency understands that robust competition generates painful job losses and that it is unfair to ask a subset of American workers to pay the full price for general prosperity. Those also interested in pragmatic politics understand that political necessity mandates attention to the displacement potential inherent in free trade. For those with leanings toward socialism or planning, the appropriate solution is straightforward: the government must use its authority to limit competition from abroad. With trade barriers in place, the domestic demand for domestic production will rise, and more American workers will keep the jobs they already have. If possible, the government should also use its authority to negotiate deals promoting exports to other countries, thereby increasing demand even further and enhancing the security of the American workforce. To those who favor government planning, mercantilism doesn't sound quite so bad—though many socialists might deny their implicit yearning to return to an era in which a few wealthy countries exploited their less developed colonies.

From a liberal perspective, the path to a solution is murkier. Free trade and comparative advantage are already liberal programs. In the long run, the market will create more new jobs than it loses, inform the public about the necessary skills, and welcome people who relocate to where they are needed. When all goes well, the long run may not take all that long to unfold; reciprocal free trade agreements may generate more jobs in export-oriented industries than they cost in domestic-oriented industries. At least, that's the theory. As in many cases, the biggest problem with a "pure" liberal agenda is that real people get hurt while economic theories work their way toward an inevitable improved equilibrium. In concrete terms, a trade policy that creates two jobs for computer programmers in Arizona for every lower-paying job that it eliminates in a West Virginia mine may help the American economy but does fairly little for West Virginia miners. Even a theory explaining that they could learn to program, move to Arizona, and increase their wages won't pay their rent, utilities, food bills, tuition, health care, or relocation expenses while they're putting the theory into play.

This human dimension explaining the problems with economic theories translated directly into economic policies also points the way toward the liberal response. If America as a whole benefits when these miners lose their jobs, and if the proper response to their job loss is for them to retrain and relocate, the country as a whole should invest in their retraining and relocation. The liberal inquiry should focus on the best ways to develop such programs. What role should the federal government play in establishing retraining and relocation aids? What role can the private sector play? Comparative advantage encourages each nation or region to sacrifice the interests of some of its industries to those that it can pursue with comparatively greater efficiency. It is not unreasonable to ask some of the winning industries to help retrain the workers trapped in the losing industries, particularly when such programs will benefit those efficient industries by muting political opposition to growth-oriented economic policies and by increasing the size and quality of the suitably skilled labor pool.

The private sector, however, cannot do this work alone. When it comes to reallocating most resources, liberal free markets work well: those who believe that they can use the resources most efficiently will invest, and investors who are correct will profit. When it comes to investing in labor, however, the Thirteenth Amendment's prohibition of slavery becomes problematic: Employers who invest in retraining potential new recruits cannot "own" their investment.[1] The workers may take their new skills elsewhere—including to competitors eager to free-ride on the investment. Structured loan programs, which might alleviate part of the problem, might also generate information-age "company stores," thereby skirting slavery with indentured servitude. It is thus hard to see how large-scale retraining and relocation programs can succeed without at least some government involvement.

The federal government already maintains two such Trade Adjustment Assistance (TAA) programs: one for workers who lose their jobs to free trade, and one for workers who lose their jobs to Canada or Mexico under the North American Free Trade Agreement (NAFTA). According to the official White House website, these programs "help trade-impacted workers gain or enhance job-related skills and find new jobs. The programs provide eligible workers with career counseling, up to two years of training, income support during training, job search assistance, and relocation allowances."[2] In order to meet those critical needs, President Bush asked Congress to allocate almost $1 billion for the 2007 fiscal year—a tad low if the goal is to help hundreds of thousands of displaced workers, but coincidentally of the same order of magnitude as the price that the U.S. economy pays to maintain countervailing and antidumping duties.[3] Furthermore, there's nothing about these programs' objectives that justifies limiting eligibility to workers whose jobs move overseas. The American economy would benefit—and political opposition to growth-oriented policies would decline—if the country enacted programs that helped *all* displaced workers maintain the education and training critical to success in the information age, and then helped them relocate as necessary.

Underfunding and narrowness of scope are hardly the only problems plaguing the TAA programs. They also suffer from maladministration and from poor design. According to Brad Brooks-Rubin, a trade lawyer in private practice, the Department of Labor's "process for investigating

TAA petitions and reaching benefits qualification decisions has yet to
provide any reasonably clear and detailed explanations of who is, and
who is not, the type of worker covered by TAA."[4] Such a lack of guidance
is crippling in

> a benefits and retraining program for workers whose jobs are lost to foreign
> trade. . . . In general, when a group of at least three workers lose, or expect
> to lose, a job because of competition from imports, they petition for TAA
> benefits. Since 2002, workers whose jobs are lost to a shift in production to
> an overseas plant, or whose facility is an upstream or downstream supplier
> to a qualifying firm, may also apply. To be certified for benefits, [a complex
> and detailed] statutory standard must be met. . . . Obviously, in order to
> demonstrate that all aspects of this standard have been met, a significant
> amount of complex information is required: information about the industry
> involved, the specific plant or location in question, and all of the workers
> joining the petition.[5]

Many workers who lose their jobs apply to the Labor Department for
the scant TAA funds and end up suing the government in the Court of
International Trade—with at least an occasional appeal to the Federal
Circuit—in large part because the criteria for eligibility remain unclear.

The Court of International Trade's Judge Delissa Ridgway expressed
her frustration in an unusually harsh rebuke of the Labor Department for
its handling of a claim from some former Chevron employees. She characterized Labor's performance as a "dereliction of duty" and a "failure to
fulfill its overarching obligations." She emphasized that the workers'
long, hard, four-year slog toward certified eligibility

> is not a case of "better late than never." The record here—perhaps
> mercifully—does not reveal the current employment status of these Work-
> ers, or how (and with what success) the men have endeavored to support
> themselves and their families in the years since their termination. But, as a
> general principle, the effectiveness of trade adjustment assistance depends
> upon its timeliness; and the effectiveness cannot be measured in dollars
> alone. There is a very human face on these cases. Workers who are entitled
> to trade adjustment assistance benefits but fail to receive them may lose
> months, or even years, of their lives. And the devastating personal toll of
> unemployment is well-documented. Anxiety and depression may set in,
> with the loss of self-esteem, and the stress and strain of financial pres-
> sures. Some may seek refuge in drugs or alcohol; and domestic violence is,
> unfortunately, all too common. The health of family members is compro-
> mised with the cancellation of health insurance; prescriptions go unfilled,
> and medical and dental tests and treatments must be deferred (sometimes
> with life-altering consequences). And college funds are drained, then
> homes are lost, as mortgages go unpaid. Often, marriages founder.[6]

In addition to her evident sympathy for these displaced workers, Ridgway also noted the danger to public policy inherent in Byzantine TAA application processes: "Trade adjustment assistance programs . . . historically have been, and today continue to be, touted as the *quid pro quo* for policies of free trade. But Congress and the Labor Department break faith with American workers if trade adjustment assistance programs are not adequately funded and conscientiously administered."[7]

Nevertheless, when the dust finally settled on Chevron's former workers, the outcome satisfied their needs without a trek to Lafayette Park. Others were not so lucky. Several relatively recent appellants have been on a *five*-year track: Former employees of Quality Fabricating applied for TAA funds in 2001. The Labor Department turned them down, but the Court of International Trade ordered Labor to provide them with benefits. In 2006, the Federal Circuit concluded that the Court of International Trade lacked jurisdiction to review Labor's relevant determination, and reversed.[8] A few years earlier, two sets of otherwise unrelated employees—gaugers on an oil pipeline and chocolatiers—shared a timetable in their abortive pursuits of TAA funding. Both sets lost their jobs in 1999. Labor denied both applications, but the Court of International Trade ruled in the workers' favor twice. The Federal Circuit reversed both cases in 2004.[9]

It is possible, of course, that the complicating factor in all three cases was that the Court of International Trade ruled for the workers over Labor's objections—an outcome that the Federal Circuit has yet to sustain. Workers who lose everywhere seem to move through the system faster. Former employees of Sonoco applied in 2002. It took only a bit more than two years for the Labor Department, the Court of International Trade, and the Federal Circuit to agree upon their ineligibility for TAA funds.[10] Something seems seriously amiss with TAA.

TOWARD LIBERAL FLEXICURITY

Why are the TAA programs such orphans? Logic suggests that they should be quite popular. They should be politically popular because they both protect workers and take the heat off corporations who move specific jobs to locations where workers can perform them more efficiently. They serve the inherent American sense of fairness by refusing to make a subset of American workers bear the full brunt of the overall increase in prosperity. They help mute the criticisms of some of free trade's harshest critics. And they help reallocate both skills and workers in directions favoring our own comparative advantage. Yet, political leaders are often much more eager to take credit for backward-looking protectionist measures that retain specific American jobs at the expense of economic growth than for forward-looking TAA measures that help specific American workers while serving the needs of the broader economy. Why?

One answer is that there is little credit to claim for the existing narrow, underfunded, poorly designed, poorly administered, ineffectual TAA programs, but such an answer is facile. The real question is why, given the enormous potential popularity latent in TAA, no one has embraced their cause and tried to craft a functioning program. The answer to that deeper question may lie in a combination of history and in the odd hybrid motivation behind TAA. Twenty years ago, trade policy scholars Judith Goldstein and Michael Borrus provided a historical review that may contain the key to understanding America's traditional inattention to TAA programs.

> The origins of the country's adjustment policies trace to a cognitive model of the proper relationship between state and society. . . . At their heart, trade adjustment policies reflect post–New Deal political norms. They are essentially compensatory. The state "pays off" industries and labor groups adversely affected by trade policy from a hopefully ever-expanding "pie." TAA was buttressed by the notion that if trade policy was going to affect constituents adversely, they were entitled to state aid. To understand TAA only as a method of selling trade liberalization, however, is to fail to appreciate the welfare function the program has played. . . . TAA was a program of transfer payments or redistribution offsetting the cost of trade liberalism. In this way, TAA acted as both a welfare policy and a way to diffuse potential opposition to liberal trade policies. . . . Adjustment assistance (or a functional equivalent) is a necessary ingredient in a liberal United States trade policy. Where an unregulated market leads to visible economic upheaval, the cognitive basis of liberalism will be questioned—the legitimacy of the free trade norm will be cast into doubt. Therefore, some agency must play the critical role of "buying off" potential opposition to state policy in order to protect the liberal norms of United States trade policy.[11]

In stark political terms, the consensus view of American TAA programs has long been that they are a concession that liberals make to advocates of government planning in order to secure the planners' tacit acceptance of a liberal trade regime. Given that characterization, the orphan status of TAA in America is easy to understand. Who would claim such an ugly bastard?

No one, perhaps, in the United States, but beauty is always in the eyes of the beholder. Denmark is a small country with a proud socialist tradition that has adopted a very liberal trade regime, at least with respect to its EU partners. In 1994, Denmark's center-left government delivered a bouncing baby adjustment assistance program, lovingly named "flexicurity" after its parents, flexibility and security. With that delivery, Denmark replaced the European preference for permanent payments to the unemployed with the American preference for time-limited unemployment insurance, pressuring displaced workers to find new jobs. The government also developed significant retraining and relocation assistance programs—programs that a center-right government maintained when it took office. Among other things, these programs assign each unemployed Dane to a labor consultant. The *Wall Street Journal* reported approvingly: "If a person hasn't found work after a year, their consultant 'activates' them, proposing specific training or work experience—and reducing benefits if they don't comply. . . . The nationwide success rate: About two-thirds of Danes who are laid off have a new job within a year." It continued:

> Its unusual mix of the free market and big government has helped Denmark cut its unemployment rate in half, from about 10% in the early 1990s to U.S.-style levels of under 5% now. The economy has been relatively robust, growing 3.4% last year. Meanwhile, France and Germany are at or above the Danish jobless rate of a decade ago. Even though Danes are among the most easily laid-off workers in Europe, polls show the country's workers are the most secure about their future. . . . Danes change jobs more frequently than any workers in the developed world except Americans and Australians. . . . Most Danes believe they can always find work in their fluid labor market. In the interim, they get security from a dole that replaces up to nine-tenths of their last wage, the highest level in Europe. Critics say the experiment might not be easy to replicate. For one thing, Denmark is small, with just 5.4 million people. And close-knit Scandinavian countries historically have had a higher tolerance for taxes. The system isn't cheap: Denmark spends about 4.4% of its GDP every year on supporting and retraining the jobless, the most expensive labor-market policy in the world.[12]

Flexicurity is well tailored to Denmark's own needs, successful, and *expensive*.

It is also a wake-up call to liberals. American support for free trade peaked in the 1990s. President Bill Clinton and House Speaker Newt Gingrich (R-GA) elevated economics over politics when they removed free trade from the arena of partisan bickering and worked together to gain ratification of the WTO and NAFTA treaties. The Bush steel tariffs put trade back in play in 2002. Democrats have been running hard in the protectionist direction ever since, and more than a few Republicans have followed. While much of the recent protectionist sentiment has been mere populist sloganeering, some of its proponents' concerns are legitimate. It *is* unfair to expect blindsided workers to pay the full cost for America's prosperity, and it *is* unreasonable to expect people to flounder in uncertainty while economic theories move between equilibria.

Transitions, even transitions to better states, involve pain—and such pain is rarely shared equally. Advocates of liberal trade must choose: Fight to the death against protectionists, bribe narrow interests with countervailing measures or safeguards, accept expensive government plans like flexicurity, or draft TAA plans in which the government provides guidelines, incentives, and, if necessary, subsidies to private-sector entities willing to help America's displaced workers retrain and relocate. The Danes showed how "big government" social planners can craft adjustment assistance programs of which they are proud. Liberals must now do likewise by following the last of these options.

Occasionally, a glimmer of hope does arise. In January 2007, Senator Max Baucus (D-MT) assumed the chairmanship of the Finance Committee, proposing "A Democratic Trade Agenda." Amidst his general push for freer trade, he explained that:

> When it comes to helping workers, we must make TAA program . . . more reflective of today's innovative economy. TAA is our commitment that America will provide wage and health benefits while trade-displaced workers retool, retrain, and find better jobs. And a renewed TAA must do what today's program does not. TAA must be available to the eight out of 10 American workers who make their money in services professions; and it must apply to all workers displaced by trade, not just those affected by free-trade agreements. In fact, we should seriously examine the idea of expanding TAA into "GAA"—Globalization Adjustment Assistance that would offer benefits not only to workers displaced by trade, but to those displaced by all aspects of globalization.[13]

Will Baucus's call lead the country to focus on forward-looking adjustment rather than on backward-looking protection? As even Baucus conceded, "Some think that the new Democratic congressional majority will be bad for trade policy," because "some candidates criticized trade in their campaigns."[14] Only time will tell.

All of these matters, of course, fall far beyond the purview of the Federal Circuit. The Federal Circuit's role in the TAA programs, as in most matters on its trade docket, is that of a detached, distant observer. Federal Circuit trade rulings tend to focus on matters of pure procedural law: Are the agency's regulations reasonable in light of the statutory instructions that Congress gave it? Did the agency apply its own regulations appropriately? Did the Court of International Trade overstep its bounds by second-guessing the agency or abdicate its responsibility by failing to do so? And if the Court of International Trade was right to rule, did it rule correctly? None of these questions implicate substantive trade policy even indirectly. Trade policy decisions are highly political, and both Congress and the president play intimate roles in shaping it. Agencies like the ITC, the Commerce Department, Customs, and the Labor Department play lesser roles in adding flesh to congressional and presidential directives that are often skeletal. The role of the judiciary is limited.

Nevertheless, the basic institutional competencies of Congress and the courts suggest that at least a brief consideration of trade policy in the context of the Court of International Trade and the Federal Circuit is appropriate for observers of those courts. In trade, as in all matters, Congress is at its best when drafting rules of general applicability and at its worst when it attempts to anticipate how these rules might apply in specific cases, particularly specific atypical cases. Courts are excellent places to see the effects that general rules have on specific parties. Nothing within congressional view can hold a candle to Judge Ridgway's observations, on the ground with displaced workers and officials from the Labor Department, that our current TAA programs don't work. The Federal Circuit may not be an ideal place to study trade policy, but it is a place where real people and real companies bring real disputes that emerged from the trade policies that the United States *has*. The information that these parties bring to the court *should* inform the future shape of our policies.

TOWARD THE BLACK MARKET

For those who nevertheless remain unconvinced of the propriety of mentioning trade policy and the Federal Circuit in the same breath, there is yet another connection: the internationalization of intellectual property. International issues arose at least twice in our exploration of patents, first in the limitations that the Agreement on Trade-Related Aspects of Intellectual Property Rights (TRIPS) placed on our ability to experiment with potential patent reforms, and then when BlackBerry maker RIM forwarded territoriality as a defense to competitor NTP's allegations of patent infringement.[15] These incursions of international law into the patent realm are interrelated. RIM's territoriality argument, although insufficient for it to win its case, did win enough to illustrate a critical point: U.S. patents operate *only* within the United States. Other national patent systems maintain similar territorial limitations. When patent rights, which possess some but not all attributes of personal property, evaporate at the border, commercial curiosities abound. Products that were legal in one country become infringements in another. Monopolies become competitive markets by crossing a border; prices plummet and opportunities for arbitrage or smuggling arise. Trading partners contemplating such anomalies often conclude that some sort of a treaty might be in order. Recent attempts to internationalize IP rights have led to numerous bilateral, multilateral, and reciprocal treaties, as well as to guidelines that may someday lead to harmonized IP systems; TRIPS is but the most important example.

The Federal Circuit plays important roles in two aspects of the internationalization of IP: the policing of domestic black markets and the reform of patent systems abroad. Its respective role in these two areas differs markedly. In the former, it plays its familiar role in appellate adjudication. In the latter, it serves at times as a muse for those trying to reform their patent systems, at others as a fury from which the reformers flee.

Black markets have been around for a long time. They arise when an otherwise legal product becomes illegal because of some irregularity in a commercial transaction. In the IP context, black markets begin when a manufacturer located outside the United States produces a legal product that is protected by a U.S. patent, copyright, or trademark, but not by an IP right in its country of origin. As long as the manufacturer also sells the product abroad, U.S. IP law has nothing to say about the matter. When anyone then tries to bring that product into the United States, however, it becomes an illegally infringing product. Trade in such patented products within the U.S. violates the IP laws *and* the trade laws, thereby creating a black market. Gray markets are similar, except that the original manufacturer holds the applicable U.S. IP right, but made and sold the product abroad in a manner that prohibited third parties from importing it into this country.

The Federal Circuit's role in policing such activity is familiar. IP owners can bring an infringement case in district court and *at the same time* file a claim at the ITC under Section 1337 of the Trade Act (known as "337 cases"). The Federal Circuit hears all 337 appeals directly from the ITC. When the IP right in question is a patent, it also hears the appeal from the district court's ruling. Judge Rader has explained:

> Patent law affords a patentee several alternative remedies against a purported infringer. For alleged domestic infringement, a patentee can file an action in a district court. For alleged infringement through importation, a patentee can also file an action in a district court or in the ITC. In fact, a patentee can bring suit both in a district court and in the ITC against an alleged infringer who is importing an allegedly infringing product. The two forums offer a patentee different types of remedies. In a district court, a patentee can seek an injunction and damages. With respect to infringing imports, however, the patentee must take the additional step of requesting the U.S. Customs Service to enforce the district court judgment by seizing the offending goods. In the ITC, the patentee may not seek money damages, but the ITC automatically enforces its judgment by directing the U.S. Customs Service to seize any infringing imports.[16]

These simultaneous attacks on foreign alleged infringers create some interesting opportunities for strategic litigation. Domestic producers have long availed themselves of these dual paths to gain maximum leverage over their foreign competitors. The Supreme Court's ruling for eBay in May 2006,[17] however, enhanced trial judges' discretion over injunctions in patent cases, but did nothing to alter the course of 337; the ITC can effectively enjoin infringement by ordering Customs to impound all infringing products. That twist introduced some new strategic opportunities. By August 2006, the *Wall Street Journal* had spotted a trend.

> Section 337 is poised to take its own turn in the protectionist limelight by potentially crippling the U.S. wireless-phone industry. Other high-tech companies could follow. . . . All of these companies are seeking an edge against their rivals via "exclusion orders," which would ban the import of products said to violate U.S. patent (yes, patent) law. . . . Incredibly, all of this takes place separately from normal judicial proceedings on patent infringement or validity. Most of the cell-phone cases mentioned above are also in court on patent-infringement grounds, but these cases can take years and are subject to lengthy appeals. The ITC tries to discharge Section 337 cases in about a year, and will not wait for the courts. . . . The big picture here is that the ITC has emerged as the patent bar's venue of choice to evade this year's Supreme Court decision in *eBay*.[18]

To throw just an added touch of irony into this "protectionist limelight," the petitioners in 337 cases don't even have to be American; anyone holding a U.S. IP right can play. As a result, 337 cases are the mechanism of choice for Japanese companies seeking to keep Chinese products away from American consumers (to pick just one example).[19]

If the *Journal* is correct in its trendspotting, 337 cases could be the face of the future. A tidal wave of trade cases could wash ashore the Federal Circuit's docket, changing the complexion of the court's caseload. What such a wave of 337 cases would not do, however, is either change or add much substance to the Federal Circuit's patent jurisprudence; claim construction, validity, and infringement analyses all proceed precisely as they would in a district court case. Judge Rader also explained that in "section 337 proceedings relevant to patent infringement, the ITC follows [the Patent Act] and the case law of this court."[20]

TOWARD THE GLOBALIZATION OF INNOVATION

When it comes to IP treaties, the Federal Circuit's role is subtler. Although some of the older IP treaties predate the Federal Circuit by a century or more, the globalization of IP ratcheted many notches forward in the

1990s. In particular, TRIPS went into effect on January 1, 1995, along with
the main WTO treaty.[21] TRIPS essentially took the basic structures of
American and European patent and copyright laws and enshrined them
as international standards. Signatory countries, including many that had
never before had IP systems, or whose IP systems were structurally quite
different from those prevailing in the developed world, agreed to conform
to the IP norms dominant in advanced industrial economies. That agreement, in turn, led to a reinvigoration of numerous older treaties and organizations capable of creating an alphabet soup of acronyms on par with
those prevalent in any other area of government activity. It also led many
countries to rewrite their IP laws, redo their IP systems, and rethink their
approaches to IP.

The most obvious effect of the growth of international IP law is the
growth of international IP lawsuits—suits that, when filed in the United
States, invariably work their way onto the Federal Circuit docket. So, for
example, when Jan Voda filed suit in the Western District of Oklahoma
alleging that Cordis Corporation was infringing his U.S. patents and
Judge Tim Leonard agreed to extend the trial to cover Voda's parallel allegations that Cordis's foreign subsidiaries were infringing his Canadian, European, British, French, and German patents, Cordis appealed
to the Federal Circuit.[22]

The court had to conduct two distinct analyses to determine whether or
not Judge Leonard had correctly allowed Voda to bundle his complaints
together. The first was relatively straightforward. U.S. law has some
pretty clear rules about when plaintiffs may combine different claims into
a single suit. For the most part, these rules consider the similarity of the
legal issues and facts relevant to the claims, the convenience of both parties, and the conservation of judicial resources. The second analysis required a full-blown inquiry into international law. What were our treaty
obligations to these other countries? How would they feel about having
U.S. courts adjudicate their patent disputes? How would the United
States feel if other countries started adjudicating disputes about infringements of U.S. patents occurring on U.S. soil? Such notions of international
"comity" are standard fare in suits implicating international and foreign
law, and they are likely to arise with increasing frequency as the pace of
IP law's internationalization quickens.

Such questions can also be complex and contentious. In Voda's case,
Judge Gajarsa concluded that foreign patents provide patentees with bundles of rights that differ from those that Congress built into the American
Patent Act; that if U.S. courts were to start hearing foreign patent cases,
they might compromise both existing treaty obligations and the broader
cause of international comity; and that several other factors also pointed

against letting Voda bring his foreign patent claims to Oklahoma.[23] Judge Newman disagreed with him on most counts.[24] Judge Prost agreed with Gajarsa. As the first Federal Circuit panel to consider the question, its ruling now binds all subsequent panels—unless the Supreme Court decides to intervene.[25]

In addition to its role as the key U.S. tribunal in an area of law with growing international implications, however, the Federal Circuit also enters the fray in an entirely unfamiliar guise. The Federal Circuit's role in this new internationalization of IP is as a model. Countries around the world—particularly around the developing world—needed crash courses in patents and copyrights. What better place to look for such a course than the United States, and who in the United States is better positioned to provide the patent course than the Federal Circuit?

To pick just one example, albeit a particularly influential one, consider the broad international ripples of an early exchange between the Federal Circuit and Congress. On January 17, 1967, the PTO granted the pharmaceutical company Roche a patent on a chemical that turned out to be the active ingredient in Dalmane, a popular sleeping pill. In the years before TRIPS pushed the United States to change its own patent laws and to extend the life of a patent to the international norm of twenty years, U.S. patents lasted only seventeen years. Dalmane was thus set to enter the public domain on January 18, 1984.

Under the patent laws, any generic drug manufacturer that chose to develop a product chemically identical to Dalmane could launch it that very day. Unfortunately for the generics, patent law wasn't the only thing keeping their products from the market; they also needed clearance from the Food and Drug Administration (FDA) before legally selling a pharmaceutical product. In early 1983, Bolar Pharmaceuticals decided to get its ducks in a row early. It began to experiment with the patented chemical so that it could develop a generic equivalent to Dalmane, submit it to the FDA, and launch as soon as the patent laws permitted. Roche sued, claiming that its exclusive patent rights to make, use, and sell precluded Bolar's experimentation and testing—both, after all, forms of use. The district court disagreed. On appeal to the Federal Circuit, Judge Philip Nichols posed the question and its answer quite succinctly:

> The district court correctly recognized that the issue in this case is narrow: does the limited use of a patented drug for testing and investigation strictly related to FDA drug approval requirements during the last 6 months of the term of the patent constitute a use which, unless licensed, the patent statute makes actionable? The district court held that it does not. This was an error of law.[26]

Nichols's conclusion caused quite a bit of consternation. If Roche was right, its patent provided de facto exclusivity long beyond its seventeen-year lifespan; generic competitors needed time to develop and test products, and if they couldn't even start until the patent expired, they certainly couldn't launch upon expiration. At the same time, though, Roche and other branded manufacturers raised a similar point. They weren't allowed to launch products as soon as they received patents, because they too needed FDA clearance. Wasn't the time that they recaptured after the patent's expiration something of a payback to the time that they lost to the FDA?

The year 1984 was an excellent time to be asking such questions, because Congress was busily rethinking many aspects of the patent system. Roche and Bolar each seemed to raise reasonable concerns. Nichols, however, was right about the law. The patent laws required Roche to lose part of its patents' valuable life, but precluded Bolar from competing for sales of some public domain drugs. Congress realized that the policy we had was not the policy we wanted—on both grounds—and reformed the law. The Hatch-Waxman Act of 1984 restored to patentees some of the patent life lost to the FDA, eased the entry of generic manufacturers by allowing them to free-ride on the results of the patentee's safety and efficacy testing as long as they could show that their product was "bioequivalent" to the original, and allowed generic companies to make and use the patented product, even though the patent hadn't yet expired, in order to demonstrate the requisite bioequivalence.[27] Congress thus overruled the Federal Circuit by statute.

These provisions have proved to be popular around the globe, despite some interesting complications. Their popularity is easy to understand. Many people believe that there is a general "right" to drugs, including those under patent, that far exceeds any general right to mechanical, electronic, or other patentable technologies unrelated to health. The Hatch-Waxman provisions improve the efficiency of drug markets and speed the transition from markets monopolized by high-priced patented drugs to competitive markets open to generic producers. Over the past two decades, many countries have adopted analogous provisions, known in the international arena as "Bolar provisions" in honor of the generic drug company whose loss impelled Congress to act rather than the American legislators who did the acting.

The complications are somewhat subtler. One of the structural aspects of American patent law that TRIPS enshrined is its unitary approach, applying a single set of standards, and providing a single set of rights, to patents and patentees from all industries and all parts of society. According to TRIPS, "patents shall be available and patent rights enjoyable without discrimination as to . . . the field of technology,"[28] subject to a few provisos and exceptions. Hatch-Waxman established a set of rules that apply only to drug patents, thereby discriminating as to the field of technology. Shouldn't TRIPS have required the United States to repeal Hatch-Waxman? Perhaps, but once again that great refuge of trade law saved the day: everything is compliant until the WTO says otherwise. Hatch-Waxman was safe unless and until challenged. That challenge eventually came, but not to the United States. In December 1997, the European Community and its member states challenged the Canadian implementation of the Bolar provisions. The WTO ruled in Canada's favor on narrow, technical grounds.[29] Nevertheless, many members of the international community saw that ruling as a statement that all Bolar provisions are TRIPS compliant and as a green light to adopt their own implementations; India, for example, trumpeted its 2005 arrival in the Bolar provision club both loudly and proudly.

Many countries have studied the American experience in patent law when developing their own patent systems. In some cases, international consensus seems to be forming that the United States arrived at the right answer; the Bolar provisions are a case in point. In other areas, the U.S. answer strikes most other countries as wrong; few if any are as liberal with software and business method patents as is the United States. The analysis preceding the Federal Courts Improvement Act's establishment of the Federal Circuit has led different countries in different directions. Over the past few decades, a number of countries have introduced specialized patent courts. At a bare minimum, patent litigation follows a path somehow different from other civil suits in Australia, Chile, China, Germany, Japan, the Netherlands, Panama, Peru, the Philippines, Singapore, South Korea, Spain, Thailand, Turkey, and the United Kingdom,[30] although much of this specialization has occurred at the trial level. The lack of circuit splits in these countries mooted at least part of the motivation for a specialized appellate court, but the specialized nature of patent law remained enough of an issue for them to agree with the American conclusion that patent litigation warrants special treatment. In all of these areas, the U.S. experience plays an important instructional and illustrative role, and the Federal Circuit figures prominently in many of the illustrations.

The key questions of international IP, though, are not questions that implicate the Federal Circuit in any significant way. TRIPS imposed an IP framework that appeared appropriate for advanced industrial economies upon economies at varying levels of development, just as the world was leaving the industrial age and entering the information age. While IP rights have proved their mettle wherever countries have tried them, and the developing world will be better off for having adopted them, the specifics of the TRIPS framework remain suspect in many ways. Are the TRIPS frameworks for patents and copyrights appropriate for developing economies, or would different approaches to IP provide a better fit?

Consider India's attempt to use its patent system to promote manufacturing, access, and employment, rather than innovation. Throughout the 1950s and '60s, Justice Rajagopala Ayyangar studied the patent systems of various countries, and he concluded that Germany's weaker patent laws had helped promote its chemical industry to a position of world leadership. He asserted that India's strategic and public policy interests in food and medicines mandated weak protection for innovations in those areas and proposed allowing patents only for process improvements, not for new products. He recommended provisions that would allow India to convert an individual patent's exclusive rights into a compulsory license, if necessary, to serve the public welfare; provisions that would require a patentee to work his invention in India in order to retain the patent; and a patent life as short as five years in some cases, and never more than fourteen years in any case. India's Patent Act of 1970 adopted all of those recommendations.[31]

Ayyangar thus demonstrated a careful consideration of the bargain that the public was striking with its innovators when it granted them exclusive rights in exchange for their innovations, set them within the context of his own country, and reached some nonstandard conclusions and recommendations. That the system produced notable successes in the areas of generic drug manufacturing and almost nowhere else is more likely a function of the starkly statist economic system in which India embedded it than of Ayyangar's ideas themselves. The imposition of a developed-world framework on TRIPS signatories suggests that Ayyangar's recommendations may be the last attempt to tailor IP rights to developing-world needs.

That same lack of experimental ability may hinder the United States—and other developed economies—as we begin to consider the sorts of changes to IP law that the shift from an industrial to an information economy might entail. The Federal Circuit may provide a reasonable view of those issues as they unfold; some hints are already evident. For the most part though, international organizations are likely to provide the best views of international IP. National institutions will inform the matter as each country determines how best to participate in this internationalization, but no single national institution will loom as large in the considerations of international IP as the Federal Circuit does in discussions of American patent law. Whereas the Federal Circuit's primary role in trade law is as an observer, its primary role in the international IP arena is as something to be observed.

TOWARD A TEST SCORE

These considerations lead to an unanswerable question: What can we say about a black-box test of the Federal Circuit's trade jurisprudence? The impossibility of deriving a meaningful answer stems not from the question itself, but rather from its context. When we looked at patents, we were able to split the policy box from the law box, evaluating Congress on the policies and focusing the Federal Circuit's evaluation on the law. A similar test of the Federal Circuit's fidelity to the limited role that Congress assigned it in the trade system might be feasible, but the answer would be meaningless. The congressional policy box—with occasional "help" from the president—is so badly corroded that it is hard to evaluate any of its individual components.

The policy we want is free trade, leading to economic specialization and comparative advantage and tempered by functioning adjustment programs. The policy we have is freer today than it has been throughout much of history, but the trade laws are directed primarily toward enforcing its unfree components. Tariffs and duties are impositions on the free market, albeit impositions generally permitted under prevailing rules. As a practical matter, the United States overuses these permitted impositions and finds problems in need of remediation far more often than they could actually exist. The policy we have seeks most of its political palliatives by helping narrow interest groups lock in their positions of the past rather than by helping them adjust to the present and prepare for the future.

The Federal Circuit has narrow authority to review the agencies charged with administering these laws. What would constitute a good black-box score under such circumstances? Recall that one of the conditions for such a test is the ability to know what the box should output before running the test (or at least to recognize whether an output is right or wrong). Under the circumstances surrounding tariffs and duties, the difference between a right decision and a wrong one is hard to recognize— which may explain why neither the Supreme Court nor the Federal Circuit has had much to say about substantive matters of trade law, and even the Court of International Trade spends most of its time reviewing agency procedure. Amendments and tariffs put in place for political reasons in evident violation of WTO rules or other international obligations make testing even murkier. And TAA programs, perhaps the only component of U.S. trade law that could promote liberal market capitalism were they overhauled to do so, are currently designed and administered so poorly that scoring is impossible.

Given these limitations, the best thing that the Federal Circuit can do is to heed Finger and Nogués's advice to the maximum extent that Congress permits: The court can insist that the ITC consider the welfare of all relevant components of the U.S. economy—and of the economy as a whole—before recommending countervailing or safeguard duties. Such transparency in agency actions *might* lay bare the political calculus and provide ammunition to those promoting forward-looking "fairness" via adjustment rather than backward-looking "fairness" via protection. In the final analysis, the trade policy we have is not the trade policy we want. The Federal Circuit can contribute little to improving the state of U.S. trade policy, other than to shine an occasional spotlight on the absurdities of a government working overtime to raise consumer prices, disburse corporate welfare, and lock workers into obsolete jobs.

9

✝

It's Good to Be the Government

FROM LONGSHANKS TO LINCOLN

In the Year of our Lord one thousand, two hundred and seventy-two, on the sixteenth day of November, His Royal Highness King Henry III of England passed to his grave. His son Edward, whose great stature had earned him the sobriquet "Longshanks," ascended the throne by the divine right of the one true God, with only a soupçon of assistance from William the Conqueror, founder of the dynasty to which Edward was heir. The cry rang out throughout the land: *The King is dead! Long live the King!* Edward, alas, could not hear his loyal subjects, for he was in the Holy Land on a taxpayer-funded Crusade against Saracen heathens. He returned to London in 1274, was crowned King Edward I in Westminster Abbey, and ruled until his death in 1307.

During his thirty-five-year reign, Edward conquered the Welsh, warred with the French, crushed the Scots, and exiled England's Jews. Nevertheless, historians seem favorably disposed toward Edward I—the greatest of the Plantagenets—a benign monarch who cared for the welfare of all who were English, Christian, and loyal. As if to prove his enlightened nature, Edward enacted numerous legal reforms, many curtailing the feudal system's most grievous excesses.

Among these notable legal reforms, one stands out. Edward I formalized an idea that had been floating around Europe for quite some time, the idea that "the King can do no wrong." Edward reasoned that those who rule by the will of God must necessarily possess at least some of God's infallibility. Those who question the statements or actions of a divine-right king must therefore be in the wrong. Given that conclusion, Edward saw no reason to allow any commoner to hail the king into court. He promulgated a law that persists to this day: the English Crown is immune from suit unless the Crown itself deigns to waive this immunity. Citizens with complaints against the Crown must petition individually for such a waiver. The sovereign's immunity from suit is an established part of the common-law heritage underpinning the Anglo-American legal tradition.

Now, one might think that this rule is fine for the Anglo portion of the Anglo-American tradition, where the spirit of Edward remains alive in the information age in the personae of Queen Elizabeth II and her fine progeny. But what of the American portion? Didn't we do away with all such claptrap when we disassociated ourselves from George III's "history of repeated injuries and usurpations, all having in direct object the establishment of an absolute tyranny"[1] in which the king could do no wrong? Didn't we develop an entire constitutional system based upon the rejection of infallible, hereditary, divine-right kings? Surely, one must conclude, we Americans dispensed with this immunity long ago, deriving as it does from a premise that we reject outright. Alas, one would be wrong. King Edward's legacy, known today as the "doctrine of sovereign immunity," is alive and well.

So what? While our government may not govern by divine right, it still has to govern—and governing requires special powers. Private citizens who conscript each other into military organizations, levy mandatory taxes against each other, or incarcerate each other are *criminals*. Governments that do these things are simply governing. The very nature of government is the monopolization of certain powers that are undesirable in general, but that remain necessary to protect and to serve the citizenry. The government *must* enjoy immunity when exercising these powers, even as private citizens who do likewise get sued—and lose. What's the big deal?

The big deal is precisely that the sovereign immunity doctrine is *not* about the government's exercise of its exclusive powers. Sovereign immunity shields the government from lawsuits for its everyday activities. Suppose you sign a contract with the government, perform your end, and the government refuses to pay you. Suppose a government agency leases an office in your building and refuses to pay rent. Suppose a government official, on official business driving a government car, slams into you on the highway and totals your car. Suppose you're a government employee and the government decides to withhold your salary. Suppose the government adopts your patented, copyrighted, or trademarked innovation for itself. Can you sue the government? Most people assume that the answer is yes, agreeing with Chief Justice John Marshall that it is "a sound principle," for example, "that when a government becomes a partner in any trading company, it devests itself, so far as concerns the transactions of that company, of its sovereign character, and takes that of a private citizen."[2] Most people would infer that a government agency signing contracts, leasing office space, hiring employees, driving on the highway, or infringing IP rights was acting as a private citizen—and thus deserved the same treatment as a private citizen. Surely, they would conclude, the law can't immunize the government from those sorts of liability.

They would be wrong—or at the very least, they would be *mostly* wrong. American law applies this distinction to *foreign* sovereigns. American courts recognize the immunity of other sovereigns acting as sovereigns. When foreign governments engage in commercial activities, however, American courts treat them as commercial enterprises, not as foreign governments.[3] When it comes to *domestic* sovereigns, however, American courts draw no such distinction. Sovereignty is sovereignty and immunity is immunity, and no suit may proceed sans waiver.

Therein lies the truly insidious nature of the sovereign immunity doctrine. Sovereign immunity shields the government from everyday behavior. And it applies not only to the federal government but to *all* domestic sovereigns—the federal government, the fifty state governments, the recognized Indian tribes, and all of their agencies, services, and companies. Sovereign immunity shields state universities and Indian casinos from liability for behavior that could sink a private university or casino. That is, it shields them from liability unless they waive their sovereign immunity. But the rules for waiver themselves are fairly intricate, and what sounds like a waiver to the common ear rarely waives *all* aspects of immunity. When suing a sovereign, there's always a catch—a special rule, a special court, a special remedy, a special *something*. Citizens never get to treat the government like a fellow citizen—even when the government behaves not only like a private citizen but like an *irresponsible* private citizen. Most people—or at the very least, most citizens—would find this situation both appalling and absurd, if only they knew how widespread it was (and could become).

But even in the American system of representative government "of the people, by the people, for the people,"[4] citizens don't get to make the rules; sovereigns do. And from the moment that Edward I first expounded it, sovereign immunity has been wildly popular among sovereigns everywhere. It is still widely accepted even among those, like the government of the United States, who no longer claim to rule by divine right. Nevertheless, and despite accepting the sovereign immunity doctrine in principle, the extreme forms of sovereign immunity have long stuck in the American craw.

Professor Erwin Chemerinsky neatly summarized the sticking points at a Stanford Law School symposium in 2001:

> American government is based on the fundamental recognition that the government and government officials can do wrong and must be held accountable. Sovereign immunity undermines that basic notion. The doctrine is inconsistent with . . . a central maxim of American government: no one, not even the government, is above the law. The effect of sovereign immunity is to place the government above the law and to ensure that some individuals who have suffered egregious harms will be unable to receive redress for their injuries.[5]

Chemerinsky's presentation was something of a lamentation, for even though "all of this seems so clear and obvious" to him, "sovereign immunity is not fading from American jurisprudence; quite the contrary, the Supreme Court is dramatically expanding its scope. . . . I do not foresee the Supreme Court eliminating sovereign immunity any time soon. The trend, unquestionably, is in the opposite direction."[6]

The trend was not always thus. In 1946, Justice Felix Frankfurter dissented strongly when a majority of his colleagues supported the sovereign State of Utah's right to declare itself immune from suit in federal court. Frankfurter saw this decision as a dangerous drift in the wrong direction, reversing a trend toward moral and responsible government that had long been under way.

> This immunity from suit without consent is . . . an anachronistic survival of monarchical privilege, and runs counter to democratic notions of the moral responsibility of the State. . . . While during the last seventy-five years governmental immunity from suit, as a doctrine without moral validity, has been progressively contracted, the Court now takes a backward step by enhancing a discredited doctrine through artificial construction.[7]

The "progressive contraction" of which Frankfurter spoke had actually begun more than ninety years earlier, driven initially by expediency rather than by morality. In the earliest days of the republic, citizens with a grievance against the government had to petition Congress for redress—much as Britons still petition the Crown. That setup let the sovereign take care of everything in one fell swoop. Congress could waive sovereign immunity, rule on the citizen's claim, and behave accordingly, or maintain its immunity and send the citizen packing whether or not his claim were otherwise viable. Needless to say, this situation worked well neither for citizens nor for an increasingly busy Congress.

In 1855, Congress passed the Claims Court Act, creating (as its name implies) the Claims Court, also known as the Court of Claims, the forerunner of both the contemporary Court of Federal Claims and the Federal Circuit. That Act represented a broad waiver of sovereign immunity—sort of. Citizens could now petition this new court to hear their claims against the government, but only if they claimed that the government owed them money because of a contract or a statute. Citizens claiming that the government's negligent behavior had damaged their property still had to go directly to Congress. Even those citizens who "won" their cases in front of the Claims Court couldn't avoid a trip to Capitol Hill, because Congress didn't really trust this new court very much; it retained to itself the power to decide whether or not to cut the citizen a check after reviewing the Claims Court's ruling.

Six years later, and with all due respect to Edward I, a long-shanked *American* leader, mired at the time "in the midst of unprecedented politi-cal troubles," entered the debate. Though some might have thought that other issues had risen to the forefront of public attention, Abraham Lincoln devoted much of his first State of the Union Address to the pressing problem of judicial reform. Among his many observations about ways to improve American justice:

> It is important that some more convenient means should be provided, if possible, for the adjustment of claims against the Government, especially in view of their increased number by reason of the war. It is as much the duty of Government to render prompt justice against itself in favor of citizens as it is to administer the same between private individuals. The investigation and adjudication of claims in their nature belong to the judicial department. Besides, it is apparent that the attention of Congress will be more than usually engaged for some time to come with great national questions. It was intended by the organization of the Court of Claims mainly to remove this branch of business from the halls of Congress: but while the court has proved to be an effective and valuable means of investigation, it in great degree fails to effect the object of its creation for want of power to make its judgments final. Fully aware of the delicacy, not to say the danger, of the subject, I commend to your careful consideration whether this power of making judgments final may not properly be given to the court, reserving the right of appeal on questions of law to the Supreme Court, with such other provisions as experience may have shown to be necessary.[8]

Lincoln's proposal seemed straightforward. He disliked some of the stronger implications of sovereign immunity and recommended an institutional way around them, a limited waiver that would serve justice while reducing the congressional workload. Two years later, Congress granted the Claims Court the authority to issue final declarations without forcing a Hill detour upon victorious claimants—though the savings in shoe leather were minimal because a Claims Court victory still required a detour by the Treasury Department for an official estimate of the government's bill. Congress removed that detour a few years later. A trend was clearly under way. "The doctrine, that of governmental immunity from suit, which, whatever claims it may have, does not have the support of any principle of justice,"[9] was eroding, at least in the American half of the Anglo-American tradition.

The erosion continued. In 1887, Congress passed the Tucker Act,[10] formalizing the Claims Court's powers and allowing it to hear claims that the government "took" private property without just compensation in violation of the Fifth Amendment,[11] along with statutory and contract claims. Eventually, Congress even dropped an 1863 abomination prohibiting Indian tribes from pressing their not-insignificant claims against the federal government in court; 1949's Indian Tucker Act finally allowed the Claims Court's judges, rather than Congress, to hear tribal claims. And in the Little Tucker Act, Congress allowed citizens with small statutory or contract claims against the government to sue in their local federal district courts rather than having to schlep to Washington, though those who enjoy a good schlep were still welcome at the Claims Court.[12] Along the way, the Supreme Court issued numerous rulings reflecting, according to Frankfurter, "a climate of opinion which ha[d] brought governmental immunity from suit into disfavor."[13]

That climate did not dissipate in 1946, the year in which Justice Frankfurter lamented the ending of the trend. In fact, 1946 was the year that the U.S. government finally admitted that maybe—just maybe—it might occasionally "do wrong" in the sorts of ways that give rise to tort liability, such as negligent behavior by a government official. That year, Congress passed the Federal Tort Claims Act (FTCA),[14] allowing American citizens to file tort suits in federal district courts *against their own sovereign government* for the first time in American history. Over the next decade, Congress twice elevated the stature of the Claims Court, so that by 1956 it stood on par with all other federal courts. That elevation continued in 1982, when Congress married the Claims Court's judges and *appellate* jurisdiction to the Court of Customs and Patent Appeals to create the Federal Circuit, a uniquely powerful court officially tied with its twelve sister circuits as the "second most powerful" court in the country. The same Federal Courts Improvement Act that created the Federal Circuit also created a *new* Claims Court, known today as the Court of Federal Claims, to inherit the *trial* portion of the old Claims Court's jurisdiction. Not bad for an institution that began life as Congress's distrusted handmaiden. All told, the progressive weakening of sovereign immunity continued for several decades after Frankfurter issued his warning.

But trends change. Although this one started before Lincoln and ran well into the Reagan years, the turn away from sovereign immunity was always more illusory than real. Through it all, the basis of the sovereign immunity doctrine had remained untouched. Even as Congress agreed to waive sovereign immunity in one class of claims after another, and the court charged with hearing many citizens' cases against their government grew in dignity and in stature, no one ever challenged a sovereign's fundamental right to *refuse* to be sued. In fact, waivers tend to strengthen the existence of that right. The entire doctrine of sovereign immunity rests upon the Crown's immunity from suit *without consent*. Waiver—whether in the form of the Tucker Act, the Little Tucker Act, the Indian Tucker Act, the FTCA, or the various other smaller statutes running throughout the U.S. Code allowing citizens to sue the government—*is* consent. No matter how many waivers Congress issues, the doctrine's health remains intact. And a healthy doctrine can always wake up one morning, join a gym, and pump itself up.

As Professor Chemerinsky noted, the trend in recent years has shifted markedly in the other direction. The Rehnquist Court developed an affinity for the sovereign immunity doctrine, particularly, though not exclusively, when it shields sovereign states from congressional edicts. This turn earned the Court accolades from those who fancy themselves staunch defenders of states' rights, while dismaying virtually everyone else. Judge John Noonan of the Ninth Circuit Court of Appeals even began to wonder whether "decisions that return the country to a pre–Civil War understanding of the nation establish a more perfect union."[15]

> Are decisions just that shield not only the states but lesser appendages of the states from paying for the wrongs they commit? Do decisions that leave the elderly and the disabled with inadequate remedies for unequal treatment establish justice? Do decisions that dislodge patents, copyrights, and trademarks from assured protection insure domestic tranquility? Do decisions that deny Congress the power to protect the free exercise of religion secure the blessings of liberty? Do decisions that leave women less protected by the law than men achieve any of the constitution's ends? The rhetorical nature of these questions points to the answers I give.[16]

This contemporary trend in the life of the sovereign immunity doctrine has brought the Federal Circuit into conflict with the Supreme Court on at least one significant occasion. A private citizen sued a Florida state board for patent infringement. This "board" wasn't engaged in a special government role; it was essentially a bank that administered a tuition prepayment program for Florida residents. Nevertheless, the board insisted that it was immune from suit. The trial judge disagreed,[17] as did the Federal Circuit.[18] As Judge Noonan alluded, however, the Supreme Court saw things differently; as a result, even commercial state agencies may now infringe patents with impunity.[19]

Conflicts of this sort are in no way unique unto the Federal Circuit. People sue government agencies, and entities that are arguably government agencies, all the time and all over the country. Trial judges routinely rule on such issues, granting immunity to some and denying it to others. All thirteen appellate courts review such rulings, and the Supreme Court reserves the right to reverse any of them. Though the application of sovereign immunity to a patent suit may have particular significance to the Federal Circuit, the sovereign immunity component of the Supreme Court's ruling does not. State agencies, including those engaged in undeniable commercial activities in direct competition with private companies, are now immune from *all* federal suits unless their state legislatures choose to waive that immunity.

Nevertheless, the Federal Circuit *does* have a unique role to play in the contemporary development of the sovereign immunity doctrine, and it does provide a unique window for those wishing to see the doctrine in action. Under the Tucker Act, the Court of Federal Claims remains the only federal court authorized to hear claims for monetary compensation from the federal government—with two notable exceptions. District courts located around the country can hear cases involving government torts (under the FTCA) and small amounts of money (under the Little Tucker Act). Anyone else, including an Indian tribe, suing the federal government for breaching a contract, for taking property without just compensation, or even for a disputed income tax refund *must* file suit in the Court of Federal Claims—and take all appeals from there to the Federal Circuit. The Federal Circuit also hears all appeals from Little Tucker Act cases, whether the trial occurred in a district court or at the Court of Federal Claims, and the court's review of the work of various government boards of contract appeals, the Merit System Protection Board, and the Court of Appeals for Veterans Claims gives it even more cases in which the government is the defendant. Even though the government's creation of each of those tribunals was an inherent waiver, sovereign immunity issues continue to creep into the law in curious and unexpected ways.

The bottom line is that any case involving a sovereign implicates special rules, rules that demonstrate the tension between a doctrine born of medieval Christian theology and an information age born of liberal market capitalism. Their interactions provide the data necessary to address several key questions: Is the sovereign immunity doctrine leading to good public policies? Is it easing government functioning at minimal cost to the public? Or is it imposing unacceptable costs by hiding traps for the unaware throughout our economy? Few contemporary institutions provide better vantage points from which to explore these questions than the Federal Circuit. That vantage point will allow us to see whether our government is entering the information age as a responsible corporate citizen—

clinging tightly to its unique governmental powers while assuming common responsibilities when it engages in common activities—or we are returning to "a pre–Civil War understanding" of sovereign immunity.

CUE THE VETERAN

Sovereign immunity is a potent weapon. Some sovereigns use their immunity as a guillotine, decapitating claims (and at times claimants) for the simple crime of opposing the king. Others use their immunity as a whittling knife, standing for suit, losing, and then cutting away undesirable portions of the judgments against it. And then there are those who simply leave their loaded weapons lying around, carelessly ignoring their latent destructive power until they hurt an innocent passerby—often one that the government would have preferred to help.

Witness one Daniel J. Sandstrom, veteran.[20] Sandstrom was one of the too many young men that our government sent to fight in Vietnam. He served with distinction in the U.S. Army for three years, receiving various combat decorations including the Purple Heart. Sandstrom's heroism came to an abrupt end in February 1969 when he lost both legs above his knees. Amputation above the knee is particularly debilitating. Amputees who retain their knees can often benefit from prosthetic devices and learn to walk again. For people like Sandstrom, no such hope remained; his amputation meant that he would never again walk. Congress recognized this distinction when it drafted the statutes governing our treatment of veterans. Disability payments are proportional to the severity of the disability, and veterans who lose their knees receive larger payments than those capable of walking with the aid of prostheses.

Veterans law, though a topic that few law students study and even fewer lawyers practice, is critical to our national security. A national government owes a unique debt to the young men and women who dedicate their youth to defending it. That debt only grows when those soldiers sustain permanent, debilitating injuries while fighting for the nation's defense. Furthermore, the lifetime care that the government promises its soldiers is a significant portion of the deal that entices young men and women to enter the military, and disability payments are an important part of that compensation package. Such economic inducements are particularly significant to liberal nations relying upon volunteer soldiers for their defense—as the United States does today. Veterans benefits, a key portion of veterans law, therefore implicate *both* the government's moral obligations *and* its utilitarian economic interests. Good public policy screams for a package of benefits substantial enough to induce would-be recruits to enlist and for government diligence ensuring that all veterans receive the benefits that they are due. Sovereign immunity appears to be particularly out of place when contemplating a disabled veteran's entitlement; the government's moral obligation alone should be enough to trump immunity. Alas, such is not always the case.

The United States maintains a program of suitable inducements and diligence—at least in theory. Congress has drafted numerous statutes governing veterans benefits and veterans rights. The Secretary of Veterans Affairs is a member of the president's cabinet. The Department of Veterans Affairs (VA) website describes its goal as providing "excellence in patient care, veterans benefits and customer satisfaction. We . . . are striving for high quality, prompt and seamless service to veterans. Our department's employees continue to offer their dedication and commitment to help veterans get the services they have earned. Our nation's veterans deserve no less."[21] And just in case the VA falls short of these objectives, Congress has passed a few statutes requiring it to be user-friendly; the VA may be the only government agency required to help its clients sue it.[22] When hearing such suits, the VA—part of the executive branch, not the judiciary—maintains its own internal trial courts and appellate courts. The Court of Appeals for Veterans Claims (CAVC), an independent executive agency, reviews their work. A veteran who remains unsatisfied with a CAVC ruling may ask the Federal Circuit to ensure that the CAVC interpreted the law correctly—thereby obtaining a judicial review of a final executive decision. Finally, Congress tends to pass new statutes enhancing at least some veterans benefits every time it sends new troops into combat.

All of this attention and care suggests that when it comes to veterans, the government has waived a fair amount of its immunity. And it has—but as Sandstrom learned the hard way, a fair amount is not always enough. In Sandstrom's case, the problem began with the statute governing disability payments.[23] In 1969, the VA classified Sandstrom as a totally disabled veteran, entitled to "special monthly compensation" because of the "anatomical loss of both lower extremities at levels or with complications preventing natural knee action."[24] That designation was incorrect; the VA should have noticed that Sandstrom had no knees, and classified him as having "suffered the anatomical loss of both legs so near the hip as to prevent the use of prosthetic appliances."[25]

Fortunately for Sandstrom, the VA is not beyond admitting its mistakes—though it can take some time. In his case, it took a quarter of a century. The VA finally noticed that Sandstrom had lost his knees and was therefore entitled to higher benefits than he had been receiving, *in 1994*. That acknowledgment of error corrected the matter going forward; Sandstrom collected the appropriate monthly amount for nearly a decade before the Federal Circuit heard of his claim. That claim dealt with the one lingering sticking point: The government had shortchanged Sandstrom for twenty-five years. Wasn't he now entitled to collect the difference?

Sandstrom thought so. And after only two more years of deliberating, the VA agreed. It took until the middle of 1996, but the VA finally admitted that it had made a "clear and unmistakable error," or a CUE—a term of art in veterans law—when it concluded that a man without knees would face "complications preventing natural knee action." What's more, the VA notified Sandstrom that, sovereign immunity be damned, though the king can do no wrong, the United States government would do the right thing. The VA told Sandstrom to expect a check for the full amount that the government had shortchanged him—all twenty-five years' worth.

True to its word, the VA cut Sandstrom a check for $55,542. Now, $55,542 might sound like a fair chunk of change, but what it doesn't sound like is a round number. Where did it come from? The VA went back to some historical compensation tables. In 1969, for example, the government had sent Sandstrom $550 per month, when it should have been sending him $625. In 1996, to fix its CUE, the VA gave Sandstrom $75. The VA then looked at the numbers for 1970, and once again gave Sandstrom the difference—and so on and so forth, making up the shortfall for each month between 1969 and 1994 to reach its grand total of $55,542.

Sandstrom was not amused. He noted what everyone knows—that $75 just didn't buy as much in 1996 as it had in 1969. Sandstrom demanded payment in real dollars, which retain their value over time, rather than in nominal dollars, which retain only their number. The rate of inflation governs the relationship between real and nominal dollars; interest paid at the rate of inflation allows payments to retain their real value. Many public—and private—programs incorporate this inflation-sensitive interest rate into payments as annual cost-of-living adjustments. The VA's disability compensation schedule was one such program, and Sandstrom contended that the government should compensate him as if he had simply saved his money in an inflation-adjusted account. In fact, by 1996, Congress had raised the compensation levels for disabled veterans to almost 450 percent of what they had been in 1969; the gap between the category in which the government had been paying Sandstrom and the correct category stood at $336 per month. Were the government to have truly restored the amount that it had been shortchanging this disabled veteran, it would have paid him $336 per month for the slightly more than twenty-five years of its CUE and cut him a check in excess of $100,000.

But Sandstrom didn't rest his request solely on sensible economics. He also made a legal argument. Congress had told the VA point-blank, "for the purposes of authorizing benefits, a . . . decision that constitutes a reversal or revision of a prior decision on the grounds of clear and unmistakable error has the *same effect* as if the decision had been made on the date of the prior decision."[26] In other words—and even simple, clear statutes typically require other words to be truly simple and clear—Congress told the VA to correct CUEs in ways that have the "same effect" as if it had never erred. To Sandstrom, the law seemed clear; the VA should have paid him in real, rather than in nominal, dollars. The VA agreed that the law was clear: "Monthly compensation rates are established by law. These monthly rates are then adjusted, usually once a year, to reflect increases in the cost-of-living. While we can understand your argument, we have no choice in the matter. We can only pay the rates authorized by law."[27] Sandstrom, who thought that he had pointed to the applicable law, asked the VA which law it had in mind. The VA responded that his request for payment in real dollars was really just a request for interest, and that the law prohibits it from paying interest, even in cases of CUE, because of—you guessed it—sovereign immunity.

That was the VA's final word on the matter. Sandstrom worked his way through the system, all the way to the CAVC, and kept getting the same answer: it's against the law for the government to pay interest. Sandstrom appealed to the Federal Circuit. Could the VA really be right about the law? Could it possibly be that even after the government waived its sovereign immunity to let veterans sue it for benefits past due; even after the VA admitted that it had committed not only an error, but a clear and unmistakable error; and even after Congress told the VA to clean up its CUEs in ways that had the same effect as correct decisions, sovereign immunity *still* made it illegal for the government to fulfill its obligations to a disabled veteran?

In any rational world, the answer would have been clear. *Of course the VA should have paid Sandstrom in real dollars!* To do anything else would violate the government's moral obligation to care for veterans disabled in the service of their country, reduce the economic incentives that we offer to convince young men and women to volunteer for the military, and thwart the clear intent of the statute. In short, the VA's insistence upon paying nominal rather than real dollars was unconscionable as a matter of public policy. The Federal Circuit, however, is part of the judiciary; law, rather than either reason or policy, governs its world. The judiciary is not supposed to wonder about policy matters and change laws to effect good public policy—even when it's clear to all what the proper policy should be. A court's job is simply to determine what the law is, and to make sure that the executive branch is applying it appropriately. And in this case, the court's role was constrained even further. Congress gave the Federal Circuit fairly little flexibility in reviewing VA decisions. Unlike decisions appealed from trial courts (whether federal district courts in patent cases, the Court of Federal Claims, or the Court of International Trade) where the Federal Circuit reviews some factual issues, all legal issues, and the application of the law to the facts, Federal Circuit review of CAVC decisions is restricted to legal questions.[28] And therein lay a problem, because the court had to concede that the "statutory language and longstanding principles governing sovereign immunity provide clear support for the VA's interpretation that payments to a veteran following a finding of CUE may not include interest adjustments."[29]

NO INTEREST

Those "longstanding principles" are indeed long standing. In April 1888, a unanimous Supreme Court rejected the claim of "Lutzarda Angarica de la Rua, executrix of the estate of Joaquin Garcia de Angarica, deceased," who had asked the court to order "Thomas F. Bayard, Secretary of State of the United States, to pay the petitioner the amount of the interest or income derived from a certain investment of money."[30] Justice Samuel Blatchford explained that her claim fell afoul of

> the well-settled principle, that the United States are not liable to pay interest on claims against them, in the absence of express statutory provision to that effect. It has been established, as a general rule, in the practice of the government, that interest is not allowed on claims against it, whether such claims originate in contract or in tort, and whether they arise in the ordinary business of administration or under private acts of relief, passed by Congress on special application. The only recognized exceptions are, where the government stipulates to pay interest and where interest is given expressly by an act of Congress, either by the name of interest or by that of damages.[31]

For the benefit of those still in doubt, Justice Horace Gray eliminated all subtlety two years later: "Interest . . . is not to be awarded against a sovereign government, unless its consent to pay interest has been manifested by an act of its legislature, or by a lawful contract of its executive officers."[32]

Anyone with even a modicum of economic understanding could be excused for thinking that this nonsense couldn't *still* be the law. These nineteenth-century cases all seem to assume that repayment of principal and payment of interest are two separate payments requiring two separate waivers of sovereign immunity. Today, everyone understands the effects of inflation, the relationship between nominal dollars and real dollars, and the importance of interest payments in assuring that compensation after a corrected CUE has the same effect as timely payments of the appropriate amount. The law should reflect that knowledge. The "no interest" rule seems even more out of place in the information age than does sovereign immunity itself.

Anyone who reached that conclusion would be right—yet wrong. There is no doubt that the law *should* reflect contemporary economic understanding. But that modality is emphatically a policy question, not a legal one. What the law *should* reflect and what the law *does* reflect are not at all the same thing. Nearly a century after his predecessors shot down Señora de la Rua, Justice Harry Blackmun summarized the sorry state and the long history of the no-interest rule—and its relationship to the general notion of sovereign immunity.

> As sovereign, the United States, in the absence of its consent, is immune from suit. This basic rule of sovereign immunity, in conjunction with the require- ment of an agreement to pay interest, gave rise to the rule that interest can- not be recovered unless the award of interest was affirmatively and sepa- rately contemplated by Congress. . . . The no-interest rule is expressly described as early as 1819, in an opinion letter from Attorney General William Wirt to the Secretary of the Treasury. . . .
>
> Prior to the creation of the Court of Claims, a citizen's only means of ob- taining recompense from the Government was by requesting individually tailored waivers of sovereign immunity, through private Acts of Congress. The administrative responsibility of hearing many of the claims was as- signed to the Treasury Department. . . .
>
> In creating the Court of Claims, Congress retained the Government's immunity from awards of interest, permitting it only where expressly agreed to under contract or statute. . . . [T]his Court has reaffirmed the notion [that] . . . "interest does not run on a claim against the United States."[33]

Blackmun prepared this summary to explain why, even after Congress had passed a special civil rights law that allowed the courts to force a de- fendant found liable for having violated a plaintiff's civil rights to pay the plaintiff's legal fees, and had further specified that in this respect "the United States shall be liable for costs the same as a private person,"[34] the government nevertheless maintained its favored position, and unlike a private person did not have to pay interest on those attorney's fees.

Once again, a Supreme Court ruling seemed to butt heads with com- mon sense. How in the world can anyone—much less a Federal Circuit judge or a Supreme Court justice—fail to appreciate that when Congress declares the federal government "the same as a private person" or tells the VA that its corrections should have "the same effect" as having never erred, the statutes mean precisely what they say. If interest payments are necessary to put the government on equal footing with private parties or to correct the government's error effectively, then so be it: let the govern- ment pay interest. How obtuse can the courts get? Does Congress have to hit judges over the head with a two-by-four marked "government inter- est payments" to get them to pay attention?

Apparently it does. In 1947, Justice Frank Murphy slammed the door on any application of common sense to the no-interest rule.

[I]n the absence of constitutional requirements, interest can be recovered against the United States only if express consent to such a recovery has been given by Congress. And Congress has indicated . . . that its consent can take only two forms: (1) a specific provision for the payment of interest in a statute; (2) an express stipulation for the payment of interest in a contract duly entered into by agents of the United States. Thus there can be no consent by implication or by use of ambiguous language. Nor can an intent on the part of the framers of a statute or contract to permit the recovery of interest suffice where the intent is not translated into affirmative statutory or contractual terms. The consent necessary to waive the traditional immunity must be express, and it must be strictly construed.[35]

Blackmun failed to see sufficient clarity in the Civil Rights Act, and by the time Sandstrom came calling to the Federal Circuit, Judge Lourie had already told Claudus Smith—a veteran shortchanged from 1961 to 1993 by a CUE misrating his eye degeneration as a 70 percent disability rather than as a 100 percent disability—that the

"same effect" language, which is at best ambiguous as to whether it refers to missed benefit payments only or missed benefit payments plus interest, is . . . not a clear waiver of the no-interest rule. Smith's appeal to public policy favoring liberal dispensation of benefits to veterans cannot change our conclusion. Public policy, no matter how compelling, cannot be a ground for finding a waiver in the absence of express statutory language. Smith's policy arguments essentially ask us to reform the law, but that is the role of Congress, not this court. . . . In sum, only express language can waive the no-interest rule, and the statutes asserted in this case lack such express language of waiver.[36]

The courts are helpless. Economically indefensible Supreme Court precedent binds them and requires them to ignore common sense, public policy, and clear congressional intent—as well as economics. When sovereign immunity is at stake, nothing else matters. Only Congress is authorized to act, and even Congress needs an occasional reminder of just how dangerous sovereign immunity can be—and just how detrimental it can be to the government's ability to help the people that it most wants to help.

Congress responded to Blackmun's comments about the apparent ambiguities in civil rights law by passing the Civil Rights Act of 1991. This time, Congress left nothing to chance. The Act's preamble declared: "The purposes of this Act are . . . to respond to recent decisions of the Supreme Court by expanding the scope of relevant civil rights statutes in order to provide adequate protection to victims of discrimination." The statute now explains that, in applicable cases that the federal government loses, the government is liable for "the same interest to compensate for delay in payment . . . as in cases involving nonpublic parties."[37] The Supreme Court got the hint and noted that Congress had superseded many of its civil rights rulings with the 1991 Act.[38] Congress had finally written the magic words allowing the courts to turn the policies we want into the policies we have.[39]

Congress really does have to go that far overboard when it wants to waive sovereign immunity. In Sandstrom's case, Congress just didn't go far enough. Judge Donald Ivers, who wrote the CAVC opinion rejecting Sandstrom's claim, seemed to recognize the logic of arguing that "same effect" should mean "same effect." The Federal Circuit's earlier ruling against Claudus Smith, however, bound him to rule against Sandstrom; the missing magic words proved fatal.[40] The Federal Circuit also saw the matter clearly, but was nevertheless unable to help. Judge Gajarsa, writing for a unanimous panel, expressed the court's frustration, showed where its sympathies lay, and then applied a binding if inequitable principle of law:

> Sandstrom submitted a number of arguments grounded in economics, logic, and public policy. His arguments have substantial merit as a matter of policy. Nominal dollars and real dollars are not the same, and late payment of devalued nominal dollars does not have the same effect as a timely payment. There is no question that Sandstrom is correct as a matter of economics and as a matter of logic. None of this is relevant, however, because the VA interpreted the existing law correctly.[41]

There lies but one tragic consequence of the anachronism known as sovereign immunity. Congress told the VA to correct its errors effectively. A veteran provided the VA with the precise formula necessary to effect that correction. The VA was sympathetic, but insisted that the law precluded effective relief. The courts agreed that the veteran was correct as a matter of economics, as a matter of logic, and as a matter of public policy—and then applied an inequitable but binding law. All three branches of the federal government knew that Sandstrom was correct. Yet Longshanks's legacy created a Kafkaesque trap, as poor Sandstrom bounced from one bureaucratic response to another, eliciting sympathy from all and ultimately losing.

Could there be any justification for such rulings? In truth, there might be one: the government's longevity. Were the government to lose a centuries-old claim, say, to an Indian tribe or an insurance company, interest liability could cripple the economy. Under such circumstances, a limitation on the interest award might be warranted. The current system inverts that treatment. The government should generally *pay* interest, with exceptions enumerated by statute. As things stand, the government generally *avoids* interest, with exceptions enumerated by statute. The government keeps its sovereign immunity weapon loaded and cocked, rather than letting Congress load it only when necessary. Outcomes like Sandstrom's are inevitable with a weapon as blunt and as powerful as sovereign immunity. Daniel Sandstrom is but one more victim of a weapon left loaded and unguarded.

Congress thought that it was helping disabled veterans recover from governmental incompetence so gross as to warrant the label "clear and unmistakable error." Instead, it sent a decorated soldier wandering legless through a maze of legal obtuseness. Few cases provide clearer illustrations of the ways that the policies we have can deviate from the policies we want. And even if Congress acts tomorrow to help future veterans avoid Sandstrom's fate, the ultimate problem will remain. The no-interest rule is a particularly odious manifestation of a flawed legal doctrine. The king *can* do wrong. The king should be liable for his mistakes. And the king's liability should include the interest necessary to effect real compensation. The King *is* dead. Long live government of the people, by the people, for the people! The time has come for it to stop acting like Longshanks and to start acting like Lincoln.

THE NAFI COMETH

It gets worse. For in the days of Lincoln, a new beast was born, a beast conceived long before Longshanks claimed immunity, gestating for lo those many centuries to emerge just as the Claims Court began tempering sovereign power in America. This beast, the dreaded NAFI, possesses the divine right of absolute immunity, yet cloaks this power from view while walking among the mortal citizenry.

Some may scoff. They may hear in the NAFI shades of the Chimera, "a thing of immortal make, not human, lion-fronted and snake behind, a goat in the middle, and snorting out the breath of the terrible flame of bright fire,"[42] a creature that though fierce, remains mythical. But they err. The NAFI has more in common with the great Roe, a "beast with the head of a lion and the body of a lion, though not the same lion."[43] Just as the Roe agglomerates parts from the king of beasts, so the NAFI agglomerates parts from our own American sovereign. To all the world, a NAFI looks like a standard government agency. But it is not; it is a NAFI. It is a government agency, yet not a government agency. As the agency that it *is*, the NAFI bears the full immunity of the sovereign. As the agency that it *is not*, it escapes the Tucker Act waiver by which Congress allowed the Claims Court to hear suits against the government.

Just ask AINS, Inc., an information technology (IT) company, about NAFIs. In April 1997, the U.S. Mint outsourced some of its IT needs to AINS. By the middle of 1999, their relationship had soured. AINS spent almost two and a half years navigating the Mint's contract dispute process, exhausted all internal appeals, and still believed that the Mint owed it more than half a million dollars. So AINS did what Abraham Lincoln would have wanted it to do: it sued this government agency in the Court of Federal Claims.[44] That's where AINS first heard the riddle: When is the government not the government? Answer: When it's a NAFI.

A NAFI is a "non-appropriated funds instrumentality." Appropriated funds are the dollars that Congress fights about every year when it prepares the federal budget. Most government agencies don't get to keep the money they earn. They return that money to the "general fund" under Congress's direct control. Congress then determines how to divide the money in the general fund among the various agencies. But NAFIs are different. NAFIs are at least essentially self-supporting. They put the money that they earn into a dedicated "revolving fund" and draw on that revolving fund to finance their operations. Though Congress reserves the right to claim any surplus in these dedicated revolving funds for the general fund—or even to terminate the NAFI's existence and seize the entire account—Congress rarely does so. Such restraint, however, is a two-way street. NAFIs that run perpetual deficits and return too often to the congressional trough for appropriated bailouts risk losing their exalted NAFI status.

The courts long ago decided that when the Tucker Act told citizens that it was safe to do business with the government despite sovereign immunity because "the United States Court of Federal Claims shall have jurisdiction to render judgment upon any claim against the United States founded . . . upon any express or implied contract with the United States,"[45] it meant only the parts of government funded by the annual appropriations process. The Tucker Act never waived sovereign immunity for self-supporting NAFIs; their immunity remains intact. Citizens who contract with NAFIs do so at their own peril. The NAFI—ironically represented in court by attorneys that the Justice Department pays with appropriated funds—can enforce the contract against the citizen, but the citizen can *never* enforce the contract against the NAFI. When AINS sued the Mint, the Mint responded that it was a NAFI and therefore immune from suit.

As a result, the only question that the courts considered was whether or not the Mint met the technical requirements for NAFIhood. (Cutting to the chase, it did.) Did AINS provide high-quality service to a client who simply refused to pay? Maybe. Was AINS a charlatan trying to squeeze its client for extra fees after providing shoddy service? Maybe. Does the truth lie somewhere in between? Maybe. But we'll never know, because no court ever examined these questions. And no court ever examined these questions because no court has the authority to consider them. NAFIs enjoy absolute immunity. Once a court determines that a government agency is a NAFI, the inquiry is over.

From whence did these strange creatures emerge and how did they enter U.S. law? It appears that the Romans knew of both sovereign immunity and NAFIs, although there is no indication that they ever put the two together. Justice David Souter dates the "natural law" conception of sovereign immunity back to Ulpian—the noted third-century jurist whose writings formed the basis first of Roman law, then of the Napoleonic Code, and today of the basic civil law governing most Continental European countries and their former colonies (including Louisiana and Quebec)—who wrote "the Emperor is not bound by statutes." Souter tracked that concept from Ulpian, through medieval jurists who extended it from the emperor "to a King, to the Pope, and even to a city-state . . . [developing] a theoretical model applicable to any sovereign body," into the writings of Thomas Hobbes, John Locke, and Samuel von Pufendorf, and finally to William Blackstone's *Commentaries on the Law of England.* Blackstone's four-volume tome, in turn, was widely considered the final word on English law in the 1780s, when our own founding fathers sat down to write the Constitution—though, at least according to Souter, the American conception of both sovereignty and immunity differed from the English view in a number of important ways.[46]

We have already seen how the story developed from there: from individual petitions to Congress, to the Claims Court Act of 1855, into Lincoln's first State of the Union Address, through numerous versions of the Tucker Act, and eventually to its present status, with monetary claims against the government triable only in the Court of Federal Claims and appealable only to the Federal Circuit. But we still haven't seen anything about NAFIs, and it remains a bit of a leap from emperors, kings, popes, and even city-states to the U.S. Mint. What happened? How did an American tradition that rejected the natural-law view of sovereign immunity, that rejected the divine right of the sovereign, and that generally recognized waivers of sovereign immunity as an important component of responsible government *still* create these absolutely sovereign creatures worming their way throughout the economy and contemporary society?

The answer returns us once again to Rome, where all roads do lead. Judge Lawrence Block, who had the unenviable task of telling AINS that the Court of Federal Claims—and by implication, all other courts—lacked the authority to hear its case, at least had the courtesy to explain the historical origins of his embarrassing conclusion:

> NAFIs have their origin in war. From the time of ancient Rome to the Europe of the seventeenth and eighteenth centuries, merchants, called "sutlers," have followed armies around and met ships of the navies in ports to supply provisions and contraband. The American Articles of War of 1775 authorized sutlers to sell troops items not provided by the government, such as "victuals, liquors, or other necessities of life," and regulated the sutlers hours, conduct and the quality of their merchandise.
>   [In 1862, Congress assessed sutlers] a fee, which was deposited in a post fund. This fund was administered by officers and its proceeds were used to aid indigent widows and children of deceased soldiers during the Civil War. This post fund was the first historically recorded NAFI. Because the sutler system was subject to abuses, such as fraud and corruption, Congress abolished the system and established trading posts and canteens on certain military posts subject to Army inspectors. . . . Although the Army regulated and operated these post exchanges [PXs], they were not considered instrumentalities of the United States because they were not funded by appropriated monies, but instead, were trading stores permitted to be kept at a military post for the convenience of the soldiers.[47]

NAFIs thus entered American law in the guise of PXs, institutions derived from a reform movement that the Lincoln administration and Congress had enacted to raise money for indigent Civil War widows and orphans—a program with intentions it is hard to fault. But good intentions pave roads leading to places far less pleasant than Rome. NAFIs, thus thrust onto the American political landscape, slowly started to make their presence felt. Their first step toward absolute immunity came in *Standard Oil v. Johnson*,[48] a short 1942 Supreme Court whose expansion of sovereign immunity was so subtle that even Justice Frankfurter failed to note it.

BEWARE THE NAFI!

The holding in *Standard Oil* was merely that PXs qualified for a federal government exemption from a California motor vehicle fuel tax, because "post exchanges as now operated are arms of the Government deemed by it essential for the performance of governmental functions," though the "government assumes none of the financial obligations of the exchange."[49] In short, it established that there are "government agencies" for which the government eschews financial responsibility—without even mentioning the sovereign immunity of such "agencies."

Shortly thereafter, the Court of Claims got into the act with a curious bit of sophistry: if the government never assumed financial liability for an agency, it could not have consented to let citizens sue that agency. In the first NAFI case, an Army PX had employed Emil Borden as its accountant. When Borden was unable to recover payroll funds stolen from his office, the PX simply withheld that amount from Borden's salary—without bothering to prove that he was liable for it. Borden sued to recover his salary. A majority of the court recognized that this case presented "a strange anomaly":

> For the Army to contend and to provide by regulation that it is not liable since it did not act in its official capacity would be like a man charged with extra-marital activity pleading that whatever he may have done was done in his individual capacity and not in his capacity as a husband.[50]

The court dismissed Borden's case anyway. In dissent, Judge Samuel Whitaker complained that

> [t]he majority recognize that [Borden] should have a right of action, but they feel compelled to hold that he has not by the decision of the Supreme Court in *Standard Oil*. . . . I do not feel so compelled. . . . Army regulations say exchange contracts are not government contracts, and, yet, the Supreme Court says that exchanges are "arms of the government." . . . By what authority does the Army say that their contracts are not government contracts?[51]

Five years later, the Pulaski Cab Co. sued the government over alleged breaches of its contract with a PX to provide taxi service within a post, but the ruling against Borden was binding; the Claims Court dismissed Pulaski's case on sovereign immunity grounds.[52]

Though Whitaker's view did not prevail and the NAFI doctrine became accepted law, he and his colleagues shared a belief that, were Congress aware of the ramifications of the doctrine, it would fix things, so that the policy we wanted would become the policy we had. This theme arose virtually every time that the Claims Court encountered a NAFI.[53]

The Court of Claims was trapped by its own bad law. The Supreme Court had ruled that although PXs were governmental agencies in some sense, they nevertheless retained their financial independence. Because of that financial independence, the federal government—or more specifically, the general fund—wasn't responsible for the PXs' finances. That relationship is hardly unique. In many ways, it mirrors the relationship between shareholders and corporations, where the corporate form shields individual shareholders from liability for the corporation's actions. The logical implication of *Standard Oil* should have been a governmental corporate shield. PXs operate independently of the federal government. The officer in charge of the PX doesn't run to Congress with budgeting decisions; he simply sets prices on goods and services, collects revenues, and then spends those revenues to keep the PX running. In a rational world, people doing business with the PX should conclude that the PX will pay its bills from those revenues and that, like all companies, if debts exceed revenues by too much for too long, the PX will go out of business. Creditors of a failed PX will then face the same meager options as do creditors of other failed businesses; those options do not include bothering the "owners," in the PX's case Congress and the general fund. Those who nevertheless choose to do business with the PX will therefore deal with it as they do with comparable small businesses, rather than as they do with the federal government: they will extend smaller credit lines on less-favorable terms to compensate themselves for the added default risk.

Apparently, only Whitaker caught this implication. Rather than telling Borden and Pulaski that a victory in court would obligate only the PX's funds and not the general fund, the court concluded that PXs, as NAFIs, were immune from suit. Rather than reading the Tucker Act to waive sovereign immunity to allow contractual and statutory suits against *all* government agencies, and then reading *Standard Oil* to limit a litigant's ability to collect its judgments to the NAFI's own revolving funds, the Court chose to read the Tucker Act as relating *only* to the general fund.

In effect, the Court of Claims created the NAFI *doctrine*—the application of divine right immunity to protect NAFIs from all lawsuits—from whole cloth. The Court of Claims applied poor logic and poor statutory construction to reach a misguided policy conclusion, and then unleashed it upon an unsuspecting public. But even when courts accidentally stumble into the realm of policy, the rules nevertheless bind them. The Court of Claims's rejection first of Borden's claim and then of Pulaski's made the NAFI doctrine real—and forced the court to apply it whenever anyone tried to sue a NAFI. The court needed help.

In 1966, Fritz Kyer came before the court. Kyer was a broker of wines and spirits who had done some work for the Grape Crush Administrative Committee, an agency that had established and maintained orderly conditions for the grape market to avoid unreasonable fluctuations in supplies or prices in the interest of producers and consumers from 1937 until 1964.[54] Though Congress had eliminated this particular blot on the free market in 1964, creditors contended that it expired with bills yet unpaid. Kyer was one such creditor. But the Court of Claims looked at the committee, concluded that it was (or at least, had been) a NAFI, and sent poor Kyer packing.

By this time, the court realized how out of hand the NAFI doctrine had gotten. It realized that it had unwittingly unleashed a dangerous policy doctrine upon an unsuspecting America, and appealed to the only people who could help it, the body actually charged with public policy decisions: Congress.

We are mindful of the fact that the result reached spells an unduly harsh outcome. Plaintiff has searched in vain for a forum in which the merits of his
claim might be aired. We add, though perhaps of little comfort, that the lack
of jurisdiction which plaintiff has faced at every turn is a matter which sorely
needs congressional correction.[55]

Four years later, Congress heard the Court of Claims' plea. Astound-
ingly, Congress *did not* eliminate the NAFI doctrine. Instead, it waived
sovereign immunity for PXs. Congress amended the Tucker Act so that it
now contains a phrase incomprehensible to anyone who has never encountered a NAFI: "An express or implied contract with the Army and
Air Force Exchange Service, Navy Exchanges, Marine Corps Exchanges,
Coast Guard Exchanges, or Exchange Councils of the National Aeronau-
tics and Space Administration shall be considered an express or implied
contract with the United States."[56]

That amendment, had it been in place a few years earlier, would have
helped Borden and Pulaski, though not Kyer. Since 1970, it has probably
helped keep PXs in line. What it did for the rest of us was hardly positive.
Congress placed its imprimatur on the NAFI doctrine. Only one slim
hope remained: the Supreme Court. The entire line of reasoning rested
upon the Court of Claims's interpretation of the 1942 *Standard Oil* decision. Perhaps if the Supreme Court ever reviewed that reasoning, it would
detect its deficiencies and correct them.

In 1976, *la veuve* Hopkins appeared before the Supreme Court on behalf
of her late husband. Mr. Hopkins had been a contract employee of the
Army and Air Force Exchange Service (AAFES)—a NAFI that Congress
had explicitly swept into the Tucker Act six years earlier—who claimed
that the AAFES had breached his employment contract. The AAFES
claimed that, despite the 1970 amendment, it was *still* immune from at
least this type of suit, because Congress had never meant to include employment contracts when it discussed "express or implied contracts." The
Supreme Court rejected this bit of sophistry and let Hopkins's suit proceed. Unfortunately for all but Hopkins, the Supreme Court also recognized the NAFI doctrine explicitly. It defined a "nonappropriated fund instrumentality" as a federal entity "which does not receive its monies by
congressional appropriation," and explained that while the 1970 amendment expressed a clear congressional intent "to afford contractors a federal forum in which to sue nonappropriated fund instrumentalities by doing away with the inequitable 'loophole' in the Tucker Act," it had done
so only with respect to those few NAFIs mentioned in the amendment. "It
is up to Congress to remedy this apparent harsh result."[57]

A year later, back at the Court of Claims, Judge Nichols noticed that "a
contract employee of an unappropriated fund agency can sue for back

pay, if deprived of it by legal wrong, but one appointed and enrolled in the ordinary non-contractual way cannot. There is no reason for this distinction. It is simply a matter of defective statutory draftsmanship. Someday, probably, it will be corrected."[58] Someday, perhaps, but not yet. Congress hasn't revisited the issue since 1970. Five years after Nichols closed on an optimistic if frustrated note, Congress merged the Court of Claims's appellate duties into the Federal Circuit, and the new court inherited the entire mess, with help along the way from the Court of Federal Claims's trial judges.

The Federal Circuit and the Court of Federal Claims were thus born having to deal with the NAFI doctrine. Congress and the Supreme Court had blessed the notion that at least most self-sufficient government agencies enjoy absolute immunity from suit. The judges left holding the bag did the only thing they could do: They began to craft rules that would help citizens recognize a NAFI when they saw one. Along the way, the courts met a number of NAFIs, as well as a number of agencies that claimed to be NAFIs but weren't. The Comptroller of the Currency, for example, claimed to be a NAFI when its landlord sued it for unpaid rent. The court disagreed and let the suit proceed.[59] The Board of Governors of the Federal Reserve fared better. The courts agreed that it is a NAFI and therefore an inheritor of the immunity due to divine-right kings (adding credence to the belief that Alan Greenspan's pronouncements emanated from Mount Sinai).[60] The Federal Housing Finance Board might have qualified as a NAFI, but Congress's willingness to bail it out with repeated injections of appropriated funds whenever it went broke cost it that exalted status.[61] Federal Prison Industries—a government-owned corporation created in 1934 to provide work simulation programs and training opportunities for inmates of federal correctional facilities—made the cut; an aggrieved contractor was unable to sue it.[62]

That's where things stood when AINS wandered into court complaining that the Mint had stiffed it. The courts decided that it was time to make the law clear—or at least as clear as possible under the circumstances. How do you know when you're dealing with a NAFI?

> A government instrumentality is a NAFI if: (1) It does not receive its monies by congressional appropriation; (2) It derives its funding primarily from its own activities, services, and product sales; (3) Absent a statutory amendment, there is no situation in which appropriated funds could be used to fund the federal entity; and (4) There is a clear expression by Congress that the agency was to be separated from general federal revenues.[63]

The Mint is a NAFI, and AINS cannot sue it. The specifics of their dispute will remain shrouded in mystery. No one will ever know whether the government held the line against a charlatan or stiffed an honest, hard-working citizen-contractor. In the divine world of sovereign immunity, facts are irrelevant.

The courts, at least, remain concerned about NAFIs, but recognize that they are helpless. Judge Block concluded his dismissal of AINS's claim with a chilling warning:

> One doubts whether our political leaders, our representatives, and certainly the general public, are aware of the problem that the extension of the NAFI doctrine presents. . . . It is indeed conceivable that the extension of the NAFI doctrine will ultimately increase the price of government goods and services by denying the efficiency of the market place to institutions, such as private enterprise funds, ironically established to mimic the market place.[64]

Judge Gajarsa conceded that Block's kind words were "likely to provide AINS with little solace. The government prevails because no judicial relief is available to contractors who choose to contract with NAFIs. Unless Congress waives a NAFI's sovereign immunity, the courts can entertain only the government's allegations of breach, not those brought by the contractor."[65]

Therein lies the sordid tale of the NAFI doctrine—and the reasons that it poses so grave a danger as we contemplate information-age economic policy. In 1993, Bill Clinton assumed the presidency vowing to reinvent government by reassessing the government's role in American life. He rejected the paternalistic view of "big government" plans that deliver services to citizens through faceless bureaucracies, and moved to a view of government as facilitator. In this view, government should assume responsibility for ensuring that citizens received critical services, but need not provide those services directly. Instead, it would engage in a variety of public/private relationships, including but hardly restricted to contracting, government-owned corporations, and genuine collaboration. Two years later, Newt Gingrich (R-GA) led the Republicans to a congressional majority promising a similarly reinventive approach to government— though one that differed with Clinton's on numerous specifics.

Clinton and Gingrich were both right—although neither of their political parties has ever championed more than a sliver of the necessary reinvention. Economic policy for the information age requires a certain amount of flexibility. Self-sufficient government agencies may be able to combine private-sector incentive systems with public-sector social commitments. They should proliferate—as they have been doing. But they can only constitute good public policy it they retain the commitment to responsible behavior that Abraham Lincoln shamed the rest of the government into accepting.

The NAFI doctrine is an impediment to the government reinvention necessary for success in the information age. At the moment, it remains an insignificant impediment only because no one knows about it. Most government agencies, including most NAFIs, pay most of their bills most of the time and resolve most of their disputes without litigation. In the case of NAFIs, there is no compelling legal reason for them to do so. When the Comptroller of the Currency claimed to be immune from suit for unpaid rent, the Court of Claims shot it down because it is not a NAFI. Had the Federal Reserve or the Mint refused to pay its rent, their landlords would have had no legal recourse. Even an explicit waiver of sovereign immunity built into the lease wouldn't help. Only Congress can waive sovereign immunity; an agency head who attempts to do so by contract is overstepping his or her authority by a wide, wide margin.

The NAFI doctrine is indefensible public policy. While the Court of Claims may have played a central role in its emergence, the matter is now far from judicial hands. The Court of Federal Claims and the Federal Circuit have no choice but to apply the law and to add yet another lamentation every time that a NAFI hides behind divine-right immunity. NAFIs, like mythical Roes, continue to bear the head of a government agency and the body of a government agency—but not the same agency. Few citizens are ever aware that the NAFIs they encounter are anything other than government agencies bound by the Tucker Act to stand behind their actions, and thus able to enter into meaningful contracts. The illusion is typically complete.

The time has come for more citizens to know about this anomaly, for more citizen complaints, and for congressional action to end the NAFI doctrine. The courts put Congress on notice of the doctrine's anomalies when Borden found himself out of luck more then fifty years ago. Perhaps the time has come for someone to put contractors on notice, as well. *Citizens: Beware the NAFI!*

10

✛

The Divine Dignity
of the Infringer

THE ELEVEN

A nomalies like the no-interest rule and the NAFI doctrine are interesting and disturbing, but the real action these days lies with fifty other domestic sovereigns: the states. In 1990, Congress passed a law called the Gun-Free School Zones Act of 1990,[1] making it a federal crime for anyone to possess a firearm in a school zone anywhere in the United States. This law was controversial for more than the obvious reasons. Beyond gun control, it generated controversy because it wasn't clear what gave Congress *the right* to make gun possession in a school zone a federal crime. Many people—including many who agreed with the sentiment behind the law—thought that that was the sort of activity that *states* typically regulated. If some state legislature wanted to legalize guns in the schoolyard, who was Congress to interfere? Congress claimed that the Constitution gave it the right to interfere in the Commerce Clause, which granted it the power "to regulate Commerce with foreign Nations, and among the several States, and with the Indian Tribes."[2] Though the connection between interstate commerce and firearms in school zones was arguably tenuous, Congress wasn't worried; the Supreme Court had stopped striking down Acts of Congress for violating the Commerce Clause in the earliest days of the New Deal.

That confidence was misplaced. On April 26, 1995, Chief Justice William Rehnquist announced that, by a five-to-four majority, the Supreme Court had determined that "[t]he Act neither regulates a commercial activity nor contains a requirement that the possession be connected in any way to

215

interstate commerce. . . . [T]he Act exceeds the authority of Congress."[3] With that declaration, the Rehnquist Court became the best friend that the states had had since the fall of the Confederacy some 130 years earlier.

The Supreme Court's rejection of Congress's tenuous Commerce Clause claim had nothing to do with sovereign immunity—but it did put the nation on notice that this Court would support the rights of the states against federal encroachment. It was but one step in a series that would soon change the relationship between the federal government and the states in a dramatic way—and in so doing change the relationship between America's domestic sovereigns and the citizens they serve. The next important step came two years later, as part of a dramatic *danse macabre* involving Congress, the Supreme Court, the states, two churches, and individual rights.

The first act opens in the mid-1980s. Alfred Smith and Galen Black have lost their jobs at a drug rehab facility in Oregon. Smith and Black are members of the Native American Church, a church whose sacraments involve ingesting small amounts of peyote—a controlled substance under Oregon law. When their supervisor discovers that two of his employees are violating Oregon's narcotics laws, he fires them. Oregon denies their claims for unemployment benefits. They sue the state. The Supreme Court agrees to hear the case.

Justice Antonin Scalia opens the second act in 1992:

> This case requires us to decide whether the Free Exercise Clause of the First Amendment permits the State of Oregon to include religiously inspired peyote use within the reach of its general criminal prohibition on use of that drug, and thus permits the State to deny unemployment benefits to persons dismissed from their jobs because of such religiously inspired use.[4]

Scalia concludes that it does. He explains that a general law that coincidentally prohibits a religious practice is hardly discriminatory and therefore cannot violate the constitutional guarantee of every citizen's right to exercise his or her faith. Congress is enraged. Within a year, it passes the Religious Freedom Restoration Act (RFRA) limiting the government's ability to interfere with the free exercise of religion—even under the guise of generally applicable laws.

Act 3 opens four years later, once again in the Supreme Court. A new character is on stage. In place of the small Native American Church, we find the mighty Catholic Church. Justice Anthony Kennedy sets the stage:

> Situated on a hill in the city of Boerne, Texas, some 28 miles northwest of San Antonio, is St. Peter Catholic Church. Built in 1923, the church's structure replicates the mission style of the region's earlier history. The church seats about 230 worshippers, a number too small for its growing parish. Some 40 to 60 parishioners cannot be accommodated at some Sunday masses. In or-

der to meet the needs of the congregation the Archbishop of San Antonio gave permission to the parish to plan alterations to enlarge the building. A few months later, the Boerne City Council passed an ordinance authorizing the city's Historic Landmark Commission to prepare a preservation plan with proposed historic landmarks and districts. Under the ordinance, the Commission must preapprove construction affecting historic landmarks or buildings in a historic district. Soon afterwards, the Archbishop applied for a building permit so construction to enlarge the church could proceed. City authorities, relying on the ordinance and the designation of a historic district (which, they argued, included the church), denied the application. The Archbishop brought this suit challenging the permit denial. . . . The Archbishop relied upon RFRA as one basis for relief from the refusal to issue the permit.[5]

The courtroom is thick with tension. Who will win this epic struggle? On one side stand the Catholic Church, the Free Exercise Clause, and Congress. On the other, the City of Boerne stands seemingly alone, protecting its prerogatives as part of the Texas sovereign to impose whatever zoning laws it chooses to adopt. The drama builds.

Will Kennedy announce that RFRA overruled *Smith* and that religious people and organizations are now exempt from all laws bearing even a tenuous connection to faith? Will he draw a sensible dividing line and announce that RFRA now protects behavior like Smith's, which is intimately intertwined with religious observance, but that it cannot override local laws for what is essentially a matter of parishioner convenience? Or will he sweep away RFRA in its entirety and reiterate the cold rule allowing local laws of general applicability to interfere with religious practice? A chorus of ghostly amici parade across the stage offering advice:

"Give every man thy ear, but few thy voice; take each man's censure, but reserve thy judgment."[6] "It is emphatically the province and duty of the judicial department to say what the law is. . . . This is of the very essence of judicial duty."[7] "This above all: to thine own self be true, and it must follow, as the night the day, thou canst not then be false to any man."[8]

Kennedy contemplates his options and their stakes. Endorsing RFRA in all its glory could eviscerate the states' ability to protect the public welfare. Drawing a line between observance and convenience would confirm Congress's right to elevate individual liberty above state regulation. Reiterating the *Smith* rule would elevate the power of the states over the rights of the individual, debilitate the Free Exercise Clause, chastise Congress, and slay RFRA. The longer Kennedy deliberates, the louder the ghostly voices become. Before succumbing to madness, he rules for Boerne. RFRA lies dead! Kennedy closes with a proud court's contumely:

RFRA is so out of proportion to a supposed remedial or preventive object that it cannot be understood as responsive to, or designed to prevent, unconstitutional behavior. . . . Sweeping coverage ensures its intrusion at every

level of government, displacing laws and prohibiting official actions of almost every description and regardless of subject matter. . . .

The stringent test RFRA demands of state laws reflects a lack of propor-
tionality or congruence between the means adopted and the legitimate end
to be achieved. [Under RFRA,] if an objector can show a substantial burden
on his free exercise, the State must demonstrate a compelling governmental
interest and show that the law is the least restrictive means of furthering its
interest. . . . If compelling interest really means what it says, many laws will
not meet the test.[9]

Final curtain. Supreme Court, Catholic Church, City of Boerne, bow.
Kennedy stands center stage. Audience applauds. House lights.

With opening night over, only the reviews remained. Some were
laudatory—but not all. An unexpected critic in San Francisco was particularly harsh. John Noonan had built his academic career as a scholar
of both Catholic canon law and American constitutional law, first at
Notre Dame and then at the University of California. He had spent
much of the 1960s, '70s, and '80s criticizing a line of Supreme Court rulings that the Warren Court started and the Burger Court continued.
This line of cases, the most famous of which are *Griswold v. Connecticut*[10] and *Roe v. Wade*,[11] established that individuals possess inherent
rights—rights that the Constitution recognizes and guarantees—to
make personal decisions without governmental interference. Noonan,
like many critics of these rulings, believed that even though the Ninth
Amendment guarantees that "the enumeration in the Constitution, of
certain rights, shall not be construed to deny or disparage others retained by the people," there is no constitutional right to privacy, and
that the Court overstepped its appropriate boundary by elevating individual autonomy over the legitimate regulatory authority of federal
and state governments. In 1986, President Ronald Reagan rewarded
Noonan's adherence to these principles by appointing him to the U.S.
Court of Appeals for the Ninth Circuit. But Noonan's loyalty was to a
philosophy rather than to a political agenda. He found himself as dis-
turbed by the Rehnquist Court's discovery of new rights for states as he
had been by earlier discoveries of new rights for individuals—again,
despite the Tenth Amendment's guarantee that "the powers not dele-
gated to the United States by the Constitution, nor prohibited by it to
the States, are reserved to the States respectively, or to the people."
Noonan's review of "the Battle of Boerne" was blistering.

[T]he Supreme Court, in repelling what it saw as an invasion of the judicial
domain by Congress, invented criteria for Congress that invaded the legislative domain. . . . [T]he Supreme Court, as the devotee of dignity and the

hitchhiker of history, has embraced with mistaken enthusiasm a doctrine of state immunity that is overextended, unjustified by history, and unworkable in any consistent way.[12]

Noonan was hardly content with that casual observation. He continued to follow the characters, perhaps awaiting a redemptive sequel. When Boerne and St. Peter's settled their differences, however, his quest for a redemptive sequel forced him to turn elsewhere. In particular, Noonan spied a critical factor lurking in the background, not only in *Boerne*, but in a whole line of Supreme Court cases that he disliked. That background factor was state sovereign immunity. Though the Constitution mentions neither sovereignty nor immunity, much less a doctrine of sovereign immunity, Noonan had the distinct "impression that some justices put the doctrine on a par with the constitution. . . . Immunity from private suits is, as the court has expressed it, 'central to sovereign dignity.'"[13]

Noonan reviewed many of the Supreme Court's recent pronouncements about the power and the dignity of the states, and about its evident decision to reign in congressional attempts to denigrate these fifty proud sovereigns. He believed that even though the Court didn't always discuss sovereign immunity, the concept was always lurking in the background. He found the missing piece in the Court's 1996 resolution of an odd dispute. Congress had passed a law allowing Indian tribes to open casinos only if they could reach agreement with the states that surrounded their tribal land. The Seminoles wanted to open a casino in Florida; Florida's government refused to negotiate on any terms. The Seminoles sued in federal court. Florida claimed immunity from suit under the Eleventh Amendment, which states, "The Judicial power of the United States shall not be construed to extend to any suit in law or equity, commenced or prosecuted against one of the United States by Citizens of another State, or by Citizens or Subjects of any Foreign State." The Supreme Court agreed. According to Chief Justice Rehnquist:

Courts have understood [the Eleventh Amendment] to stand not so much for what it says, but for the presupposition which it confirms. That presupposition, has two parts: first, that each state is a sovereign entity in our federal system; and second, that it is inherent in the nature of sovereignty not to be amenable to the suit of an individual without its consent. Federal jurisdiction over suits against unconsenting states was not contemplated by the U.S. Constitution when establishing the judicial power of the United States. . . .

The principle of sovereign immunity is a constitutional limitation on the federal judicial power. . . . The entire judicial power granted by the Constitution does not embrace authority to entertain a suit brought by private parties against a state without consent given.[14]

Noonan found this sentiment animating many of the Supreme Court's recent decisions favoring state sovereign immunity over congressional attempts to secure individual rights. He used that observation to fashion his own sequel, a feature-length docudrama of the people and the principles that the Rehnquist Court was trampling in pursuit of its state-centric agenda.

This simultaneous damage to individual rights and federal power is critical to understanding sovereign immunity. Noonan captured this simultaneity by opening his critique with sympathy for the people that the Court has hurt and closing it with a lamentation for the principles that the law has lost. The people do indeed deserve sympathy: a writer alleging that her ethnic-press publisher infringe her copyright; a professor alleging that his university discriminated against him because of his age; a female student raped by several of her college's football players against whom state authorities refused to take action—all were blocked from filing their suits in federal court because to do so would offend the dignity of a sovereign.[15] His lamentations likewise deserve to be sung:

> Why should a state not pay its just debts, why should it be saved from compensating for the harm it tortiously causes? Why should it be subject to federal patent law, federal copyright law, and federal prohibitions of discrimination in employment and not be accountable for the patent or copyright it invades, not accountable for its discriminatory acts as an employer? No reason in the constitution or in the nature of things or in the acts of Congress supplies an answer. The states are permitted to act unjustly only because the highest court in the land has, by its own will, moved the middle ground and narrowed the nation's power.[16]

That narrowing of national power is where the real action in sovereign immunity is today. Not in side effects like the no-interest rule or the NAFI doctrine, and not even in the Claims Court's modern progeny, the Court of Federal Claims and the Federal Circuit. No, the action today is in constitutional interpretation, and in particular, in the Supreme Court's decision to emphasize Tenth Amendment states' rights and Eleventh Amendment state immunity from suit, while ignoring Ninth Amendment individual rights. But Noonan's closing comments hint at why the Federal Circuit continues to play a central role in the sovereign immunity debate even in guises other than as the Claims Court's appellate successor. Roughly three years after announcing that the sovereign state of Florida was immune from the Seminoles' suit, the Supreme Court determined that Florida's sovereign immunity also protected it from suits alleging patent infringement.[17] And when patents are in the game, the Federal Circuit always takes center stage.

INFRINGEMENT IMMUNITY

Assuming center stage can take a while. In fact, the clash between patent rights and the Eleventh Amendment rose to the fore slowly, beginning with events that occurred more than thirteen years before the Federal Circuit was born. In 1969, the Patent and Trademark Office granted Marian Chew a patent on her newly invented method for testing automobile fuel emissions. Somewhere along the line, Chew came to believe that the State of California had incorporated her method—without her authorization—into its standard auto inspection procedures. She asked the state for royalties. When the Board of Control turned her down, she sued. California insisted that the Eleventh Amendment rendered it immune from patent infringement suits. The trial judge agreed. Chew then appealed to the Federal Circuit.[18] The clerk of court spun his assignment wheel, and it landed on Chief Judge Markey and judges Friedman and Nies. Judge Helen Nies affirmed the trial judge on behalf of a unanimous panel.

In 1990, of course, the current round of Eleventh Amendment jurisprudence was still a glimmer in the Supreme Court's eye; the trend toward narrower interpretations of immunity that ran from Lincoln through Frankfurter was ending, but no new trend had taken its place. That left a bit more ambiguity about the Eleventh Amendment's scope than one might find today—but not an infinite amount. Nies noted a number of then recent Supreme Court cases discussing the Eleventh Amendment.

> While the Justices have expressed differing opinions on the limits of congressional power to abrogate states' immunity . . . even under the broadest view . . . Congress must make its intent to do so unmistakably clear. . . . Congress must express its intention to abrogate the Eleventh Amendment in unmistakable language in the statute itself. Evidence of such congressional intent must be both unequivocal and textual.[19]

Congress knew that it couldn't override state sovereignty casually even before the Supreme Court buddied up to the states. When Congress passed the Patent Act, all that it had said was that patentees could sue "whoever" infringed their patents—hardly an unambiguous insistence upon ignoring so critical a divine right as a state's sovereign immunity.

Nies further explained that the absence of a clear congressional intent to hold states liable for infringement tied her hands. She rejected Chew's public-policy arguments as wholly inadequate—even "assuming that the constitutional and statutory goal of 'promot[ing] the Progress of Science and useful Arts' would be better effectuated by subjecting states to patent infringement suit in federal court."[20]

But Chew's public-policy arguments were not lost on everyone. Congress thought that she had made some pretty good points, and unlike the courts, Congress is supposed to let public policy sway it. In 1992, Congress translated Chew's policy argument into law. The Patent Remedy Act included clear, unambiguous, unmistakable language. Congress first clarified any lingering ambiguity: "The term 'whoever' includes any State, any instrumentality of a State, and any officer or employee of a State or instrumentality of a State acting in his official capacity."[21] Then it removed any lingering doubt: "Any State, any instrumentality of a State, and any officer or employee of a State or instrumentality of a State acting in his official capacity, shall not be immune, under the eleventh amendment of the Constitution of the United States or under any other doctrine of sovereign immunity, from suit in Federal court by any person . . . for infringement of a patent."[22] The congressional removal of ambiguity and doubt settled the matter. States were not immune from allegations of patent infringement.

Or so it seemed for several years—until the Floridians entered the picture. The 1990s were heady times for the State of Florida—Hurricane Andrew notwithstanding—and the growing state found itself embroiled in a number of legal squabbles. At least one of them involved allegations of patent infringement.

Back in the 1980s, Peter Roberts, founder of the College Savings Bank of Princeton, New Jersey, had devised a clever way to help people save money for college. His method was so clever that the PTO let him patent it. He incorporated it into a commercial product, the CollegeSure® Certificate of Deposit. But CollegeSure may not have been the only product on the market incorporating the patented method; the Florida Prepaid Postsecondary Education Expense Board, a state agency charged with helping people save enough money to attend Florida's public colleges and universities, offered something similar. College Savings sued Florida in 1994, confident that the Patent Remedy Act would let it fare better than had Chew.

While the case was pending, the rules began to change. Flush from its Supreme Court victory over the hapless Seminoles, Florida surveyed the legal terrain to see if anyone else was challenging its dignity as a sovereign. It noticed College Savings. "In light of the Court's ruling in *Seminole Tribe*, Florida Prepaid moved to dismiss College Savings' claim as barred by the Eleventh Amendment."[23] At trial, Judge Garrett Brown explained that Congress still had the power to abrogate a state's immunity under at least some circumstances; that the amendments to the Patent Act fell within those circumstances; and that Congress had been more than clear about insisting that states had to follow the patent laws.

Florida appealed to the Federal Circuit, but by the time that the assignment wheel landed on judges Clevenger, Rader, and Bryson, the analysis had grown even more complicated; the proud court's contumely from *Boerne* had become the law of the land. Nevertheless, Judge Clevenger, writing for a unanimous panel, agreed with Brown. Along the way to that conclusion, he hurdled the numerous painstaking obstacles that the Supreme Court had recently introduced into Eleventh Amendment jurisprudence:

> Protecting a privately-held patent from infringement by a state is certainly a legitimate congressional objective under the Fourteenth Amendment, which . . . empowers Congress to prevent state-sponsored deprivation of private property. It is, of course, beyond cavil that the patent owned by College Savings is property. . . . In subjecting the states to suit in federal court for patent infringement, Congress sought to prevent states from depriving patent owners of their property without due process through infringing acts, an objective that comports with the text and judicial interpretations of the Fourteenth Amendment.
>
> Unlike the statute at issue in City of Boerne, the burden that the Patent Remedy Act places on states is slight, and it is not disproportionate or incongruous with the significant harm to patent holders who, absent abrogation of Eleventh Amendment immunity, would be unable to enforce fully the rights conveyed by their patent. The Patent Remedy Act thus achieves the congruence between the injury to be prevented and the means adopted to remedy the injury that distinguishes a permissible, remedial exercise of Congress' power under the Fourteenth Amendment from an impermissible extension of the substance of the Fourteenth Amendment rights themselves. . . . Because Congress clearly expressed its intent to abrogate the sovereign immunity of the states to suit for patent infringement, and because Congress exercised its intent pursuant to a valid exercise of power, the decision of the district court denying Florida Prepaid's motion to dismiss the claim as barred by the Eleventh Amendment is affirmed.[24]

Clevenger had jumped through all of the necessary hoops. He had considered the Supreme Court's two recent rulings; looked at what Congress had done and how it had justified its actions; made certain that they were grounded in constitutional law; commented on the important public policy goal of protecting private property; and explained why, even in this new, state-friendly environment, sovereign states are still no freer to infringe patents than is the federal government. His analysis was compelling; his conclusion seemed sound.

The Supreme Court would have none of it. Chief Justice Rehnquist could hardly argue that Congress had been insufficiently clear about abrogating state sovereign immunity in patent infringement cases. He could, however, wonder whether Congress really had the authority to "compel States to surrender their sovereign immunity for these purposes."[25] In 1992, Congress had justified the Patent Remedy Act on three grounds: the

Commerce Clause, the Patent Clause, and the Fourteenth Amendment. The Supreme Court had knocked out the Commerce Clause with its recent jurisprudence about guns in school zones and Indian casinos, and for technical legal reasons, the elimination of the Commerce Clause as a potential justification also wiped out the Patent Clause. The entire analysis came down to the Fourteenth Amendment—which was, in fact, where Judge Clevenger had hung the Federal Circuit's hat. Was Clevenger correct in seeing the Patent Remedy Act as a reasonable way for Congress to protect private property from state seizures? Rehnquist—and a majority of his colleagues—thought not. In fact, he seemed particularly peeved at Congress for insisting that state patent infringement was an important problem when in reality, it was only a *potentially* important problem.

> Testimony before the House Subcommittee in favor of the bill acknowledged that states are willing and able to respect patent rights. . . . At most, Congress heard testimony that patent infringement by States might increase in the future, and acted to head off this speculative harm. . . .
>
> Congress . . . barely considered the availability of state remedies for patent infringement and hence whether the States' conduct might have amounted to a constitutional violation under the Fourteenth Amendment. . . .
>
> The provisions of the Patent Remedy Act are [therefore] so out of proportion to a supposed remedial or preventive object that they cannot be understood as responsive to, or designed to prevent, unconstitutional behavior. An unlimited range of state conduct would expose a State to claims of direct, induced, or contributory patent infringement. . . . Congress made all States immediately amenable to suit in federal court for all kinds of possible patent infringement and for an indefinite duration. . . .
>
> The historical record and the scope of coverage therefore make it clear that the Patent Remedy Act cannot be sustained under . . . the Fourteenth Amendment. The examples of States avoiding liability for patent infringement by pleading sovereign immunity in a federal-court patent action are scarce enough, but any plausible argument that such action on the part of the State deprived patentees of property and left them without a remedy under state law is scarcer still.[26]

Enough said. The Federal Circuit is overruled, College Savings loses, the State of Florida keeps it winning streak going, Eleventh Amendment immunity gets stronger, and fifty state sovereigns are now aware that they may infringe patents with relative impunity.

THE SOVEREIGN ACADEMY

Critics of the new trend in Supreme Court sovereign immunity analysis turned toward San Francisco. Judge Noonan did not disappoint—nor, for that matter, did he miss the opportunity to remind his erstwhile friends on the political right that it was he, not they, who remained true to the institutional focus of philosophical conservatism:

> In the case of the right to an abortion, the Supreme Court had explained its adherence to precedent by emphasizing the reliance of millions of persons on the availability of abortion. The court now did not mention the reliance of millions of patentees on the protection of patent laws. The damage to them was treated not only as collateral but as so inconsequential as not to be worthy of mention. Patents were a cherished creation of the constitution; it had scarcely been thinkable that a hole could be made in their protection. There was only one word for the court's decision: bizarre. . . . The consequences for "IP-dependent sectors of the American economy like biotechnology, software, entertainment, and pharmaceutical manufacturing" were seen as "potentially devastating."[27]

That potential devastation remains. And the potential may be greatest at some of the very institutions upon which the nation is relying to maintain American economic leadership into and throughout the information age. The Supreme Court's announcement that states are exempt from the patent laws threatens to destabilize American higher education. State universities are "arms of the state," or state agencies. Private universities are not. As a result, the Eleventh Amendment creates a giant rift within the world of academia. Even among our top schools, the playing field has suddenly become uneven: the University of California, the University of Virginia, and the University of Michigan are all immune from suit; Columbia, Georgetown, and the University of Southern California are not. This new reality alters any contractual relationships or regional consortia that combine the talents, skills, faculties, and facilities of public and private institutions. But it threatens to hit particularly hard in the realm of patents.

Virtually anyone who has spent any time at a major research university over the past two decades has noticed the growing importance of patents. Government policy has encouraged universities to patent its innovations. This policy emphasis has both sped the transfer of technology from academic laboratories to retailer's shelves and created a new source of revenue to fund American higher education. Neither of these results was coincidental; the congressional drive to promote university patenting emerged from the same set of concerns that motivated it to create the Federal Circuit. Former Harvard president Derek Bok explained:

> In the late 1970s, the slowdown in economic growth and the challenge of strong industrial competitors in Europe and Japan caused Congress to search for new ways to stimulate economic growth. As the Cold War waned, the

emphasis of science policy in Washington shifted to place less weight on maintaining military superiority and more on ensuring America's competitiveness in the world economy. This change in priorities led the government to consider new ways of linking university research to the needs of business. In 1980, Congress passed the Bayh-Dole Act, which made it much easier for universities to own and license patents on discoveries made through research paid for with public funds. Federal and state legislation offered subsidies for a variety of university-business cooperative ventures to help translate the fruits of academic science into new products and processes. Tax breaks encouraged industry to invest more in university-based science. By all accounts, these initiatives achieved their purpose.[28]

Bok cited numerous statistics to bolster his conclusion: By 1990, there were more than two hundred university offices exploring licensing and commercialization opportunities. By 2000, universities were earning more than $1 billion per year in royalties and license fees; more than twelve thousand academic scientists were collaborating with local companies through more than a thousand "official" collaborative programs; and numerous campuses had established incubators for small business development and entrepreneurship. A few universities had even launched venture capital funds to invest in the companies that their professors founded.[29] In short, Congress had detected a need (an injection of innovation into the U.S. economy), found participants already in the American economy poised to fill that need (the research universities), and drafted a statute that motivated these private actors to serve the needs of public policy. Congress turned the policies we want into the policies we have—kudos to Congress on a job well done.

Even those less sanguine about the role of the Bayh-Dole Act agree. According to professors David Mowery, Richard Nelson, Bhaven Sampat, and Arvids Ziedonis, the empirical data establish

> that the Bayh-Dole Act was one of several factors that contributed to the growth of patenting and licensing by U.S. universities during the 1980s and 1990s. The Act provided a strong congressional endorsement for academic institutions' involvement in patenting and licensing research discoveries and simplified the formerly complex administrative processes through which U.S. universities gained title to the IP resulting from publicly funded research. . . . There is little doubt that U.S. universities now are more heavily and directly involved in patenting and licensing of research results than at any previous time in their history. . . . Another factor behind the growth of university patenting is the extension of definitions of "patentable material" into the realm of science. . . . But this extension . . . reflects developments in a much broader set of policies and institutions (notably, the U.S. Patent and Trademark Office) than university patent and licensing policies or the Bayh-Dole Act.[30]

In other words, the policy has worked; the only remaining debate is precisely how much of the credit Bayh-Dole deserves and how much belongs to complementary decisions at the congressional, administrative, or even judicial levels. But public policy remains a challenging task. Congress, the administrative agencies, and the courts must remain ever vigilant for the possibility that last year's policy success sowed the seeds of this year's failure.

America's research universities are still digesting the cultural changes of the past twenty-five years. The rules are changing rapidly in academia, and technological innovation underpins many of the changes. Are universities navigating the transition well, turning themselves from engines of industrial-age research and education into information-age institutions? Appropriate technology transfer policies are central to the reorientation. Mowery, Nelson, Sampat, and Ziedonis caution:

> The issues raised by university patenting and licensing are complex, and the course of action that is likely to yield the greatest public benefit . . . varies among inventions and fields of technology. Nevertheless, for the foreseeable future, U.S. universities . . . will be patenting more intensively. A key challenge for policy concerns the appropriate design of licensing policies for universities engaged in patenting of inventions financed with public funds to ensure that publicly funded research yields the greatest possible societal benefit. . . .
>
> Ultimately, U.S. universities . . . will retain their privileged institutional status as entities that deserve extensive public financial support and prestige to the extent that they are seen by the public as serving its broad interests. . . . U.S. universities must exercise considerable responsibility and political sensitivity in managing their IP if the remarkable achievements of the past century are to be sustained in the new century.[31]

The Supreme Court threw a massive monkey wrench into the policy formation process when it eliminated Congress's attempt to enforce patent laws against the states. Should federal research funds continue to flow to state universities—funds that will lead to patents whose possessors need not follow patent law? How can any private-sector company accept a license on such a patent—knowing that it is enforceable only in one direction? Who will collaborate with a state university, or join with one in a patent pool, knowing of the inequitable distribution of rights and responsibilities? Though there have been few reports of such problems to date, the Federal Circuit has heard rumblings of trouble looming ahead.

Consider, for example, the tale of Galen Knight and Terence Scalen, cancer researchers at the University of New Mexico whose work led to three university-owned patents.[32] After they left the faculty, they went to work elsewhere, applying the expertise they had gained along the way to obtaining those patents. The university believed that their new efforts infringed the patents and sued; Knight and Scalen countersued. The university asked the court to dismiss Knight and Scalen's counterclaims because it offended its dignity as a sovereign and ran afoul of the Eleventh Amendment. The trial judge agreed and threw out all of their counterclaims. At the Federal Circuit, Judge Lourie described a complicated set of technical rules that determined which of their counterclaims could stand and which the Eleventh Amendment precluded—and then reinstated only some of them.

About a year later, the University of Illinois attempted a comparable maneuver in its litigation with Fujitsu; this time, Judge Dyk found technical grounds upon which to refuse the university's request.[33] Talk about chutzpah! A state university and a private party dispute their commercial relationship. The university sues the private party. The courts must consider all issues that the university decides to raise and must refuse to consider some of the issues that the private party would like to raise. So much for "exercising considerable responsibility and political sensitivity in managing IP." The incidence of such irresponsibility seems likely to increase with each passing year.

To make matters worse, while state universities were beginning to grasp that, despite Rehnquist's confidence that "states are willing and able to respect patent rights," there was no law requiring them to do so, the Federal Circuit issued a ruling that made life harder for private universities. For decades, universities had paid insufficient attention to some aspects of patent law because of a rule known as the "experimental use" exception.[34] Under this rule, anyone who uses a patented invention "solely for amusement, to satisfy idle curiosity, or for strictly philosophical inquiry" is not liable for infringement. Universities long assumed that because they were in the business of philosophical inquiry, they didn't have to worry all that much about infringement. So when Professor John Madey left Duke University and Duke continued to use his patented inventions, the university insisted that experimental use shielded it from liability. The trial judge agreed. The Federal Circuit didn't. Judge Gajarsa pointed out that "solely" means "solely." The Federal Circuit had ruled many times in the past that if the use of a patented invention furthered the user's business interests in any way, the experimental-use exception couldn't shield it. Because universities unquestionably conduct research, at least in part, to attract students, faculty, and research grants, Duke was using Madey's patented inventions in part to further its own business interests.[35]

As a matter of patent law, the ruling against Duke was straightforward. To the academic community, it struck like a bolt from the blue. It panicked the American Association for the Advancement of Science (AAAS). In

October 2004, its Science and Intellectual Property in the Public Interest (SIPPI) project did what academics do best—it organized a working group to study the issue and to "explore options for developing a national and internationally recognized research exemption." It complained that "the *Madey v Duke* decision court characterized Duke as being in the business of conducting research and obtaining grants." Though AAAS could hardly dispute that characterization, it nevertheless asserted that "the US scientific and academic communities are concerned that this ruling may have a chilling effect on their research, by adding legal costs and delays. This is a particular concern for disciplines in which foundational discoveries and research tools are commonly patented."[36]

Without disparaging that particular concern, however, the AAAS overlooked what is likely an even more important point. In the space of less than five years, state universities learned that they are immune from patent infringement suits, while private universities learned that many of their research laboratories expose them to liability as infringers. The entire terrain of academic research and patenting shifted, leaving public and private universities on opposite sides of a gaping chasm. How will this rift play itself out? While little of consequence has happened to date, it does appear likely to damage the delicate and successful technology transfer policy that served the country so well through the 1980s and '90s. But this question is simply part of a broader quandary. The world is still digesting what it means to have fifty sovereigns who are exempt from the patent laws. The Supreme Court sacrificed patent rights, like interstate commerce and religious freedom before it, on the altar of states' rights. We have a new trend: ignore Ninth Amendment individual rights; exalt Tenth Amendment states' rights; and watch Eleventh Amendment state sovereign immunity march on. The law is clear: federal courts may not even consider infringement claims against states and state agencies.

TAKEN

The Supreme Court's ruling against College Savings seemed to free America's domestic sovereigns to infringe patents with impunity. Yet, one slim possibility to protect patentees from marauding sovereigns remained: takings law. The Fifth Amendment's Takings Clause forces the federal government to exhibit at least a modicum of responsibility when expropriating private property: ". . . nor shall private property be taken for public use, without just compensation." The Fourteenth Amendment extends that requirement to the states.

Takings law goes straight to the heart of government functioning, dignity, and responsibility. "Eminent domain," or the seizure of private property for public use, is a critical and necessary function of government. A government unable to seize property could never develop infrastructures requiring rights-of-way, such as railways, roads, or wired communication networks. The framers of the Constitution included a takings clause precisely because they recognized that their new government needed this seizure authority. Their limitation of such seizures to "public uses," and their insistence that the government provide "just compensation," attempted to guarantee that the government would use this authority sparingly and responsibly. The takings clauses force domestic sovereigns applying this necessary power of government to stand for suit without crying that it degrades their sovereign dignity.

When a government agency infringes a patent, has it "taken private property for public use without just compensation"? Judge Clevenger's arguments in *College Savings* suggest an affirmative answer. The Supreme Court's rejection of his arguments with respect to infringement didn't preclude the possibility that state appropriation of patent rights might be a taking. Could takings law alone force state agencies to behave responsibly? This question has particular salience for at least two reasons, one grounded in a recent high-profile Supreme Court decision and the other in the Federal Circuit's special role in takings jurisprudence. Appreciating that salience requires a bit of background on both counts.

The matter that got takings law out of the seminar rooms and onto the front pages started in 2000, when New London, Connecticut, approved a development plan that would help revitalize the city. The municipal government turned the plans over to a private development corporation and authorized it to level and rebuild the city's potentially attractive waterfront. Unfortunately, a working-class neighborhood was in the way, and some of its residents preferred to stay in their homes. So the city did the expedient thing: it took their property, determined what it considered to be just compensation, and turned the entire area over to the developer. Susette Kelo, one of the evicted residents, sued the city. The matter went all the way to the Supreme Court. Were the city's stated purposes of promoting economic development and enhancing its tax base really "public uses"? In a bitterly contested five-to-four opinion, Justice John Paul Stevens issued one of the Court's most restrained opinions in decades:

> When the legislature's purpose is legitimate and its means are not irrational, our cases make clear that empirical debates over the wisdom of takings—no less than debates over the wisdom of other kinds of socioeconomic legislation—are not to be carried out in the federal courts. . . . Just as we decline to second-guess the City's considered judgments about the efficacy of its development plan, we also decline to second-guess the City's determinations as to what lands it needs to acquire in order to effectuate the project. . . . Once the question of the

public purpose has been decided, the amount and character of land to be taken for the project and the need for a particular tract to complete the integrated plan rests in the discretion of the legislative branch.[37]

The *Kelo* ruling achieved several things simultaneously: First, it energized the property rights advocates who had been warning about the excesses of takings for years; it instantly magnified the scope of the issue and catapulted it from one that engaged a small community into very public scrutiny. Second, it impelled several states to repudiate their newfound power to condemn private property and transfer it to private parties likely to pay higher taxes. Third, it forced many people who had been railing against "judicial activism" for years to reassess the merits of judges that are at least a little bit activist; after all, judicial deference to a City Council's decision about the "uses" most likely to serve the "public" that elected it is the height of judicial restraint. Fourth, it adopted a definition of "public use" broad enough to include a state agency's unauthorized use of a patent and added impetus to those of us wondering whether such a public use mandated just compensation.

So much for the question's first source of salience. The second source, the Federal Circuit's special role in takings jurisprudence, derives from the Court of Federal Claims's special role in takings jurisprudence. Citizens complaining that a federal agency took their property in violation of the Fifth Amendment must bring their suits in the Court of Federal Claims, with appeals going to the Federal Circuit.

To take but a few simple examples of federal takings, consider first the dastardly "Rails to Trails Act," a bit of federal legislation designed to convert old unused railway tracks and the areas around them into parks and hiking trails. Menno and Evelyn Toews owned some property in Clovis, California, that happened to have such unused rail lines running across it. The folks who had owned that land back in 1891 had granted the San Joaquin Valley Railroad Company the right to lay those tracks and operate its trains, "Provided, however, that if said Railroad Company shall permanently discontinue the use of said railroad the land and Rights of Way shall at once revert to the undersigned." Rail service ended in 1994. In 1995, the City of Clovis convinced the federal government to designate the abandoned tracks for public use, as part of a 4.5-mile walking trail. The Toews claimed that this designation constituted a taking. Judge Bruggink at the Court of Federal Claims agreed, as did a unanimous Federal Circuit panel of judges Plager, Bryson, and Linn.[38]

Next consider a tougher claim, that of Tuthill Ranch. In 1953, Tuthill's predecessor in interest had granted the Bonneville Power Authority a perpetual easement to lay the cables necessary to provide electricity to the Pacific Northwest, to lay additional accompanying communication cables, and to update the facilities on appropriate occasions. When Bonneville decided to upgrade its communication facilities from copper wires to fiber optics, it laid enough fiber to accommodate its projected needs several decades into the future. That decision resulted in a fair amount of dark fiber filling the same space that the copper wire had previously occupied. So far, so good; Tuthill had no complaints. The problem arose when Bonneville decided to lease that dark fiber to private concerns. Tuthill argued that these private companies, shooting photons through fibers on its ranch, were physically invading its domain—and that since they did so with government approval, their invasion constituted a "physical taking." Was Tuthill right? The complexities of takings law render that question more difficult than it was in the Toews' case. Judge Hodges at the Court of Federal Claims thought not. At the Federal Circuit, Judges Gajarsa and Lourie agreed; Chief Judge Mayer did not. Tuthill lost its claim for a physical taking by a score of two to one.[39]

Or consider a clever move by Lion Raisins, a large family-owned Central California raisin producer. Lion found itself embroiled in a dispute with the mighty Raisin Administrative Committee (RAC), the federal agency charged with ensuring the smooth functioning of America's critical raisin industry. But Lion had a problem. The RAC is a creature of the Agriculture Marketing Agreement Act of 1937 (AMAA),[40] the same Act that created the Grape Crush Administrative Committee whose demise left poor Fritz Kyer holding a stack of unpaid bills in 1964. In other words, the RAC is a NAFI. When Lion asked the Court of Federal Claims to consider its allegations that the RAC's regulatory activities amounted to federal takings, Judge Nancy Firestone dismissed the case as an affront to the RAC's sovereign dignity. On appeal, the assignment wheel selected judges Bryson, Linn, and Dyk. On behalf of a unanimous panel, Judge Dyk declared:

> We see no basis in the text of the Tucker Act itself; the legislative history of the 1970 amendments; or in the decisions of the Supreme Court or this court, for limiting the scope of the jurisdictional grant over claims "against the United States . . . founded upon the Constitution" to exclude takings claims against the United States based on actions by NAFIs. If there is a taking, the claim is founded upon the Constitution and within the jurisdiction of the Court of Claims to hear and determine. The RAC is an agent of the United States, and the United States may properly be sued in the Court of Federal Claims for any takings that are allegedly consummated by the acts of its agent.[41]

Finally, a chink in a NAFI's armor! Though a NAFI may be a government agency that is not a government agency, it is still a government agency. When it expropriates a citizen's property, or when the regulations that it administers have the effect of expropriation, the government is liable for just compensation. That liability emerges from the Constitution itself, not from the statutory waivers of the Tucker Act. The entire NAFI doctrine derived from a series of inquiries into the Tucker Act's scope. The Fifth Amendment both predates the Tucker Act and binds Congress. The Fifth Amendment establishes liability for *all* federal government expropriations. Congress lacks the authority to absolve the government of some of that liability simply by choosing to organize selected agencies as NAFIs. For the first time in fifty years, a plaintiff had cleared the jurisdictional hurdle: the courts would hear Lion's case against a NAFI.

Of course, none of that did Lion much good, because Dyk also rejected its two takings claims. Nevertheless, it adds impetus to our query: If the Fifth Amendment establishes that NAFIs might nevertheless face takings liability for seizing property, does the Fourteenth Amendment similarly establish that state universities might nevertheless face takings liability for infringing patents? The complexities and possibilities of takings law grow with each new case and with each passing year.

A PATENT CASE OF TAKING

Those complexities and possibilities ratcheted several notches higher a year after Lion left Lafayette Park. The Zoltek Corporation arrived, alleging that the federal government had taken its property by infringing its patent claiming several methods for manufacturing "carbon fiber sheets with controlled surface electrical resistivity." The Department of Defense had given the F-22 fighter jet contract to Lockheed. Lockheed subcontracted for two types of fiber sheets, the first manufactured in Japan and imported into the United States and the second made mostly in Japan but completed in the United States. The fiber sheets themselves didn't infringe Zoltek's patents, but the methods used to manufacture them did— or at least, they would have infringed had they occurred in the United States.[42] Zoltek nevertheless had two theories about why it should be able to sue the government. The first rested upon Congress's helpful explicit waiver of sovereign immunity:

> Whenever an invention described in and covered by a patent of the United States is used or manufactured by or for the United States without license of the owner thereof or lawful right to use or manufacture the same, the owner's remedy shall be by action against the United States in the United States Court of Federal Claims for the recovery of his reasonable and entire compensation for such use and manufacture.[43]

Unfortunately for Zoltek, Congress had also included an inconvenient limitation on that waiver: "The provisions of this section shall not apply to any claim arising in a foreign country."[44] That limitation, combined with the general rules about territoriality, doomed Zoltek's infringement claim. Chief Judge Edward Damich of the Court of Federal Claims, however, thought that Zoltek had the makings of a decent takings claim; the Fifth Amendment has no territoriality restrictions. The Federal Circuit accepted a rare interlocutory appeal.

The Clerk of Court spun his assignment wheel, and it landed on Judges Gajarsa, Plager, and Dyk. The complexities of Zoltek's questions hit this panel hard; its three judges managed to crank out four opinions. Judges Gajarsa and Dyk were, however, able to agree that the Supreme Court had answered at least one of the questions long ago—in 1894, to be precise—when it told John Schillinger that the federal government's infringement of his patent for an improvement in concrete paving could not constitute a Fifth Amendment taking. Sixteen years later, Congress responded with the explicit Tucker Act waiver that allows patentees to sue the federal government for domestic infringement.[45] That 1910 amendment certainly changed the rules, but did either the waiver itself or the Supreme Court's subsequent discussions of the waiver change the rules enough to let Zoltek succeed where Schillinger had failed? Gajarsa and Dyk said no.

> As the Supreme Court has clearly recognized when considering Fifth Amendment taking allegations, property interest . . . are not created by the Constitution. Rather, they are created and their dimensions are defined by existing rules or understandings that stem from an independent source such as state law. Here, the patent rights are a creature of federal law. . . . In response to Schillinger, Congress provided a specific sovereign immunity waiver for a patentee to recover for infringement by the government. Had Congress intended to clarify the dimensions of the patent rights as property interests under the Fifth Amendment, there would have been no need for the new and limited sovereign immunity waiver. The manner in which Congress responded to Schillinger is significant.[46]

In other words, although patents are property rights, they are not necessarily identical in scope to other types of property derived through bodies of law other than the Patent Act. Fifth Amendment takings claims apply differently to different types of property, and when it comes to patents, the Supreme Court answered the question when speaking to Schillinger in 1894.

Judge S. Jay Plager disagreed vehemently. In his opinion, Gajarsa and Dyk had misconstrued the nature of property, the property rights inherent in a patent, the full constitutional dimension of a takings claim, and the scope of the 1910 waiver.

[The Takings Clause] has a long and noble history of protecting and preserving property rights against unfettered Governmental seizure, and in so doing of protecting individual freedom and personal integrity from undue government authority. It is well understood that this constitutional provision does not preclude the Government from taking private property for public use. Rather, the Constitution guarantees that the citizen will be fully compensated for such a taking. By requiring just compensation the Constitution makes the property owner whole, and it also places a constraint on government action by imposing the cost of such action on the Government's fisc, thus subjecting administrative action to the discipline of public decision-making and legislative authorization. . . .

[Zoltek] alleges that the Government took its property—its government-granted patent right—when the Government's subcontractors used the patented method in the production of certain products employed in the F-22 production. On its face, the claim seems straightforward. Property rights are created by law. In the ordinary course, the law is state law. In the case of patents, the law is federal, and the patent statute expressly declares that the rights in an issued patent are property. . . .

[W]hen the Government chooses to acquire a patent right without prior permission of the owner, there is a way, unrelated to infringement law and unique to the Government, through which a patentee's right to exclude others may be obtained. The Government can exercise its power of eminent domain and simply seize or, as we say, "take" the property it needs for a public use. In effect, the Government forcibly acquires a license to use the invention. However, because of the Constitution, the Government may do this only if it pays the just compensation demanded by the Fifth Amendment.[47]

Plager was particularly dismayed with Gajarsa's opinion that "it is the responsibility of Congress, and of Congress alone to decide whether, and to what extent, it will permit the courts to help it fulfill its Constitutional obligations under the Takings Clause."[48] Plager saw that position as "a remarkable view of the Constitution."[49] He wondered: "Can it be that Congress, by a stroke of the legislative pen, may withhold the remedies and revoke the protections given to the citizenry by the Fifth Amendment, not to mention the other Articles of the Bill of Rights to the Constitution?" and answered his own question: "Fortunately no authority exists for such a radical doctrine of legislative preemption over constitutional right."[50] Finally, for good measure, he also opined that Gajarsa and Dyk had misconstrued *Schillinger* and misapplied the limitation to sovereign immunity.

Buried within Judge Plager's eloquent exposition on takings lie insights relevant to many lingering questions. He evidently sees no difference between patents and other types of property, at least with respect to Fifth Amendment takings. His dispute with Gajarsa and Dyk on this point may someday be of great consequence. Suppose that Congress decides that the

Patent Act overprotects innovation and, in a step toward optimality, reduces some aspect of patent strength. Would patentees whose existing
patents became weaker have a valid takings claim? Under the Gajarsa/
Dyk view, probably not. Under the Plager view, quite likely

   As to the idea of bringing a takings claim against a state university, it's
clear that Judge Plager would allow it. Under the Gajarsa/Dyk view, such
a claim appears less likely to stand. As Plager noted—and as Dyk himself
explained to Lion Raisins—if an activity is a taking, Congress can't retract
individual rights that the Constitution recognizes. If Zoltek's takings
claim failed because the congressional decision to allow infringement
claims in 1910 included a geographic limitation, one of three things must
be true: either a patent is not property and infringement is not a taking, a
patent is a special kind of property that evaporates at the border, or the
limitation is invalid. Gajarsa and Dyk seem to imply that the Supreme
Court decided that the first was true in 1894 and has never retracted that
ruling. Because the Fourteenth Amendment simply applies Fifth Amendment rules to the states, if infringement is not a taking for the federal government, it can hardly be one for state governments—Judge Clevenger's
implications to the contrary in *College Savings* notwithstanding.[51] Gajarsa
and Dyk do not, however, say so outright—and if the true implication of
their ruling is merely that the limitation captures the standard territorial
limits of U.S. patents, the question as to whether or not infringing states
are liable for a taking remains open.[52]

   This intrapanel debate thus implicitly reiterates the basic philosophical
dilemma from which so many of the gaps between patent law and patent
policy seem to stem: Are patents most like houses, cars, or licenses?
Everyone agrees that patent law is a regulatory system that creates property rights, but the debate over precisely what type of property it creates
continues to rage. It is clear that Judge Plager finds himself staring at his
panel colleagues across a gaping chasm.

   Finally, the entire nature of the takings dispute returns us foursquare to
the basic dilemma of sovereign immunity. No one doubts that governments need special privileges to function. Eminent domain is among
them. Even a system that restricted sovereign immunity to critical government powers—rather than expanding it to cover anything that a government might choose to do—would keep eminent domain in place. The
Fifth Amendment would still require just compensation, and *Kelo* might
even continue to allow governmental entities to seize private property for
questionable public uses. When it came to questions like Zoltek's, however, the matter would be more straightforward. A government might infringe a patent for two distinct sets of reasons: it might be operating as an
economic actor (say, a university), or it might be serving some public purpose that only governments serve (say, building advanced military fighter

jets). Where the line between them is blurry, the courts might have to decide to which category the activity in question belongs, but such decisions are hardly beyond the competence of the judiciary. If the activities fall within the standard economics category, patentees would be able to sue the government as they would all accused infringers, with no special rules applying to the government as defendant; prevailing patentees might even enjoin the government's infringement. If the activities fall within the government *qua* government category, patentees could never get an injunction, but they could certainly bring a takings claim for just compensation. And when they did, we might finally get an answer to the philosophical conundrum: How, if at all, do the property rights that the Patent Act created differ from other forms of property?

In the meantime, the best that we can do is to defer the philosophical inquiries into the nature of patents and to refocus instead on a key question of public policy. Overall, is sovereign immunity a good thing? Is it a net bane or a net boon to American society? And either way, does its manifestation in the patent realm make things better or worse? We have amassed the material that we need to test our black box. We first set out, along with Lincoln, to promote a responsible, just government. How are we doing?

THE CONSERVATIVE BOX

If a responsible, just government is truly our goal, sovereign immunity is a step in the wrong direction. Abraham Lincoln had his way for a while, but contemporary American law is trending toward Longshanks. The past decade or two have been good for American sovereigns. The Supreme Court has even reminded us that "Indian tribes are domestic dependent nations that exercise inherent sovereign authority over their members and territories. Suits against Indian tribes are thus barred by sovereign immunity absent a clear waiver by the tribe or congressional abrogation."[53] Just ask John Demontiney, a member of the Chippewa Cree tribe. In 1992, the Bureau of Indian Affairs (BIA) contracted with his tribe to build the Bonneau Dam on reservation land. The tribe subcontracted part of the task to Demontiney's engineering firm. A contract dispute ensued. Demontiney sued both the tribe and BIA for breach of contract. He started his suit in the tribe's own courts, moved from there to federal district court in Montana, on to the Ninth Circuit, over to the Court of Federal Claims, and then to the Federal Circuit—all to no avail.[54] The message was clear: sovereign immunity protected the tribe, and because he was only a subcontractor to the BIA, he couldn't sue the federal government. Did his claim have any merit? Once again, we'll never know. Sovereign immunity cases have a way of working out that way.

Though sovereign immunity arises in only a small fraction of the cases in which the government finds itself defending its behavior as an economic actor against allegations of impropriety, the cases in which it does arise are uniquely important. Sovereign immunity, and more broadly sovereign dignity, underpins the very notion that the government follows unique rules even when engaged in commonplace economic activities. Without sovereign immunity, the Claims Court would have been superfluous—citizens would have been able to sue the government in federal district courts. The Eleventh Amendment would similarly have established special rights for state governments only with respect to their governmental activities; commonplace commercial rules would govern the commonplace commercial activities in which states chose to engage. But such is not the world in which we live, nor does it describe the black box that we must test. The defining feature of *that* black box is the current state of the sovereign immunity doctrine.

One of the Rehnquist Court's famous five-to-four splits was at the epicenter of this black box. Though there are always exceptions to such generalizations, Justice Anthony Kennedy and Chief Justice William Rehnquist became consistent, vocal advocates for the "sovereign dignity" of the states, typically with the support of justices Sandra Day O'Connor, Antonin Scalia, and Clarence Thomas. They saw the states' immunity from suit—formalized in the Eleventh Amendment, but hardly begun there—as a critical element of sovereign dignity and an important legal concept with deep historical roots. As Kennedy explained it:

> The generation that designed and adopted our federal system considered immunity from private suits central to sovereign dignity. When the Constitution was ratified, it was well established in English law that the Crown could not be sued without consent in its own courts. In reciting the prerogatives of the Crown, Blackstone—whose works constituted the preeminent authority on English law for the founding generation—underscored the close and necessary relationship understood to exist between sovereignty and immunity from suit. . . . Although the American people had rejected other aspects of English political theory, the doctrine that a sovereign could not be sued without its consent was universal in States when the Constitution was drafted and ratified.[55]

But that view of history and of dignity is hardly definitive. Other historical trends, other interpretations of those trends, and above all, other important values lead to very different conclusions. They also split the Supreme Court. Justice David Souter, typically backed by justices John Paul Stevens, Ruth Bader Ginsburg, and Stephen Breyer, values the dignity of the individual citizen above the dignity of the sovereign. His interpretation of history—including the same passage from Blackstone and its impact on constitutional-era thinking—differs greatly from Kennedy's:

> The Court calls "immunity from private suits central to sovereign dignity," and assumes that this "dignity" is a quality easily translated from the person of the King to the participatory abstraction of a republican State. The thoroughly anomalous character of this appeal to dignity is obvious from a reading of Blackstone's description of royal dignity, which he sets out as a premise of his discussion of sovereignty: "First, then, of the royal dignity. Under every monarchical establishment, it is necessary to distinguish the prince from his subjects. . . . The law therefore ascribes to the king . . . certain attributes of a great and transcendent nature; by which the people are led to consider him in the light of a superior being, and to pay him that awful respect, which may enable him with greater ease to carry on the business of government. . . ." It would be hard to imagine anything more inimical to the republican conception, which rests on the understanding of its citizens precisely that the government is not above them, but of them, its actions being governed by law just like their own. . . .[56]
>
> The very essence of civil liberty certainly consists in the right of every individual to claim the protection of the laws, whenever he receives an injury. One of the first duties of government is to afford that protection. "In Great Britain the king himself is sued in the respectful form of a petition, and he never fails to comply with the judgment of his court." . . . To the Americans of the founding generation it would have been clear . . . that if the King would do right, the democratically chosen Government of the United States could do no less.[57]

This tension between the dignity of the individual and the dignity of the sovereign provides the key to our black-box test. Where does sovereign immunity fit into the sorts of policies likely to maximize America's prospects for success in the information age? What are the relative roles of America's institutions, America's ideals, and the philosophies that they embody in shaping the necessary policy terrain? Different philosophical orientations suggest different answers—and different black-box tests. At one conservative extreme, Kennedy and Rehnquist would ignore the question. Sovereign immunity is neither good nor bad—it simply *is*. It is a historical doctrine, an accepted fact. Immunity from suit is a basic attribute of sovereign dignity. Some sovereigns may conclude that waiving that immunity increases their credibility and their ability to govern by example and by moral suasion, rather than by fiat. Some sovereigns may conclude that waivers help them obtain more favorable terms from private parties with whom they engage in voluntary commercial activities, such as contracting and employment. Such sovereigns are certainly free to waive their immunity—in whole or in part—for that, too, is a sovereign's prerogative.

From this perspective, most of the questions that we would like to ask in testing this particular black box are misplaced. Does the system constitute good public policy? Was it appropriate in an agrarian age, an industrial age, or an information age? Kennedy, Rehnquist, and those who agree with them would argue that such questions are irrelevant—or even worse, dangerous. Imperial immunity was hardly radical when Ulpian described it in the third century. The extension of immunity from the monarch to lesser sovereigns was hardly radical when Longshanks formalized it a millennium later. No one challenged it for the next five centuries or so; its inclusion in Blackstone's writing, the thinking of our Constitution's framers, the Eleventh Amendment, and the letters of the early attorneys general all *assume* sovereign immunity from suit. If Congress determines that some doctrinal implications of immunity are inappropriate for the information age, Congress can repeal those implications by passing a law. If its very roots prove incompatible with the needs of an information-age society, the people will have to elect federal and state representatives to amend the Constitution appropriately. In other words, if sovereign immunity, as currently understood, meets our societal and economic needs as we transition into the information age, we can consider ourselves fortunate; otherwise, we must consider ourselves less so. In neither case can the courts play a helpful role. And in the meantime, the Supreme Court's job is to apply the sovereign immunity doctrine precisely as the framers of the Constitution and its Eleventh Amendment would have understood it. All other courts must follow suit.

The conservative philosophy underlying this view is everywhere evident: It animates Kennedy's abhorrence of RFRA as an unacceptable congressional incursion upon the Court's right to interpret the Constitution, Rehnquist's protection of states from federal legislation designed to avoid only potential problems, and Kennedy's historical review of the founders' views on sovereignty. In all of these opinions, what comes across is a visceral belief that the legislation in question alters the delicate power balance among America's institutions and thus threatens to undermine the fabric of American society. Recall that to a conservative, the brilliance of our constitutional institutions provides the best guarantee of our continued freedom and prosperity. Attempts to impose one institution's views on another—no matter how well guided or grounded in legitimate policy concerns they might be—are unacceptable.

But theirs is not the only conclusion consistent with philosophical conservatism. Judge Noonan, also a philosophical conservative, has emerged as one of their harshest critics. In his opinion, the Supreme Court, not Congress, threatens the delicate balance of power among our various institutions. Noonan opposed the Warren and Burger Courts' privacy decisions because they altered the balance of power between state and federal governments. He opposed the Rehnquist Court's sovereign immunity decisions *for precisely the same reason*. And to those who argue—for either or both sets of decisions—that the Supreme Court did not "alter" the relationship but rather restored the one embodied in the Constitution, philosophical conservatives like Noonan can simply note that both lines of decisions were surprising deviations from *stare decisis*; whether they imposed a radical power rebalancing or restored a long-lost balance, they certainly represented a discontinuity in societal thinking. It is this discontinuous rebalancing, rather than the actual outcomes of the Supreme Court's rulings, that infuriates many philosophical conservatives—and that differentiates them most clearly from political conservatives.

This conservative critique challenges sovereign immunity only as applied, not as an overall concept. Noonan's primary concern is with the appropriate balance of power among sovereigns. He has not complained about "side effects" like the no-interest rule or the NAFI doctrine, though he might well concede that we would be better off without them. The infringement of individual rights clearly bothers him, but it is equally clear that this concern is secondary. As a philosophical conservative, Noonan likely believes that robust American institutions provide the greatest long-term assurance of individual rights and liberties. This belief likely leads him to oppose significant shifts in the powers balanced between the federal and state governments.

The black box of sovereignty therefore fails *this* conservative test, albeit with diffuse blame. Congress has failed both by elevating federal supremacy over the states' rights to regulate individual behavior and by allowing anomalies like the no-interest rule and the NAFI doctrine to persist. The courts—again, primarily the Supreme Court—have failed by rebalancing power among American institutions. Preparedness for the information age remains a secondary consideration. The conservative focus on traditions and institutions implies that things that have worked well in the past will continue to work well. Experience validates this belief often, though not always. The true challenge for conservatives transitioning to the information age lies in allowing robust institutions to change just enough to accommodate information-age realities, and no more. Noonan's critique is clear: he believes that the Supreme Court is enforcing a radical adaptation while calling it stability. To a conservative, such a program fails on numerous counts.

THE LIBERAL BOX

To a liberal, analyses begin with the rights of the individual, not with institutions. American institutions are important precisely because they

enforce liberal values. When institutional or historical constraints interfere with contemporary liberal values, the institutions must adapt. But
philosophical liberals, like their conservative counterparts, can follow
this basic belief to different conclusions. Professor Erwin Chemerinsky
placed himself at one liberal extreme by arguing that sovereign immunity is more than merely *not* a constitutional doctrine but a downright
*un*constitutional doctrine concocted by five justices proud of their adherence to the "originalist" school of constitutional interpretation. As
Chemerinsky explained it:

> Originalists maintain that rights should be found in the Constitution only if
> stated in the text or clearly intended by its framers. Sovereign immunity, as
> applied by the Rehnquist Court, is a right of governments to be free from suit
> without their consent. Yet . . . [t]he text of the Constitution is silent about sov-
> ereign immunity . . . [and] silence is inherently ambiguous. Perhaps Justice
> Kennedy is correct that the framers were silent because they thought it obvi-
> ous that states could not be sued in state court. Alternatively, it could mean
> they thought it clear that states could be sued in state court. . . .
>
> Simply put, my point is that sovereign immunity cannot be found in the
> Constitution from an originalist perspective. The power in this argument is
> that it is the originalists on the Court who are the champions of state sover-
> eign immunity. A nonoriginalist, like me, would argue that the framers' in-
> tent as to sovereign immunity, even if it could be known should not be con-
> trolling. The Constitution's text neither mandates nor prohibits sovereign
> immunity. Therefore, the Court's decisions about it should be based on con-
> temporary functional considerations, not the framers' intent. The framers'
> conception of government is radically different from how government oper-
> ates in the twenty-first century. Therefore, their views about sovereign im-
> munity should not be binding upon us today.[58]

Were Chemerinsky in charge of either public policy or the courts, the
solution would be simple. The absence of an explicit discussion of sovereign immunity in the Constitution frees us to incorporate a full range
of "contemporary functional considerations" into our thinking about
sovereignty. It is therefore impossible to justify either the no-interest
rule or the NAFI doctrine, and while some of the state prerogatives elevated above federal law might survive a contemporary functional consideration test, most would likely fail. History is ambiguous, and nothing explicit in the Constitution prevents us from adopting policies
tailored to our information-age needs.

In the information age, "immunity" should apply only to necessary
governmental activities—say, collecting taxes, waging war, policing the
country, and eminent domain—that are prohibited to private citizens.
From this perspective, the courts, primarily but not exclusively the

Supreme Court, are responsible for this black box's failure. Congress rarely if ever asserts immunity explicitly, but it has passed numerous laws that promote equitable, responsible behavior. The courts have elevated an archaic doctrine over these contemporary laws to preclude responsible government behavior. The black box fails and the fault lies with the courts.

The typical retort to such arguments is that Chemerinsky's "nonoriginalism" removes *too much* structure from constitutional law. Whereas hard-core originalism risks turning the Constitution from a living document into an ossified mummy of enlightened eighteenth-century thinking, hard-core nonoriginalism risks turning it into an amoeba (or at the very least, an invertebrate). Living societies deserve living foundations. But complex living documents, like complex living organisms, are hardly amorphous. They adapt and evolve slowly, over time. Chemerinsky's somewhat glib conclusion that the framers' "views about sovereign immunity should not be binding upon us today" hardly means that they should be irrelevant. At a bare minimum, constitutional evolution should evoke the aphorism "The past has a vote, not a veto."[59]

Critiques along the lines of Justice Souter's flow from a liberal tradition that permits institutional evolution without amorphousness. In 1850, the liberal economist and French parliamentarian Frederic Bastiat, writing with his characteristic terseness, explained the incompatibility between liberty and sovereign immunity in a few simple sentences:

> It is not true that the legislator has absolute power over our persons and property. The existence of persons and property preceded the existence of the legislator, and his function is only to guarantee their safety. It is not true that the function of law is to regulate our consciences, our ideas, our wills, our education, our opinions, our work, our trade, our talents, or our pleasures. The function of law is to protect the free exercise of these rights, and to prevent any person from interfering with the free exercise of these same rights by any other person.[60]

In many ways, this sentiment is more American than French. For whereas Thomas Jefferson proclaimed "governments are instituted among men, deriving their just powers from the consent of the governed,"[61] revolutionary France found that "the principle of all sovereignty resides essentially in the nation."[62] In the context of sovereign immunity, the difference is significant. The French Declaration of the Rights of Man and of the Citizen establishes that men have inherent rights, but discusses law only in the context of men, citizens, and persons; it imposes no explicit boundaries on the nation's exercise of its sovereignty and insists only that "society has the right to require of every public agent an account of his administration." When the dignity of the sovereign and the dignity of the individual conflict, whose takes precedence? Either answer is possible; the document is silent.

To Bastiat and Jefferson, on the other hand, individual liberty precedes sovereignty. Far from being above the law, the sovereign that Jefferson foresaw existed not because of any divine or natural right, but rather because it served the public interest—or at the very least, had yet to prove intolerable.

> Whenever any form of government becomes destructive of these ends, it is the right of the people to alter or to abolish it, and to institute new government, laying its foundation on such principles and organizing its powers in such form, as to them shall seem most likely to effect their safety and happiness. Prudence, indeed, will dictate that governments long established should not be changed for light and transient causes; and accordingly all experience hath shewn, that mankind are more disposed to suffer, while evils are sufferable, than to right themselves by abolishing the forms to which they are accustomed.[63]

The long-standing historic justification for sovereign immunity therefore evaporates; what remains is Justice Souter's conclusion that the dignity of the individual precedes the dignity of the sovereign.

That conclusion is prescriptive. Sovereign immunity is incompatible with philosophical liberalism. The liberal's sovereign possesses no rights other than those that the governed choose to grant it—those necessary "to protect the free exercise of these rights, and to prevent any person from interfering with the free exercise of these same rights by any other person."[64] When the government acts within the sphere of those rights, it possesses the full force of the sovereign. It escapes liability, and thus need not stand suit, not because of immunity, but rather because what is prohibited to others is permitted to it. Philosophical liberals may differ over this sphere's size, but all see it as finite and bounded. The moment that government steps outside that sphere, the rules that bind others must also bind it.

When the federal government moves to protect rights that some states might infringe, liberals side with the feds. When a state moves to permit individual decisions that the federal government would restrict, liberals side with the states. A liberal government would pay its debts in real dollars, adhere to all of its contractual obligations, and respect all forms of property rights—including patents. Liberals see these conclusions as grounded not only in sound policy, but also in the Constitution—a document designed to maximally constrain government's ability to infringe individual rights. In a passage that has long inflamed the passions of political conservatives, Justice Arthur Goldberg argued that:

[T]he Ninth Amendment shows a belief of the Constitution's authors that fundamental rights exist that are not expressly enumerated in the first eight amendments and an intent that the list of rights included there not be deemed exhaustive. . . . The Ninth Amendment simply shows the intent of the Constitution's authors that other fundamental personal rights should not be denied such protection or disparaged in any other way simply because they are not specifically listed in the first eight constitutional amendments. . . . Liberty also gains content from the emanations of specific constitutional guarantees and from experience with the requirements of a free society.[65]

This belief in nonenumerable fundamental individual rights defines the constitutional dimension of philosophical liberalism.

Justice Souter's liberal critique is the only one specifically attuned to the information age. Individual empowerment is the beating heart of the information age. A system that elevates the individual over the sovereign completes an inversion of medieval priorities that has been under way for several centuries. It is unclear precisely how far Souter himself would follow this inversion's implications, but he has positioned himself as the true heir to an American tradition that includes both Jefferson and Lincoln. In this view, individual rights and liberties will allow the country to develop and maintain robust institutions.

Sovereign immunity is, at its very core, antithetical to this belief. Rather than strengthening and enhancing the dignity of America's institutions—including the American sovereign—immunity weakens and degrades them. Assertions of sovereign immunity hurt governmental attempts to lead by example. An immune sovereign is incapable of anything other than amoral behavior and thus devoid of moral authority. Unanticipated side effects of immunity hamper the government's ability to solve real problems. A NAFI's refusal to stand and defend its behavior as one party to a contract elevates power over justice. A court's inability to compensate veterans for admitted government errors because well-intentioned statutes omit some magic words adds needless complexity to the law. A state's refusal to abide by the patent laws generates contempt for both patents and states, and undermines legitimate congressional attempts to promote the progress of science and the useful arts. Many of these problems disappear among those who believe that a divine-right sovereign can do no wrong—but few who live in the information age share that belief.

This liberal test is thus the only one capable of determining how well the black box of sovereignty addresses the needs of today's transitional society. The box's performance is dismal. The Supreme Court has consistently read a preconstitutional notion of sovereignty into our republican Constitution—from its nineteenth-century embrace of the no-interest rule to its contemporary elevation of the Eleventh Amendment. Lower courts—including the Federal Circuit—find their maneuvering room dwindling, along with their ability to address obvious miscarriages of justice.

Those who see in all of this enhanced sovereign dignity are delusional. The doctrine of sovereign immunity is degrading the American sovereign and constraining its ability to respond to transitional challenges. The Claims Court's living descendants—the Court of Federal Claims and the Federal Circuit—share a bird's-eye view of this problem, but they are hardly alone. Far from their courtrooms, adherents of liberal and conservative philosophies are converging. Whether the sovereign's disregard of individuals threatens the nation's institutions or the doctrinal rebalancing of institutional power threatens individuals, both threats are real. Contemporary sovereign immunity jurisprudence has no place in the information age. If we are to succeed, we must finally abandon Longshanks's legacy and plunge headlong into Lincoln's reminder that "it is as much the duty of Government to render prompt justice against itself in favor of citizens as it is to administer the same between private individuals."[66] Government *qua* government may warrant special rules. Government as economic actor deserves none. Every exception undermines the government's credibility as arbiter and standard-setter. In a networked economy of empowered individuals, a contract must be a contract, an employer an employer. On the Internet, no one knows you're a doge.

IV

THE CIRCUIT'S SECRETS

The Federal Circuit is much more than just "the patent court." Between the surprising breadth of the federal claims docket and the concept of "pendent jurisdiction," whereby any issue raised in conjunction with a patent issue accompanies the patent question on appeal, the court's purview extends into areas that few associate with Federal Circuit jurisprudence. That antitrust and copyright questions should accompany patent disputes on more than rare occasions is perhaps unsurprising. But foreign affairs, war powers, abortion, tax, banking, bankruptcy, and housing also work their way onto the Federal Circuit docket. How does the court's consideration of these issues expand its worldview? What does its approach to the interplay among patents, copyrights, and antitrust say about its view of intellectual property in the information age? And perhaps above all, how does the court's consideration of innovation within a broad commercial and social context affect our perception of its performance?

11

✛

Peripheral Vision

THE JURISDICTION HAWKS

"The Bishop of Rome hath no jurisdiction in this Realm of England."[1] At least, that's what the Church of England proclaimed in 1571. That bishop of Rome, better known as Pope Pius V, might have had a different opinion. One point on which the pope and the Anglicans would have agreed, though, is that jurisdiction is a big deal. They would have been right. In the information age, jurisdiction is still a big deal. At times, in fact, jurisdiction can be *the whole* deal.

What is "jurisdiction?" Jurisdiction today is perhaps best known as a topic that glazes over the eyes of first-year law students during their mandatory Civil Procedure class. *Black's Law Dictionary* defines *jurisdiction* as

> a term of comprehensive import embracing every kind of judicial action. It is the power of the court to decide a matter in controversy and presupposes the existence of a duly constituted court with control over the subject matter and the parties. Jurisdiction defines the powers of courts to inquire into facts, apply the law, make decisions, and declare judgment. The legal right by which judges exercise their authority. It exists when court has cognizance of class of cases involved, proper parties are present, and point to be decided is within powers of court. Power and authority of a court to hear and determine a judicial proceeding; and power to render particular judgment in question. The right and power of a court to adjudicate concerning the subject matter in a given case. The term may have different

meanings in different contexts. Areas of authority; the geographic area in which a court has power or types of cases it has power to hear.[2]

. . . which probably explains the glazed eyes. When it's not being used to bore law students or to diss the Pope, jurisdictional analysis plays a critical role in the American legal system. It defines which courts have the right to hear which cases. A plaintiff who sues in the wrong court, or an appellant who appeals to the wrong court, will never get a hearing on the merits; a court that lacks jurisdiction to hear a case is acting without legal authority if it tries.

Sometimes, *no* court has jurisdiction to hear a case—as anyone who has ever tried to sue a sovereign sans waiver has learned. Most of the time, some court somewhere at some point has jurisdiction to hear a case. But every court, on every case, must ask itself whether *this court* has jurisdiction to hear *this case* at *this point*. That question is so critical—and so central to the American system of justice—that we have dispensed with all of the normal rules concerning the ordering of questions. An objection to a court's jurisdiction is the *only* question that either party can raise at any time, or that the court can raise at any time all by itself. If a court ever decides that it lacks jurisdiction to hear a case, it *must* dismiss it for lack of jurisdiction—even if it has held an entire trial and the jury is already out deliberating.

With stakes this high, you would think that lawyers must spend a lot of time, and a lot of their clients' money, conducting jurisdictional analyses. For the most part, you would be wrong. Jurisdiction is typically pretty straightforward. Most plaintiffs wave their hands at it in a sentence or two, few defendants challenge it, and most judges don't bother looking into it on their own. Why? Because by and large, the most common jurisdictional questions in the federal courts hinge on geography and on numbers, and neither one is terribly subtle. A citizen of one state disputing a suitably large sum of money with a citizen of another state can sue in federal court, as can anyone suing anyone on a question of federal law. The location of the trial court determines which regional circuit hears the appeal. Simple, straightforward, and no reason to burn a clients' money—with one exception: some of those cases go to the Federal Circuit rather than to the geographically ordained regional circuits.

The Federal Circuit's judges are all jurisdiction hawks. After all, much of what they own is subject matter. While they get all the appeals from the Court of Federal Claims, the Court of International Trade, the Court of Veterans Appeals, the Patent and Trademark Office, and numerous boards and commissions, the heart of their work lies in the world of patents, and they don't "own" any of the district courts that hear patent cases. Those trial judges are used to taking their marching orders from the regional circuits that govern their regions. All of a sudden, a patent case arrives on their docket, and some but not all of the rules change—along with the appellate judges who will soon review their work. If the Federal Circuit didn't take a hawkish view of jurisdiction, making sure that it heard all proper appeals and only proper appeals, the system might fray at the edges. What's more, those few courts that the Federal Circuit *does* own all have complicated jurisdictional rules themselves. So it's hardly surprising that jurisdictional analyses at the Federal Circuit are often more complicated—and on occasion, even more interesting—than those at most other courts. Nor, for that matter, is it surprising that a review of Federal Circuit jurisdictional analyses can lead to bodies of law far beyond those that people normally associate with the court—areas like foreign affairs, war powers, abortion, housing, copyright, and antitrust, to name but a few. If you want to escape the tunnel vision that a docket packed with patent, trade, and federal claims cases can engender, jurisdictional analysis is a fine place to start. The Federal Circuit's peripheral vision begins with the scope of its jurisdictional analyses.

Consider a pair of foreign affairs cases. In the space of less than a year, the Federal Circuit had to determine whether or not the Court of Federal Claims had jurisdiction to consider the merits of cases brought by Cuban citizens claiming that the federal government owed them retirement benefits, and by a Saudi-born Sudanese citizen claiming that the United States blew up his pharmaceutical plant under the mistaken belief that he was producing chemical weapons for al Qaeda. Judge Clevenger handled both cases for unanimous panels.

How did the court approach these questions? Clevenger explained that the key to determining jurisdiction lay in the Reciprocity Act.[3] The remaining trappings of medieval sovereign immunity notwithstanding, the U.S. government is pretty generous about letting citizens of foreign countries sue it—but it does have its limits. Our government will only let a foreigner sue it if the plaintiff's country "accords to citizens of the United States the right to prosecute claims against their government in its courts."[4] After all, turnabout is fair play. The jurisdictional questions were thus whether the governments of Cuba and the Sudan would afford U.S. citizens the same rights to sue them that they afford their own citizens. Do they?

Back in World War II, a number of Cuban citizens enlisted in the U.S. Armed Forces, and they subsequently became Civil Service retirees. Since Fidel Castro seized power and imposed authoritarian rule in 1959, however, Cuba and the United States have not been the best of friends. Nevertheless, these folks drew Civil Service retirement benefits until 1963, when the Treasury Department sent them a letter explaining that "there is no reasonable assurance that a payee living in Cuba will actually receive

United States Government checks or be able to negotiate them for full value." Rather than escrowing the benefits checks until the retirees could provide such guarantees, Treasury terminated their benefits. In November 2000, some of them (or their heirs) finally got around to filing suit in the Court of Federal Claims. The U.S. government claimed that the court lacked jurisdiction to hear the case. When the court sat down to see what the Reciprocity Act had to say about the matter, the plaintiffs submitted an affidavit from Jorge Cobas, a Cuban attorney, who explained that "a citizen of any country, including those of the United States, has the ability to seek judicial relief in a Cuban court, even if the claim is against the Republic of Cuba . . . [although] from time to time the Cuban Government and the Communist Party have enjoyed some influence in judicial proceedings."[5] The government, for its part, submitted a State Department statement that "any right of a U.S. citizen to pursue a claim against the Cuban government in Cuban courts is subject to the political interference of the Cuban government and, thus, that there are serious impediments to the ability of a U.S. citizen to pursue effectively a lawsuit against the Cuban government."[6] With that, the Court of Federal Claims dismissed the suit for lack of jurisdiction.

On appeal, Clevenger pointed out that political control is not the test—nor, for that matter, is a competent, trustworthy judiciary. The only relevant test is reciprocity, and the standards for determining reciprocity are pretty low. So low, in fact, that when a group of Latvians sued the United States for a tax refund back in 1959, the Court of Claims found

> reciprocity between the government of the Republic of Latvia in exile and the United States even though the former country did not maintain courts, but rather, determined administratively claims against the state. . . . The Republic of Latvia, which had been invaded by forces of the U.S.S.R., was still recognized by the United States and the two countries had concluded a treaty prior to the invasion permitting American citizens free access to Latvian courts. It . . . would [have been] a "harsh construction of [the Reciprocity Act]" to deny Latvian citizens access to the Court of Claims simply because the state of affairs required all claims brought against the Latvian government, including those brought by American citizens, to be adjudicated administratively.[7]

With that, Clevenger concluded that "precedent cautions, if not compels, us to refrain from interpreting the Reciprocity Act rigidly. . . . Equal treatment is the paramount requirement. . . . Reciprocity is not defeated by a modicum of political interference from the foreign sovereign, by the differing extent to which a foreign sovereign has waived immunity from suit, or even by the nonexistence of a court system in the foreign country."[8] He sent the Cubans back to the Court of Federal Claims for a full-blown evidentiary hearing.

So much for the Cubans. How about the Sudanese? They claimed that when the United States mistakenly identified their El-Shifa Pharmaceutical Company as a manufacturer of al Qaeda's chemical weapons and destroyed their factory, the government effectively took their property for a public use. They thus brought a takings claim. At the Court of Federal Claims, Judge Baskir concluded that the "Constitution of the Republic of the Sudan guarantees for all persons the right to prosecute claims against the government," without delving into whether the Constitution of the Republic of the Sudan was worth the paper on which it was written. The plaintiffs had cleared the "hurdle" of the Reciprocity Act. The government raised a few other jurisdictional challenges, but they too fell to careful analysis. The Court of Federal Claims concluded that it had jurisdiction to hear the case—so it did.[9]

Before getting to the punch line, though, it's important to understand what was at stake here. As Clevenger vividly described:

On August 7, 1998, the United States Embassies in Nairobi, Kenya, and Dar es Salaam, Tanzania, were bombed in nearly simultaneous attacks that were linked to Osama bin Ladin and the terrorist organization al-Qaeda. On August 20, 1998, President William Jefferson Clinton ordered the armed forces of the United States to conduct strikes in Afghanistan and Sudan intended to "disrupt bin Ladin's terrorist network and destroy elements of its infrastructure" there. In particular, the stated purpose of the strikes was to "destroy, in Sudan, [a] factory with which bin Ladin's network is associated, which was producing an ingredient essential for nerve gas."

The day after the strikes, the president sent a letter to Congress in which he stated that the Plant was being used to produce chemical weapons. The president stated the United States had acted in self-defense, and that the strikes were a necessary and proportionate response to the imminent threat of further terrorist attacks against U.S. personnel and facilities. These strikes were intended to prevent and deter additional attacks by a clearly identified terrorist threat. The targets were selected because they served to facilitate directly the efforts of terrorists specifically identified with attacks on U.S. personnel and facilities and posed a continuing threat to U.S. lives.[10]

What's more, it seems that the trial record contained evidence showing that there were good reasons for Clinton to have believed that El-Shifa *was* producing chemical weapons—as even the plaintiffs conceded. So here's what it all came down to: The president of the United States responded to an act of war by selecting what appeared to be a legitimate military target, but in fact was not. Its owners, citizens of a country known for harboring anti-American terrorists (not to mention for committing numerous ongoing atrocities unrelated to Americans), who admitted to having disguised their factory, came to Washington to sue the U.S. government for destroying it. The U.S. courts, acting pursuant to American rules of fair play, concluded that these plaintiffs had a right to come to town, to make their case, and to petition for redress—and that the courts had to hear them out.

But things are not quite as bizarre as they might seem. All judges studying the matter reached the same conclusion: there's jurisdiction and there's jurisdiction. Although the courts had the authority to hear the case, they lacked the authority to second-guess the President's decisions about how to conduct a war. This claim raised a "nonjusticiable political question," a fancy way of saying that though the court was allowed to *hear* the case, it wasn't allowed to *decide* the case. Baskir dismissed the case and the Federal Circuit affirmed.

That's how the Federal Circuit gets to see issues like foreign affairs and war powers. Jurisdictional inquiries really can broaden the Court's view of the world—at times even by forcing it into areas in which few jurists would choose to wade. Recall that one of the Federal Circuit's greatest strengths is that the esoteric nature of many of the issues that it investigates keeps its work out of the political limelight. It would be hard to imagine a better way to destroy this apolitical reputation than by saddling the court with an abortion case. Yet, when Jane Doe and Maureen Britell, two military wives, became pregnant (independently), that's precisely what happened. Both women learned that their fetuses suffered from anencephaly, an abnormality that is invariably fatal either before or shortly after birth. Both applied to their military health care providers for funding to perform abortions. Both providers denied the claims, citing applicable government regulations restricting the funding of abortions other than those necessary to protect the mother's life. From there, however, things took slightly different turns.

Both women filed suits for less than $10,000 in convenient federal district courts pursuant to the Little Tucker Act—Doe in Washington State and Britell in Massachusetts.[11] In Doe's case, the district court enjoined the insurer from withholding payment. The government appealed immediately to the Ninth Circuit. The Ninth Circuit refused to stay the ruling pending appeal, the insurer released the money, Doe got the abortion, and the matter landed straight back in the district court, where the government sought reimbursement from Doe and a reinstatement of its enjoined regulation. The district court then ruled against the government on the grounds that its regulation lacked a rational justification. The government, apparently now wary of the Ninth Circuit, appealed to the Federal Circuit, claiming that jurisdiction was proper because of Doe's Little Tucker Act claim.

In Britell's case, she and her husband paid their own $4,000 bill and had to sue for reimbursement. The Britells won in the trial court, and the government appealed to the First Circuit. The First Circuit concluded that it lacked jurisdiction. Though the Little Tucker Act let Britell sue in Massachusetts, all appeals in Little Tucker Act cases go to the Federal Circuit—to which the First Circuit transferred the case.

The two cases arrived at the Federal Circuit at the same time, where it made sense to assign them to a single panel—if for no other reason than to assure coherence in Federal Circuit abortion jurisprudence. The clerk of court spun his wheel, and judges Michel, Bryson, and Prost landed the unenviable task of handling the "patent court's" first real abortion cases. The three judges all started by agreeing with the First Circuit's analysis: the Federal Circuit had jurisdiction if the cases really were about forcing the federal government to pay money, but *only* if that's what they were about.

Judge Bryson analyzed Doe's situation, and concluded that, while Doe may have cited the Little Tucker Act, the relief that the court actually awarded wasn't cash, but rather an injunction precluding a further withholding of cash. With an evident sigh of relief on behalf of a unanimous panel, Bryson wrote: "Although the underlying question presented by this case is whether the government's ban on paying for certain kinds of abortions is unconstitutional, we do not reach the merits of that issue. Instead, we hold that we lack jurisdiction over the appeal from the district court's judgment, and we therefore transfer the case to the court with jurisdiction over the appeal, the United States Court of Appeals for the Ninth Circuit."[12]

In Britell's case, Judge Michel spoke for the unanimous panel: "Although this court, and surely all humankind, feels great sympathy for any parent faced with the truly horrifying diagnosis of anencephaly, we find that the law is clear: the state has a legitimate interest in potential human life from the outset of a woman's pregnancy, regardless of a diagnosis of a severe birth defect or fetal abnormality."[13] Given the clarity of binding Supreme Court precedent on that point, the court ruled in the government's favor.

Jurisdictional rulings can cut in either direction—some days they let you punt and others they force you to play. But one way or another, they do inject the "patent court" into areas far beyond the progress of science and the useful arts.

This little *pas de trois* involving the First, Ninth, and Federal Circuits illustrates how courts are supposed to behave when tough jurisdictional questions arise: conduct the analysis and then make sure that the right court decides the case. Most judges in most courts are pretty good about following this rule; it's hard to imagine an instance of judicial overreach greater than a judge who takes it upon herself to decide a case that her court lacks jurisdiction to hear. Nevertheless, such overreaching does occur—as a housing law controversy involving the Fifth and Federal Circuits demonstrates.

THE PREDICATE

The setting for this housing fracas was Mockingbird Run, a low-income housing project in Bryan, Texas, subject to a complex regulatory scheme that the Department of Housing and Urban Development (HUD) had developed to entice property owners to provide habitable housing for the poor. Participation in the program was voluntary; participating property owners relinquished many of their normal property rights to HUD's regulatory oversight in exchange for mortgage guarantees and various other tax and financing benefits. Participating landlords, for example, agree to maintain their properties in good repair and condition and relinquish their right to set rents without HUD's approval. Furthermore, because HUD pays the rent for residents of some low-income housing, participating landlords essentially agree to let their tenants (in the form of HUD) set the rents. In exchange, HUD promises to take the landlord's costs into consideration and to behave reasonably in evaluating requested rent increases.

Christopher Village, a limited partnership, owned Mockingbird Run and had been operating it (poorly) under these HUD programs since 1983. By 1995, the place was a shambles. HUD demanded that Christopher Village bring it up to minimal levels of habitability. Christopher Village requested a rent increase. HUD refused to consider the request unless and until Christopher Village escrowed $2 million for repairs. Christopher Village refused. HUD foreclosed. Christopher Village sued HUD in the Southern District of Texas, seeking the return of its property and a declaratory judgment that HUD had behaved in an arbitrary and capricious manner by refusing to consider its requested rent increase. The district court ruled in HUD's favor. Christopher Village appealed to the Fifth Circuit. When neither the district court nor the Fifth Circuit was willing to stay the ruling pending appeal, HUD sold Mockingbird Run to the City of Bryan for $10. The city razed the property.[14]

That's where the jurisdictional controversy began. By the time the Fifth Circuit actually got to hear the appeal, it had a problem: When Christopher Village first sued, it wanted its property back—a claim that district courts have jurisdiction to hear and regional circuits have jurisdiction to review. However, by the time the Fifth Circuit heard the case, Christopher Village's only remaining claim was for money—a remedy that only the

Court of Federal Claims can order and only the Federal Circuit can review. To play by the rules, the Fifth Circuit *was required* to tell Christopher Village that it lacked jurisdiction and was precluded by law from considering the merits of its claim. And that claim was hardly without merits; even if Christopher Village was the world's worst slumlord, it's still wrong for the government to blackmail taxpayers *as a prerequisite to handling their forms.*

Judge Edith Jones, writing for a unanimous Fifth Circuit panel, didn't play by the rules. She claimed that "[a] declaration that HUD violated its regulations and contracts grants [Christopher] Village adequate relief because, even without regaining title to the property, [Christopher] Village could use the declaration as a predicate for a damages action against HUD in the Court of Federal Claims."[15] The availability of adequate relief, she explained, allowed the Fifth Circuit to retain jurisdiction. With the jurisdictional question thus settled, she launched into a lengthy discourse on federal housing policy:

> Nothing . . . requires [Christopher] Village, as a low-income property owner, to absorb or subsidize operating and maintenance deficiencies. Instead, the programs are designed to ensure that HUD establishes rental rates so that property owners receive enough revenue to cover all of the property's expenses including maintenance, repairs, debt service, taxes, and a six percent return on investment. Thus, the HUD reimbursement scheme resembles cost-plus contracts or public utility regulation, in either of which situations the private party who performs the work is assured of recovering reasonably incurred costs as well as a reasonable return on investments.[16]

In other words, a landlord who chooses to enter the HUD low-income housing program need *never* make a further capital investment in the property, is guaranteed a rent that covers *all* costs and yields a 6 percent operating profit, and can also take advantage of the various tax and financing benefits. As they say, nice work if you can get it. Christopher Village not only got the work but also got a fair amount of Jones's sympathy: "There is no statutory or regulatory basis for imposing on a conscientious low-income housing operator the risk of uncompensated dilapidation or deterioration; the federal government, not the private contractor, is charged with funding the public program."[17] Jones ruled for Christopher Village on a narrow point of administrative law, issued a precedential ruling in Fifth Circuit housing law, and sent Christopher Village to the Court of Federal Claims armed with a "predicate."

All of which would have been well and good, except that there is no such thing in U.S. law as a predicate that one court sends to another. The Fifth Circuit lacked jurisdiction to hear the appeal—and Jones knew it.

Twenty-five years earlier, in an opinion that remains binding law in the Fifth Circuit, Jones's predecessors had explained that:

> Congress established the Court of Claims to determine claims of this type and magnitude but deliberately withheld equitable powers from it. Since the United States by reason of its nature acts only through agents, it is hard to conceive of a claim falling no matter how squarely within the Tucker Act which could not be urged to involve as well agency error subject to review [in district court] under the [Administrative Procedures Act]. Little imagination is needed to foresee the consequences of a holding that such claims as this may be reviewed either in a court having power to grant equitable relief against the United States or in one having none. We refuse to believe that Congress intended, in enacting the [Administrative Procedures Act], so to destroy the Court of Claims by implication.[18]

Jones should have dismissed the appeal and sent Christopher Village to the Court of Federal Claims without pretending that she had the authority to tell another court how to rule. Instead, she gave Christopher Village a predicate—which it dutifully took to Lafayette Park, fully expecting the Court of Federal Claims to rubber-stamp its hard-won Fifth Circuit victory.

Jones also made at least one other error unrelated to jurisdiction: she chose the wrong slumlord to label "conscientious." Christopher Village was part of a network of partnerships and corporations run by the same group of people. These folks—under the guise of a different member of the *keiretsu*—pled guilty to an insurance fraud scheme in which their insurer padded its premiums, the *keiretsu* claimed higher costs to HUD, HUD agreed to rent increases commensurate with these costs, and the *keiretsu* and its insurer split the difference. By the time Judge Firestone of the Court of Federal Claims looked at the case, the battle lines were drawn. Christopher Village said, "Judge Jones already told you that we win." The government noted that even if Jones were correct in finding that HUD had violated its own regulations and thus breached its contract with Christopher Village, Christopher Village's earlier fraud meant that it had breached first. Firestone ruled for the government.

Christopher Village appealed to the Federal Circuit. Judge Dyk, speaking for a unanimous panel of aggrieved jurisdiction hawks, used relatively restrained language to explain that Judge Jones had not only overstepped her judicial authority but had done so in a way that wasn't even a close call. Her ruling had violated not only Fifth Circuit precedent, but comparable rulings in most of the other circuits and analogous rulings of the Supreme Court. "Although we are reluctant to conclude that one of our sister circuits has acted beyond its jurisdiction," Dyk explained, "we find that it plainly did so here. The Fifth Circuit's ruling . . . did not merely exceed the court's jurisdiction, it 'directly implicated issues of sovereign immunity' and is therefore void. Because the Fifth Circuit's judgment is void, it is not entitled to preclusive effect" in the Court of Federal Claims. He then reviewed Judge Firestone's ruling against Christopher Village and affirmed.[19]

Cases like *Christopher Village* raise more questions than answers. What was Judge Jones trying to do? Was she expressing outrage at the government for blackmailing its citizens? Was she showing sympathy for a plaintiff whom she believed to be a conscientious provider of low-income housing being tormented by the bureaucracy? Was she looking for an excuse to set Fifth Circuit housing law? Did she really believe that a judge on another court would simply rubber-stamp her ruling? It's hard to believe that she missed the jurisdictional analysis so completely— particularly given that she spoke for a unanimous panel of the Fifth Circuit. Sometimes it's just not possible to know what's going on behind the scenes—but a good court full of jurisdiction hawks can shine some light on these legal anomalies.

PATENT PENDENT

Jurisdiction hawks or not, there was at least one occasion when the Federal Circuit itself ruled in a case where it knew it lacked jurisdiction— though in the court's defense, it was staring into the barrel of a gun at the time. The story started in 1983, when Colt Industries filed a patent infringement suit against several manufacturers of M16 rifle parts, including one that Charles Christianson, a former Colt employee, owned and operated. That case eventually settled, but not before making a brief if uneventful stop at the Federal Circuit. Three days after settling, Christianson filed his own suit against Colt in Illinois, alleging that Colt had misappropriated his trade secrets and violated the antitrust laws. The absence of patent issues suggested that this case, unlike the first one, had nothing at all to do with Federal Circuit jurisdiction. Along the way to resolution, however, Christianson backed up one of his antitrust theories by showing that Colt had misused some of its patents. When the district court looked at the pertinent facts, it not only ruled in Christianson's favor but also invalidated nine of Colt's patents.

Colt, who had had some luck at the Federal Circuit in its earlier patent infringement claim, took the appeal to Lafayette Park. Christianson complained, arguing that the Seventh Circuit should hear the appeal. The Federal Circuit agreed with Christianson and transferred the case. The Seventh Circuit conducted a detailed jurisdictional analysis to determine whether or not this case "arose under" the patent laws—the operative phrase that Congress had used in specifying precisely which cases the Federal Circuit had exclusive jurisdiction to hear:

> This appeal . . . was originally filed in the Federal Circuit, a coordinate jurisdiction, that . . . sent the suit here. The question then arises whether we are bound by that court's ruling that this court is to hear the case. We think not. . . . We also note that the Federal Circuit has never considered itself constrained by the jurisdictional rulings of other circuits. . . . We will, therefore, consider whether we possess appellate jurisdiction in the instant case. To do so, we must determine whether the Federal Circuit has exclusive jurisdiction over the appeal because, in the absence of [the 1982 statute that created the Federal Circuit], we clearly would.[20]

With that introduction in place, the Seventh Circuit concluded that the case arose under the patent laws. It transferred the matter *back* to the Federal Circuit, pausing only long enough to commiserate that Congress's decision to grant the Federal Circuit exclusive jurisdiction over all appeals arising under the patent laws "may save costs by promoting uniformity, but initially at least, it imposes new costs generated by jurisdictional uncertainty . . . at considerable expense to the parties and the judicial system and no doubt considerable bewilderment to laymen."[21]

The undoubtedly bewildered laymen wandered back to Lafayette Park, where Chief Judge Markey told them:

> The present appeal reflects a monumental misunderstanding of the patent jurisdiction granted this court. An appeal in a pure and simple antitrust case is here solely because an issue of patent law appears in an *argument* against a *defense*. Christianson asserted rights that arise under, and only under, antitrust law. . . .
>
> As evidenced by our respectful disagreement with our sister circuit in this opinion, this court's jurisdiction in some cases is less than crystal clear. With five years of experience under the Act, it may be time for Congress to make its intention even more clear to those willing to look for it in the statute and legislative history. In the meantime, . . . we can still, as was said in our original transfer order, "discern no basis for jurisdiction in the Court of Appeals for the Federal Circuit." . . .
>
> However, now that the transferee court has transferred the case back to this court, new considerations arise. . . . A dismissal of this appeal would . . . risk leaving the parties with no avenue of appellate review of the district court's judgment. For that reason, and because a dismissal would not be in the interest of justice, we deny Christianson's motion to dismiss. . . . The parties have briefed and argued in both circuit courts and have not yet received a disposition on the merits of the appeal. It is time they did.[22]

And they did. Despite concluding that his court lacked jurisdiction, Markey reversed the summary judgment in Christianson's favor and sent the matter back to Illinois for a trial.

The situation needed a referee, and the Supreme Court was the only candidate. Justice William Brennan, writing for a unanimous court, agreed with the Federal Circuit—sort of. He agreed with Markey's jurisdictional analysis, but concluded that the Federal Circuit should have reached the logical conclusion that its Ping-Pong match with the Seventh Circuit was alive and well, rather than ruling in a case that it lacked jurisdiction to hear.[23]

That's how the Federal Circuit came to rule in a case despite knowing that it lacked jurisdiction. It was also pretty much the final word on the meaning of "arising under" until 2002, when the Supreme Court considered a related question: Suppose a plaintiff files a lawsuit that has nothing at all to do with patent law, and the defendant counterclaims with a patent suit. Where does the appeal go? A strict interpretation of "arising under" suggests that it should go to the regional circuit; the lawsuit itself did not arise under the patent laws. A policy-oriented analysis suggests that it should go the Federal Circuit; if the court's purpose is to maintain the coherence of the patent laws, letting patent suits flow across the country just because they arrived as counterclaims rather than as original claims hardly makes sense. Justice Antonin Scalia answered this question in a short opinion for a unanimous Supreme Court: If Congress wants to get *all* patent cases in front of the Federal Circuit, it can change the statute. In the meantime, "not all cases involving a patent-law claim fall within the Federal Circuit's jurisdiction."[24]

With that, Scalia unleashed at least one interesting follow-up question on the courts: What happens to patent cases that land at the regional circuits? Does Federal Circuit law govern? If not, what does? No one is quite certain, but the Eighth Circuit, the first regional circuit to consider the issue, announced that Federal Circuit law, not its own twenty-plus-year-old precedent, was binding.[25]

Questions of this sort are called "choice of law" questions, and they can be even more of a law-student soporific than are jurisdiction questions. They arise because of the country's dizzying array of courts and legislatures, including fifty state legislatures, fifty state court systems (along with a few more of each thrown in to cover territories like the District of Columbia, Puerto Rico, or Guam), Congress, twelve regional circuits, and the Federal Circuit. Unless and until the Supreme Court feels like intervening to impose uniformity, each lawmaking body retains a fair degree of autonomy—as the existence of circuit splits demonstrates. Perhaps the greatest source of confusion about choice-of-law questions, though, is that few lawsuits involve only a single issue. The very act of suing someone suggests a certain amount of tension. Whether the suit is between strangers or between parties who know each other well, it's rare to find a situation in which a plaintiff has but a single grievance against the defendant and the defendant has no claim in return. For the most part, plaintiffs claim numerous wrongs and defendants respond in kind. As a result, most lawsuits raise numerous issues, and different issues are subject to different bodies of law. Contracts, for example, often contain a choice-of-law clause, in which both parties agree to resolve their *contractual* differences subject to the laws of a specific state. Tort claims, on the other hand, are typically judged under the law of the state in which the tortious act occurred. Issues that arise under federal law are subject to federal law—as interpreted by the appropriate circuit—and so on and so forth.

When suits involve claims implicating different sources of legal authority, there are only three ways to go, and the choice among them is a matter of public policy: We could force parties to segment their suits into individual claims and to bring each claim in the appropriate court, we could impose the law of the court in which the parties appear on all claims, or we could have a single court apply different bodies of law to different parts of a lawsuit. American law has chosen the third route; a court that has jurisdiction to hear at least one part of a case also has "pendent jurisdiction" to hear all of its other parts. Whenever a case involves multiple claims, though, the presiding court must determine not only that it has jurisdiction but also which body of law applies to which claims. The Federal Circuit has to conduct a choice-of-law inquiry on almost every patent case. For the most part, the Federal Circuit has adopted a straightforward and sensible rule: it applies its own law to patent issues, and the law of the appropriate regional circuit to everything else.

Pendent jurisdiction is a significant source of the Federal Circuit's peripheral vision. Although lawsuits can combine arbitrary issues and bodies of law, some combinations are more common than others. People who hold patents frequently hold sizable intellectual property portfolios, combining copyright and trademark portfolios with their patents, and the very nature of a patent as an exclusive right means that patentees will often butt heads with antitrust law's aversion to exclusivity. Pendent jurisdiction provides the Federal Circuit with a panoramic view of IP and antitrust—the commercial contexts in which patentees convert their patents into business strategies. This view helps curb the myopia that a narrow focus on patents might otherwise engender. It gives the Federal Circuit's judges the opportunity to consider bodies of law that are related yet distinct and to see the ways that patent law interacts with the other laws shaping America's innovative, creative, and commercial communities. Our inquiry into the Federal Circuit's performance must therefore consider what happens when the Court wanders beyond the comfortable confines of patent law and into the related realms of copyright and of antitrust.

12

✛

Dawn of the
Digital Millennium

ANNIE

Patent law has a younger sister named Anne. Anne, unfortunately, is quite ill. Anne caught her first bout of technophobia more than a century ago, but she was able to secure congressional treatment. The pathology proved recurrent, and poor Anne had to return to Congress again and again. In the 1990s, Anne heard of a particularly potent strain of malignant technology beginning to spread. She sought preventive care. Congress responded with its strongest vaccine ever, a risky experimental inoculation that would either nurse poor Anne back to health or raise the cost of her death throes to untold heights. But the new technology is too strong. Anne is dying; the prognosis shows no possibility of her returning to robust health. Her family is split into warring camps: some seek to perpetuate her life support by steadily increasing her dosage of government-granted medication without heed to its public cost; others feel that it is time to give this grand old dame a dignified burial and to focus instead on her ultimate and inevitable resurrection. While this intrafamily squabble rages, Anne writhes in pain, racked with terminal technophobia. Each new pang pushes her to visit yet another emergency room, seeking succor at the hands of the judiciary while lobbying Congress for increasingly stronger doses of its high-risk narcotic. One day, she entered the emergency room in Lafayette Park.

But enough with the allegories. Patent law's younger sister is none other than copyright law, born under the Statute of Anne of 1710. Way back in 1557—when the English Crown was still distributing monopolies to its favored interests—Queen Mary granted a charter of exclusivity in the printing and book trades to the "Worshipful Company of Stationers of London," or the English printers guild. Her goal was simple. These monopoly providers could censor any and all of the perfidious literature then circulating that was encouraging her subjects to forsake the one true Church in favor of the blasphemy known as Protestantism. That didn't work out too well. Mary died in 1558, and in 1559 Queen Elizabeth renewed the charter with the slightly modified goal of protecting her God-fearing citizens from the Papist conspiracy known as Catholicism—thereby allowing the Stationers to publish the 1571 declaration that the pope lacked jurisdiction in England. And so things go in the wonderful world of censorship.

The Stationers Company's charter somehow survived the Statute of Monopolies of 1624. In 1643, the parliamentary Puritans then running England renewed it once again—recasting its censorious intent in a direction of their own choosing. This reauthorization earned the ire of one John Milton, a wordsmith of no small renown, who urged Parliament to judge "over again that order which ye have ordained to regulate printing. That no book, pamphlet, or paper shall be henceforth printed, unless the same be first approved and licensed by such."[1] Alas, Milton's entreaties were to no avail; the charter outlasted the brief English Republic of Lord Cromwell. By 1694, however, concepts like monopoly, royal privilege, and censorship seemed strangely out of tune with Enlightenment values. Parliament let the charter lapse. Independent competition arose virtually overnight. England's hapless citizen-consumers were suddenly flooded with affordable books of questionable moral and political content. The Stationers were not pleased. They lobbied to restore their monopoly, but to no avail; Parliament refused all such overtures.

Finally, in an act of some desperation, the Stationers hit upon the perfect front men: *authors!* Rather than urging Parliament to act on its own behalf, this guild of large wealthy printers would urge Parliament to protect the poor starving authors who, shorn of their corporate protectors, were at the mercy of every unscrupulous independent who happened to own a printing press. This tactic worked. In 1710, Parliament officially noted that "printers, booksellers, and other persons have of late frequently taken the liberty of printing, reprinting, and publishing, or causing to be printed, reprinted, and published, books and other writings, without the consent of the authors or proprietors of such books and writings, to their very great detriment, and too often to the ruin of them and their families"[2] and moved to prohibit this grave injustice. The Statute of Anne, "an act for the encouragement of learning, by vesting the copies of printed books in the authors or purchasers of such copies, during the times therein mentioned,"[3] reestablished the principle of monopoly ownership of written works, though only for a time-limited period rather than in perpetuity, and in the hands of the author "or his assigns" rather than in the hands of a printer or publisher.

The key to the Stationers' ploy lay in the clause "or his assigns." To whom does an author assign his rights? If he wants to get his book published, he assigns them to his publisher. The circle was complete. The olde printers' guild of England managed to recast the virtue of its monopolistic position from the promotion of Reformation morality to the promotion of Enlightenment education. Quite a sleight of hand.

The rights that the Statute of Anne granted to authors and their assigns gained clarity through several high-profile mid-eighteenth-century lawsuits pitting guild publishers against their nonguild competitors.[4] The outcomes of these suits were very much in the minds of our own founding fathers when they penned the Constitution's intellectual property clause and of the First Congress when it enacted the Copyright Act of 1790. Over the years, Congress occasionally codified (and much less frequently overruled) further judicial developments and expanded the Copyright Act's scope to accommodate new media and technologies. By the time Congress passed the Copyright Act of 1976, the regime's contours were familiar: Creators *or their assigns*, including musicians, artists, and filmmakers in addition to authors, held exclusive but incomplete rights to their works for a fixed period of time. The "incompleteness" allowed the public to make "fair use" of copyrighted work even without authorization, and the "or their assigns" portion continued to elevate the interests of publishing companies, record companies, and movie studios above those of authors, musicians, and filmmakers.

In many ways, the 1976 revisions to the Copyright Act marked the culmination of nearly three centuries of deliberation, debate, scholarship, and legal development. By the 1970s, creators knew more or less which rights they retained; the public knew more or less which rights *it* retained. Traditional copyrights and traditional fair uses led to occasional marginal disputes, but nevertheless formed a relatively predictable system underpinning creative industries that also served many public interests. Then a momentous event occurred: Technology shifted beneath our feet, and this seemingly coherent system became increasingly incoherent. That shift set the stage for the Federal Circuit's cameo in the debate over the future of copyright.

The genesis of this tectonic technological shift is worth considering because technology and economic opportunity have shaped copyright laws since the Statute of Anne. Until quite recently, the reproduction of creative works was difficult, time consuming, and expensive. It was so expensive, in fact, that mass reproduction was out of the question; even orders of monks laboring for centuries with quills couldn't satiate the latent European demand for bibles. Much of the Christian public responded to this shortage by keeping itself blissfully illiterate. The Church—effectively the controller of this important work, though hardly its owner—regarded translations and other unauthorized "derivative works" as blasphemous, and punished transgressors with penalties that even today's aggrieved copyright holders might find draconian. The reproduction of paintings and sculptures, though arguably less controversial, was even more difficult, time consuming, and expensive.

For a time, the Chinese experimented with movable type, a capital-intensive process that appeared to have some potential for mass consumption, but the absence of sufficient demand for printed matter among an illiterate peasantry rendered the technology cost-ineffective and led to its dismissal. In the mid-fifteenth century, Johannes Gutenberg developed Europe's first printing press. His bibles were inappropriate for mass consumption; they appeared in a technical language that only those with ample training could understand, and he priced them around three times the average annual white-collar salary. Several decades later, however, the technology had improved, prices had plummeted, and Martin Luther had devised a "killer ap": the vernacular bible. All of a sudden, Christendom had a reason to embrace literacy. With a literate public, creative sorts developed a new impetus not only to create but also to express themselves in writing. Though reproduced paintings and sculpture remained beyond the reach of most of "the public," the printed word began to permeate throughout society.

That permeation, in turn, led to new business opportunities in the generation and distribution of copied creative works. But whereas the primary inputs into creativity remained personal time, effort, and inspiration, the primary inputs into copying and distribution were capital-intensive printing presses, paper mills, inks, and sales networks—and capital was, is, and always will be much more fungible than inspiration. In other words, once some individual creator revealed something worth distributing, *anyone* blessed with the necessary capital could distribute it. That fungibility, set within the proto-market economy of sixteenth- and seventeenth-century England, led to a seeming paradox. The growing literacy and cultural appreciation that mass distribution had wrought generated a significant demand for mass-produced, widely distributed creative works—but competition and the absence of pricing power dampened the expected returns on the capital investments necessary to meet that demand. Simple economics made it undesirable to invest in the technologies necessary to meet consumer demand without a guaranteed return, such as the one that the various charters granted the Stationers Company.

Eighteenth-century copyright law adopted a clever fix—notwithstanding the gyrations of Stationers intent upon preserving their perpetual monopoly. In contemporary terms, the new copyright laws recognized the conflict between economics and technology as a market failure. Its framers understood that an unfettered free market might not motivate enough investment in creativity, production, or distribution to meet the bourgeoning demand. In response, they devised a surprisingly sophisticated regulatory system to meet the societal imperative of increased supply. Unlike many of the socialistic command-and-control regulations promulgated throughout the middle decades of the twentieth century, these eighteenth-century regulators adopted a more liberal market-based approach. They chose to employ a property-like regime, under which the public granted a set of "exclusive rights" to creators for a "limited time."

The original relationship among technology, economics, and the regulatory regime known as "copyright" is critical to understanding just how complete a betrayal technology's current attack represents. The eighteenth-century regulators' goal was not simply to increase the quantity (or even the quality) of creative works being produced. Their goal was to increase the quantity of such works *reaching the public*, or "commercialization" in contemporary parlance. Commercialization, in turn, required a regulatory scheme that motivated investment in every phase of the process that placed a creator's creation into the public's hands. Because the vagaries of the free market seemed to make underinvestment in creation, production, and distribution inevitable, a suitable regulation had to motivate additional investment in each of creating, producing, and distributing.

Though it's unlikely that the eighteenth-century founders of copyright law viewed the world in these contemporary terms, there's little doubt that they understood the technological and economic framework within which any market in creative works would have to develop. They crafted their package of "exclusive rights" responsively and carefully. What rights would the creator retain? Given the technological requirement of significant capital investment in production, an exclusive production—or copying—right seemed critical. Given the further technological requirement of significant capital investment in distribution, an exclusive distribution right seemed equally critical. From the very inception of copyright law, these two central rights dominated. Only the creator (or his authorized agents) could create new copies of the work, and only the creator (or his authorized agents) could distribute copies of the work. This regulatory scheme responded to the perceived failures of the free market. It delineated a contract between the broad public and its creative classes. The public accepted restricted access over a larger set of creative works for a limited time.[5] Creators were able to exploit those restrictions to extract economic compensation for their efforts and investments.

Technology, economics, and regulation combined to yield a coherent body of copyright law. Congress propertized the rights necessary to motivate commercialization. "Content creation industries" flourished; popular culture exploded; and books, periodicals, songs, plays, and movies proliferated. Every now and again some member of the public created and/or distributed a copy of a creative work without authorization, proclaiming her action necessary to serve some important public policy goal, and the creator—or more likely, the creators' "assigns," who had invested in copying and distribution—disagreed. The courts considered both arguments and ruled on a more or less case-by-case basis. From these seemingly ad hoc roots grew the "fair use" doctrine. By and large, technology remained wedded to the copyright holders; even "fair" public uses required significant capital outlays.

HIGH INFIDELITY

Over the centuries, technology began to stray from the legal bed that it shared with creators. A series of clever innovations began to reduce the costs of copying. Between the late nineteenth and the late twentieth centuries, the cost of copying text, image, music, and video spiraled downward; the mass production of creative works no longer required significant capital outlays. With each cost reduction, members of the public discovered new capabilities. They learned to copy, distribute, reconfigure, and combine creative works—works protected by copyright—in new and creative ways. Each of these new uses led to a new clash between copyright holders asserting a lack of authorization and accused members of the public citing a higher purpose of public policy. The courts continued to evaluate these claims on an ad hoc basis. Finally, roughly 185 years after first codifying the basics of copyright, Congress took it upon itself to codify the lessons of fair use that the courts had teased from these many cases; the Copyright Act of 1976 contained a new, statutory fair-use provision.[6]

The years following the 1976 congressional imprimatur on fair use proved tumultuous for copyright holders and the public alike. Copying technology continued to improve in quality, expand in scope, and decline in price. Mass production of text, pictures, music, and film became progressively easier, and the capital required to own and master the necessary technology plummeted. Copyright holders waged a massive attack on one such technology, the videocassette recorder (VCR).[7] They claimed—correctly—that Sony's VCR rendered trivial the unauthorized reproduction of their copyrighted work. Sony conceded that point, but asserted—equally correctly—that its VCRs also enabled numerous non-infringing and otherwise fair uses. The copyright holders conceded *that* point. This considerable concord over the range of uses of the VCR notwithstanding, a critical policy question remained: Should the law allow Sony to manufacture and sell a device that facilitates infringement? Wouldn't such a machine lead to myriad infringements and force the copyright holders to chase millions of small infringers in suits across the country? Or should the law terminate the development and commercialization of a potentially useful and popular technology simply to prevent its likely misuse? Which policy did we want? Would we have to change the law to get it? By a five-to-four vote, the Supreme Court ruled in favor of Sony,[8] setting the dominant contemporary test for new technologies: Any technology that enables "substantial noninfringing uses" is legal, even if it also paves the way for significant infringement. The copyright holders stewed over this loss, but quickly accommodated themselves to the new technological terrain and learned how to profit despite this setback.

The *Sony* case put copyright law on notice: technology was no longer its loyal bedmate. With each passing year, the mass production of high-quality copies got easier and less expensive. In the mid-1990s, when Congress next reconsidered the Copyright Act, copyright holders arrived armed with a laundry list of measures that recognized its erstwhile partner as an imminent threat. Chief among their desiderata for a preemptive attack was "anticircumvention," which became law as part of the Digital Millennium Copyright Act (DMCA) of 1998.[9] The anticircumvention provisions marked a radical change to copyright law—in many ways, the most radical change since copyright's basic contours were set in the eighteenth century. For nearly three hundred years, the substantive contract between the public and the creative classes had been set. Creators obtained limited (though significant) exclusive rights to produce and distribute works of their creation. The public obtained an ostensibly larger collection of creative works, retained the right to make fair use of these works with or without authorization, and eventually assumed full ownership of all creative works. Creators and the public had renegotiated specific contract terms over the centuries: the time limit had increased markedly; the rules for contracting had changed (e.g., by removing the rule that copyright law protected only works registered at the Copyright Office); new and novel fair uses arose; new classes of creative works entered the contract; special cases and terms led to a proliferation of statutory clauses; and the general complexity of the copyright contract grew over time. But the fundamental substantive bargain remained unchanged between 1710 and 1998.

The anticircumvention provisions created a new claim for copyright holders, adding a new rider to their contract with the public. This right had nothing to do with either the mass production or the distribution of creative works; it related entirely to the technological attack on copyright law. These new provisions allowed copyright holders to prohibit people from using otherwise legal technologies and, in some cases, outlawed those technologies in their entirety. Subject to numerous qualifications and exceptions, these new provisions made it a violation for people to "circumvent a technological measure that effectively controls access to a [copyrighted] work."[10] They also prohibited various activities related to helping others circumvent such access controls—and in particular, to aiding circumvention by developing and circulating enabling technology. Like most new statutes (or new riders to existing contracts), the DMCA's language included a certain amount of ambiguity; the sheer complexity of the task that it undertook injected even more uncertainty into its actual scope or meaning.

Numerous commentators noted that these inherently expansive provisions would soon likely curtail many uses that would otherwise have qualified as fair. How they felt about that expansion tended to hinge on their view of copyrights—or more broadly, of IP rights. Those who view IP as property emphasized the need to protect property rights, even at the expense of forcing the public to pay a higher cost. Those who view IP as regulation emphasized the system's policy objectives and found the inevitable erosion of fair-use rights distressing. This seemingly abstract philosophical question took an even bigger bite out of copyright law than it did out of patent law.

Professor Jane Ginsburg, known for her resounding defenses of copyright holders enduring the new technological onslaught, conceded that the DMCA could in theory have unintended and undesirable effects, but shed few tears for those hurt only in theory:

> As a general matter, one should recognize that, in granting copyright owners a right to prevent circumvention of technological controls on "access," Congress may in effect have extended copyright to cover "use" of works of authorship. . . . In theory, copyright does not reach "use"; it prohibits unauthorized reproduction, adaptation, distribution, and pubic performance or display. Not all "uses" correspond to these acts. But because "access" is a prerequisite to "use," by controlling the former, the copyright owner may well end up preventing or conditioning the latter. . . . It may in fact be misleading to condemn (or to celebrate) the DMCA's impact on the "copyright balance" between owners and users. After all, which "balance" do we mean? . . . From a user's point of view, the owner's "bundle of rights" never extended to *all* uses of works; owners now are relying on legal protection of technological measures to secure the airtight coverage the substantive

tion only.

law never previously afforded. From a copyright owner's point of view, if in the past low technology imposed a tolerance for widespread copying, that state of affairs should not be confused with a legal *right* to engage in widespread convenience copying. Newer technology undermines the factual premise for the tolerance; if the tolerance is to persist as a prerogative, it requires a legal basis.[11]

David Nimmer, one of the country's preeminent copyright lawyers and the author of a leading treatise on copyright law, asked many of the same questions and derived many of the same answers as Ginsburg, but through a lens less deferential to copyright holders and more concerned with the public at large. His evident concern for the public interest stemmed, at least in part, from his willingness to take an overt stand on the nature of the property interests inherent in copyright: "Copyright is a right less absolute than the real property interests in one's domicile."[12] It likely also stemmed in part from his reading of the history of copyright law: "Copyright owners have always had the right to retain their works confidentially," but once they publish the work and place into the stream of commerce, "they have historically lost control over its subsequent flow."[13] Nimmer thus saw the same quandary as did Ginsburg, but he framed it quite differently:

> If copyright owners package their "published" goods in digital envelopes accessible only through passwords, then perhaps they can, indeed, levy a unilateral royalty upon such activities as resales and reviews. . . . In turn, the legal issue arises of how to conceptualize the browsing activities of users in decades past. Why is it that reviewers could traditionally quote scattered passages from copyrighted works? Is it because they had a right to do so? Could chefs review the techniques of their predecessors as contained in published cookbooks of the past as a matter of right? If so, was the right of constitutional magnitude, safeguarding First Amendment interests of free speech and the advancement of knowledge? Or did the law simply allow those activities, as it would have been economically unproductive to pursue such small scale utilization? These fundamental questions exert practical consequences. Under the first point of view, any danger to the public's right to browse posed by the digital environment must be negated. Under the second point of view, by contrast, the marketplace can be left to develop—if browsing rights are extinguished in the process, the only lesson to derive is that the economics evidently have changed.[14]

With that, the DMCA left Congress, passed through some commentators, and began to haunt the federal judiciary. The first few courts to consider the new statute encountered it in settings quite close to those that Congress had anticipated when it chose to turn anticircumvention into the policy we have. These courts not only ruled in favor of the copyright holders but also applied language and created a trail of dicta more sympathetic to anticircumvention than to fair use. Courts quickly ruled that the anticircumvention provisions prohibited Streambox's virtual VCR from capturing images streamed over a RealNetworks player,[15] and more significantly, that they rendered illegal an open-source program that enabled users to decrypt and copy DVDs without the explicit authorization of the movie studios.[16]

Defendants in these cases argued that they were simply providing technologies protected under the *Sony* standard, technologies that enable significant noninfringing uses along with the infringements that had landed them in court. They also argued that many of their customers were simply making fair use of copyrighted works—by, for example, decrypting legally purchased copies of DVDs to view on unauthorized playback devices.[17] Trial and appellate judges alike appeared unmoved by these arguments. While all conceded that the cases might have been closer prior to the DMCA, the anticircumvention provisions rendered the question moot. The defendants developed and circulated decryption devices that circumvented algorithms put in place specifically to "control access" to copyrighted works. Infringement or the simultaneous enablement of significant noninfringing activity was more or less irrelevant. Anticircumvention was not a "copyright." Though part of the Copyright Act, it was an entirely new beast—a beast whose form and powers appeared formidable, but were still ill understood.

By the time the courts finished ruling on these few cases, the fair-use doctrine appeared imperiled, despite its continued statutory home in the DMCA. Technology had challenged copyright law, copyright law came back with anticircumvention guns blazing, and the fair-use doctrine lay bleeding in the crossfire. Judicial dicta suggested that the DMCA might have overruled the *Sony* test for "significant noninfringing uses," and pro-copyright-holder commentators like Ginsburg asserted that unauthorized access in the name of fair use remained illicit. It started to seem as if the DMCA had destabilized the bargain between the public and its creative classes, much as technology had destabilized the enforcement mechanisms necessary to secure the rights that copyright law grants to America's creative class.

COPYRIGHT CAMEO

Rumors of the fair-use doctrine's demise piqued the curiosity of a broader class of copyright holders. Whereas Congress *had* considered the growing impact of inexpensive production technologies on media products like movies and songs, it *had not* anticipated the implications of anticircumvention to more mundane products. In early 2003, two consumer-goods manufacturers filed suit under the anticircumvention provisions. In both cases, the manufacturers had built weak encryption into base products in order to monopolize their aftermarkets. When competitors broke the encryption algorithms, the manufacturers sued.

In one case, Chamberlain, a manufacturer of automatic garage door openers, introduced a kluge that it claimed could confound illicit entry. Skylink hacked its way around Chamberlain's algorithm and sold universal clickers capable of operating multiple types of garage door base units—including Chamberlain's.[18] In the other, the printer company Lexmark encrypted the handshake between its printers and replacement toner cartridges. Static Control Systems decrypted the handshake and sold replacement cartridges compatible with Lexmark's printers.[19] Both plaintiffs forwarded the same DMCA argument: Their products contained embedded software, which, like all software, was copyrighted. Their encryption algorithms controlled access to their copyrighted software. Anyone who decrypted these algorithms to interact with the software therefore circumvented their access controls. Anyone who sold devices that enabled such circumvention was a trafficker subject to DMCA liability.

These prima facie cases sounded strong, and the policy implications seemed obvious: The DMCA had destroyed the possibility for competitive aftermarkets. Increasing numbers of products contain embedded software (i.e., any product that contains a microchip), and much of that software must communicate with other products. According to Chamberlain and Lexmark, the DMCA provided manufacturers with an ironclad way to restrict the devices with which its own devices may communicate. No one believed that Congress had anticipated this outcome—including Professor Ginsburg, whose unwillingness to shed any tears for users denied access as a matter of theory melted away when she met users denied access in practice:

> I do not believe that [the anticircumvention provisions] cover the circumvention of a technological measure that controls access to a work not protected under [the Copyright Act]. And if we're talking about ballpoint pen cartridges, printer cartridges, garage doors and so forth, we're talking about works not protected under [the Copyright Act]. As has already been stated here and in many of the filings, there's nothing in the legislative history that would suggest that such a result was intended. The legislative history points to Congress' desire to protect copyrighted works against circumvention.[20]

Ginsburg's beliefs and general incredulity notwithstanding, the question for the courts was whether the statute's words, not its intent, mandated the outcome that Chamberlain and Lexmark advocated. Meanwhile,

Nimmer, whose sympathy for users denied access had existed even in theory, signed on as one of Skylink's lawyers.

That's when poor, sick Anne landed in Lafayette Park. Chamberlain's original claim was that Skylink had circumvented its access control and infringed its copyrights *and its patents*—a claim that "arose under" the patent laws at least in part. Though the patent claims faded to insignificance early in the proceedings, the Federal Circuit's pendent jurisdiction thrust it into the center of this major copyright controversy. The clerk of court's assignment wheel landed on Judges Gajarsa, Linn, and Prost. Though the rules of pendent jurisdiction required this panel to rule as a matter of Seventh Circuit law, the Seventh Circuit had not yet said anything about the relevant DMCA provisions. The panel thus set out to interpret this complex question about the DMCA in a way that allowed the entire Copyright Act to make sense; the court could only assume that its best efforts at statutory construction on the Seventh Circuit's behalf would reach the same conclusion that the Seventh Circuit would reach on its own.

The panel's judgment was unanimous: Chamberlain had tried to push the new anticircumvention laws too far. In addition to simply announcing that Chamberlain lost, however, Judge Gajarsa's opinion addressed many of the key issues underlying a provision that the Seventh Circuit, in its only even remotely relevant statement on anticircumvention, had called "an attempt to deal with special problems created by the so-called digital revolution."[21] Gajarsa, for instance, weighed in on the nature of copyrights as property:

> The essence of the DMCA's anticircumvention provisions is that [they] establish causes of action for liability. They do not establish a new property right. The DMCA's text indicates that circumvention is not infringement, and the statute's structure makes the point even clearer. This distinction between property and liability is critical. Whereas copyrights, like patents, are property, liability protection from unauthorized circumvention merely creates a new cause of action under which a defendant may be liable. . . .
>
> The anticircumvention provisions convey no additional property rights in and of themselves; they simply provide property owners with new ways to secure their property. Like all property owners taking legitimate steps to protect their property, however, copyright owners relying on the anticircumvention provisions remain bound by all other relevant bodies of law.[22]

Whatever type of property copyrights may be—whether more closely akin to houses or to licenses—the DMCA did not expand the scope of the property rights already built into copyright law. Instead, Congress recognized that the digital data of the information age poses new challenges for copyright holders and responded by creating a new protective mechanism to help them enforce their rights. By the time the case reached the Federal Circuit, Chamberlain had dropped all of its infringement claims; it was no longer even arguing that Skylink had invaded its property, but sought to protect its exclusive commercial position nonetheless. Like the Stationers of yore, Chamberlain believed that copyright law should protect its monopoly. Gajarsa shot it down cold; in the absence of an extended property right, Chamberlain's claim of entitlement seemed particularly weak.

Gajarsa also spent some time pondering the deal that Congress had cut between the public and its creative classes when it passed the DMCA. "Congress attempted to balance competing interests, and endeavored to specify, with as much clarity as possible, how the right against anticircumvention would be qualified to maintain balance between the interests of content creators and information users."[23] Congress crafted the new provisions

> to help bring copyright law into the information age. Advances in digital technology over the past few decades have stripped copyright owners of much of the technological and economic protection to which they had grown accustomed. Whereas large-scale copying and distribution of copyrighted material used to be difficult and expensive, it is now easy and inexpensive. . . . Congress therefore crafted legislation restricting some, but not all, technological measures designed either to access a work protected by copyright or to infringe a right of a copyright owner.[24]

The logical implication of Chamberlain's position, Gajarsa explained, is that Congress had surreptitiously split the world of copyright in two. In one regime, the long-accepted contours of copyright law still governed. In the other, copyright holders who availed themselves of encryption technologies possessed unrestricted rights and cut the public out of the equation entirely. He rejected that implication outright: "Even under the substantial deference due Congress, such a redefinition borders on the irrational."[25] He continued:

> Chamberlain's proposed construction would allow copyright owners to prohibit exclusively fair uses even in the absence of any feared foul use. It would therefore allow any copyright owner, through a combination of contractual terms and technological measures, to repeal the fair use doctrine with respect to an individual copyrighted work—or even selected copies of that copyrighted work. Again, this implication contradicts [the new anticircumvention provisions] directly. Copyright law itself authorizes the public to make certain uses of copyrighted materials. Consumers who purchase a product containing a copy of embedded software have the inherent legal right to use that copy of the software. What the law authorizes, Chamberlain cannot revoke.[26]

The DMCA thus did nothing to alter the fundamental balance between the public and its creative classes. Creators possess only the rights they had possessed under the 1976 Act, and the public retained every right that had ever fallen under the fair-use banner. The DMCA's only real accomplishment was its introduction of a new enforcement mechanism designed to make life a little easier for the copyright holders that technology had betrayed. Once again, Gajarsa slammed shut the idea that the DMCA might have given the manufacturer of garage door openers the lost monopoly of the Stationers.

So is the policy we have the policy we want? That's a question that courts rarely address, and the Federal Circuit's ruling against Chamberlain was no exception. Nor, for that matter, was the Sixth Circuit's parallel ruling against Lexmark. Judge Jeffrey Sutton's only real comment about congressional choices in his majority opinion focused on the inapplicability of claims like Lexmark's (or, by implication, like Chamberlain's) to anything that was even on the congressional radar:

> Nor can Lexmark tenably claim that this reading of the statute fails to respect Congress's purpose in enacting it. . . . Nowhere in its deliberations over the DMCA did Congress express an interest in creating liability for the circumvention of technological measures designed to prevent consumers from using consumer goods while leaving the copyrightable content of a work unprotected. In fact, Congress added [a] provision in part to ensure that the DMCA would not diminish the benefit to consumers of interoperable devices in the consumer electronics environment.[27]

The courts seem intent upon doing their interpretive jobs and leaving the tough policy calls to Congress. Those of us who dwell in the land of the commentators need show no such deference. Did Congress's decision to augment copyright law with anticircumvention provisions move us closer to or further from sound copyright policy? Is the policy we have the policy we want?

BUZZ FROM THE BLOGOSPHERE

Fortunately, the information age has given us a new medium for instant commentary, a medium neither humble nor bashful, a medium known as the blogosphere. Professor Michael Madison spoke for many IP bloggers:

> The court emphatically sided with consumers' rights to open their garage doors with the openers of their choosing. Hurrah, and all that, for the court's rejection of an obviously abusive attempt to use IP law to advance an anticompetitive agenda. But still. . . .

The broader issue is that this is precisely the kind of case that should engage everyone, showing how IP law can touch the day-to-day lives of everyone, not just alleged "pirates." My guess, though, is that aside from IP lawyers and non-lawyer IP policy wonks (who seem to be hard-wired to care about this stuff), this won't get the mass media attention that the P2P cases attract. It's not sexy. . . .

Out of the blogosphere and into the garage. That's what we need to sell. How do we market the message?[28]

Many other bloggers echoed Madison's "hurrah and all that." Jason Schulz of the Electronic Frontier Foundation (EFF)—a cyberlibertarian organization that has taken the lead in fighting attempts to counter technological advances with legal restrictions—described the case as "a lengthy and interesting unanimous opinion by Judge Gajarsa, with some real gems reining in some of the overbroad and much-abused language."[29] Adam Thierer, director of telecommunication studies at the libertarian Cato Institute, mused that he could "only imagine the can of worms this case would have opened if it went [in the] opposite direction. If Chamberlain would have prevailed, then using similar logic, TV manufacturers could have prevented other companies from creating universal 'integrated' remote controls for our televisions and audio/video equipment."[30]

Most practicing IP lawyers in the blogosphere more or less agreed with Thierer's assessment that the court *had* to rule against Chamberlain, if for no reason other than that a ruling for Chamberlain would have upended significant swaths of the American commercial terrain.[31] Professor Ed Felten, a Princeton computer scientist and one of Madison's nonlawyer IP policy wonks, focused his analysis on the policy we have—a policy that he sees as unduly burdensome on technological progress—and on the judiciary's limited ability to fix that policy:

In the end, the court [finds] that (1) tools whose only significant uses are non-infringing cannot violate the DMCA, and (2) in construing the DMCA, courts should balance the desire of Congress to protect the flanks of copyright owners' rights, against users' rights such as fair use and interoperation. In this case, the court said, the balancing test was easy, because Chamberlain's rights as a copyright owner (e.g., the right to prevent infringing copying of Chamberlain's software) were not at all threatened by Skylink's behavior, so one side of the balancing scale was just empty. The court's decision to leave us with a balancing test, rather than a more specific rule, seems motivated by caution, which seems like a wise approach in dealing with uncharted legal territory.

Of course, this entire exercise is predicated on the assumption that Congress had a clear idea what it meant to do in passing the DMCA. Based on what I have seen, that just isn't the case. Many lawmakers have expressed surprise at some of the implications of the DMCA. Many seemed unaware that they were burdening research or altering the outlines of the Sony rule (and clearly some alteration in Sony took place). Many seemed to think, at the time, that the DMCA posed no threat to fair use. Partly this was caused by misunderstanding of the technology, and partly it was due to the tendency to write legislation by taking a weighted average of the positions of interest groups, rather than trying to construct a logically consistent statutory structure. So the DMCA is still a mess. It still bans or burdens far too much legitimate activity. This court's ruling has gone some distance toward resolving the inherent contradictions in the statute; but we still have a long, long way to go.[32]

Felten's fellow nonlawyer IP policy wonk, Seth Finkelstein, seemed less attuned to the niceties of judicial process. He essentially shrugged off *Chamberlain* as gloss on a poor policy choice, only to arrive at the same conclusion as Felten: the policy we have is not the policy we want, or as he expressed it, "the whole opinion boils down to the judicial version of a Monty Python-ese statement of: 'Stop that! It's silly.'"[33]

A rare blogospheric consensus seemed to be emerging. The policy that Congress enacted under the DMCA's anticircumvention provisions is not the policy we want, but the Federal Circuit's insistence that these new provisions continue to make sense within the overall scheme of copyright law nevertheless blunted some of its most odious policy implications. Yet something seemed wrong. If there really is a consensus that anticircumvention is bad policy, who would lobby Congress to keep it? All that had to happen was for the forces of IP blogdom to march to Washington and demand IP reform. Why wasn't it happening?

It wasn't happening because the blogosphere is only a small part of the story. The DMCA's strongest backers—the record companies and movie studios who pushed it into law and who continue to push for its expansion—knew that Chamberlain and Lexmark made them look bad. These consumer goods companies argued that the DMCA reversed the long-standing American preference for competitive markets. *No one* believes that that is the policy we want. Had that view of the DMCA prevailed, Congress might well have weakened the anticircumvention provisions. The pro-DMCA copyright holders wisely chose to say little and to let their opponents dominate the discussion. As far as they were concerned, the Federal Circuit's ruling against Chamberlain, followed in short order by the Sixth Circuit's ruling against Lexmark, helped to rationalize a law that they liked by blocking some its more disturbing implications—and did so in a manner that hurt only people in industries unrelated to their own. Saying nothing seemed wise; they could save their objections for another day.

That day took less than eighteen months to arrive. The dispute on that day pitted StorageTek, a manufacturer of automated tape cartridge libraries capable of storing massive amounts of computer data, against CHE, an independent business that repairs StorageTek-manufactured data libraries. StorageTek alleged that CHE's repairs violated the DMCA's anticircumvention provisions. CHE responded that its repairs fell squarely within a new "safe harbor" provision that Congress also first introduced in 1998 as part of the DMCA, specifically to protect software maintenance and repair organizations. A trial court in Boston agreed with StorageTek. Because the original complaint included patent claims, the appeal came to the Federal Circuit. The assignment wheel selected Judges Rader, Schall, and Bryson.

Most of the action in this dispute hinged on the safe harbor—a provision whose interpretation proved sufficiently contentious to split the panel and to cause Judge Rader to dissent. Nevertheless, Judge Bryson's majority opinion explained that, following *Chamberlain*, anyone alleging an anticircumvention violation "must prove that the circumvention of the technological measure either 'infringes or facilitates infringing a right protected by the Copyright Act.'" Because the majority had found that CHE's behavior fell within the contentious safe harbor, it wasn't infringing any of StorageTek's copyrights. Thus, "[t]o the extent that CHE's activities do not constitute copyright infringement or facilitate copyright infringement, StorageTek is foreclosed from maintaining an action under the DMCA."[34]

To no one's surprise, StorageTek petitioned for a rehearing. What might surprise some was the solidarity that copyright holders showed in lining up behind StorageTek. In a joint amicus brief, the Software and Information Industry Association (SIIA), the Association of American Publishers (AAP), the Entertainment Software Association (ESA), the Motion Picture Association of America (MPAA), the National Music Publishers' Association (NMPA), and the Recording Industry Association of America (RIAA) all urged the Federal Circuit to rehear the case *en banc*—not because they agreed with StorageTek and Judge Rader about the safe harbor provision, but specifically to overrule *Chamberlain*. They described *Chamberlain* as "manifestly contrary to Congress's purpose and intent":

> The *Chamberlain* analysis fundamentally misread the statute. . . . [It] imported into [the DMCA] a requirement that Congress deliberately chose not to put there. It ignored other provisions of the same statute, enacted at the same time, that make its interpretation of an additional requirement untenable. And it misapplied [a] provision which was enacted in part to prevent precisely the misreading to which the *Chamberlain* panel succumbed. By following this aspect of the *Chamberlain* opinion and applying it [here], the panel in this case compounded the error.[35]

The Federal Circuit denied StorageTek's petition, provided a brief expansion of its thoughts about the safe harbor provision (from which Judge

Rader again dissented), and said nothing at all about the DMCA, anticircumvention, *Chamberlain*, or the amici.[36]

So much for an emerging consensus. Though the many powerful lobbying groups had bitten their tongues after *Chamberlain* and *Lexmark*, they believed that Congress did give us the policy we want when it enacted the anticircumvention provisions, and that the courts had taken a turn that they saw as both weak judicial interpretation and bad public policy.

No one could say that we weren't warned. Back in the instantaneous analysis of the post-*Chamberlain* blogosphere, Ernest Miller, a fellow of Yale Law School's Information Society Project, explained why the courts should not have wasted their time performing intricate analyses and balancing tests.

> Since the law is this ridiculous, jurists are being forced to find distinctions to prevent this nightmare while preserving Jack Valenti's wishes. [*Chamberlain*] shows the logic twisting in action. . . . How the DMCA can be interpreted in this way, I don't understand. . . . The judge's argument in the present case is mere assertion that rejects the ridiculous logic of the DMCA, however it is not much of an argument, if it can be characterized as an argument at all.[37]

Jack Valenti, of course, was the long-time head of the MPAA, one of the organizations that derided Gajarsa's efforts as "manifestly contrary to Congress's purpose and intent."

Miller's comments were more than a mere potshot at Valenti and his colleagues. They were also an indication of a problem that some legal scholars were beginning to cite with both *Chamberlain* and *Lexmark*. In the land of the law journals, where analyses are longer, more detailed, more reflective, and less instantaneous than in the blogosphere, several commentators disagreed with Gajarsa's analysis—as well as with Sutton's analysis in *Lexmark*. These commentators believed that the DMCA compelled rulings that created the absurd implications of which Gajarsa, Sutton, the bloggers, and others had warned. Though most conceded that these judges ruled in a manner consistent with the policy we want (or need), they nevertheless remained troubled about judicial fidelity to the policy we have. After all, the policy we have is the one that the statute captures. If it's not the policy we want, we will have to convince Congress to change it—and if the courts take the heat off Congress whenever the implications of poor congressional policy decisions become too odious, what will motivate Congress to act in the face of concerted opposition from the amicus dream team?

The message behind this scholarship remains unclear. International IP scholar Zohar Efroni, for example, presented a detailed consideration of the *Chamberlain* and *Lexmark* legal analyses. Using the rarefied language of scholarship, he concluded that neither opinion was "immaculately facile," which hardly sounds like a compliment. Most of his other conclusions were more readily comprehensible from a linguistic perspective, if not from the perspectives of law and of policy.

Efroni noted—with apparent disapproval—that "both courts, while carrying out the task of interpreting and applying the DMCA anticircumvention rules, occasionally resorted to the parameters of common sense and the rule of reason."[38] He then pivoted to downplay the implications of his own careful legal analysis: The courts "achieved the only reasonable results considering the settings presented before them. So what does copyright law have to do with restrictions on competition in the aftermarket for peripheral devices? The correct answer is nothing, and this message was lucidly delivered by the courts."[39] Finally, he attempted to reconcile his feelings about these rulings by reference to Justice William O. Douglas's rule of thumb: good laws should make sense. "When courts are forced, in the course of their interpretational endeavors, to 'strip' a statute from its letter (if not from its spirit) in order to achieve reasonable results, something is likely wrong with that statute."[40]

Indeed there is. Mathematical logic teaches that within any given system, if one contradictory statement is true, all contradictions are true. The anticircumvention provisions introduced a contradiction into copyright law: they authorized copyright holders to eliminate fair uses while announcing that the fair-use doctrine remained unchanged. Any competent logician could thus derive that Chamberlain and Lexmark behaved in ways that were simultaneously permissible and impermissible. Judges, however, cannot rest upon such triumphs of logic (or illogic); they must break the impasse by determining which of these contradictory statements takes precedence over the other. Under the circumstances, "immaculately facile" reasoning may not have been an option. Though Efroni seems to believe that the Federal Circuit in *Chamberlain* and the Sixth Circuit in *Lexmark* both got their cases right despite getting the law wrong, it's not clear how he, as a legal scholar, believes that these courts should have ruled. It is clear, however, that he sees much work ahead if Congress is ever to give us the policy we want.

> In a technology-oriented environment, the application of the DMCA as an attempt to hinder competition demonstrated by companies like Lexmark and Chamberlain may be only the tip of the iceberg. Applied to our digitized society, in which more and more aspects of everyday life are dependent on and managed by data manipulation and computer programs, a literal reading of the DMCA could provide copyright owners with outrageously excessive control over too many things. . . . One step in the right direction would be to

narrow the scope of either the former or the latter. The stakes involved cannot be underestimated, and as one commentator has phrased it, they can put no less than the integrity of copyright law into question. Our ability to appreciate the big picture of what the DMCA actually means, or rather, what it should mean, cannot be confined to its letter. The current juncture indicates that courts are ready and willing to prove themselves an essential and alert safety valve.[41]

Efroni would thus point Congress in two promising directions: either weaken the protections that we grant to software providers, or weaken the DMCA's anticircumvention provisions.

SENSE SANS SENSIBILITY

The key to Efroni's critique is simple: copyright law no longer makes sense. The digital technologies of the information age have done more than simply betray copyright. They have turned a sensible regulatory system that balanced the needs of the public and its creative classes to motivate creativity and its commercialization into a regulatory system that distributes unenforceable rights. It's hard to imagine a less sensible system—or a weaker approach to public policy. The DMCA is a reflection of that inherent shortcoming. Some scholars who share Efroni's belief that the DMCA is untenable legislation in an information age have proposed radical solutions. Professor Terry Fisher, for one, has proposed rethinking the entire copyright bargain between the public and its creative classes by severing the right to compensation from the right to control distribution. He would replace the current copyright system with "a governmentally administered reward system":

A creator who wished to collect revenue when his or her song or film was heard or watched would register it with the Copyright Office. With registration would come a unique file name, which would be used to track transmissions of digital copies of the work. The government would raise, through taxes, sufficient money to compensate registrants for making their works available to the public. Using techniques pioneered by American and European performing rights organizations and television rating services, a government agency would estimate the frequency with which each song and film was heard or watched by consumers. Each registrant would then periodically be paid by the agency a share of the tax revenues proportional to the relative popularity of his or her creation. Once this system were in place, we would modify copyright law to eliminate most of the current prohibitions on unauthorized reproduction, distribution, adaptation, and performance of audio and video recordings. Music and films would thus be readily available, legally, for free.[42]

Efroni and Fisher are hardly alone in believing that information-age challenges may require significant shifts to the ways that we think about copyrights. It's hard to find anyone who *disagrees* with that assertion—though corrective policy proposals range from draconian vigilante enforcement mechanisms to the abolition of copyright. The reason for such broad agreement is that, as we foretold allegorically, poor Anne is dying. Unlike patent law, where robust debates over policy reforms engage issues large and small, structural and tactical, legislative and judicial, the copyright debates of the information age are existential.

Digital technology has driven a stake through the heart of the copyright bargain. From the Statute of Anne of 1710 to the Copyright Act of 1976, copyright law gave copyright holders the exclusive right to control distribution. Technology and economics have rendered those rights unenforceable. Copyright policy chose to grant these rights to motivate investment in large-scale copying and distribution. Technology and economics say that copying and distribution are no longer capital-intensive tasks worthy of regulatory motivation.

This pattern is common and becoming increasingly prevalent: Technology creates new opportunities. Economics dictates the opportunities that people choose to pursue. Those who stand to lose under the new rules of technology and economics fight back, frequently trying to use law and regulation to reinstate transaction costs that technology eroded. Policymakers decide which costs to reinstate by law. Technologists work within the new legal and economic realities. The entire process repeats itself over and over again.[43] Here, technology made copying and distribution cheap and easy. People availed themselves of this technology to make and distribute numerous copies of their digital files, paying little heed to the niceties of copyright law. Copyright holders fought back and petitioned Congress to enact the anticircumvention provisions. Congress responded favorably in the DMCA. Chamberlain and Lexmark sought to avail themselves of these legally imposed transaction costs to monopolize their aftermarkets. The courts stopped them cold.

Today, no one believes that the situation is stable. Some advocates flock to Congress seeking a repeal of the anticircumvention provisions—if not a rethinking of copyright law itself. Others flock to Congress seeking a strengthening of the anticircumvention provisions and additional enforcement mechanisms. Who will prevail? The answer depends, in large part, on the view of intellectual property that Congress decides to adopt. If IP is property, sacred like all property, increased enforcement seems appropriate. If IP law simply uses property rights to achieve a market-based regulatory scheme, Congress must rethink that scheme in light of contemporary technological and economic realities. Under this latter route—the return to the first principles of the copyright system to develop a regulatory structure better aligned with our policy goals—some variant of Fisher's drive to sever distribution rights from compensation rights seems reasonable. Yet his proposal threatens to supplant long-standing tradable rights with government administrators and taxes—a disturbing step away from a liberal market economy at the dawn of the information age.

As we noted when considering compulsory licenses in the patent context, a government bureaucracy is not strictly necessary; judicially crafted guidelines governing "reasonableness" and "nondiscrimination" would leave most salient decisions where they belong—in the hands of the rights holder. Could such a scheme also work in a copyright context despite the difficulty of tracking infringement? That's a question that all good liberals should ponder whenever we encounter schemes like Fisher's: Can we keep the salient regulatory restructuring without bureaucratizing private decisions and transactions?

Or perhaps it is time for liberals to ponder even more radical possibilities, such as whether free-market principles would still lead to an undersupply of new creativity. Perhaps it is time to ask: If technology has eliminated the need to motivate investments in the mass production and distribution of creative works, do we really need a regulatory mechanism governing creativity? If the essence of the information age is cheap, abundant information, won't new communication media provide consumers with more text, photos, and music than they can possibly absorb? Won't consumers begin to value people who scout and filter that mass of freely contributed creativity to tell then which small fraction is worthy of attention? Haven't we begun to see such businesses emerge across the Internet? Perhaps such models suggest that technology alone has overcome the market imperfection that undersupplies creative works, so that law and regulation no longer need to do that work.

The data, I suspect, do not yet sustain a case strong enough to eliminate this long-standing regulatory system altogether. They are clear, however, that as technology comes closer to perfecting the market, law will have to choose between either relinquishing its hold and letting market forces take over or working ever harder to retain existing business models and expectations by prohibiting many natural benefits of digital media's newfound fluidity. The liberal approach—at least among those of us who see IP systems as reformable regulatory mechanisms rather than as sacred property rights—is to begin with the goal of promoting progress, to survey the terrain to see which aspects of promotion are unachievable within a free market, and to regulate only as necessary to overcome those perceived shortcomings.[44] Much work lies ahead. The limitations on IP experimentation that TRIPS imposed notwithstanding, it is almost inconceivable that copyright will end the twenty-first century in recognizable form; it is simply an untenable body of law in the information age.

So where do we stand? What does our brief glimpse of the black box of copyright law say about the state of copyright policy? What does it say about the Federal Circuit's performance on its excursion into the part of the IP terrain that it shares with its twelve sister circuits? And what does it say about the future of copyright law within a liberal market system? From what we have seen, only the first two of these questions have straightforward answers: The policy we have is not the policy we want. Congress gets a failing grade for misaligning copyright policy with the technological and economic realities of the information age. The Federal Circuit gets a high grade, either for teasing out a sensible interpretation from a complex statute or for elevating common sense above a formalistic statutory reading that threatened to strangle the American economy (depending on whom you ask). On the third question, liberal IP scholars have their work cut out for them.

The best feature of copyright law has always been its reliance on tradable rights set within a market-oriented regulatory scheme. If technology has rendered those rights unenforceable, what alternative set of rights (if any) should supplant them? Compensation rights, some other set of rights, or no rights at all? And regardless of the rights awarded, how can we continue to use market mechanisms to motivate the rapid dissemination of high-quality creative products—which is, after all, the ultimate goal of IP policy? Perhaps we should return to the structural problem that we detected in patent law—the insistence on a unitary system despite the varying needs of different industries—fold our creative industries into the analysis, and rethink our entire approach to IP law (TRIPS permitting, that is).

These are the questions that will engage copyright scholars, Congress, and the courts over the next few decades. The Federal Circuit's unique role in patent law more or less guarantees that it will gain additional glimpses of the copyright wars and that it will remain a significant voice in all discussions of IP reform. It also implies, however, that the Federal Circuit is unlikely to adjudicate more than a few key copyright cases. *Chamberlain* may prove to be the sole exception. But the mere exercise of viewing copyright law through the eyes of a patent court renders the entire excursion worthwhile. We must wish poor Anne well in her remaining time, but we cannot expect to see her in Lafayette Park on more than the rare occasion.

13

✛

Sherman's March

OLD BEDFELLOWS

The court's panorama turns next to antitrust. Antitrust and patents are *very* old bedfellows. King James declared "monopolies are things contrary to our laws," with the sole exception of "projects of new invention," nearly four centuries ago. For a while, the linkage seemed to break somewhere in the North Atlantic. The framers of the Constitution took the new-invention exception to heart when they drafted the Intellectual Property Clause, as did the First Congress when it enacted the Patent Act of 1790, but the general principle rendering all other monopolies illegal appeared nowhere in American statutory law for an entire century. Into the breach rode Senator John Sherman (R-OH), a former Secretary of the Treasury, a future Secretary of State, and the younger brother of General William Tecumseh Sherman, to champion what became the Sherman Antitrust Act of 1890.[1] From that day forward, monopolies were things as contrary to the laws of the United States as they were to the laws of England.

That day also marked the arrival of two enduring philosophical conflicts in American legal circles. The first of these conflicts relates to the nature of antitrust law itself, the second to its relationship with its fraternal twin, patent law. On the first front, Adam Smith had framed antitrust's existential quandary in 1776:

People of the same trade seldom meet together, even for merriment and diversion, but the conversation ends in a conspiracy against the public, or in some contrivance to raise prices. It is impossible indeed to prevent such meetings, by any law which either could be executed, or would be consistent with liberty and justice. But though the law cannot hinder people of the same trade from sometimes assembling together, it ought to do nothing to facilitate such assemblies; much less to render them necessary.[2]

Smith considered it inevitable that conspiracies in restraint of trade would operate to the detriment of the public and eviscerate the viability of the free markets that he advocated, but he was even less comfortable with the thought of laws that prohibited such conspiracies. In his opinion, laws designed to protect competition seemed likely to suppress more liberty than they unleashed—notwithstanding the critical role that competition plays in the capitalist system.

Was Smith right? The debate still rages among advocates of the free market. Liberals favor free markets because they are the most effective, fairest mechanisms for distributing scarce resources among the members of the public. Free markets promote competition, and competition impels producers to offer consumers increasingly attractive products at increasingly attractive prices. Free markets thus serve the public interest by maximizing consumer welfare. Most free-market economists, however, concede that there are circumstances in which "anticompetitive" producers can interfere with the appropriate functioning of the market—though the debate about the frequency of such market imperfections remains vigorous. U.S. antitrust law relies upon both private parties and government enforcement agencies to police the markets by detecting, punishing, and deterring anticompetitive behavior.

So far, none of this is controversial—at least among advocates of liberal markets. The controversies arise in trying to determine how often anticompetitive behavior actually occurs, how strict antitrust enforcement should be, and whether such enforcement causes more damage than it cures. Two top Industrial Organization economists, professors William Baumol and Janusz Ordover, echoed Smith's discomfort in a classic 1985 paper:

> There is a specter that haunts our antitrust institutions. Its threat is that, far from serving as the bulwark of competition, these institutions will become the most powerful instrument in the hands of those who wish to subvert it. More than that, it threatens to draw great quantities of resources into the struggle to prevent effective competition, thereby more than offsetting the contributions to economic efficiency promised by antitrust activities. This is a specter that may well dwarf any other source of concern about the antitrust processes. We ignore it at our peril and would do well to take steps to exorcise it.[3]

Alan Greenspan, whose interest in antitrust predated his lengthy stint
as God of Finance, was even harsher in his criticism: "The entire structure
of antitrust statutes in this country is a jumble of economic irrationality
and ignorance. It is the product: (a) of a gross misinterpretation of history,
and (b) of rather naive, and certainly unrealistic, economic theories."[4] According to Greenspan, the only reason that antitrust intervention might
ever be warranted was to clean up bad government policies of the past;
he argued that if we had fewer interventionist economic policies, we
would need fewer antitrust remedies.[5]

Even those who find Greenspan's criticism excessive nevertheless recognize that Baumol and Ordover's specter is real. Antitrust law *can* be oppressive, and during various decades of the twentieth century—including
the period including 1961, when Greenspan penned his withering critique, and ending shortly before Baumol and Ordover issued their cautionary note—American antitrust law *was* oppressive. According to
prominent historian Richard Hofstadter, writing in the 1960s, "the managers of the large corporations do their business with one eye constantly
cast over their shoulders at the antitrust division."[6]

> Economists and lawyers differ profoundly on how effective the antitrust
> laws have been . . . but there is hardly a major industry that has not seen a
> significant lawsuit or two, and in most industries in which intervention
> might be thought desirable, government action has had more than negligible
> effects. . . . The existing state of enforcement conforms to the state of the pub-
> lic mind, which accepts bigness but continues to distrust business morals.
> . . . Visitations by the Department of Justice are a nuisance, lawsuits are ex-
> pensive, and prosecution carries an odious stigma, but the antitrust proce-
> dures can be considered an alternative to more obtrusive regulation such as
> outright controls on prices.[7]

Other alternatives, however, are also possible. Over the past twenty-
five years, antitrust scrutiny has shrunk from oppressive to almost non-
existent before growing back to fall somewhere in between. At the same
time, Americans' willingness to accept obtrusive regulations like outright
price controls has declined steadily.

The adventures of antitrust law and the businesses it scrutinized
throughout that period bring us squarely to the second great philosophical conflict: defining the appropriate relationship between antitrust law
and patent law. When antitrust enforcement is so intense that it qualifies
as oppressive, who is it likely to oppress? Not surprisingly, those whom
the law suspects of illicit monopolistic behavior. Who is more suspicious
than a patentee, blessed with a government-authorized license for exclusivity? During eras of oppressive antitrust enforcement, the law typically

scrutinizes patentees' behavior closely, ready to pounce at the sight of any attempted extension, expansion, or leveraging of that exclusivity beyond the narrowest confines of the patent. Conversely, policymakers who favor patentees tend to hold antitrust enforcement at arm's length.

Contemporary conventional wisdom accommodates a joint statement of purpose. Under prevailing policy norms, all laws that regulate commercial activity are supposed to be pro-consumer.[8] Conventional wisdom today asserts that intellectual property rights foster innovation—leading to long-term consumer benefits—while antitrust enforcement fosters competition, which leads to nearer-term consumer benefits. The two bodies of law work together to ensure that consumers gain rapid access to high-quality, low-cost products.

It was not always thus. In the more than two decades since Professor Louis Kaplow wrote, "The intersection of antitrust law and patent policy has proved to be a source of perpetual confusion and controversy since the passage of the Sherman Act nearly a century ago," neither the confusion nor the controversy have abated.[9] Not long ago, conventional wisdom held that antitrust and IP were in hopeless, eternal conflict. Patents (and to a lesser extent, copyrights) confer monopolies, while antitrust opposes and seeks to terminate monopolies. The former is pro-producer, the latter pro-consumer. The former restricts competition; the latter promotes it. Conflict is thus inevitable and irreconcilable.

Such conventional wisdom dominates eras when antitrust regulators oppress anyone who would use her property—intellectual or real—to gain competitive leverage. The last such era ended in 1981, when Ronald Reagan arrived in Washington intent upon unshackling America's markets. In the space of a few short years, American policymakers inverted their attitudes toward patents and antitrust. "Chicago School" economics directed a significant change in antitrust policy. Members of the Chicago School believe that nearly all anticompetitive behavior is inherently self-defeating and that antitrust enforcement is appropriate only in exceptional circumstances. As Robert Bork, one of the leading Chicago School voices on antitrust, explained:

> Antitrust is . . . a set of continually evolving theories about the economics of industrial organization. . . . The capture of the field by anti-free-market theories will have impact far beyond the confines of antitrust itself. The struggle between economic freedom and regulation also reflects and reacts upon the tension in our society between the ideals of liberty and equality. . . . Within the limited frame for observation provided by antitrust, . . . it is worth noting that the general movement has been away from . . . the ideal of competition and toward the older idea of protected status for each producer, away from concern for general welfare and toward concern for interest groups, and away from the ideal of liberty towards the ideal of

enforced equality. . . . If, as I believe, [these trends] have already gone much too far in antitrust as elsewhere in our polity, they should be recognized and reversed, for they are ultimately incompatible with the preservation of a liberal capitalist social order.[10]

In the early 1980s, the Federal Trade Commission and the Antitrust Division of the Department of Justice, the two government antitrust enforcement agencies, developed guidelines consistent with the economic theories of the Chicago School, reduced the scrutiny they applied to various activities that their predecessors had considered anticompetitive, and allowed American businesses to grow in ways that previous enforcement efforts had stymied. The Supreme Court soon followed the agencies' lead toward realigning antitrust law with economic rationality—in essence moving the antitrust policy we have toward the antitrust policy we want.[11]

The changes in patent policy were even more profound. The Federal Courts Improvement Act creating the Federal Circuit, the Bayh-Dole Act promoting industrial technology transfer programs, the Hatch-Waxman Act improving the efficiency of drug markets, and the Supreme Court's announcements that software and microorganisms were patentable subject matter revolutionized American patent policy in the space of less than five years.[12] Taken as a whole, the first half of the 1980s ushered out an era of weak patents and oppressive antitrust in favor of an era of strong patents and laissez-faire antitrust.

Perhaps the most obvious sign of this shift came in some of the nomenclature that the antitrust authorities used to discuss the antitrust implications of various patent licensing practices. In 1970, Bruce Wilson, special assistant to the assistant attorney general for antitrust in the Nixon administration, presented the administration's thoughts about patent licensing at an antitrust conference. After assuring the audience that "we are not anti-patent," he proceeded to outline nine verboten licensing practices—soon dubbed the "Nine No-Nos."[13] In 1981, Tad Lipsky, deputy assistant attorney general of the Antitrust Division in the Reagan administration, revisited the question:

> For the better part of the last decade, Division enforcement policy toward patent licensing has been advertised using a list of forbidden practices commonly known as the "Nine No-Nos." Each of these practices is thought to be especially deserving of antitrust condemnation by virtue of some inherently anticompetitive feature. . . . [M]y predecessor identified "the most important single concern of the Antitrust Division in this area, namely, whether one or more licenses are being used as part of a broader conspiracy to restrain significant actual or potential competition among affected firms." I would enthusiastically endorse this last conclusion in particular. Where I depart from my predecessor, however, is in his assertion that the "Nine No-Nos" have

much independent validity as economically rational antitrust rules. . . . When one makes the analysis, one finds that the "Nine No-Nos," as statements of rational economic policy, contain more errors than accuracy.[14]

From that day forward, the patent and antitrust communities were both on notice. Not only were the Nine No-Nos history, so was the thinking that led to them. Economic rationality was the order of the day. Antitrust law and patent law would be subject to economic scrutiny—both individually and when they came into conflict. Public policy would flow in directions believed most likely to promote economic growth.

Eleven months after Lipsky repealed the Nine No-Nos as an affirmative statement of antitrust policy, the Federal Circuit held its opening session as the most important institutional player in the new era of patent law. Like most new institutions, the Federal Circuit's birth raised as many questions as answers. Of particular interest to the members of the antitrust community was the posture of this unknown court vis-à-vis their own field. The Reagan administration, Congress, and even the Supreme Court had all implied the dawn of a new era in both antitrust law and patent law. Lipsky's announcement removed many of the shackles that had prevented patentees from exploiting their patents fully. Congress had created a new court to rationalize the patent law, and the administration had explained that its view of "rationality" was economic rationality. But patent law and antitrust law had been tripping over each other since the days of King James. How would this new court behave at this trickiest of all legal interfaces, the juncture where the blessed monopolies on projects of new invention meet the accursed monopolies restricting general commerce?

HUMBLE BEGINNINGS

In July 1983, less than a year after its birth, the Federal Circuit issued its very first statement about antitrust. A trio of German inventors had received a U.S. patent for their vibration-sensing machine, useful in balancing tires, and assigned it Carl Schenck AG. Schenck sued the Nortron Corporation and two other American companies for infringing its patent. The trial itself was vanilla; Schenck won on both validity and infringement. Nortron appealed. In addition to trying to reargue both the facts and the law, Nortron took the low road. It tried to capitalize on both the then-prevailing protectionist spirit sweeping America and the long-established distaste for monopolists that had subsided so recently that Nortron had apparently missed the memo.

Chief Judge Markey would have none of it. He took Nortron to task for calling Schenck a "German monopolist" and for mimicking King James with a pronouncement that "patents are an exception to the general rule against monopolies."

> Disclosure of an invention found to have revolutionized an industry is but a classic example of the ideal working of the patent system. If a patentee or licensee enjoys widespread sales, that too is but an example of the incentive-useful arts promoting element in the patent system. Patents and licenses are exemplifications of property rights. Further, and happily, participation in the U.S. patent system, as patentees and as licensees, is available to citizens and non-citizens alike.
>
> A patent, under the statute, is property. Nowhere in any statute is a patent described as a monopoly. The patent right is but the right to exclude others, the very definition of "property." That the property right represented by a patent, like other property rights, may be *used* in a scheme violative of antitrust laws creates no "conflict" between laws establishing any of those property rights and the antitrust laws. The antitrust laws, enacted long after the original patent laws, deal with appropriation of what should belong to others. A valid patent gives the public what it did not earlier have.[15]

Markey's passion revealed at least two beliefs—particularly given that antitrust was irrelevant to the case at bar, and many judges would simply have ignored Nortron's rhetoric. First, on the property-or-regulation question, Markey viewed patents as property. Second, at least with respect to antitrust law, Markey saw no difference between patents and other forms of property.[16]

The Federal Circuit's first actual ruling on a question at the interface of antitrust and patent law arrived five months later. It hinged on a rather technical point, but one for which the Supreme Court provided ample guidance long before the Federal Circuit was born. In 1943, the Food Machinery and Chemical Corporation had secured a patent on machinery useful for sewage treatment systems. Many years later—near the end of the patent's lifetime—Food Machinery sued Walker Process Equipment for patent infringement. Walker Process responded as almost all accused infringers do—by arguing, first, that the patent was invalid and, second, that even if it were valid, it hadn't been infringed. While litigating its validity case, however, Walker Process made a startling discovery: the only reason that Food Machinery had ever secured the patent was that it had defrauded the Patent and Trademark Office! Walker Process smelled blood. Not only did it win the infringement suit, but it also added a counterclaim that Food Machinery's use of a fraudulent patent to monopolize a market violated the antitrust laws. The trial court threw the claim out, and the Seventh Circuit affirmed. The Supreme Court thought that Walker Process's theory might have some merit. It announced a new rule: patentees who use fraudulently obtained patents in an anticompetitive manner *may* have violated the antitrust laws—provided that the plaintiff can also prove all of the other elements of an antitrust violation. Thus was born an important class of patent/antitrust cases, the *"Walker Process* cases."[17]

Many years later, American Hoist and Derrick sued Sowa and Sons for infringing its patent. Sowa countered that American Hoist had defrauded the PTO to obtain its patent and brought a *Walker Process* claim. A district court in Oregon agreed with Sowa on validity and fraud, but concluded that the fraud in question was insufficient to qualify as an antitrust violation. On appeal, the Federal Circuit applied its standard choice-of-law rule; the new body of Federal Circuit law governed the patent issues, and Ninth Circuit law governed the nonpatent issues. Judge Rich restated Markey's comments to Nortron in gentler terms, rejected some but not all of Sowa's arguments, highlighted a critical flaw in the judge's instructions to the jury, and remanded the matter for another trial.[18] The upshot of the Federal Circuit's first true antitrust ruling was thus that regional circuit law applies to antitrust cases, and *Walker Process* plaintiffs must prove *all* elements of their antitrust claims—precisely as the Supreme Court had instructed Walker Process itself almost twenty years earlier. Good to know and all, but hardly earthshaking. Anyone who had been paying attention could probably have predicted both of these points.

That's pretty much where things stood for more than fourteen years. Throughout that period, occasional *Walker Process* claims passed through the Federal Circuit. The court applied regional circuit antitrust law to decide some cases in favor of the plaintiffs and others in favor of the defendants. Some antitrust cases raised challenging procedural issues—questions of jurisdiction, standing, statutes of limitations, and whatnot—but little of interest to substantive antitrust law, the relationship between patents and antitrust, or even economic rationality. Throughout that period, the Federal Circuit averaged fewer than a half-dozen substantive antitrust matters per year—including *Walker Process* claims—and few of them generated issues of interest to the antitrust community. The long-standing and seemingly inherent relationship between patent law and antitrust law notwithstanding, the patent court remained a rather minor player in the antitrust world.

Throughout at least much of this period, that result was hardly surprising. The Chicago School economics that dominated antitrust in the 1980s led to a sharp decline in antitrust enforcement. The Federal Circuit's birth in 1982 came amidst a tectonic shift whipsawing the American economy from a period of weak patents and strong antitrust into one of strong patents and weak antitrust. The Federal Circuit's job was to help strengthen the patent system. When it came to antitrust, the new court's rules were simple. First, patentees have a legal exclusive over the market that their patents define, whether or not the monopolization of such a market might otherwise violate the antitrust laws. Second, defrauding the PTO works to the detriment of the patent system. Because fraudulently obtained patents can't protect anyone from anything, a fraudulent patentee who monopolizes a relevant antitrust market is liable under the antitrust laws. Third, because antitrust issues are not unique unto the patent laws, regional circuit law governs all Federal Circuit antitrust analyses. And fourth, attempts to leverage patents to monopolize markets beyond those that the patent covers are subject to the same analysis as attempts to leverage *any* property right to monopolize a market—which at the time, meant relatively lax scrutiny and enforcement. In retrospect at least, though some may have disagreed with the court's resolution of specific disputes, no one should have been surprised by anything occurring at the Federal Circuit's patent/antitrust interface.

But things change and eras end. By the early 1990s, many people believed that the Chicago School had overplayed its hand. A new band of economists rode into Washington. This "Post-Chicago School" agreed with Bork's description of antitrust as "a set of continually evolving theories about the economics of industrial organization" and evolved them beyond the strong laissez-faire theories that Bork himself had favored. While the distinction may appear subtle to some, the shift from a Chicagoan belief that successful anticompetitive behavior is truly exceptional to a Post-Chicagoan belief that successful anticompetitive behavior is merely rare opened the door to yet another reassessment of antitrust policy.

The first hint of a shift in the Federal Circuit's thinking about antitrust came in March 1998, in an odd place: an *en banc* footnote. It arrived by way of a dispute among dentists. In 1977, Dr. Per-Ingvar Branemark published a book about dental implants. Two years later, Branemark and a colleague filed patent applications, first in Sweden and then in the United States, claiming an invention related to dental implants. Though the inventors' notes to their Swedish patent agent mentioned the 1977 book, the agent helpfully deleted the reference before filing either application. The inventors then cut an exclusive licensing deal with Nobelpharma and received their U.S. patent in 1982. Nobelpharma asserted the patent on at least three occasions and emerged victorious each time. The fourth time was the charm. In July 1991, Nobelpharma sued Implant Innovations for infringing its patent. Implant Innovations came roaring back, claiming that Branemark had intentionally omitted any mention of his 1977 book from his U.S. patent application, that material in the book would have led the PTO to reject Branemark's patent application, that Nobelpharma possessed its patent solely because Branemark had defrauded the PTO, that the patent was therefore invalid, and that Nobelpharma was liable for violating the antitrust laws. In short, yet one more *Walker Process* case. The case went to trial in Illinois, where the judge ruled Nobelpharma's patent invalid as a matter of Federal Circuit patent law, the jury found Nobel-pharma liable under the antitrust laws, and the judge upheld the jury's finding as reasonable under Seventh Circuit antitrust law.

Nobelpharma appealed to the Federal Circuit.[19] The Clerk of Court spun his assignment wheel, and it landed on Judges Rich, Plager, and Lourie. Judge Lourie penned a careful, detailed opinion affirming the district court on all issues—with one hidden little twist. Footnote 5 read: "Because precedent may not be changed by a panel, the issue of 'choice of circuit' law set forth [here] has been considered and decided unanimously by an [e]n banc court."[20] Thus armed with a unanimous *en banc* license, Lourie overturned fourteen years of precedent:

> As a general proposition, when reviewing a district court's judgment involving federal antitrust law, we are guided by the law of the regional circuit in which that district court sits. However, we apply our own law, not regional circuit law, to resolve issues that clearly involve our exclusive jurisdiction. Whether conduct in the prosecution of a patent is sufficient to strip a patentee of its immunity from the antitrust laws is one of those issues that clearly involves our exclusive jurisdiction over patent cases. It follows that whether a patent infringement suit is based on a fraudulently procured patent impacts our exclusive jurisdiction.
>
> Moreover, an antitrust claim premised on stripping a patentee of its immunity from the antitrust laws is typically raised as a counterclaim by a defendant in a patent infringement suit. Because most cases involving these issues will therefore be appealed to this court, we conclude that we should decide these issues as a matter of Federal Circuit law, rather than rely on various regional precedents. . . . However, we will continue to apply the law of the appropriate regional circuit to issues involving other elements of antitrust law such as relevant market, market power, damages, etc., as those issues are not unique to patent law, which is subject to our exclusive jurisdiction.[21]

With that, Lourie introduced "Federal Circuit antitrust law." For the very first ruling of Federal Circuit antitrust law, he announced that it reached precisely the same conclusion that the district court had reached in ruling against Nobelpharma as a matter of Seventh Circuit antitrust law.

Legal scholars were quick to note that something significant had happened, but they weren't quite sure what it was. As long as the Federal Circuit used its own law to reach conclusions identical to those that the regional circuits would reach, its declaration was of purely academic interest. Scholars could only wonder, though, whether Lourie's announcement was tantamount to a fox announcing that it would guard the henhouse. The Federal Circuit's raison d'être was the strengthening of patent rights. Did we really want a court widely perceived as the champion of patents refereeing potential conflicts between patent law and an-

titrust law? That might have sounded like a good idea in the Chicagoan
heyday, but by 1998 that day had come and gone. Was it still a good idea?

THE INEVITABLE BUTTING OF HEADS

For about two years into the life of Federal Circuit antitrust law, few commentators saw anything of earthshaking significance to either substantive
antitrust law or substantive patent law. By 2001, however, Professor James
Gambrell was able to publish a troubling critique:

> While there has been a warming trend in the relationship between the patent
> and antitrust laws . . . it would be inaccurate to say they are really friends.
> . . . While this "warming" trend is evident in the Antitrust Guidelines and
> elsewhere, a "warning" trend is evident in a number of recent decisions by
> the Federal Circuit, a court created primarily to handle all patent appeals.
> These recent decisions find the court concluding that it should develop the
> principles governing the relationship between patent rights and antitrust re-
> straints instead of looking to antitrust precedents in the appropriate regional
> circuits. . . . Instead of patent rights being circumscribed by core antitrust
> principles, the fear is that the Federal Circuit will emasculate the patent-
> antitrust interface by taking too liberal a view of the bundle of rights granted
> to the patent owner when antitrust principles are involved.[22]

Gambrell cited four fundamental problems with the emerging body of
Federal Circuit antitrust law: He chided the court for elevating patent
rights over "core antitrust principles that it was not given the jurisdiction
to control," for squeezing the regional circuits out of their role in "con-
structing antitrust principles that should properly circumscribe the bundle of rights the IP laws protect," for promulgating expansive views of
patents that "create uncertainty when other IP rights are involved," and
for requiring "district courts to have the sophistication of Houdini and the
imagination of Alice in Wonderland to sort out what principles the Federal Circuit has responsibility for and what principles the regional courts
have the final say on."[23]

The Federal Circuit addressed Gambrell's fourth challenge in 2004:

> Federal Circuit antitrust law centers on a single critical question: What be-
> havior by the patentee in procuring or in enforcing a patent can strip the pat-
> entee of antitrust immunity? When the courts consider a patentee's behavior
> under Federal Circuit law and determine that it involved nothing more than
> an appropriate attempt to procure a patent and an appropriate attempt to en-
> force a legitimately obtained patent, the antitrust inquiry is over with respect
> to the behavior at issue. When, on the other hand, the courts consider a
> patentee's behavior under Federal Circuit law and determine that it involved

either an inappropriate attempt to procure a patent or an inappropriate attempt to enforce a patent, the remainder of the antitrust inquiry must proceed under the law of the regional circuit.[24]

With that clarification, the Court applied Federal Circuit law to determine that the patentee in question had defrauded the PTO, and then turned to Tenth Circuit law to evaluate the remaining elements of the antitrust claim. The Supreme Court, ever helpful, granted cert on a narrow point of procedural law, chastised the Tenth Circuit for having deviating from the other circuits on that point, reversed the Federal Circuit's ruling under the overruled point of Tenth Circuit law, and said nothing about Federal Circuit antitrust law.[25]

In fact, the Supreme Court has never said anything about the Federal Circuit's decision to inject its own law into the world of antitrust. As Gambrell's critique suggests, many commentators wish that it would. For though its 2004 clarification explains that the scope of Federal Circuit antitrust law is really quite narrow, Gambrell's fourth complaint was always the least significant. His first three went right to the heart of public policy at the patent/antitrust interface. Is the introduction of Federal Circuit antitrust law a step toward aligning the policy we have with the policy we want, or a step away from such an alignment? Critics like Gambrell began to suspect that the answer was "away" when the Federal Circuit started to decide cases under its own law in ways that seemed to differ with the conclusions that the regional circuits would have reached.

The "warning" trend that Gambrell identified suggested that the Federal Circuit was emerging as odd man out among America's institutional antitrust players. The FTC, the Department of Justice, the Supreme Court, and the regional circuits all seemed to favor a 1990s Post-Chicago formulation: Patent rights are great as long as they don't distort competition, but if they start interfering with competitive markets, antitrust should assume center stage. The Federal Circuit seemed mired in a 1980s Chicago School view of the world: Patentees may use valid patents as they see fit. Even antitrust law recognizes that most monopolies are legal if the monopolist acquired them legally—and monopolies derived through patents are not only legal but also demonstrations of what Chief Judge Markey had called the "incentive-useful arts promoting element in the patent system." If you want to hold a patentee liable for violating the antitrust laws, you're going to have to prove that he did something more than just exert his patent rights.

Once again, the philosophical debate about patents seemed be rearing its ugly head. Though the issues are not identical, those viewing patents as sacred property rights often feel most comfortable around Chicagoans; those viewing patents as a clever form of regulation prefer the company of Post-Chicagoans. The antitrust bar, and in particular its Post-Chicagoans, saw the first real "warning" in the context of an antitrust violation called a "refusal to deal."

Under normal circumstances, people are free to conduct business with whomever they please and likewise to refuse to do business with whomever they please. Antitrust law recognizes that under some unusual circumstances, a monopolist who refuses to deal with a supplier or with a distributor may be attempting to monopolize a market. The case in question began in 1993, when Intergraph, a computer manufacturer that held several patents related to the "Clipper Chip," stopped making Clipper machines and shifted its production to use Intel chips. Intel designated Intergraph a "strategic customer" and granted it access to proprietary information that helped Intergraph maintain a competitive position within the computer market. By 1996, Intergraph suspected that Intel was infringing its Clipper patents. Intergraph started by chasing some of its direct competitors who were using Intel's products, but in November 1997 it filed suit in Alabama against Intel itself, alleging fraud, misappropriation of trade secrets, negligence, wantonness and willfulness, breach of contract, intentional interference with business relations, breach of express and implied warranties, and violation of the Alabama Trade Secrets Act as well as patent infringement. When Intel threatened to terminate Intergraph's status as a strategic customer, Intergraph added an antitrust claim. At the district court, Judge Edwin Nelson sided with Intergraph, concluded that Intel was a monopolist likely to lose in the event of a full-blown trial, and preliminarily enjoined Intel from terminating Intergraph's rarefied status while the trial was pending. Nelson justified his ruling by enumerating six theories under which Intel's behavior violated the antitrust laws: five standard antitrust theories, and a red flag that he called "improper use of IP."

Intel appealed, arguing that "no law requires it to give such special benefits, including its trade secrets, proprietary information, IP, pre-release products, allocation of new products, and other preferences, to an entity that is suing it on charges of multiple wrongdoing and is demanding damages and the shutdown of its core business."[26] At the Federal Circuit, the clerk of court's assignment wheel landed on Judges Newman, Smith, and Plager. Judge Newman's framing of the dispute left little doubt as to her leanings:

> Intel states that its commercial response to Intergraph's suit is not an antitrust violation, and that this "garden-variety patent dispute" does not warrant the antitrust remedy here imposed. . . . Intergraph's response is that it cannot survive in its highly competitive graphics workstation business without these services and benefits from Intel, and that the district court simply

acted to preserve Intergraph's prior commercial position while the parties litigate unrelated patent issues. Intergraph states that the national interest requires that patentees be free to enforce their patents without risk of retaliatory commercial response from the accused infringer. Intel disputes these
premises, and also points out the incongruity of Intergraph's statement that
it is essential to Intergraph's business that it have the products for which it is
demanding the shutdown of Intel's production.[27]

From there, things went straight downhill for Intergraph, as Newman
reversed one after another of the district court's rulings in its favor.
Along the way, she provided some choice language that left few commentators with any doubt about how she, at least, viewed the relationship between antitrust law and patent law, beginning with the old
bromide: "The antitrust laws were enacted for 'the protection of competition, not competitors."[28]

> [T]he Sherman Act does not convert all harsh commercial actions into an-
> titrust violations. . . . Courts have recognized that the relationship between a
> manufacturer and its customer should be reasonably harmonious; and the
> bringing of a lawsuit by the customer may provide a sound business reason
> for the manufacturer to terminate their relations. . . . [N]o case has held that
> the divulgation of proprietary information and the provision of special or
> privileged treatment to a legal adversary can be compelled on a "refusal to
> deal" antitrust premise. . . . In response to Intel's argument that its propri-
> etary information and pre-release products are subject to copyright and
> patents, the district court observed that Intel's IP "does not confer upon it a
> privilege or immunity to violate the antitrust laws." That is of course correct.
> But it is also correct that the antitrust laws do not negate the patentee's right
> to exclude others from patent property. . . .The patent and antitrust laws
> serve the public in different ways, both of importance to the nation.[29]

She closed by noting that "despite the district court's sensitive concern
for Intergraph's well-being while it conducts its patent suit against Intel,
there must be an adverse effect on competition in order to bring an antitrust remedy to bear."[30] Because she saw no such adverse effect here, and
because the "compulsory disclosure of proprietary information and provision of pre-production chips and other commercial and IP is a dramatic
remedy for antitrust illegality,"[31] she reversed the district court and dissolved the preliminary injunction.

That's what the Federal Circuit had to say about refusals to deal, and
why large parts of the antitrust bar found the experience unsatisfying; it
seemed as if the patent court had announced that patentees could never be
liable for a refusal to deal. Meanwhile, in climes that antitrust experts, and
in particular Post-Chicagoans, find more agreeable, the FTC saw enough
in Intergraph's complaints to bring a government case against Intel.

CHICAGO?

This emerging rift between the Federal Circuit and the FTC seemed intriguing. Was it really a matter of Chicagoans reasserting themselves against a Post-Chicago onslaught? And perhaps more to the point, why should anyone other than an antitrust scholar care?

Although some might view a battle between Chicago School economists and Post-Chicago School economists as little more than academics splitting hairs, the public policy consequences are profound. When it comes to the structure of the U.S. economy—particularly during its transition to a fully information-age economy—disputes about the prevalence of dangerous anticompetitive activities and the role of IP have consequences that emanate far beyond the ivory tower. In fact, this Chicago vs. Post-Chicago debate is merely the antitrust world's contribution to a larger debate whose significance is beyond doubt: the one between 1980s-style Reaganomics and 1990s-style Clintonomics. The terms *Chicago* and *Post-Chicago* are merely antitrust-specific labels for the underlying economic theories—labels that carry less political baggage than does anything attached to the names Reagan or Clinton.

Shortly after the Federal Circuit's 1999 ruling for Intel, the American Antitrust Institute (AAI)—a self-proclaimed Post-Chicago organization of ivory-tower types—invited FTC chair and Post-Chicago icon Robert Pitofsky to address its 2000 annual conference.[32] Pitofsky told his audience that the Federal Circuit had upset the traditional balance between antitrust and IP "in a way that has disturbing implications for the future of antitrust in high-technology industries."[33]

Why did Pitofsky, despite clarifying that he has "no quarrel with the fundamental rule that a patent holder has no obligation to license or sell in the first instance," nevertheless have to wonder what the rules will be "when the patent holder conditions the availability of its patented products or inventions on terms that affect competition?" As he saw it, the emerging body of Federal Circuit antitrust law "could be read to say that the invocation of IP rights settles the matter, except in [some exceptional] narrow situations . . . regardless of the effect of the refusal to deal on competition or the importance of the refusal to deal to protect incentives to innovate." He concluded: "That should not be the way these issues are addressed."[34]

Pitofsky's concern did not stem from the ways that the Federal Circuit's treatment of Intel's refusal to deal differed from the one that his own agency took—at least, that wasn't his primary concern. It stemmed instead from a dispute about Xerox and its copiers, a dispute that threatened to undermine the most significant Post-Chicago victory of the 1990—and a dispute that the Federal Circuit had resolved just weeks before his AAI talk.

The facts were straightforward. Xerox makes copiers. Xerox also makes patented replacement parts and copyrighted manuals to help people repair its copiers, should the need arise. For many years, Xerox allowed independent repair shops to buy its parts and manuals. CSU was one such shop. It used Xerox's parts, Xerox's manuals, and its own expertise to offer Xerox's customers lower-cost repair services than they could obtain from Xerox itself. One day, Xerox changed its mind and decided to stop selling patented parts and copyrighted manuals to its competitors in the service market. CSU claimed that Xerox was violating the antitrust laws; Xerox claimed that CSU just wanted to infringe its IP rights. The district court in Kansas sided with Xerox, and the Federal Circuit affirmed.[35]

Several years earlier, however, a group of independent service organizations (ISOs) had sued Kodak—one of Xerox's smaller competitors in the copier market—on what appeared to be identical facts. The trial judge had granted Kodak's motion for summary judgment, reasoning that Kodak couldn't really violate the antitrust laws by monopolizing the market for repair parts for its own machines. Because Kodak didn't raise a formal patent issue, the appeal went to the Ninth Circuit, which reversed the district court. Kodak appealed to the Supreme Court, which chose this moment to intervene. In its first Post-Chicagoan opinion, the Supreme Court said that the district court had been too hasty in ruling for Kodak and sent the case back for trial.[36] Kodak lost that trial, and the Ninth Circuit affirmed.[37]

For the first time, there appeared to be a clear split between the Federal Circuit and one of the regional circuits on a matter of antitrust law. As many would have predicted, the Federal Circuit elevated the patent rights above antitrust concerns; the Ninth Circuit took the opposite route. This *Kodak/Xerox* controversy, more than anything else, created the ruckus about Federal Circuit antitrust law. To many observers, it seemed a stake in the heart of Post-Chicago analysis.

To appreciate why many saw—and see—it that way, it's important to look at the full sweep of Post-Chicago analysis, from the Supreme Court's 1992 *Kodak* ruling, through the *Kodak/Xerox* controversy and Pitofsky's AAI speech in 2000, to June 2006, when the AAI titled its annual conference "The IP Grab" and invited *me* to speak about the role of IP rights in aftermarket antitrust analysis.

An aftermarket is precisely what it purports to be: a market that comes into existence only *after* some initial transaction closes. Consider, for example, the Kodak and Xerox cases. No one needs replacement parts, manuals, or repair services until he buys a copier—known in the trade as "original equipment," marketed by "original equipment manufacturers," or OEMs. What's more, the specific nature of the parts, manuals, and services that any given consumer will eventually need is contingent upon their choice of OEMs. Once a consumer purchases a copier, she's pretty much eliminated one of the OEMs from her future; consumers with Kodak copiers have little use for Xerox, and those with Xerox copiers are unlikely to do much business with Kodak. From that point on, these consumers are essentially captive, or "locked in," to OEM-specific aftermarkets. Consumers will likely soon need parts and manuals that *either but not both* Kodak and Xerox produce. They will also need other auxiliary products and services that they may have to buy from the OEM they chose, or for which that OEM may face independent competitors.

An OEM has significant power in all aftermarkets related to its own products, though as Chamberlain demonstrated, that power need not translate into a monopoly. At times, OEMs may choose to exploit that power to the detriment of both their customers and their independent competitors—as service-aftermarket competitors alleged that both Kodak and Xerox did. Can such exploitation give rise to antitrust liability? The Supreme Court addressed this question in 1992, when it sent Kodak back to California to stand trial for allegedly violating the antitrust laws. Justice Scalia gave the Chicagoan answer:

> A rational consumer considering the purchase of Kodak equipment will inevitably factor into his purchasing decision the expected cost of aftermarket support. If Kodak set generally supracompetitive prices for either spare parts or repair services without making an offsetting reduction in the price of its machines, rational consumers would simply turn to Kodak's competitors for photocopying and micrographic systems. . . . In my view, if the interbrand market is vibrant, [it] functions as an infinitely more efficient and more precise corrective to such behavior, rewarding the seller whose intrabrand restraints enhance consumer welfare while punishing the seller whose control of the aftermarkets is viewed unfavorably by interbrand consumers.[38]

That view, however, did not prevail. Instead, Justice Blackmun rallied a majority behind his Post-Chicagoan analysis:

> [Even assuming] that all manufacturers possess some inherent market power in the parts market, it is not clear why that should immunize them from the antitrust laws in another market. The Court has held many times that power gained through some natural and legal advantage such as a patent, copyright, or business acumen can give rise to liability if a seller exploits his dominant position in one market to expand his empire into the next. . . . While it may be, as the dissent predicts, that the equipment market will prevent any harms to consumers in the aftermarkets, the dissent never makes plain why the Court should accept that theory on faith rather than requiring the usual evidence needed to win a summary judgment motion. . . . In the end, of course, Kodak's arguments may prove to be correct. . . . But we cannot reach these conclusions as a matter of law on a record this sparse.[39]

The contemporary antitrust debate in a nutshell: Either market discipline will impose automatic corrections making any attempts at anticompetitive behavior self-defeating, or it won't. How do we know which one is true? And perhaps more to the point, how can such a formalistic academic question really define the shape we want the industrial terrain to assume? The answer lies in a closely held secret that antitrust economists all know but that few share with the public at large. Economic theorists following Justice Scalia's lead are often right as a matter of theory *in the long run*, unless the monopolist's anticompetitive behavior changes the structure of the market. The question is how long that long run will take to unfold.

Most anticompetitive behavior is tough to sustain forever. Sooner or later, one wrong move by even the most powerful monopolist, or one simple difference among the conspiratorial members of a cartel, can create an opening. When enough openings appear, some outsider will pounce, enter the market, and offer consumers a new alternative. Consumers will unleash their pent-up anger at those who have been exploiting them through anticompetitive behavior, abandon the incumbent, embrace the new entrant as savior, and the entire monopolistic edifice will crumble. Industrial history is full of such stories, and Chicagoans love to cite them.

Unfortunately, the requisite long run can take an unacceptably long time to arrive, particularly given that Alan Greenspan's critique is also right: misregulation, including mistakes within IP systems, can complicate the free market's normal autocorrective mechanisms and push that long run to a distant horizon.[40] While the future is unfolding, monopolists and conspirators can wreak havoc on markets, consumers, and, on occasion, the economy at large. If a monopolist can reap extraordinary profits for a few years—or even a few months—the prospect may prove so enticing that it warrants the risk of ultimate self-defeat. Economic empiricists following Justice Blackmun's lead like to compile detailed, data-driven records. Where the data suggest that the theoretical autocorrection lies too far in the future to simply sit around and wait, or that a structural change to the market will drive so many competitors out of business that the autocorrection may never arrive, these pragmatic Post-Chicagoans prefer to use antitrust law to hasten its arrival.

Both sides in this debate remain wedded to the power and importance of liberal market capitalism (though Chicagoans do like to impugn the Post-Chicagoans' purity). Both sides recognize that monopoly is and should be legal—a reward for insight and business acumen. Both sides concede Adam Smith's observation about businessmen's desire to leverage their strengths to the detriment of the consuming public, as well as his observation that their desire does not diminish when that leverage would harm the very markets that they need for the economy to function. The Chicagoans also accept Smith's admonition that attempts to use the law to correct these anomalies risk doing more harm than good. The Post-Chicagoans believe that if the legal remedies are restricted to cases in which the facts scream for legal help, the benefits can outweigh the costs. The statist attempts to use a heavy antitrust hand to micromanage the organization of an industrial economy never make it to the table. No one in this debate wants to resurrect any No-Nos.

This intraliberal squabble has dominated the past few decades of debate within the antitrust community—much as the debate between Reagan's and Clinton's economic policies has dominated discussions of the broader American economy. This debate's impact on the patent community—or even on the wider IP community—has been less direct and less obvious. Yet, it reflects the primary philosophical dispute that keeps raising its ugly head. Are patents property just like any other property, or are they property of a sort fundamentally different from houses or cars? Or are they regulatory permits, set within a regime that captures some but far from all characteristics of property?

A pure Chicago approach is most likely to see patents in stark property terms. As a matter of theory, patents are neither harder nor easier to misuse in an anticompetitive manner than are other forms of property. That they may confer more leverage over a market than does real estate is interesting, but of no real consequence. To a Post-Chicagoan more likely to see patents in regulatory terms, that distinction is hugely consequential. If patents create great opportunities for exploitation, antitrust law should scrutinize patentees closely, examine the data, and identify abuses. If the abuses are systematic, the policymakers in Congress should consider rewriting the patent laws to frustrate their recurrence. If such a rewrite weakens patent rights, so be it; the entire purpose of a liberal regulatory mechanism is to serve the public by filling an economic gap that the free market is unable to fill on its own. In the patent context, that means rewarding innovation to generate innovation. At the patent/antitrust interface, it means curtailing those rewards before they harm the competitive markets that we want them to bolster.

All of which returns us to the Federal Circuit. The Supreme Court veered toward the Post-Chicagoans in 1992. At the time, the Bush *père* administration had filed an amicus brief supporting Kodak and the Chicagoans. Less than a year later, the Clinton administration came to town favoring economic policies aligned with Post-Chicago analysis. By early 1995, Clinton had appointed Pitofsky chairman of the FTC. Yet in 2000, the Federal Circuit was still issuing opinions that made people doubt that the court had ever evolved its antitrust thinking beyond its roots in Reaganomics-friendly Chicago.

CREATIVE DESTRUCTION

This concern remained at the forefront of Post-Chicagoan thinking about the Federal Circuit in 2006, when the AAI invited me to address its 2006 conference. I approached my assignment wondering: Are the courts resolving disputes at the intersection of IP law and antitrust law in a manner consistent with sound public policy?[41]

The answer lies in understanding what happens at that intersection. Suppose that a patentee holds one of those rare critical patents that, unlike Schenck's, does confer a monopoly in the technical sense relevant to antitrust law. The patentee uses his patent in a manner normally considered legitimate, but that in this case reduces competition in a market somewhat broader than the one that the patent claims—say, an aftermarket. The patentee sues a competitor for infringement. The competitor counterclaims that the patentee is victimizing it in violation of the antitrust laws. What's more, both parties are right: the competitor as a matter of antitrust law and the patentee as a matter of patent law. Under this scenario, a patent analysis unconcerned with antitrust counterclaims would unequivocally rule that the patentee's behavior was proper, but an antitrust analysis unconcerned with a patent defense would just as unequivocally find a violation of the antitrust laws. Patent and antitrust laws seem to point toward irreconcilable results. What would we like to see a black box output under such circumstances?

The key to devising a meaningful test sequence for a black-box test lies in understanding the uneasy truce between the antitrust and the IP laws, a truce that rests upon understanding the role that IP rights play in a free-market economy generally wedded to competition. Joseph Schumpeter presented the classic explanation in 1942, as part of his theory of "creative destruction":

> Capitalism is by nature a form or method of economic change and not only never is but never can be stationary. . . . The fundamental impulse that sets and keeps the capitalist engine in motion comes from the new consumers, goods, the new methods of production or transportation, the new markets, the new forms of industrial organization that capitalist enterprise creates. . . . The opening up of new markets, foreign or domestic, and the organizational development from the craft shop and factory to such concerns as U.S. Steel illustrate [a] process of industrial mutation—if I may use that biological term—that incessantly revolutionizes the economic structure *from within*, incessantly destroying the old one, incessantly creating a new one. This process of Creative Destruction is the essential fact about capitalism. . . .
>
> [I]n capitalist reality as distinguished from its textbook picture, it is not [price] competition which counts but the competition from the new commodity, the new technology, the new source of supply, the new type of

organization . . . competition which commands a decisive cost or quality advantage and which strikes not at the margins of the profits and the outputs of the existing firms but at their foundations and their very lives. This kind of competition is as much more effective than the other as a bombardment is in comparison with forcing a door, and so much more important that it becomes a matter of comparative indifference whether competition in the ordinary sense functions more or less promptly; the powerful lever that in the long run expands output and brings down prices is in any case made of other stuff.[42]

According to Schumpeter, mechanisms like patents that promote a competitive drive to discover, exploit, and commercialize the next great technological innovation "will in the long run enforce behavior very similar to the perfectly competitive pattern."[43]

In short, the evolutionary concepts that Bork attributed to antitrust are an essential component of capitalism. Patent rights promote "savings" by motivating competitors to think about long-term revolutionary change. As painful as some of these investments might seem in the short run—say, in the form of markets that appear to be less competitive than we might otherwise like—they will pay off in the long run, where they promise both to preserve our liberal system and to impel it toward further growth. In an economic policy designed to promote consumer welfare, antitrust law serves the general purpose of promoting competition, while IP law provides the special purpose of allowing selected participants to avoid competition long enough to overcome the barrier to entering innovative ventures. Courts should resolve any situation in which these two important bodies of law come into conflict subject to a fact-intensive, case-by-case analysis. A "patent supremacist" assertion that patents are property and thus absolute is unlikely to serve the public interest. Nor is an "antitrust supremacist" insistence upon ignoring patent rights likely to do much better.

The normatively appropriate analysis for these complex cases is correspondingly complex. First, the court needs to establish whether patent law protects the patentee's behavior, ignoring the antitrust allegations. Second, the court needs to determine whether the patentee's behavior violates the antitrust laws, ignoring any potential patent defense. If the court answers either question in the negative, the analysis is over. If the court answers one question in the affirmative and the other in the negative, the resolution is straightforward. If, however, the court finds affirmative answers to both, the court must then balance the costs and benefits of ruling either way.[44]

So much for resolving patent/antitrust conflicts in a manner consistent with the consumer welfare standard and the goals of a free market. It's one thing to describe a normative framework for a black-box test, and another thing entirely to run the test. How have the courts been doing? The answer lies in the *Kodak/Xerox* controversy. During the first eight years after the Supreme Court's ruling against Kodak, few of the follow-on lawsuits related to patents—or even to IP more generally.[45] After the Supreme Court sent Kodak back to stand trial, its case continued to work its way through the courts until the Ninth Circuit eventually ruled that Kodak had, in fact, violated the antitrust laws—an outcome of interest to the antitrust community but of little consequence in the patent world. Shortly thereafter, however, the independent repair companies suing Xerox arrived in Lafayette Park expecting to achieve the same success that their predecessors had found in California. They were sorely disappointed—and the patent community suddenly found itself deep inside an antitrust debate pitting Chicagoans against Post-Chicagoans.

INCOMPLETE

How did the patent community find itself mired deep within an antitrust debate? As noted, Xerox, like Kodak, sold copiers in the competitive OEM market. Xerox, like Kodak, also sold replacement parts, manuals, and repair services. In the repair market, many independent service organizations competed with both Kodak and Xerox. Xerox, again like Kodak, chose to change its policies concerning the availability of replacement parts to third-party service technicians. And finally, the independent service organizations driven from the market for servicing Xerox copiers alleged that Xerox's policy shift had an anticompetitive effect in the service aftermarket—much as those driven from the Kodak copier service aftermarket had sued Kodak.

At that point, things started to diverge. Xerox based its defense in IP law, pleading that patents protected its parts and copyrights its manuals. According to Xerox, CSU was complaining because Xerox had conditioned the sale of its patented replacement parts and its copyrighted manuals on the sale of its repair services. Xerox then went even further and counterclaimed that CSU was attempting to infringe its patents and its copyrights. Kodak, on the other hand, had forwarded only an IP-based defense—never an infringement counterclaim—and even its IP defense was but a small part of the business justification for its actions. When the matter reached the Ninth Circuit, the court appreciated the complexity of the antitrust/IP conflict, but determined that the facts dominated the case's resolution:

> The effect of claims based upon unilateral conduct on the value of IP rights is a cause for serious concern. Unilateral conduct is the most common con-

duct in the economy. After [the Supreme Court's ruling in] *Kodak,* unilateral conduct by a manufacturer in its own aftermarkets may give rise to liability and, in one-brand markets, monopoly power created by patents and copyrights will frequently be found. Under current law the defense of monopolization claims will rest largely on the legitimacy of the asserted business justifications. . . .

Without bounds, claims based on unilateral conduct will proliferate. The history of this case demonstrates that such claims rest on highly disputed factual questions regarding market definition. Particularly where treble damages are possible, such claims will detract from the advantages lawfully granted to the holders of patents or copyrights by subjecting them to the cost and risk of lawsuits based upon the effect, on an arguably separate market, of their refusal to sell or license. The cost of such suits will reduce a patent holder's "incentive . . . to risk the often enormous costs in terms of time, research, and development." Such an effect on patent and copyright holders is contrary to the fundamental and complementary purposes of both the IP and antitrust laws, which aim to "encourage innovation, industry and competition."[46]

With this concern at the forefront of its appellate review, the Ninth Circuit examined the facts of the case, the parties' presentations to the jury, and the judge's jury instructions and concluded that the jury had understood Kodak's IP defense and had reasonably rejected it.

Xerox, as noted, fared better in its own journey through the courts. The district court in Kansas ruled in its favor. CSU appealed to the Federal Circuit,[47] where Chief Judge Mayer, speaking on behalf of a unanimous panel, explained that

in the absence of any indication of illegal tying, fraud in the Patent and Trademark Office, or sham litigation, the patent holder may enforce the statutory right to exclude others from making, using, or selling the claimed invention free from liability under the antitrust laws. We therefore will not inquire into his subjective motivation for exerting his statutory rights, even though his refusal to sell or license his patented invention may have an anticompetitive effect, so long as that anticompetitive effect is not illegally extended beyond the statutory patent grant. It is the infringement defendant and not the patentee that bears the burden to show that one of these exceptional situations exists and, in the absence of such proof, we will not inquire into the patentee's motivations for asserting his statutory right to exclude. Even in cases where the infringement defendant has met this burden, which CSU has not, he must then also prove the elements of the Sherman Act violation. We answer the threshold question of whether Xerox's refusal to sell its patented parts exceeds the scope of the patent grant in the negative. Therefore, our inquiry is at an end. Xerox was under no obligation to sell or license its patented parts and did not violate the antitrust laws by refusing to do so.[48]

The appellate courts seemed to have headed in opposite directions. Under such circumstances, is it even possible to assign a systemic black-box score? Or must one of these courts have failed while the other performed well? Patrick Moran, a J.D./MBA candidate at Marquette University who wrote his case note on *Kodak* and *Xerox*, spoke for large parts of the antitrust community when he asserted that only the Ninth Circuit had succeeded in promoting sound public policy:

> [T]he Federal Circuit and Ninth Circuit have reached diametrically opposed holdings in cases involving essentially identical fact patterns and legal issues. This graphically illustrates the potential for conflict between the patent laws and the Sherman Act. Although both bodies of law serve important social goals, these goals must be harmonized. The Federal Circuit's [*Xerox*] decision does not contribute to these goals in any meaningful way. The [*Xerox*] decision serves only to extend the already expansive patent holder rights beyond those intended by modern Congress while ignoring competitive concerns. . . . In addition, patent holders will be allowed to create and extend monopolies unimpeded, to the detriment of small businesses.[49]

FTC chairman Pitofsky would undoubtedly have agreed. Chief Judge Mayer's protestations to the contrary notwithstanding, the community at large saw these rulings as a circuit split—with sympathy flowing overwhelmingly in the Ninth Circuit's direction. And why shouldn't the community see a split? After all, such a perception requires little more explanation than noting that the Federal Circuit expressed less interest in entering the Post-Chicago era than did many other institutions.

That perception, however, is hardly the only one possible. In fact, a very different picture emerges from reading these two rulings at face value. Under an objectively neutral reading, both courts recognized the room for tension between an otherwise legitimate exertion of IP rights and anticompetitive effects in a single-supplier aftermarket. Both asserted that the resolution lies in fact-specific analyses. In *Kodak*, a jury concluded that the plaintiffs had presented strong evidence of an antitrust violation, while Kodak had presented only weak evidence of a defense rooted in IP. The Ninth Circuit affirmed. In *Xerox*, the district court granted summary judgment because Xerox had presented strong evidence of infringement, while the plaintiffs presented only weak evidence of an anticompetitive effect. The Federal Circuit affirmed. In other words, it is entirely possible that despite the similarity between the facts in these cases as they unfolded in the real world, the legal presentations of the IP-owning parties differed greatly—and proved to be dispositive. Lawyering might matter after all.

If we assume—for just a moment—that both appellate courts meant what they said, then their conclusions appear to be not only consistent but also mutually reinforcing of the normatively correct approach and worthy of a strong systemic black-box test score. Both courts recognized that ruling in favor of the IP holder would risk reduced competition and higher prices in the aftermarket in question. Both courts also recognized that ruling in favor of the antitrust plaintiffs would reduce the value of the IP in question and thus the incentives on offer to all similarly situated IP holders. Under the proposed balancing test, the courts *should have* reviewed the evidence and considered the strength of the two arguments. Had a single court applied such a test explicitly, it would likely have concluded that the best way to preserve *most* competition and *most* motivation would be to allow a convincing showing of anticompetitive effect to override weakly asserted IP claims *and* to allow solid IP claims to override unsubstantiated antitrust allegations.

Of course, the downside of such a ruling is that it creates uncertainty. How should a third copier manufacturer—or any other company whose products create aftermarkets—know whether it is closer to Kodak or to Xerox? The answer is straightforward, if intellectually unsatisfying: it can't. The very nature of a balancing test creates uncertainty. As time progresses and lawsuits proliferate, market participants will gain data with which to gauge the propriety or impropriety of their behavior.

In the meantime, although it may appear that *Xerox* is part of a Federal Circuit IP grab while *Kodak* represented the Ninth Circuit falling in line with a Post-Chicago program, that appearance *may* be deceiving. (Then again, it may not.)[50] Had the Federal Circuit followed a strong-form reading of the Ninth Circuit's *Kodak* opinion, the implicit emerging rule would have been that there is no difference between IP rights and other property rights in antitrust analysis *and* that there is no difference between an aftermarket emerging solely from an IP right and any other market. Such an antitrust-supremacist view would likely have reverberated throughout the world of potential innovators to effect an undesirable reduction in the motivation to invest in innovation. Schumpeter would not have been pleased. The different fact-specific analyses that the Ninth and Federal Circuits followed to differing outcomes at least preserves the notion of balancing the short-term concerns of antitrust with the longer-term concerns of IP law. The implicit substitution of fact-specific analysis for bright-line rules appears to preserve the balance between competition and innovation, albeit at the expense of a bit of uncertainty—not to mention discomfort among Post-Chicagoans.

So where does all of this leave us? What can we say about the status of the interface between patent law (or IP law, more generally) and antitrust law? How is our big black box of policy doing in this respect? What about our smaller black box of Federal Circuit performance? None of these questions lend themselves to simple answers. The Reagan administration's injection of Chicago School theories into antitrust analysis rates an easy A. It eliminated many of the most damaging constraints that statist thinking had imposed on the U.S. economy. The further evolution of those theories through Post-Chicago analysis was also an important step toward a balanced antitrust policy. As we have already discussed, the Federal Circuit's strengthening of patent rights earned it a high grade—though there are those who say that the court never knew when to stop, continued strengthening patents beyond any reasonable limits, and is watching its grade erode by the minute. But as to the interface? More than six years after *Xerox*, the data remain sparse. We derived a normative black-box test and concluded that the courts' (including the Federal Circuit's) performance to date is "not necessarily inconsistent" with good policy. But double negatives will never earn anyone much of a grade. It remains unclear whether our policymakers have really taken the time to think through the systemic issues that arise at the interface. It remains equally unclear whether any of the courts have really applied the correct case-by-case analyses.

This critical arena, where more and more of our economic growth lies, remains a morass of uncertainty. When it comes to the patent/antitrust interface, the only grade that we can offer to anyone is an "incomplete."

14

✛

Misuse Abuse

BULLY PULPIT

Peripheral vision is a wonderful thing, and pendent jurisdiction is an excellent source of it. In the final analysis, though, the expansion of the Federal Circuit's worldview is of little value if it provides only an occasional postcard from the worlds of copyright and antitrust—or even of abortion, housing, or foreign affairs. The point of any panorama is enhanced context and understanding. A court focused myopically on the "four corners" of a patent as a self-contained legal document, or even on the "four corners" of the Patent Act as a stand-alone statute, may resolve disputes between parties, but it is unlikely to serve the critical role that Congress assigned it. Patents, and intellectual property more generally, are but part of American industrial policy—a policy that attempts to promote innovation and productivity within a free competitive environment. The ultimate question concerning the Federal Circuit's peripheral vision is whether the court appreciates the role of patent law within this overall economic policy framework.

One thing that the court could do is to use its bully pulpit. The judges of the Federal Circuit could view any seeming anomaly, any instance in which patent law seems to lead to an unjust result or run counter to public policy, as an opportunity to inform the debate. As Judge Michel told the attendees of a Case Western Reserve Law School symposium, "we have to write more carefully perhaps, but not write less. . . . We must do this for several reasons: credibility of the courts, development of law, clarification of the law, and predictive power."[1] One more reason seems to suggest it-self: to inform those charged with setting public policy about the facts on the ground. This view of the facts on the ground is really the best source of a court's peripheral vision, and the one most relevant to understanding whether or not the legal environment in which our courts are a significant player—but hardly the *only* significant player—corresponds to our as-serted policy pronouncements. It is the only way that we can really un-derstand whether the policies we have are the policies we want.

These questions are actually *easier* to address in the context of IP law and at the Federal Circuit than they are elsewhere. IP is unique in Ameri-can law, in that the Constitution itself provides the policy pronounce-ment: promote progress. The discussions surrounding the Federal Cir-cuit's birth made its raison d'être no subtler: enhance the role of innovation as an engine of economic growth. There is no way to assess our systemic progress toward either goal without studying facts on the ground. How are our patent-driven companies operating within the broad commercial environment? Are patents creating more new business models than they are destroying? The answers to these questions are the essence of the court's peripheral vision—and provide insights, if not an-swers, to the most important of our black-box tests.

The best place to seek answers may well be in a stand-alone doctrine of patent law that looks quite similar to antitrust law, yet remains doctrinally distinct. The doctrine of "patent misuse" determines which of a patentee's potential business strategies are illegal. The doctrine itself is easy to ex-plain. A patent grants a patentee exclusive rights over the invention de-scribed in its claims section for the life of the patent. It does not grant a patentee *any* exclusive rights over anything else. Suppose, however, that a patentee tries to leverage her patent into a somewhat broader market (pos-sibly an aftermarket) or beyond the life of the patent. In that case, she has *mis*used her patent and reduced the competitive nature of some market for some product or service. The penalty for misusing her patent is harsh: the courts will not enforce it until she can prove that she has restored the mar-ket that she damaged to its rightful level of competitiveness—or in legal terms "purged" the effects of her misuse.

Regrettably, though misuse is not hard to understand, it appears to be *very* hard to apply. In 1998, Judge Newman explained that patent misuse

relates generally to the use of patent rights to obtain or to coerce an unfair commercial advantage. Patent misuse relates primarily to a patentee's ac-tions that affect competition in unpatented goods or that otherwise extend the economic effect beyond the scope of the patent grant. The concept of patent misuse arose to restrain practices that did not in themselves violate any law, but that draw anticompetitive strength from the patent right, and thus were deemed to be contrary to public policy. Patent misuse is viewed as a broader wrong than antitrust violation because of the economic power that may be derived from the patentee's right to exclude. Thus misuse may arise when the conditions of antitrust violation are not met. The key inquiry is whether, by imposing conditions that derive their force from the patent, the patentee has impermissibly broadened the scope of the patent grant with anticompetitive effect.[2]

She offered that explanation because a jury had found that C. R. Bard had misused its patents despite the absence of antitrust allegations. Citing previous concerns that patent misuse is "too vague a formulation to be useful," and agreeing that "the law should not condone wrongful commercial activity," she nevertheless cautioned that "the body of misuse law and precedent need not be enlarged into an open-ended pitfall for patent-supported commerce" and reversed the jury's finding.[3]

Rulings of this sort led Judge Richard Posner—among the most influential of all Chicago School legal thinkers—to wonder, "If misuse claims are not tested by conventional antitrust principles, by what principles shall they be tested? Our law is not rich in alternative concepts of monopolistic abuse; and it is rather late in the day to try to develop one without in the process subjecting the rights of patent holders to debilitating uncertainty."[4] He asked that question shortly before the Federal Courts Improvement Act eliminated Seventh Circuit patent law—and with it his opportunity to play a significant role in shaping the patent-misuse doctrine. Nevertheless, his question remains a challenge to the judges of the Federal Circuit: How, if at all, does the common form of patent misuse, in which a patentee conditions patent licenses or sales on the simultaneous licensing or purchase of some other unpatented product, differ from antitrust tying, where a monopolist conditions the sale of his monopoly product on the simultaneous purchase of some other product?

The answer is not clear. Posner implies that there is no difference, although he did find an instance of misuse unrelated to antitrust tying when he encountered GSK's paroxetine patent.[5] Newman, on the other hand, contends that patent misuse is broader than antitrust tying, even though some of her earlier rulings suggested that the two are identical—and she was unable to identify any concrete differences. In a curious twist, many of the Post-Chicago critics unhappy with the Federal Circuit for elevating patent rights above market needs when conducting antitrust analyses also complain that in the few areas where alleged infringers traditionally found it easier to prove that a patentee had misused his patent than to prove a full-blown antitrust allegation, the Federal Circuit has imported the complications from antitrust law into its misuse analysis. In other words, the Federal Circuit's critics are unhappy that the court seems

to be moving toward Posner's asserted equation of tying and misuse—
a fine Chicagoan formulation.

That equation hardly puts the court in the minority on this point; most
analysts agree with Posner. Congress, however, was never a body bound
by the dictates of either sensible analysis or the federal judiciary. In keeping with its general willingness to let the courts conduct case-specific
antitrust analyses while micromanaging IP analyses, Congress injected a
special clause into the Patent Act in which it used the legislative prerogative of double, triple, and quadruple negatives to explain what patent
misuse *is not* (which might not have been quite so odd were there also a
statutory provision explaining what patent misuse *is*).[6] In particular, one
of these limitations built Chief Judge Markey's aversion to the term
patent monopoly into patent law; anyone accusing a patentee of misuse
must prove that the patent in question defines a relevant market susceptible to anticompetitive behavior. Unfortunately, no one bothered to alert
the keepers of antitrust law to this development. The relevant Supreme
Court precedent—dating back to the pre-Chicago era of weak patents
and strong antitrust enforcement—embraced the concept of a patent monopoly, presumed that every patent defined a relevant antitrust market,
and let antitrust plaintiffs move on to the other elements of their tying allegations without forcing them to prove that the allegedly harmed market was susceptible to anticompetitive manipulation.

AIN'T MISBEHAVIN'

That anomalous split between antitrust and patent law misled some litigants to expend enormous amounts on meaningless litigation, culminat-
ing in the Supreme Court's announcement of the obvious: the mere possession of a patent is insufficient to establish possession of a "patent
monopoly" in the meaningful sense necessary to sustain an antitrust-tying allegation. The expensive dispute that led to this announcement began with Trident, a company that manufactures and sells a system combining its patented equipment for printing Universal Product Code (UPC)
symbols directly onto corrugated cardboard with its unpatented ink. Independent Ink claimed that Trident's patented equipment defined an
original equipment manufacturer (OEM) market in which Trident possessed market power by dint of its patents, that replacement ink defined
a relevant antitrust aftermarket, and that Trident's insistence that its OEM
customers buy only its own replacement ink constituted an anticompetitive tying arrangement in violation of the antitrust laws. Trident, predictably, rejected those characterizations. *Neither party submitted any evidence to the trial judge.* Independent Ink rested its argument on the

long-standing if misplaced antitrust rule that every patent defines a relevant antitrust market. Trident countered with the patent rule that *only some* patents define the sorts of product markets prone to misuse. Trident then moved for summary judgment, asserting that in the absence of any evidence that it monopolized a relevant antitrust market, its exertion of leverage into an adjacent market could not violate the antitrust laws. The trial court agreed with Trident and granted summary judgment.

On appeal, the Federal Circuit agreed with Independent Ink—up to a point. The Federal Circuit explained that under binding Supreme Court precedent—precedent with which it did not necessarily agree—possession of a patent does, in fact, define a relevant antitrust market *as a matter of antitrust law*. Given this precedent, its only room for flexibility lay in deciding whether this market definition was conclusive or only presumptive. Judge Dyk, on behalf of Judges Clevenger and Prost, chose the second route. He announced that, as a matter of antitrust law, possession of a patent *presumptively* defines a relevant antitrust market; sent the matter back down to the trial court to allow Trident to rebut the presumption; and suggested that the Supreme Court might want to clean up its antitrust jurisprudence.[7]

The Supreme Court took the bait. On behalf of a unanimous court, Justice John Paul Stevens announced that from this point forward, antitrust law would adopt the patent law rule that only some patents define relevant antitrust market, thereby moving patent misuse a step closer to antitrust tying.[8] This ruling sets up a small black-box test: Is the shift normatively correct? The answer hinges upon a standard calculus. Bright-line or "per se" rules, like the one that says that all patents confer meaningful monopolies, are appropriate only when the activities in question are so likely to be objectionable, and so unlikely to be justifiable, that the expenditure of additional legal and judicial resources is unlikely to excuse the defendant's behavior—and is, in fact, more likely to lead to errors than to epiphanies. It seems unlikely that behavior related to conditioning sales in aftermarkets derived from patents meets such a strenuous test. Under the new set of rules, plaintiffs alleging anticompetitive effects in such markets will have the opportunity to prove their cases. Defendants will have the opportunity to counter and to justify their behavior. In short, we can give the Supreme Court an A on this limited black-box test; this substitution of fact-specific rule-of-reason analysis for a stark bright-line rule appears to preserve the balance between competition and innovation, albeit at the expense of a bit of uncertainty.

This new antitrust-tying rule also leads to an interesting observation about the practical relationship between tying and patent misuse—as well as about the philosophical posture of the Federal Circuit in the Chicago vs. Post-Chicago debate. The "patent monopoly" rule in antitrust-tying cases isn't the only vestige of the pre-Chicago era. The Supreme Court's *entire treatment* of tying is more consistent with an overregulated statist economy than it is with a liberal market economy. As far as Supreme Court precedent is concerned, tying itself is one of those business activities that is objectionable so often that the law can label it per se illegal without even looking to see whether or not is has had any anticompetitive effect in the specific market under consideration. Few contemporary economists believe that the current legal treatment of tying represents sound economic policy. Chicagoans believe that tying is *never* objectionable and at times—say, when a vendor substitutes an integrated product for two old stand-alone products—can be beneficial. Post-Chicagoans are a bit more skeptical; they believe that tying can be anticompetitive at times. But *no one* believes that binding Supreme Court precedent is right. As a result, lower courts go through great gyrations to explain why business models that very clearly *are* ties really are not "ties," but rather bundles, packages, systems, or integrated products. Sometimes the lower courts are even more audacious than that. In the high-profile and still bitterly contentious government challenge to Microsoft, for example, a unanimous *en banc* D.C. Circuit announced that "the rule of reason, rather than per se analysis, should govern the legality of tying arrangements involving platform software products."[9] As many commentators noted at the time, while this announcement is questionable as a statement of antitrust law, it is unassailable as a matter of antitrust economics.

All of which explains why it is significant that it was Justice Stevens—hardly one of the court's Chicagoans—who announced that the patent-misuse rule trumped the antitrust-tying rule, thereby at least nudging tying analysis in a more appropriate direction. It also points, once again, to the nagging feeling that even in the Post-Chicago era, the Federal Circuit remains a very Chicagoan type of place—which in turn explains the seeming anomaly that most of the AAI's Post-Chicagoans viewed Stevens's ruling as a contribution to the "IP grab" rather than as a step toward rational, case-specific analyses of anticompetitive effects in real markets.

The source of that feeling is that Judge Newman's reversal of the jury verdict against C. R. Bard was hardly unusual. In the entire history of the Federal Circuit—more than twenty-four years as I write these words—the court has found *exactly one* instance of patent misuse. In 1986, Chief Judge Markey commended a trial judge who had applied an antitrust-tying analysis that equated a patent with a relevant antitrust market to conclude that the Senza-Gel Corporation had misused its patented process for cooking hams.[10] That commendation led Congress to create the anomaly that landed Independent Ink in the Supreme Court nearly two decades later, by ending the presumption that patents create relevant monopolies as a matter of patent law. Perhaps feeling sheepish for having been thus chastised, the Federal Circuit developed a deep aversion to misuse claims. According to the Federal Circuit, during a twenty-year period in which the Patent and Trademark Office has granted almost two and a half million patents, numerous companies have leveraged patents to commercial success, and thousands of patent disputes have made their way to Lafayette Park, *no one* has "draw[n] anticompetitive strength from the patent right" in a manner that the court would "deem to be contrary to public policy." Such a track record boggles the mind. There is only one possible way for it to make sense. The Federal Circuit *must* believe that no one has misused a patent in a manner contrary to public policy because it is impossible (or at least nearly impossible) to do so. No other explanation is even remotely plausible.

This evisceration of the patent-misuse doctrine has hardly gone unnoticed. Professors Burk and Lemley lamented that "while patent misuse has the potential to serve as a policy lever, its use by the Federal Circuit to date has been minimal, and seems to have diminished over time."[11] An anonymous 1997 student case note in the *Harvard Law Review* opened: "The continuing vitality of the patent misuse doctrine is in doubt. Both judges and commentators have argued that this equitable doctrine should be eliminated, primarily because they believe that the antitrust laws more adequately address the same concerns." A few paragraphs later, the author explained that at least part of this aversion to the doctrine arose because "the expansion of the doctrine occurred mostly before the 1970s, a time when the courts held a more critical view of monopolies in general and of the rights that accrued to inventors in particular. Critics contend, in part, that the doctrine is therefore an 'anachronism'"[12]

Without naming the city (or its eponymous university), this author pointed directly toward the most likely source of the patent-misuse doctrine's disappearance: the shift in economic thinking away from 1970s statism toward Chicago School liberalism. The debate over the propriety of even having a patent-misuse doctrine mirrors the antitrust debate. Unfortunately—at least for the hardest-core Chicagoans and apparently also for the Federal Circuit—the Supreme Court created the patent-misuse doctrine, and only the Supreme Court or Congress can destroy it. That creation occurred amid an earlier controversial shift in thinking about economic policy, in a period of American economic and legal history known as the "Lochner era."

UP FROM LOCHNER

That era takes its name from the case of *Lochner v. New York*, a Supreme Court ruling that had nothing at all to do patents, misuse, or antitrust. The

State of New York had passed a law limiting a baker's workweek to sixty hours. Lochner ran a bakery, where he "required and permitted" his employees to work more than sixty hours. When New York sued him for violating its labor law, Lochner complained that the regulation interfered with his right to contract with his employees on whatever terms they found agreeable. In 1905, Justice Rufus Peckham, writing for a majority of a divided Court, agreed with Lochner and threw out New York's maximum workweek. From that point on, *Lochner* came to represent a profound and critical debate about the relationship between America's industrial development and its constitutional system.

According to one view, America's transition from an agrarian economy to the world's leading industrial power required new approaches to regulation. Proponents of this view recognized that regulations like labor laws represented a break from historical practice, but they contended that new economic conditions mandated new social structures and legal responses. They also implicitly favored a good liberal interpretation of the Constitution analogous to the one that Justice Souter followed in his consideration of sovereign immunity; they saw the Constitution as a living document, flexible but not amorphous, as capable of protecting liberty in the new industrial age as it had been in the agrarian age.

According to the other view, our founding fathers had constructed an economic system in which the rights of property owners were paramount. One critical protected property right was the right to contract, or to craft any terms agreeable to both parties as a condition of transferring property—including labor. Though they, too, used different terms, their view approximated the conservative rigid originalism that Chief Justice Rehnquist and Justice Kennedy apply to sovereign immunity.[13]

With that background in mind, the controversy over patent misuse becomes clear. To those who see a patent as property like all other property, who believe that property rights are paramount, and who view the right to contract as among the most fundamental of all property rights, *of course* a patentee can set arbitrary conditions in a patent license, including those that relate to unpatented aftermarkets. To those who see patents as a regulatory scheme working to promote innovation within an overall attempt to maximize consumer welfare, *of course* restrictions on license terms are consistent with the constitutional order; license terms that deter progress—say, by interfering with otherwise competitive markets not subject to a patent's explicit terms—run directly counter to the IP Clause's imperative of promoting progress.

That's almost precisely the debate that unfolded as Congress and the Supreme Court began to grapple with the proliferation of aftermarkets in an industrial economy—a trend that has only accelerated with our current transition to an information economy. In 1912, under facts that eerily foreshadowed Independent Ink's recent visit to the Supreme Court, the A. B. Dick Company sold its patented rotary mimeograph machine to Christina Skou, on the condition that she use only Dick's unpatented ink. The inscrutable Miss Skou, however, purchased some ink from Sidney Henry. Dick sued Henry; Henry responded that Dick was trying to extend its patent illicitly from mimeograph machines to ink. On behalf of a divided Court, Justice Horace Lurton upheld "the right of a patentee owner of a machine to license another to use it subject to any qualification in respect of time, place, manner or purpose of use which the licensee agrees to accept."[14] A patentee who is up front and clear about the terms of sale can impose pretty much any conditions to which he and the buyer agree.

Congress responded in the Clayton Act of 1914, the second major American antitrust statute, which (among other things) declared it "unlawful for any person engaged in commerce . . . to lease or make a sale or contract for sale of goods . . . whether patented or unpatented, for use, consumption, or resale . . . where the effect of such lease, sale, or contract . . . may be to substantially lessen competition or tend to create a monopoly in any line of commerce."[15] It seemed pretty clear that Dick's attempt to corner the aftermarket on unpatented mimeograph ink would, at the very least, have substantially lessened competition in a line of commerce. So when Universal arrived at the Supreme Court in 1917 to argue that the Motion Picture Patents Company's attempt to restrict the sorts of movies that people could show on its patented projectors was anticompetitive, the Court overruled its precedent, pointed the law in the opposite direction, and introduced the concepts that would become the patent-misuse doctrine. Justice John Clarke, writing for a still-divided Court, shuddered at the thought of

> a restriction which would give to the plaintiff such a potential power for evil over an industry which must be recognized as an important element in the amusement life of the nation, [which] is plainly void, because wholly without the scope and purpose of our patent laws and because, if sustained, it would be gravely injurious to that public interest, which we have seen is more a favorite of the law than is the promotion of private fortunes.[16]

The controversy continued to rage. The very next year, the Executive Branch weighed in on the side of prohibiting restrictive licenses. The Department of Justice (DOJ) arrived at the Supreme Court in an early round of what turned into a fifty-plus-year attempt to break up the United Shoe Machinery Company, a monopolist whose position and leverage may have disadvantaged those who make or wear shoes, but posed no serious threat to the amusement life of the nation. This time, Justice Joseph McKenna swung a majority of the Court behind his view that the

aggrieved shoemakers must have accepted United Shoe Machinery's
lease terms "upon a calculation of their value—the efficiency of the machines balanced against the restrictions upon and conditions of their use."

> Let us guard against confusion and not confound things which must be kept
> in distinction. A patentee is given rights to his device, but he is given no
> power to force it on the world. If the world buy it or use it the world will do
> so upon a voluntary judgment of its utility, demonstrated, it may be, at great
> cost to the patentee. If its price be too high, whether in dollars or conditions,
> the world will refuse it; if it be worth the price, whether of dollars or condi-
> tions, the world will seek it. To say that the world is not recompensed for the
> price it pays is to attack the policy of the law, is to defy experience and to de-
> clare that the objects of inventive genius all around us have contributed noth-
> ing to the advancement of mankind. . . . We see nothing else in the circum-
> stances of the parties than that which moves and may move the transactions
> of men.[17]

McKenna's argument notwithstanding, the patent-misuse doctrine
somehow managed to stay alive throughout the Lochner era. When the
Supreme Court finally capitulated in the face of Franklin Roosevelt's 1936
landslide, repudiated *Lochner*, accepted the New Deal, and allowed the
nation to move into its next phase of industrial organization, patent misuse not only felt right at home but also picked up its name and its full-
blown formulation as an idea worthy of the title "doctrine."[18] By 1957,
Justice John Marshall Harlan felt comfortable saying that it "is now, of
course, familiar law that the courts will not aid a patent owner who has
misused his patents to recover any of their emoluments accruing during
the period of misuse or thereafter until the effects of such misuse have
been dissipated, or 'purged' as the conventional saying goes."[19]

That was more or less the state of the patent-misuse doctrine when the
Federal Circuit became its primary custodian in 1982. It has not fared well
there. According to many observers, it reached its nadir in 1992, surrounding the licensing conditions that Mallinckrodt applied to its
patented device for diagnosing and treating pulmonary disease by deliv-
ering a radioactive aerosol mist to a patient's lungs. Mallinckrodt marked
its products "single use only" and sold them to hospitals. At least some
hospitals used Mallinckrodt's products and then shipped them off to
Medipart, which reconditioned them and returned them to the hospitals
for a second use. Mallinckrodt sued Medipart. The district court ruled in
Medipart's favor, finding that Mallinckrodt had misused its patent
(though without referring to the patent-misuse doctrine explicitly). At the
Federal Circuit, Judge Newman, on behalf of judges Lourie and Clevenger, not only reversed but also reached back to a pre-*Lochner* case to
support her position that a patentee's

right to exclude may be waived in whole or in part. The conditions of such waiver are subject to patent, contract, anti-trust, and any other applicable law, as well as equitable considerations such as are reflected in the law of patent misuse. As in other areas of commerce, private parties may contract as they choose, provided that no law is violated thereby: "The rule is, with few exceptions, that any conditions which are not in their very nature illegal with regard to this kind of property, imposed by the patentee and agreed to by the licensee for the right to manufacture or use or sell the [patented] article, will be upheld by the courts."[20]

Armed with that 1902 description of the relationship between patent law and other bodies of law, Newman noted with disapproval, "The district court's holding that Mallinckrodt's restriction to single patient use was unenforceable was, as we have remarked, based on 'policy' considerations."[21]

Newman's analysis then took two interesting twists, one predictable, the other less so. The predictable twist was her conclusion that, given that she did not believe Mallinckrodt had misused its patent, Medipart was liable as an infringer. Her less predictable twist came in a single undeveloped sentence: "To sustain a misuse defense involving a licensing arrangement not held to have been *per se* anticompetitive by the Supreme Court, a factual determination must reveal that the overall effect of the license tends to restrain competition unlawfully in an appropriately defined relevant market."[22] In other words, Newman equated patent misuse with antitrust tying, in contrast to the comments that she would make to C. R. Bard six years later. According to Newman—or at least, according to Newman in *Mallinckrodt*—an accused infringer claiming that a patentee has misused his patent must show that the alleged misuse has had an anticompetitive effect on some relevant antitrust market. What sorts of proof are acceptable? The accused infringer has a choice: either she can show that the patentee has committed some act so heinous that the Supreme Court has labeled it a per se violation of the antitrust laws, or she can engage in the long, hard, factual slog that all antitrust plaintiffs must undergo to win their cases under a rule-of-reason analysis.

Once again, Newman's decision to equate patent misuse with antitrust law seems like the sort of ruling that would make the Post-Chicago parts of the antitrust bar happy as a shift beyond IP law's narrow focus on activities toward antitrust law's broader consideration of effects. And once again that might well have been the Post-Chicagoans' response were it not for their sneaking suspicion that the Federal Circuit also takes a strict Chicagoan view of antitrust. Put the two pieces together, and you get a doctrine that says that it's almost impossible for a patentee to misuse a patent, because the market itself will discipline all seemingly illicit misuses.

THE SILENCE OF THE DOGS

Many commentators disapproved of this apparent emerging doctrine. Robert Hoerner, who had been an official at DOJ's Antitrust Division in the 1960s, issued a scathing critique:

> In its decision establishing the patent misuse doctrine, the U.S. Supreme Court did not require a finding of either an antitrust violation or an anticompetitive effect. The Federal Circuit in its recent decisions, however, has almost uniformly required proof of an anticompetitive effect before the doctrine can be invoked. Those recent decisions cannot be squared with the patent misuse doctrine established by the Supreme Court. . . .
>
> Stepping back and looking at the issue from a larger perspective, it could be argued that the Federal Circuit appreciates that the patent applicant has made an irrevocable but valuable disclosure, to the benefit of the public, in his patent application, and that he should be regarded as having a *property right* to enforce it. Misuse destroys that right until purge. The difficulty with the above speculation is that in our system of justice appellate courts are "inferior" to the U.S. Supreme Court, the decisions of which control and must be followed. If the Supreme Court holds that . . . an "anticompetitive effect" is not required for a finding of . . . misuse, by what warrant does the Federal Circuit ignore such holdings?[23]

As far as Hoerner was concerned, the matter was clear. The Supreme Court had gotten public policy right when it dictated a misuse doctrine broader than antitrust. The Federal Circuit was thus simultaneously overstepping its charge, ignoring its proper institutional role, and working to the detriment of public policy. The Federal Circuit had abused the misuse doctrine.

Is Hoerner right? The best indication about his claim that the Federal Circuit is usurping Supreme Court authority lies in a "dogs that don't bark in the night" type of analysis. The Supreme Court considered patent misuse in 2006, when it reviewed Independent Ink's claims against Trident. Though the issue at stake there was not quite the one that earned the Federal Circuit Hoerner's ire, it was close enough to open the door for a truly irate Supreme Court. Were even a single justice as incensed as Hoerner about the overall doctrinal development of the patent-misuse doctrine in the Federal Circuit's hands, there probably would have been at least a concurring opinion. The absence of even a snide dictum suggests that the Supreme Court is less troubled by the Federal Circuit's narrowing of the patent-misuse doctrine than is Hoerner.

The more interesting question that Hoerner's critique raises is whether or not the Federal Circuit's treatment of patent misuse represents sound public policy—in other words, it's time for another black-box test. To those seeking a return to the weak-patent, strong-antitrust era of the 1970s, the court's sparing use of misuse must be a raging disappointment. Given America's disastrous economic performance in that decade, though, a return to its attitudes about IP and antitrust would hardly serve the public interest. No, the more interesting question is how to evaluate the policy consequences of the patent-misuse doctrine's current state within the intraliberal squabble that pitted Reaganomics against Clintonomics in the large, or the Chicago against the Post-Chicago schools in the more specialized realm of antitrust scholarship.

It's hard to see how a good Chicagoan could differ with a policy that reserves the right to curtail selected patentee behavior *in theory*, while permitting virtually all patentee behavior *in practice*—other than possibly arguing that it generates wasteful litigation. Post-Chicagoans might have a different take on the matter. From a Post-Chicago perspective, the rules are fine—the problem lies in their application. In principle, a patent-law rule that actually looks beyond the confines of the patent to see the *effect* of a patentee's behavior on the market is a great leap forward for patent law, as Burk and Lemley argued in advocating that the Federal Circuit make better use of the policy levers already at its disposal. The public would be well served by a massive injection of context-sensitive rules of reason into all of our IP laws. In addition, even if large parts of patent-misuse analysis and antitrust-tying analysis collapse into each other, misuse still adds two important arrows to the quiver of liberal market enforcement—at least as a matter of theory. First, there is another branch of misuse, as Judge Newman recognized in *C. R. Bard* and Judge Posner recognized when he confronted *ice-nine*, that lets a broad array of policy and equity considerations work their way into the calculus. Second, the misuse *remedy* of refusing to enforce the rights inherent in misused patents is immensely useful. Could an antitrust court impose this sort of remedy without reference to a patent claim? The answer is unclear.

The Supreme Court has stated numerous times that antitrust courts have broad authority to craft remedies necessary to overcome the effects of anticompetitive behavior. One such statement of this principle is particularly relevant. Back in the 1960s the federal government brought an antitrust suit against two British drug companies, Glaxo and ICI, claiming that they had conspired to fix prices on the antifungal griseofulvin. Both firms claimed that they each had patents relevant to griseofulvin production and that they were doing little more than exerting their legitimate patent rights. In the course of this antitrust investigation, the government contested the validity of those patents. When the matter finally reached the Supreme Court in 1973, Justice Byron White explained that not only could an antitrust court consider issues related to patent validity even in the absence of an explicit patent claim but it can also order a patentee to make and sell more of the patented product than the patentee might want and even compel the patentee to license the patent—all in the name of correcting a market that the patentee's anticompetitive behavior had damaged.[24]

Given White's blessing to these antitrust remedies that trample a patentee's rights, other impositions, including a refusal to enforce the patent altogether, should also be available. As I argued in detail (and quite persuasively, if I may say so myself) in *Digital Phoenix*, this sort of remedy might have been the only one that the government could have implemented had it truly desired to change Microsoft's behavior at the end of their lengthy antitrust battle.[25] Nevertheless, and my own persuasiveness notwithstanding, it's probably not a good idea to read too much into White's 1973 ruling against Glaxo. Though any Supreme Court precedent that the Court itself has not overruled explicitly remains binding law, this particular ruling emerged during an era of disastrous economic thinking about patents and antitrust—an era whose basic premises the country has long since repudiated. Furthermore, even within the realm of antitrust opinions that the Supreme Court issued during that era, this one stands out as unimportant. For whatever reason, *no court* has ever cited this case in more than passing, much less relied upon it to invalidate a patent or to compel a license to remedy a violation of the antitrust laws. As any good lawyer could tell you about a case with that kind of profile: act upon it if you must, but do so at your own peril.

ALL IN THE POOL

People—even good lawyers—rely on all sorts of things at their own peril all the time. Just look at what happened when three practicing patent lawyers took it upon themselves to present "A Patent Lawyer's View" of the patent-misuse doctrine as of 2005—to the Federal Circuit Bar Association, no less. They opened with the somewhat surprising assertion: "Patent misuse, an equitable defense to the enforcement of a misused patent, appears to be enjoying a resurgence."[26] Their primary evidence of this resurgence? The International Trade Commission had recently declared six patents related to recordable and rewritable CDs (CD-Rs and CD-RWs, respectively) unenforceable under the doctrine of patent misuse.

Four companies—Philips, Sony, Taiyo Yuden, and Ricoh—all held patents related to the production of CD-Rs or CD-RWs. That situation put them in a quandary that is becoming increasingly common in the electronics industry: each of them controlled a different critical step in the production. If they all held tight to their own patents, none of them would be able to manufacture either CD-Rs or CD-RWs. Instead, they set up a patent-pooling system. Philips administered the pool, and even took the unusual step of asking the DOJ's Antitrust Division whether it had any problems with the pooling arrangement. The department saw that Philips had set up four different packages, each relevant to the production of a specific product, and then offered these packages on "reasonable and nondiscriminatory" (or RAND, a term of art in the patent-licensing world) terms to anyone interested in manufacturing CD-Rs or CD-RWs. DOJ expressed its opinion—not binding anywhere, but still potentially persuasive—that the pooling arrangement was fine. A few years later Philips subdivided the packages even further, splitting each one into a collection of patents "essential" for manufacturing the products and those that were "nonessential." A few years after that, some foreign CD manufacturers decided that Philips's terms weren't quite so reasonable after all, and stopped paying royalties.

Philips filed a 337 petition, asking the ITC to prevent these infringers from importing their products into the United States The importers responded that Philips had misused its patents by including nonessential patents in the essential group, and thus forcing them to buy patents that they neither wanted nor needed as a condition for buying those that they did want. The ITC agreed with everyone: It ruled that the importers were infringing but that the patents were unenforceable because Philips had misused them. The patent-misuse doctrine was alive and well at the ITC in December 2003.[27]

The ITC, however, hardly has final say in such matters. Philips appealed to the Federal Circuit, where the patent-misuse doctrine had been asleep for a long, long, long time. The Clerk of Court's assignment wheel landed on Judges Bryson, Gajarsa, and Linn. On behalf of a unanimous panel, Judge Bryson agreed that patent pooling is a reasonable way to get around difficulties like the one that the various contributors to these pools faced and thus is a critical element of supporting of both the patent system and economic growth in the information age—a policy conclusion consistent with positions that both Reagan's and Clinton's economic teams had adopted, and thus with which both Chicagoans and Post-Chicagoans would agree. He explained that, contrary to the ITC's characterization, no one was

> "forced" to "take" anything from Philips that they did not want, nor were they restricted from obtaining licenses from other sources to produce the relevant technology. Philips simply provided that for a fixed licensing fee, it would not sue any licensee for engaging in any conduct covered by the entire group of patents in the package. By analogy, if Philips had decided to surrender its "nonessential" patents or had simply announced that it did not intend

to enforce them, there would have been no way for the manufacturers to decline or reject Philips's decision. Yet the economic effect of the package licensing arrangement for Philips's patents is not fundamentally different from
the effect that such decisions would have had on third parties seeking to compete with the technology covered by those "nonessential" patents.[28]

Judge Bryson also took the time to explain the importance of patent-
pooling arrangements from a public policy perspective—and why a well-
organized patent pool advances technology without imposing an illicit restraint on competition.

> It is entirely rational for a patentee who has a patent that is essential to par-
> ticular technology . . . to charge what the market will bear for the essential
> patent and to offer the others for free. . . . For the patentee in this situation to
> offer its nonessential patents as part of a package with the essential patent at
> no additional charge is no more anticompetitive than if it had surrendered
> the nonessential patents or had simply announced a policy that it would not
> enforce them against persons who licensed the essential patent. In either
> case, those offering technology that competed with the nonessential patents
> would be unhappy, because they would be competing against free technol-
> ogy. But the patentee would not be using his essential patent to obtain power
> in the market for the technology covered by the nonessential patents. This
> package licensing arrangement cannot fairly be characterized as an exploita-
> tion of power in one market to obtain a competitive advantage in another.[29]

As a stand-alone matter, this ruling probably nudged public policy in
the right direction (though such nudging is hardly the Federal Circuit's
job); patent pools are likely to grow in importance, and few patentees
would attempt them if the courts overrode the DOJ opinion letters so
lightly. As part of a pattern of Federal Circuit misuse cases, however, it
brought the doctrine's "apparent resurgence" to a screeching halt. Once
again, the Federal Circuit reiterated the tests necessary to find patent misuse, applied those tests to the facts in front of it, and concluded that no
misuse had occurred—though to be technically accurate, the panel determined only that the ITC had not proved misuse.

A STANDARD FRAUD

Is the patent-misuse doctrine dead, or just asleep? Perhaps the answer lies
outside the doctrinal branch paralleling antitrust, in the more general notion of a patent used in a manner contrary to public policy. Perhaps a case
involving allegations of good old-fashioned fraud might wake the sleeping doctrine—or at least poke it enough to reveal some sign of life. Yet
when such a case arose, the doctrine did not even stir.

The case in question involved the Joint Electron Device Engineering Council (JEDEC), a standard-setting body affiliated with the Electronic Industries Association (EIA). Standard-setting bodies play a critical role in the modern economy. They coordinate the participants in a given industry and try to get them to pool their technologies to create "industry standards." Such industry standards are often necessary if different companies are to make mutually compatible products. In the absence of industry standards, large parts of the economy would collapse to single-company aftermarkets. Competition would dwindle in market after market, and consumers would lose time after time. Standard-setting bodies allow competitors to pool their knowledge and their technologies—particularly their knowledge of relatively mature technologies—to incorporate the best elements of what had been competing products into an industry standard. Such bodies typically require participants to disclose relevant patents, patents pending, trade secrets, and so forth, and to make anything that works its way into the standard available on RAND terms. Different manufacturers can then license anything necessary to the standard and produce compatible products. Competition "within the standard" replaces competition "for the standard," and consumers win.

Rambus, though perhaps best known as a microchip company, doesn't actually produce any chips. Instead, it employs research engineers and patent lawyers and makes its money by licensing its chip patents to manufacturers. At various points throughout the 1990s, Rambus was a guest, a member, a nonmember, and an active participant in JEDEC. Of particular relevance to the fraud story, Rambus has an impressive collection of patents related to dynamic random access memory chips (DRAMs), and JEDEC developed standards for synchronous DRAM (SDRAM) and for double data rate SDRAM (DDR-SDRAM). Rambus neglected to inform JEDEC that some of its patents, and in particular some of its pending patent applications (which were secret and known only to Rambus and the PTO), were relevant to the SDRAM and DDR-SDRAM standards. When the standards came out and various manufacturers started working toward them, Rambus filed a patent infringement suit against Infineon. Infineon countered, in part, with a fraud claim against Rambus. That counterclaim raised some interesting questions. Did Rambus's failure to disclose its patents constitute fraud on JEDEC? Did it constitute patent misuse in its broad sense? According to a Virginia jury, Rambus defrauded JEDEC twice. According to a Virginia trial judge, Rambus defrauded JEDEC when it failed to disclose its patents relevant to SDRAM, but not when it failed to disclose its patents relevant to DDR-SDRAM—largely because of the timing with which Rambus joined and quit JEDEC.[30]

What did the Federal Circuit have to say? The panel was split. Judge Rader found no fraud. He began his inquiry by applying the standard pendent jurisdiction choice-of-law rule and thus delved into the peculiarities of Virginia's state laws describing fraud. He wondered whether Rambus had a clear, well-defined duty to disclose the patents in question to JEDEC. He looked at various of JEDEC's bylaws, announcements, rules, and publications for an answer, only to find that "[t]he language of these policy statements actually does not impose any direct duty on members."

> While the policy language advises JEDEC as a whole to avoid standards "calling for the use of" a patent and the manual obligates the chairperson to remind members to inform the meeting of any patents or applications relevant to the work of the committee, this court finds no language—in the membership application or manual excerpts—expressly requiring members to disclose information. There is no indication that members ever legally agreed to disclose information. . . .[31]

In fact, Rader almost seemed more peeved with JEDEC than with Rambus:

> [T]here is a staggering lack of defining details in the EIA/JEDEC patent policy. When direct competitors participate in an open standards committee, their work necessitates a written patent policy with clear guidance on the committee's IP position. A policy that does not define clearly what, when, how, and to whom the members must disclose does not provide a firm basis for the disclosure duty necessary for a fraud verdict. Without a clear policy, members form vaguely defined expectations as to what they believe the policy requires—whether the policy in fact so requires or not. JEDEC could have drafted a patent policy with a broader disclosure duty. It could have drafted a policy broad enough to capture a member's failed attempts to mine a disclosed specification for broader undisclosed claims. It could have. It simply did not.[32]

Judge Sharon Prost disagreed. She noted that "at the time Rambus joined JEDEC, it had several pending patent applications . . . spawning more than a thousand claims in dozens of continuation and divisional applications. Rambus also had a specific plan for using its pending patent applications against anyone using the SDRAM standard," a plan of which she was aware because it appeared in a 1992 Rambus business document that was part of the appellate record. Furthermore, she noted, Rambus didn't tell JEDEC about its relevant pending patent applications. "Instead, Rambus continued to attend JEDEC meetings for three more years, watching the SDRAM standard evolve and then amending its patent applications to try to cover features of the standard. Richard Crisp, Rambus's JEDEC representative, testified at trial about how 'Rambus was intentionally drafting claims to intentionally cover the JEDEC SDRAMs.'"[33]

Prost then disagreed with Rader's fine parsing of JEDEC's disclosure policies, indicated that she found them clear enough to let Rambus know that what it was doing was wrong, suggested that Rader was making the case so complicated that any future allegations of similar failures to disclose patent applications would require such detailed claim constructions that "an action for fraud will become more a federal patent case than a case arising under state law," and agreed with both the jury and the trial judge that Rambus had committed fraud with respect to the SDRAM standard.[34]

Judge Bryson, the third member of the panel, agreed with Rader. Rambus was off the hook. Or was it? If not technically fraud, how about misuse? Could there be a better illustration of what Judge Newman had called an action that "did not in [itself] violate any law, but that drew anticompetitive strength from the patent right" and should thus be deemed "contrary to public policy"? If ever there were a perfect opportunity to resurrect the general branch of the patent-misuse doctrine, this had to be it.

What did the Federal Circuit have to say about misuse? Although the court had not found Rambus to be a fraud, even Rader conceded that that was only because JEDEC's bylaws and policies were insufficiently clear. Everyone knew what had happened here: Rambus took advantage of a standard-setting body and its pending (hence secret) patent applications to achieve unfair leverage and to "draw anticompetitive strength." So what did the court have to say about patent misuse? Would you believe . . . *nothing!* Not a single word. No one even brought it up—not Infineon, not the trial court, not Rader for the majority, and not Prost in dissent. The doctrine seemed to have fallen into such disuse that no one even thought to raise it.

No one, that is, at the Federal Circuit. And when it comes to patent law, the Federal Circuit usually has final say. But when it comes to anticompetitive strength, other institutional actors share the limelight. In this particular case, the Federal Trade Commission got involved. In August 2006, nearly four years after the Federal Circuit ruled in Rambus's favor, the FTC agreed with Judge Prost. According to Commissioner Pamela Jones Harbor's opinion for a unanimous commission:

> Standard setting occurs in many industries and can be highly beneficial to consumers. . . . Typically, the procompetitive benefits of standard setting outweigh the loss of market competition. . . . But when a firm engages in exclusionary conduct that subverts the standard-setting process and leads to the acquisition of monopoly power, the procompetitive benefits of standard setting cannot be fully realized. . . . JEDEC operated on a cooperative basis and required that its members participate in good faith. According to JEDEC policy and practice, members were expected to reveal the existence of patents and patent applications that later might be enforced against those practicing the JEDEC standards. In addition, JEDEC members were obligated to offer

assurances to license patented technologies on RAND terms, before members voted to adopt a standard that would incorporate those technologies. The intent of JEDEC policy and practice was to prevent anticompetitive hold-up. Rambus, however, chose to disregard JEDEC's policy and practice, as well as the duty to act in good faith. Instead, Rambus deceived the other JEDEC members.[35]

The FTC found that Rambus's actions had violated the antitrust laws, but that it needed additional briefings before it could determine the appropriate remedy. In an uncharacteristic understatement, the *Wall Street Journal* commented:

> A series of judges have looked at the same set of facts and come to different conclusions about Rambus's behavior in connection with [JEDEC]. . . . [A] Federal Circuit court concluded Rambus didn't have an obligation to disclose the patent information, overruling a finding by a district court that Rambus's conduct constituted fraud. But the FTC's 120-page ruling sends a warning signal it plans to deal harshly with companies that hide patents from industry groups who demand their disclosure.[36]

Even five and a half years into the Bush *fils* administration, Post-Chicago analyses receive a warmer reception at the FTC than they do at the Federal Circuit. The pattern that emerges from the Federal Circuit's misuse jurisprudence is unmistakable. While it's hard to argue with the court's reading of any specific fact pattern (though at times, it's as easy as simply agreeing with a dissenter), only one message is possible. If *no one* has misused a patent in more than twenty years, it must be damn near impossible to misuse a patent. Patent rights have achieved an almost sacred status, perhaps even greater than that of other forms of property—where antitrust courts find at least occasional violations. Sensible rules and statements about the importance of balancing patent rights against other bodies of law notwithstanding, it seems as if a patentee holding a valid patent can do no wrong. Would it be misuse to attach unacceptable license terms to a patent license? Absolutely, as a matter of theory, but no one has ever seen an unacceptable license term in practice. Would it be misuse to defraud a professional organization? Absolutely, as a matter of theory, but as Judge Prost noted, unlikely in practice. The court's inability to find even a single instance of patent misuse in over two decades speaks volumes. It is yet another dog not barking in the night.

THE POST-CHICAGO ILLUSION

Is the Federal Circuit a Chicagoan court? Is it truly hostile to Post-Chicago analysis? The answers remain elusive because one of the relevant terms is ill defined. There *is* a Chicago School of economics. Chicago School economists believe, among other things, in economic libertarianism, a laissez-faire approach to regulation, and the power and the beauty of markets. From the school's inception, Chicagoan economists were interested in the interaction of law and policy. They pioneered "law and economics," applying analytic principles from economics to the study of the law. They also championed the lighter-touch antitrust reforms of the early 1980s, although some might have gone farther and eliminated antitrust enforcement altogether.

There *is not*, however, a Post-Chicago School—at least, not beyond the confines of a very narrow antitrust community. It is a term that several antitrust scholars and organization (such as the AAI) apply to themselves to differentiate their views, analyses, and policy recommendations from both the Chicagoans of the 1980s and the industrial planners who had preceded them. It's tough to be precise about the Federal Circuit's receptiveness to Post-Chicago analyses of patent law because there is no clear consensus as to what such analyses would entail.

Nevertheless, the construction of a virtual dialog about IP law between Chicagoans and Post-Chicagoans remains valuable because the debate in the antitrust world mimics a broader debate in the political and economic realms—and as noted, it does so using terminology that carries little enough political baggage to focus on substance rather than on labels. Debates pitting "Reagan" against "Clinton" can get needlessly visceral for reasons unrelated to the specific topics under consideration. In contexts like antitrust and IP, the basic dividing questions are simple and fundamental—Adam Smith raised them in 1776: How often do imperfections creep into the workings of a free market? Is it possible for interventions to correct those imperfections without doing more harm than good? The answers provide the Federal Circuit with its test score on the black box known as "misuse." If imperfections are either rare or too tough to correct, its score is high. Otherwise, it is low. The Chicago/Post-Chicago split captures the debate over this score.

With that score decided—or rather, undecided—the Federal Circuit's panoramic view is complete. Its brief glance into the world of copyright reiterates what we know from reading the newspapers: A broken copyright system grants the creative classes unenforceable rights and increasingly draconian enforcement methods. In the world of patents, the Federal Circuit's critics converge to a common complaint: patents have become so strong that they are interfering with the rest of the economy. The Federal Circuit, of course, is only empowered to address a fraction of the causes and a slightly larger fraction of the effects of this virus; the primary remedy lies in Congress. Nevertheless, because the Federal Circuit is the primary arena for viewing the relationship between our patent laws and actual markets—the relationship that teaches us what policies we actually have—it should also be the primary source of questions about the policies we want. Is the Federal Circuit asking such questions? Our look beyond the narrow confines of patent law, through the periphery, out to the horizon, reveals that such questions are few and far between. The greatest frustration in trying to put our IP systems in context is not that our institutions are deriving incorrect answers; it's that they aren't even asking the critical questions.

All of which leads us to the mother of all Federal Circuit black-box questions: How does the *patent* policy we have relate to the *economic* policy we want? Commentators seem to feel that the relationship is poor. The Federal Circuit seems to shy away from the question. Congress seems willing to consider some minor details, but not to revisit the big issues. The regrettable answer is that this critical box is insufficiently defined to lend itself to testing. Inattention rarely succeeds through anything other than dumb luck. A court unable to find a single instance of patent misuse, or a single example of a patentee wielding a valid patent in an anticompetitive manner, must either believe that patent rights are incorruptible (or at least nearly so) or be delinquent in identifying their abuse. If the former is true, the Federal Circuit should announce it, solicit support from scholars, and encourage the Supreme Court and Congress to address the issue. If the latter is true, the Federal Circuit must remedy this serious deficiency in its work. Outsiders cannot know which belief actually guides the court, but we might be able to encourage it to reveal the answer—and to pick an appropriate course of action. Until then, all that we can do is to warn the court that it is heading for a poor grade on this, the most important of its tests. The Federal Circuit's entire existence hinges upon our desire to align American patent law with an economic policy that will empower the U.S. economy throughout the information age. It would be nice to believe that the court is at least considering the relationship between patent law and economic policy. It's never too late to start.

15

✛

The Permanent Experiment

THE HUMAN COURT

The Federal Circuit's "patent court" moniker notwithstanding, even a myopic focus on this single court yields a surprising panorama of the contemporary legal terrain. Any selection of topics thus remains at least somewhat idiosyncratic. While the court's history, its patent docket, and its trade and federal claims dockets dominate the view, institutional analysts maintain significant flexibility when choosing specific topics within those areas; the court's forays into other legal arenas provide even greater flexibility. I organized my own institutional analysis around my thesis that the liberal policy perspectives that helped motivate the Federal Circuit will also lead to a successful information-age economy, subject to a conservative respect for institutional competencies and boundaries. The idiosyncrasies underlying both my selection of topics and my definition of normative black-box tests all flowed from that objective.

Beyond these mandatory dockets, the inclusion of at least some "optional" topics in an institutional analysis is critical to conveying the richness of an institution that falls so easily into narrow stereotyping. My personal interests and experience led me to explore sovereign immunity, the no-interest rule, NAFIs, takings, copyright, antitrust, misuse, and disappearing polymorphs. Others could just as easily have opted to explore food and drug law, trademarks, tax, government contracting, banking, bankruptcy, or Indian law.

The Federal Circuit's involvement in the first of the latter set of topics is an offshoot of the Hatch-Waxman Act; the *sui generis* bargain between generic drug companies and branded patentees exempts otherwise-in-fringing activities to the extent necessary for a generic company to file an Abbreviated New Drug Application (ANDA) with the Food and Drug Ad-ministration.[1] Trademark disputes arrive from the Patent and Trademark Office; after all, "trademark" is this regulatory agency's middle name, and the Federal Circuit has appellate jurisdiction over all disputes emanating from the agency.[2] The court's involvement in the other arenas stems from their potential as federal claims. Taxpayers who believe that they are due a refund must sue the government in the Court of Federal Claims.[3] Gov-ernment contractors must bring their claims to either a specialized review board, such as the Armed Forces Board of Contract Appeals or the Veter-ans Administration Board of Contract Appeals, or to the Court of Federal Claims;[4] an interesting and large class of such claims arose from the gov-ernment's mishandling of the savings and loan crisis of the 1980s, result-ing in numerous banking and bankruptcy cases passing through the Court of Federal Claims, the Federal Circuit, and, in the critical *Winstar* case, the Supreme Court.[5] The Indian Tucker Act puts the Court of Federal Claims, and thus the Federal Circuit, at the forefront of Indian law.[6] All of these in-quiries add richness and texture to the court's work.

The "agenda" guiding my own selection of topics, however, was my desire to share the (philosophically) liberal and conservative windows that this nonpartisan, high-impact, low-profile institution has on the un-folding rules of the information age—and in particular, of the information economy. Former chief judge H. Robert Mayer framed this challenge in his foreword to a 2002 book celebrating the Federal Circuit's twentieth birthday: "Some have said this court is a permanent experiment. That of course is a contradiction in terms."[7] Oxymoronic or not, the Federal Cir-cuit truly *is* a permanent experiment, and as with any experiment, it's never a bad idea to review some interim data. As *The Secret Circuit* heads to press, the court is nearing a quarter-century of data generation—more than enough to permit the sort of evaluation that we have undertaken. What have we learned?

Perhaps the first and most obvious lesson is that the Federal Circuit is not really a "people's court." To some extent, no appellate court is a peo-ple's court, because parties rarely attend appellate hearings; lawyers and judges typically discuss some finer points of law, paying scant attention to factual or emotional issues. Parties who do attend oral arguments could find the proceedings cold and impersonal. In the Federal Circuit's case, the human dimension is removed even further because the overwhelming majority of the litigants it sees are either corporations or government agencies. Nevertheless, the occasional solo inventor does wander in, and the Federal Circuit does hear two entire categories of "people cases": those appealed from the Merit Systems Protection Board (MSPB) and those from the Court of Appeals for Veterans Claims (CAVC). The former tribunal protects the rights and benefits of civil servants; the latter, those of veterans. Though some of these matters are quite complex, the court possesses minimal tools with which to help even worthy appellants—as Daniel Sandstrom learned in his fruitless attempt to secure government interest payments. Congress has limited the Federal Circuit's authority to overrule these tribunals to narrow instances of egregious error. As a result, the overwhelming majority of these cases end either in summary affirmances or in brief unpublished opinions. The *results* of the Federal Circuit's people cases thus convey little of the cases' actual flavor. The *experience* of those cases that unfolds in open court can be quite different.

Lawyers representing MSPB and CAVC appellants understand that the severe congressional limitation on Federal Circuit jurisdiction means that creativity and stridency are often preconditions for a successful appeal. Even a quick perusal of MSPB, CAVC, and related Federal Circuit cases reveals that it's far too difficult to discipline a civil servant and far too easy to screw a veteran. Typical requests for MSPB review tend to elicit the feeling of "You must be kidding." Typical requests for CAVC review elicit a "There must be some way we can help" (or at least, those are my feelings). By and large, the answer to both sentiments is no. They're not kidding and the court can't help. But anyone sitting in the courtroom can learn—and the very unfamiliarity of people cases on the Federal Circuit docket means that the lessons are often both poignant and important.

For example, I witnessed an MSPB appeal involving a Social Security Administration (SSA) benefits analyst who perpetually botched more than 30 percent of the forms she administered. SSA, which had given her ten months of classroom training before giving her these responsibilities, crafted nine months of personal mentoring. No improvement. No matter how slowly she worked (and she did work slowly), her accuracy fell in the 50- to 70-percent range. Reluctantly, SSA realized that it could no longer inflict her incompetence on Social Security recipients and demoted her. She appealed to the MSPB. She submitted many documents suggesting that she had received some favorable reviews, but to no avail; during more than a year of mentoring and monitoring, her performance remained inadequate. The MSPB affirmed her demotion. She secured new counsel and appealed to the Federal Circuit.

Her new counsel came roaring out of the starting gate. He discovered a favorable memo that his client had failed to submit to the MSPB. He saw the MSPB's refusal to reopen the matter in order to include this additional memo as a sign of a (possibly criminal) government violation of due process and an obstruction of justice.

My experience with corporate clients had left me unprepared for this sort of lawyering. While I agreed that the SSA had to demote a file clerk incapable of achieving even minimal levels of accuracy, I still felt sorry for a woman watching her salary get cut from about $35,000 to about $30,000. I was less than enamored with her attorney. Did he really see a constitutional violation? Could he possibly believe that his client had received something other than due process? Was he appealing merely to placate an implacable client? Or was he simply taking money from a poor client who seemed unlikely to have the cash to spare?

Oral argument answered my questions. Counsel was a young man in way over his head. The judges were much kinder to him than they would have been to a comparably overwhelmed corporate lawyer. They let him speak his piece—which he did without histrionics—and asked him a few questions. Before my eyes (and at least in my own mind), he morphed from a scoundrel inflating his client's notion of her constitutional rights and consequently his own bill, into an inner city kid who had somehow pulled himself through law school and stayed to represent his working-class neighborhood. He lost, but he did so with dignity. Perhaps I remain the scoundrel for using minimal information to substitute one weak stereotype for another, but this simple case proved invaluable to my own education.

I also watched the case of a Vietnam vet who had returned home from his tour of duty shell-shocked (or technically, exhibiting symptoms of Post-Traumatic Stress Disorder). He came home in 1972 and filed for benefits. The VA rejected his application. Twenty years later, still suffering from various symptoms, he applied again. This time—perhaps in part because American attitudes toward veterans had changed—he was able to qualify. But he then discovered something curious: his medical records were missing from his service file. The VA had rejected his 1972 application because the Navy had misplaced his files, and no one had bothered to look for them. In 1995 he asked the VA to find his files and grant him back benefits for his twenty-plus missing years.

So began his Kafkaesque journey from the Board of Veterans Appeals to the CAVC up to the Federal Circuit and back and around and around—virtually all on procedural nonsense. No matter how hard he tried, he just couldn't get the VA to ask the Navy for his files to help him prove that he was entitled to back benefits. On his first trip to the Federal Circuit, the panel thought that it had found a way to help him, but an *en banc* court told the panel that it was wrong; the attempted assistance simply lengthened the veteran's bureaucratic nightmare. Two and a half years later, he returned to Lafayette Park, still seeking some way to secure his missing files. The court had run out of legal options to help him, and the VA stood firmly behind its insistence that he file a new request and move to the back of its queue. When his turn came around the next time, the VA conceded that it would have to help him, because Congress had passed some new laws in late 2001 requiring the VA to assist veterans facing such circumstances. The VA was under no obligation to help him in 2003, though, because he had filed his request prior to 2001, and the new law's benefits were not retroactive.

Oral argument gave the Federal Circuit one slim chance to get the government to behave reasonably. An appellate panel in black-robed person peering down into the well of the court has significant bully-pulpit potential. While the Federal Circuit may not use it often, it is a wonder to behold what happens when three judges see a conflict between institutional boundaries and a just cause. All three judges peppered both attorneys with questions. Why had the VA refused to ask the Navy for the papers? Even the VA admitted that the full limit of its search had been a single phone call in 1972. Every time the judges asked, the government lawyers provided the same response: We don't have to call the Navy to request the papers.

Finally, in open court, Judge Paul Michel shared a bit of wisdom that we should chisel into every government building in America: "The fact that there's no obligation doesn't mean that you're prohibited from doing something sensible." By the end of oral argument, the VA lawyer had made a personal promise to the bench that she would call the Navy. Sometimes, it seems, justice can prevail. And sometimes the corporate court called the Federal Circuit can show a human face. A critical first lesson learned.

THE BOURGEOIS COURT

A second lesson is that political and economic context is critical to appreciating the Federal Circuit's performance. While such context is likely important to most institutional assessments, the circumstances surrounding the Federal Circuit's birth suggests that context is particularly important in its case. At the same time, the complexity of the issues with which it deals, the absence of clean partisan splits on most of those issues, and the general context-insensitive nature of intellectual property law, all combine to guarantee that Federal Circuit observers spend less time considering the political and economic environment in which the court operates than do observers of most other institutions. That inattention to context likely also leads to another common misconception, namely, that the Federal Circuit warrants primary blame for all of the patent system's shortcomings.

As we have seen, though, the Federal Circuit is but one important component in a complex patent system—and the patent system is but one component in an even more complex market economy. The Federal Circuit's role in the modern economy is more than simply as a component of a component. The Federal Circuit was among the first new U.S. government institutions created to address the challenges of an economy in transition from the industrial age to the information age. The weak patent system that it inherited, for all of its flaws, was sufficient to power the American economy through the middle decades of the twentieth century—precisely those decades in which the United States most clearly dominated the global economy. That dominance extended throughout the creation process. Americans—American scientists, American engineers, American universities, American companies—led the world in innovation, in creativity, in commercialization, in production, and in distribution. Then something happened. By the mid-1970s the U.S. lead had dwindled to the point that many saw its disappearance as imminent. Malaise set in. The country needed new approaches, new modes of thinking, new models, and new institutions.

What ground did these new institutions have to cover? The key insights emerge from one of the most piercing critiques of the nineteenth-century European economy, a critique written during the Continent's transition from an agrarian society to an industrial economy. The critique was called *The Communist Manifesto*.

> The bourgeoisie, historically, has played a most revolutionary part. The bourgeoisie, wherever it has got the upper hand, has put an end to all feudal, patriarchal, idyllic relations. . . .
>
> The bourgeoisie has . . . been the first to show what man's activity can bring about. It has accomplished wonders far surpassing Egyptian pyramids, Roman aqueducts, and Gothic cathedrals; it has conducted expeditions that put in the shade all former exoduses of nations and crusades.
>
> The bourgeoisie cannot exist without constantly revolutionizing the instruments of production, and thereby the relations of production, and with them the whole relations of society. . . . All fixed, fast frozen relations, with their train of ancient and venerable prejudices and opinions, are swept away, all new-formed ones become antiquated before they can ossify. . . .
>
> The need of a constantly expanding market for its products chases the bourgeoisie over the entire surface of the globe. It must nestle everywhere, settle everywhere, establish connections everywhere. . . . To the great chagrin of reactionaries, it has drawn from under the feet of industry the national ground on which it stood. All old-established national industries have been destroyed or are daily being destroyed. They are dislodged by new industries, whose introduction becomes a life and death question for all civilized nations, by industries that no longer work up indigenous raw material, but raw material drawn from the remotest zones; industries whose products are consumed, not only at home, but in every quarter of the globe. . . . And as in material, so also in intellectual production. . . .

The bourgeoisie, by the rapid improvement of all instruments of production, by the immensely facilitated means of communication, draws all, even the most barbarian, nations into civilization. . . .

The bourgeoisie, during its rule of scarce one hundred years, has created more massive and more colossal productive forces than have all preceding generations together. Subjection of nature's forces to man, machinery, application of chemistry to industry and agriculture, steam navigation, railways, electric telegraphs, clearing of whole continents for cultivation, canalization or rivers, whole populations conjured out of the ground—what earlier century had even a presentiment that such productive forces slumbered in the lap of social labor? . . .

At a certain stage in the development of these means of production and of exchange, the conditions under which feudal society produced and exchanged, the feudal organization of agriculture and manufacturing industry, in one word, the feudal relations of property became no longer compatible with the already developed productive forces; they became so many fetters. They had to be burst asunder; they were burst asunder.

Into their place stepped free competition, accompanied by a social and political constitution adapted in it, and the economic and political sway of the bourgeois class.[8]

It's hard to imagine a more prescient description of the Federal Circuit's docket: Though the Constitution ended most "feudal, patriarchal, idyllic relations," those few that remain attach to sovereign immunity. The modern "wonders far surpassing Egyptian pyramids" and the constant revolutions in the instruments of production and the relations of production form the patent system's métier. "The need of a constantly expanding market for its products chases [American entrepreneurs] over the entire surface of the globe," necessitating rules governing international trade. "Free competition, accompanied by a social and political constitution adapted in it" defines the operating context for the Federal Circuit (and all other institutions playing important roles in the contemporary economy).

The Federal Circuit was made to serve Marx's hated bourgeoisie. The Federal Circuit helps to guide the rules that motivate the constant technological revolution underpinning the new modes of production; it oversees the emergence of global trade and distribution, and it highlights the limitations that vestigial feudal privileges impose upon a liberal system. The rules governing innovation, globalization, and sovereigns conducting business are as central to our own transition to the information age as they were to Europe's transition to the industrial age. The Federal Circuit provides a window where we can watch them unfold. Since 1982, the court has helped usher in an era in which the inventive class continued the exponential growth of invention—a century and a half after Marx

credited it with having already surpassed the combined efforts of all preceding generations.

Nevertheless, and despite all of the wonderful accomplishments that
Marx attributed to the bourgeoisie, Marx was hardly a fan of these fine
producers, inventors, and deliverers of civilization to "even the most barbarian" of nations. He saw them as rigid protectors of their own privilege,
just as reluctant to evolve beyond nineteenth-century capitalism as their
ancestors had been to evolve beyond feudalism. He believed that the system, despite its obvious penchant for production, innovation, invention,
creativity, rebirth, and revolution, nevertheless contained the seeds of its
own destruction. He failed to appreciate the system's adaptivity, its internal autocorrective capabilities, and the possible paths of its evolutionary
development. He believed that once a society entrenched "free competition, accompanied by a social and political constitution adapted in it, and
the economic and political sway of the bourgeois class," no further
growth was possible; those possessing political sway would refuse to
share it with the lower classes and would instead wield it like a sword, decapitating those who tried to climb above the station that life had assigned them.

Those beliefs were misplaced. Capitalism, liberalism, and their accompanying institutions continue to evolve—as both Schumpeter and Bork
noted. Some of the steps that they have taken since Marx's day were mis-
steps; others were corrective. Most were simply steps forward—and with
each such step, increasing portions of the world's poor saw their lives improve and their opportunities expand.

In the years since the U.S. economy underwent its own industrialization, the country has passed through several different eras, each guided
by a differing variant of liberalism making different concessions to conservatism and socialism. During the *Lochner* era of the early twentieth century, the Supreme Court stood as guardian of the view that property rights
and contracts rights are sacrosanct. That theory gave way to the New Deal
and the rise of the regulatory state; property and contracts hardly became
profane, but their halos dimmed considerably as the government imposed
numerous restrictions that would have been unthinkable in earlier eras. In
terms of industrial policy, the leading thinkers of this era viewed the economy as a massive, complex machine—a machine that they set out to manage using the finest management theories then available. Though American economic policy never reached the socialist extremes that it did in
other countries, the middle of the twentieth century was clearly a high-
water mark for planning and micromanagement—the "mixed economy"
in which social planning and free markets coexisted, at times more ami-
cably than at others. That view gave rise to intrusive antitrust scrutiny and
strict enforcement—imposed whenever a market seemed poised to devi-

ate from its planned course. It also let the patent system fall into a state of disuse and contempt; not only are entrepreneurship and innovation notoriously hard to plan, control, and manage, but they often lead to Schumpeterean creative destruction, discontinuities, and deviations from government plans.

Setting aside the still-contentious question as to whether or not the New Deal philosophy and the policies it engendered were necessary or appropriate responses to the Great Depression, by the late 1970s it was clear that they were no longer working. President Carter commissioned studies that confirmed that failure and their impropriety for the future, yet took only a few modest steps away from them. President Reagan and his economic team shattered them beyond all recognition. Their deregulatory and free-market reforms fundamentally reoriented the American economy and ended once and for all the notion that the economy is a machine. Antitrust scrutiny and enforcement plummeted in importance. Patents, a venerable regulatory system that employs property rights and market mechanisms to empower individual innovators and entrepreneurs, skyrocketed in esteem.

The Federal Circuit was born under that philosophy. Through a quirk of history, it was charged not only with reinvigorating our patent system but also with overseeing our trade laws and the government's economic behavior. In one fell swoop, Congress created an institution where innovation, globalization, and the role of government all unfolded—just as we began to enter the information age, and in apparent mockery of all that Marx despised. The Federal Circuit took its charter seriously and injected the new anti-planning, pro-market ethos into everything that it touched—or at least into every opening that Congress permitted it.

The economic era that Reagan ushered in continued to evolve. The Clinton administration identified market imperfections and moved to correct them, all the while being pilloried both by those who had hoped that a Democratic president would return to the days of mechanistic planning and by those who disbelieved in the very notion of a "market imperfection." Toward the end of the Clinton era, we began to grasp the answer to a question that had eluded us for twenty years: If the economy is not a machine, what is it? In the late 1990s we came to see the economy as a *network*. Networks, like markets, allow empowered individuals to interact freely wherever connections exist. Also like markets, networks require basic rules and standards to function; without them, they devolve into anarchy. Unlike classical markets, however, networks can propagate viruses quickly and broadly.[9] In a networked economy, a certain amount of monitoring and intervention appear inevitable.

The 1980s and '90s thus witnessed a concerted effort to liberalize the U.S. economy, bearing the lessons of both socialism and conservatism in mind. It left functioning government plans untouched, tried to reform those that no longer worked, and respected the institutional boundaries that define American society. It is within that framework that the Federal Circuit was born, and it is within that framework that the vantage point it provides is most valuable. From the Federal Circuit, it is possible to see the rules governing innovation, globalization, and the government as an economic actor—precisely the areas that Marx highlighted as central to the bourgeois agenda.

Even though the prescriptive portions of Marx's work inspired untold misery for untold millions, many of his diagnostic analyses were poignant and insightful. Joseph Schumpeter built upon these very insights in developing his theory of creative destruction.[10] More recently, William Baumol posited that entrepreneurial activity exists—in roughly comparable amounts—in all societies. In most societies, entrepreneurs try to outperform expectations in antisocial ways, through crime, corruption, or "rent-seeking" behavior that maximizes their own return while reducing overall societal welfare. Capitalist societies, as Marx noted, are inherently revolutionary. The constant need for change and innovation impels innovation, productivity, competition, and efficiency. Baumol posited that capitalism provides a socially beneficial outlet for entrepreneurial behavior.[11] A functioning patent system is thus a critical contributor to social welfare; it directs clever energy away from antisocial outlets and toward productive pursuits. If Baumol's theory is correct, the Federal Circuit's role in America's economic growth in the years since the court's birth looms larger than ever—as does the importance of considering this young American institution within an appropriate political and economic context. A second lesson learned.

THE CONSERVATIVE COURT

A third key lesson is that the Federal Circuit is a profoundly conservative court. Once again, that characterization is philosophical, not political—the court's evident preference for Chicago-style Reaganomics over Post-Chicago Clintonomics notwithstanding. Hints of this conservatism abound. The court's announcement of Federal Circuit antitrust law in 1998 provides a useful illustration: Many observers saw it as a flagrant imposition of Federal Circuit authority into an inappropriate area. Yet the Federal Circuit was careful to limit its own body of antitrust law to the elements of an antitrust claim that implicate patent law directly, rather than to all elements of an antitrust claim brought to counter an infringement suit.[12] Similarly, there is no clear reason that the Federal Circuit could not insist that its own procedural law governed all elements of cases "arising under" the patent laws, yet from the court's inception, regional circuit procedural law has governed. The Federal Circuit's overall choice-of-law posture suggests a humble reluctance to inject its own opinions beyond the subject matter that Congress assigned it explicitly.

The court's deference to Supreme Court opinions, including those that are quite old and were arguably overruled by statute, demonstrates a similar humility. For three simple examples, consider: Judge Dyk's refusal (on behalf of a unanimous panel) to conclude that Congress eliminated the "patent monopoly" concept from an antitrust-tying analysis when it amended the Patent Act accordingly—forcing Independent Ink and Trident to trek all the way to the Supreme Court;[13] Judge Rich's insistence (again, on behalf of a unanimous panel) that despite widespread and long-standing assumptions to the contrary, the Supreme Court's diktat that patentable subject matter extended to "anything under the sun that is made by man" authorized the PTO to patent business methods;[14] and Judges Gajarsa and Dyk's rejection (against Judge Plager's strong dissent) of the idea that Congress had overridden the Supreme Court's announcement that government infringement does not constitute a taking in 1910.[15] Clearly, this is a court that walks timidly when an institutional boundary draws near.

The best evidence of this conservatism lies in the Federal Circuit's cautious deference to Congress on matters of patent law. Professors Burk and Lemley catalogued numerous policy levers that they assert Congress gave the Federal Circuit to ensure that patent law makes sense and conforms to sound public policy.[16] They then showed that the Federal Circuit systematically ignores virtually all of these policy levers. Whether such caution is appropriate in whole or in part, the point remains: a less conservative court would be less cautious.

Such caution extends even where it is clearly unwarranted. When issues like patent misuse and antitrust *force* the court to consider behavioral effects and the underlying policy implications, the Federal Circuit mouths suitable analytic inquiries and balancing tests. When it applies those tests, however, all of its rulings seem to fall on one side of the scale. Why? Perhaps because rulings that recognize patents as property and then protect the rights of property owners surely fall within the Federal Circuit's bailiwick, while rulings that restrict the rights of property owners under certain circumstances risk injecting impermissible policy considerations into the law. Only the latter set *may* overstep the court's legitimate boundaries. Why risk it? Better to play it safe whenever an institutional boundary comes into view.

This excessive caution has likely flamed the fires beneath some of the Federal Circuit's harshest critics. Contemporary critiques of the patent system all assert that the system is "too strong." That strength leads to two problems. The first is largely hypothetical: As the web of improvidently granted patents increases, fewer innovators will be able to bring their products to market without infringing. They will stop innovating, and the patent system will freeze scientific research and technological evolution. Though all concede that such a catastrophe could occur as a matter of theory, and that if current growth trends in patenting continue it will eventually become a certainty, there is little or no hard evidence that it has yet to cripple a single American industry. The second problem is already quite real: Actual patentees are using their patents in ways that harm competitive markets, deter entry, chase competitors, and raise prices. Are such activities nevertheless worthwhile? In all likelihood, some are and some are not. Federal Circuit jurisprudence to date, however, seems to think that all are fine. Until patentees and accused infringers can point to concrete examples of impermissible behavior, attempts to leverage patents in anticompetitive manners are likely to increase. The court's inherent conservatism seems to have made it impossible for it to address this growing class of problems.

This shortcoming transcends mere respect for institutional boundaries; it runs smack into a clash of institutional competencies. Once again, Congress bears primary responsibility for having seized aspects of IP law that lie beyond its own institutional competence, but the Federal Circuit's willingness to accede without even mentioning the problem is disconcerting. It runs afoul of the economic justification for the separation of powers.

The primary purpose of the separation of powers, namely, "checks and balances," is to prevent too much power from accumulating in a single person or institution. America works best when its three branches of government eye each other warily, exercise suitable oversight, and refuse to rubber-stamp pet programs or political agendas popular in another branch. From this perspective, the separation of powers injects intentional inefficiencies into a system that we the people may not always trust when it's operating at peak efficiency. The separation of powers does, however, have an economic upside: it represents a division of labor. In the black box that is our legal system, Congress is well positioned to read public opinions about policy matters and to draft general statutory rules. But good general rules, by their very nature, only point in the right direction most of the time. Myriad special and unforeseen circumstances can shade the proper resolution of any particular dispute. Congress is in a poor position to consider individualized fact patterns. The judiciary, on the other hand, is well positioned to consider individualized facts within a congressionally set context.

The Anglo-American "common law" tradition, unlike the Napoleonic Code–based "civil law" tradition dominant on the European continent, recognizes the importance of individual circumstances to conflict resolution and therefore reserves significant powers to the judiciary. Parliaments in countries with civil law traditions tend to draft lengthy, detailed statutes that consider numerous contingencies. Judges in those systems apply the facts to those laws with little interpretive flexibility. Believe it or not (and anyone who has ever seen our Internal Revenue Code should doubt it), statutes in the Anglo-American system are relatively short and straightforward. For political reasons, Congress leaves many of them intentionally ambiguous and relies upon judicial interpretations to flesh out their meaning. The division of labor is clear. Congress, unable to consider the specifics affecting any individual, translates vague policy pronouncements into gross statutory prescriptions. Judges, immersed in individualized specifics, fine-tune the statutes to derive appropriate judgments.

Over the past few decades, many commentators have noted an erosion of the barriers separating our supposedly coequal branches of government. Conflicts between the president and Congress always make headlines, and typically motivate analysts to explain how a failure to uphold their preferred political agenda would represent an inappropriate power shift and thus herald the end of the republic. In most such cases, the executive and legislative branches each have their supporters, and something resembling a public debate is possible.

The reporting of conflicts between the legislative and judicial branches, on the other hand, tends to be much more one-sided. Over the past few decades, numerous authors have decried activist judges who usurp the legislative policymaking prerogative. In the days of the Warren Court, these cries came mostly from the political right despite the Court's repeated insistence that it was simply applying federal constitutional policy that state legislatures had abrogated. Most of the Warren Court's controversial decisions led to an American social policy fiercely protective of privacy, individual rights, and the equality of opportunity. The political left joined the fray in full force when the Rehnquist Court's rulings impinged upon Congress's ability to hold the states to standards that the left favored. Today, activism is decried across the political spectrum. "Judicial restraint" and "strict construction" are recognized virtues, and judges whose rulings favor creationist teachers or atheistic parents become immediate targets of partisan venom. Judges perceived to have usurped legislative prerogatives, whether or not a reading of their rulings can justify that perception, had best duck for cover.

Legislative usurpation of judicial prerogatives receives substantially less attention. Over the past few decades, both Congress and state legislatures have passed numerous statutes that reduce judicial flexibility—and debates about still more such statutes reverberate throughout the political ether. Significant political movements argue against allowing judges to ensure that rulings in criminal sentencing, tort law, damage awards, bankruptcy, and other legal arenas are appropriate given case-specific facts and individualized circumstances. Judicial flexibility also varies widely across different bodies of law. Under the antitrust law rule of reason, judges must consider the effects of a defendant's behavior upon a specific market before deciding whether or not a violation has occurred. Under patent and copyright law, no such formal rule of reason exists; behavior is either permissible or impermissible with little regard to context or effect. From time to time, Congress moves to hem in judicial review of administrative agency decisions—the tight constraints on Federal Circuit review of the CAVC is but one example of this phenomenon. Political pressure to reduce judicial flexibility cuts across broad swaths of social and economic law. Some of these political movements have succeeded at the federal level, others in some of the states. The Supreme Court has upheld the constitutionality of some of these statutes and invalidated others.

Just because something is constitutionally permissible, however, doesn't mean that it's wise. The division of labor inherent in the separation of powers recognizes the need for flexibility and individual responsiveness. Only our judges can provide the necessary attention and insight. As we move into the information age, our judges will need *more* flexibility, not less. Statutory law simply cannot keep pace with the technology-driven changes shaping our economy and our society. Specific cases that seem anomalous—but that actually represent the forefront of a new trend—will necessarily reach the courts before the pattern that they will soon reveal reaches congressional ears. Our judges need the flexibility to hear why these cases are new and why changed circumstances should shift the ruling one way or another within the permissible statutory grounds. The more often Congress insists that it can foresee all circumstances and craft tight, universally applicable rules, the more often Congress will be wrong.

As with any flexible system, abuse is possible. The correct response to abuse is to improve guidelines, increase oversight, and stiffen penalties. Guidelines emerge from a combination of legislative statutes and judge-made law; the antitrust rule of reason is again a prime example. Increased oversight strengthens the hand of appellate judges relative to trial judges, thereby decreasing the potential emotional appeal of factual specifics and facilitating a dispassionate discussion of the matter. Stiffer penalties and judicial sanctions will ensure that judges—at both the trial and appellate level—will provide enough information to explain why they concluded that a specific case was sufficiently anomalous to deserve treatment at the perimeters of the permissible range rather than near its center. In other words, the best response to abuse is to motivate improved performance to reduce abuse, enhanced oversight to increase detection of abuse, and increased penalties to deter future abuse. It *is not* to eliminate legitimate, socially beneficial behavior.

Congress must work to better align patent law with institutional competencies. It must reserve for itself only the general rule-making component, assign the PTO the task of fleshing out regulations, and authorize the courts to make the law make sense. As a fine conservative court, the Federal Circuit will undoubtedly accept this new liberal assignment swimmingly and begin to craft meaningful rules to ensure that the patent system is not only internally coherent but also a functioning part of a competitive free-market economy. Therein lies lesson three.

THE EXPERIMENTAL COURT

That need for congressional restructuring points to the fourth, and perhaps most important, lesson to emerge from our institutional study of the Federal Circuit's role in industrial transformation and economic renaissance: the court is ready for the next stage of its permanently experimental existence.

The Federal Circuit, operating in conjunction with the other significant changes to patent policy of the early 1980s, helped reinvigorate the American patent system. But the court has already achieved its first great assignment: it strengthened the American patent system, restored respect to U.S. patents, and turned them into useful commercial tools. Critics such as professors Lerner and Jaffe contend that the court's button is stuck in the "on" position; they see the Federal Circuit as a strange judicial automaton, working to make the U.S. patent system stronger and stronger and stronger and stronger and stronger and stronger and stronger with no end in sight.[17] Others, like Professor Dreyfuss, believe that the court's initial "pro-patent" reputation has abated, although it's not clear what reputation has replaced it.[18] Either way, the court is ready for a revised congressional assignment.

This need ties the court's past to its future. This book opened with a central thesis, namely, that the liberal policy perspectives that helped motivate the Federal Circuit will also lead to a successful information-age economy. In an era of information abundance, inexpensive information exchange, and numerous amorphous networks, public policy must empower individuals. Liberty and autonomy are the keys to success. In the Federal Circuit's primary areas of responsibility, these keys unlock bold policy pronouncements. On patents: *Promote innovation!* On trade: *Strengthen the American economy and make Americans richer!* When it comes to government business: *Adhere to the highest standards of ethical business*

behavior! These simple pronouncements describe the policies that most citizens *think* we have, that our judges *must assume* that Congress captured in
statutes, that most citizens would like to believe our judges implement—
and that we input into the various black boxes. Are these beliefs warranted? Our institutional study of the Federal Circuit identified numerous
policies screaming for reform if we are to align the American economy
with the needs of the information age. These needs defined the black box
outputs and played an important role in scoring the tests.

What were these outputs? Some, but not all, trace to that still-unan-
swered metaphysical question of IP: Is "intellectual property" really property, and if so what type of property? Or are our IP systems "merely" regulatory regimes that employ property rights? The answers dictate the
amount of flexibility available in contemplating policy reform. An explicit
announcement that patents and copyrights are regulatory systems employing property rights would clear the way for:

- A structural change away from the current unitary patent system (or
  technically the bipartite patent/copyright system) toward a system
  that incorporates elements of industry-specificity;
- A realignment of institutional responsibilities with institutional competencies, and the consequent injection of rule-of-reason analyses
  throughout IP law;
- An explicit balancing test to resolve true conflicts between antitrust
  and IP law;
- A "first principles" review of copyright law leading to a system that
  aligns the law with contemporary economic and technological realities;
- A reinvigorated patent-misuse doctrine, in which courts detects and
  deters misuse of both the antitrust-tying and the general nontying
  varieties.

Most of these reforms become more difficult as the explication moves
away from a regulatory view of IP. Some may become either impossible
or prohibitively expensive if IP is as sacred as more traditional forms of
property—particularly if Judge Plager's view of takings is correct. Metaphysics is thus central to some black-box test scores.

For the policy reforms emerging from other black boxes, metaphysics
are irrelevant. Even within the patent realm, a "narrowest reasonable interpretation" of disputed claim terms in issued patents could clean up
claim construction considerably and in an economically efficient manner
without implicating property issues.

When it comes to trade, the most effective policy reform would remove
all barriers immediately and unilaterally, but political considerations ren-

der such an approach impossible. Smaller reforms might try to inject greater elements of sense into Customs proceedings and to limit safeguards and antidumping and countervailing duties to those few cases where they are truly warranted. In at least some settings, the Federal Circuit already possesses the power to require administrative inquiries as broad as those that Finger and Nogués advocate;[19] the consistent enforcement of such a requirement could go a long way toward reconciling trade practice with sound economic policy. The most significant viable reform to trade policy, however, would be a broad adjustment assistance program, in which government facilitators helps private educators, trainers, employment advisors, and job brokers help displaced workers relocate within the dynamic American economy of the information age. That reform alone would recast trade law from a backward-looking form of protection to a forward-looking form of preparation.

On sovereign immunity, the best step would be to apply to domestic sovereigns the rule that U.S. law already applies to foreign sovereigns. In the information age, sovereign immunity should shield only those activities central to the exercise of sovereignty; sovereigns engaged in commercial transactions should play by general commercial rules. In the meantime, it could hardly hurt to eliminate the NAFI doctrine and the no-interest rule. Anything that might force states and their universities to follow the IP laws would also be welcome.

Given these articulated policy goals as inputs and desirable reforms as outputs, what did our black-box tests reveal? In the nonpatent areas, systemic performance was poor. Congress gave the country bad policies when it chose to interfere with free trade and when it introduced anti-circumvention provisions into the copyright law. The Supreme Court's broad reading of sovereign immunity applied to government actors engaged in everyday commercial transactions hurts both the economy and the credibility of the government. The Court of Claims created a mess called the NAFI doctrine, and the Supreme Court and Congress made matters worse by entrenching it. All of these policies deserve low to failing grades. The policies we have are not the policies we want, and the longer they remain, the more harm they do.

The Federal Circuit seems to rule in a manner consistent with the laws that enact these bad policies. Given that the court's job is to implement laws whether they represent good policy or bad, it's tough to give this performance anything other than a solid grade. For extra credit, the Federal Circuit has even used its bully pulpit to highlight some policy problems inherent in the Digital Millennium Copyright Act, the NAFI doctrine, the no-interest rule, and other selected implications of sovereign immunity. On trade, the court could use that same bully pulpit to promote transparency by becoming a stickler for sound, broad-based economic analyses in all agency proceedings; to date, it has done so only infrequently. By and large, though, while these nonpatent policies that we have may not be the policies we want, the Federal Circuit has generally handled them as well as it could under the circumstances.

On the patent side of the docket, the test scores become a bit more interesting. Claim construction lies entirely within the bailiwick of the judiciary, and the Federal Circuit's test score there is poor. In 1995, the court admitted that it had been bungling it for more than a decade; in 2005, it found the need to try yet again. In the interim, the Supreme Court removed at least some options from the table. The court's score on claim construction remains disappointing, although the results are not yet in on its most recent effort.

Validity and infringement also lie largely within the Federal Circuit's control. Aside from the doctrine of equivalents, where the Supreme Court's meddling turned what should have been a Federal Circuit A into a shared B, the Federal Circuit's scores are quite high. In the past quarter-century, the Federal Circuit has injected significant certainty into the patent system. Though patent litigation remains unduly expensive— a burden for which the Federal Circuit bears partial blame—litigants today have a better understanding of both validity and infringement issues than they had at any point in history prior to the Federal Circuit's birth. The court has turned patents into useful tools of business strategy and rewards genuinely capable of motivating innovation. Given that this test represents the Federal Circuit's primary assignment, its high grades here are particularly noteworthy.

In the other aspects of the patent system, as well as in the interaction between patents and other market realities, the Federal Circuit shares the limelight with several other institutional actors. When it comes to remedies, the congressional decision to treat patents as "sort of property" without further clarification led to the Federal Circuit's general preference for injunctions; Congress and the Federal Circuit both deserve poor grades, but the Supreme Court picks up a few points for at least nudging the system in a more reasonable direction.

On the unitary structure of patent law, Congress receives a poor grade. In all fairness, a poor grade might not have been warranted when Congress first chose a unitary system in 1790, but the limitations of a unitary system were already evident by the 1990s when TRIPS etched the concept into an international norm. The poor systemic grade stands. As to the Federal Circuit's performance, the answer lies in the policy levers. If professors Burk and Lemley are right about the flexibility that the Patent Act actually contains,[20] the Federal Circuit deserves a poor grade for failing to use tools at its disposal to better align the policies we have with the policies we want. If Professor Wagner and I are correct and the Patent Act is rigid,[21] the court deserves to lose only a few points for underusing the more modest set of policy levers that it nevertheless possesses (though Wagner would likely disagree with my grade assignment).

The Federal Circuit's weakest scores arise from its consideration of patents within a broad market context. On antitrust matters, virtually every other major player—the Federal Trade Commission, the Department of Justice, the Supreme Court, Congress, and the regional circuits—deserves two A's, one for supplanting 1970s thinking with 1980s Chicago School liberalism and another for allowing the law to evolve further into 1990s Post-Chicago analysis. In that stellar class, the Federal Circuit stands alone with an incomplete. The situation is even darker in the Federal Circuit's own special misuse corner, for despite reciting the proper standards as if they were a mantra, the court seems unable to apply them objectively. It is hard to give the Federal Circuit anything other than an F for its dismal mistreatment of the patent-misuse doctrine.

These black-box scores combine to tell two stories, one favorable, the other cautionary. The favorable story describes where we have been. The American economy was a mess in the late 1970s. Serious thinkers in Washington, from both political parties, from all branches of government, and from private sector volunteers, brainstormed about the best ways to address the enormous economic challenges. They concluded that America needed less regulation and more liberal markets. They saw a functioning innovation system as central to those needed reforms. They rethought many aspects of the U.S. patent system and created a new institution to oversee its renaissance. They gave that institution further responsibilities, both to enhance its prestige and to stave off the dreaded curse of tunnel vision. They elevated it to a position of prestige and authority, as one of the thirteen "second most powerful courts in the land." That new institution was the United States Court of Appeals for the Federal Circuit. The Federal Circuit took its charge seriously and helped usher the American patent system through two and a half decades of increased liberalism and unparalleled growth. It received high scores on its primary assignment and passing grades on most others. The American public has been served well by the visionaries who rethought American industrial policy in the late 1970s, and by those who implemented the new liberal policies in the 1980s and '90s.

The cautionary tale lies mostly in the future—although it may have already begun. In this tale, economic reality has changed yet again. The American economy of the late industrial age met and conquered the challenges of the 1970s, but both those problems and their solutions have already run their course. The early twenty-first century poses a full range of information-age challenges—challenges that deserve attention, thought, and new approaches to policy.

Our innovation system remains critical to our continued success, but it's not clear that anyone is doing anything more than tinkering around its edges. The copyright system has collapsed into an abyss of unenforceable rights; Congress responds by tightening enforcement rather than by revisiting first principles to craft more appropriate motivators. The patent system's unitary structure leads to misallocations of resource investment and potential inconsistencies in the patent law; the international community enshrines unitary structure in a major IP treaty. The trade system imposes barriers to imports while jobs move offshore; Senators and Presidents reward inefficient domestic producers while starving adjustment assistance programs. Patents become powerful, valuable levers of business strategy; the Federal Circuit seems unable to find any limits on acceptable use. American economic policy no longer seems attuned to the times.

America's economic successes of the past twenty-five years should be inspiring a new generation of thinkers to move boldly into the information economy. An institutional study of the Federal Circuit should be motivational: It is a rare example of an unequivocal success. Congress created it to achieve a specific objective within a broader policy terrain. The institution, the objective, and the policy terrain all worked. Research, commercialization, and economic welfare all soared. The Federal Circuit is ready for its next assignment. American innovation and entrepreneurship are ready for their next boost. The American economy awaits further liberalization. And the world awaits the emergence of the full-blown information age, where information is abundant and inexpensive to all, and where we have learned to manipulate information well enough to make better decisions, to devise better strategies, and to craft better public policies. Those of us who live at the dawn of the information age face many challenges. Only a few of them have answers residing in that red brick office building on Madison Place, along the east side of Presidents Park.

Notes

These notes do not all adhere to the strict legal conventions known as *The Bluebook*, but rather looser conventions of scholarly research: I attempted to provide pointers necessary for readers to track quotes and controversies back to original sources. To the extent that I may have failed to provide some curious readers with adequate guidance, I apologize in advance. On more technical points, I have been less than meticulous in indicating changes between capitals and lowercase in quotes, and I may have omitted some ellipses. I also omitted indications to internal quotes except where critical. I did not correct errors that I found in original sources, though I might have introduced some of my own. I also left all archaic, alternative, and English spellings as I found them (though my spell-check program may have overridden some inadvertently). All Web addresses are subject to change.

PREFACE

1. H. Robert Mayer, foreword to Kristin L. Yohannon, ed., *The United States Court of Appeals for the Federal Circuit: A History, 1990–2002* (Washington, DC: Court of Appeals for the Federal Circuit, 2004), xxi–xxii.

CHAPTER 1

1. H. Robert Mayer, foreword to Kristin L. Yohannon, ed., *The United States Court of Appeals for the Federal Circuit: A History, 1990–2002* (Washington, DC: Court of Appeals for the Federal Circuit, 2004), xxi–xxii.

2. Congress has not overruled the Federal Circuit by statute in more than a decade. Between 1982 and 2005, the Supreme Court reviewed only fifty-two Federal Circuit rulings and reversed only a fraction of them. See Arthur J. Gajarsa and Lawrence P. Cogswell III, "The Federal Circuit and the Supreme Court," 55 *Amer. U. L. Rev.* 821 (2006).

3. See Gajarsa and Cogswell, "Federal Circuit."

4. See, for example, Adam B. Jaffe and Josh Lerner, *Innovation and Its Discontents: How Our Broken Patent System Is Endangering Innovation and Progress, and What to Do about It* (Princeton, NJ: Princeton University Press, 2004); William M. Landes and Richard A. Posner, *The Economic Structure of Intellectual Property Law* (Cambridge, MA: Harvard University Press, 2004); *To Promote Innovation: The Proper Balance of Competition and Patent Law and Policy* (Washington, DC: Federal Trade Commission, 2003); Stephen A. Merrill, Richard C. Levin, and Mark B. Myers, eds., *A Patent System for the 21st Century* (Washington, DC: National Academies Press, 2004).

5. For good discussions of the Federal Circuit's origins by people involved in its founding, see Marion T. Bennett, "The United States Court of Appeals for the Federal Circuit—Origins," in Yohannon, *United States Court of Appeals*, 3–11 (reprinted from *Court History (1982–1990)*); Daniel J. Meador, "Origin of the Federal Circuit: A Personal Account," 41 *Amer. U. L. Rev.* 581 (1992); Pauline Newman, "Origins of the Federal Circuit: The Role of Industry," 11 *Federal Circuit Bar Journal* 541 (2001); Donald R. Dunner, "Reflections on the Founding of the Federal Circuit," 11 *Federal Circuit Bar Journal* 545 (2001); and Daniel J. Meador, "Retrospective on the Federal Circuit: The First 20 Years—a Historical View," 11 *Federal Circuit Bar Journal* 557 (2001). Not surprisingly, these historical reviews tend to be rather laudatory. For recent historical discussions by those who are less than complete Federal Circuit fans, see Jaffe and Lerner, *Innovation*, chap. 4; Landes and Posner, *Economic Structure*, chap. 12. Though these discussions may differ in emphasis and analysis, they all agree on all significant facts.

6. U.S. Const. Art. I § 8 cl. 8.

7. Newman, "Origins of the Federal Circuit," 542–43.

8. William J. Clinton, State of the Union Address, January 23, 1996.

9. See 35 U.S.C. §§ 200–12.

10. See 21 U.S.C. § 355.

11. See Public Law 97-164, 96 *Stat.* 25 (1982).

12. See *Diamond v. Chakrabarty*, 447 U.S. 303, 309 (1980); and *Gottschalk v. Benson*, 409 U.S. 63 (1972).

13. Though the Semiconductor Protection Act of 1984 was technically an amendment to copyright law rather than to patent law, the concerns motivating it had more in common with the typical patent-law focus on innovation, commercialization, and competitiveness than with the typical copyright-law focus on creativity. See 17 U.S.C. §§ 901–14.

14. See *International Soc'y for Krishna Consciousness v. Lee*, 505 U.S. 672, 677 (1992).

15. See, for example, *Dickerson v. United States*, 530 U.S. 428 (2000), eliminating a circuit split that occurred when the Fourth Circuit, alone among the circuits, concluded that Miranda warnings were not required and that a defendant aware of

his rights without being Mirandized could nevertheless confess in a manner admissible in court.

16. See, for example, *Bank of Am. Nat'l Trust & Sav. Ass'n v. 203 N. Lasalle St. P'ship*, 526 U.S. 434 (1999), resolving in favor of creditors a split in which the Seventh and Ninth Circuits allowed debtors to take certain restructuring actions protecting their assets, while the Second and Fourth Circuits rejected similar restructuring plans.

17. See *Krishna Consciousness*, 505 U.S. at 685.

18. Rochelle Cooper Dreyfuss, "The Federal Circuit: A Case Study in Specialized Courts," 64 *NYU L. Rev.* 1, 7.

19. Meador, "Origin of the Federal Circuit," 558.

20. Meador, "Origin of the Federal Circuit," 559.

21. Bennett, "United States Court of Appeals," 14–15. Examples of "later need" that added to the Federal Circuit's jurisdiction included appeals from the United States Court of Veterans Appeals, appeals concerning the vaccination liability act, appeals from the General Accounting Office Personnel Appeals Board, and appeals from judgment against the Trust Territory of the Pacific Islands.

22. As a technical matter, the preexisting Court of Claims had *two* dockets. Like many administrative agencies, it held trials and then considered appeals of those trials at an internal appellate board. The proposed judicial reform was to combine the appellate component with other appeals as part of what became the Federal Circuit. The trial portion of the old Court of Claims's task remained distinct; it is now the responsibility of the Court of Federal Claims.

23. H. Rep. 97-312 at 21–22 (1981).

24. S. Rep. 97-275 at 30 (1981).

25. Public Law 97-164, 96 *Stat.* 25 (1982).

CHAPTER 2

1. Abraham Lincoln, Second Inaugural Address, March 4, 1865.

2. Franklin D. Roosevelt, First Inaugural Address, March 4, 1933.

3. John F. Kennedy, Inaugural Address, January 20, 1961.

4. George W. Bush, Second Inaugural Address, January 20, 2005.

5. *New Orleans v. Dukes*, 427 U.S. 297, 303 (1976). See also *Lewis v. Casey*, 518 U.S. 343, 388 (1996) (Thomas, J., concurring) ("The Constitution is not a license for federal judges to further social policy goals."); *County of Sacramento v. Lewis*, 523 U.S. 833, 865 (1998) (Stevens, J., concurring) ("[F]or judges to overrule [a] democratically adopted policy judgment on the ground that it shocks *their* consciences is not judicial review but judicial governance"); and *Am. Ins. Ass'n v. Garamendi*, 539 U.S. 396, 427 (2003) ("Our business is not to judge the wisdom of the National Government's policy; dissatisfaction should be addressed to the president or, perhaps, Congress").

6. Felix Frankfurter, "Some Reflections on the Reading of Statutes," 47 *Colum. L. Rev.* 527, 534–35 (1947). Available at http://www.criminology.fsu.edu/faculty/gertz/felixfrankfurter.html.

7. Edsger W. Dijkstra, "On the Reliability of Programs," EWD303, available at http://www.cs.utexas.edu/users/EWD/transcriptions/EWD03xx/EWD303.html . Throughout Dijkstra's career, he circulated his thoughts in a series of unpublished "EWD manuscripts," many written in Dutch and subject to differing translations. Because of Dijkstra's prominence, these manuscripts have circulated widely and led to widely varying Dijkstra quotes at differing levels of pithiness capturing the same basic thought. These quotes are likely not apocryphal, but rather an artifact of the way that Dijkstra circulated his ideas. The University of Texas has established an on-line archive of EWDs at http://www.cs.utexas.edu/users/EWD/.

8. Lawrence Lessig, *Code and Other Laws of Cyberspace* (New York: Basic Books, 1999), 6.

9. This highly simplified treatment omits all references to procedure and the exceptions that exist at the end of every declarative sentence. It cannot substitute for a formal legal education.

10. According to a well-known and allegedly age-old adage that I have been unable to track to any source earlier than 1984: "If the law is against you, argue the facts; if the facts are against you, argue the law; and if they both are against you, pound the table." Assistance in attributing this quote is appreciated.

11. *Planned Parenthood v. Casey*, 505 U.S. 833, 866 (1992).

12. 28 U.S.C. § 1295 (numerous technical definitions and exceptions and a few minor clauses omitted).

13. 38 U.S.C. § 7292.

14. *Moba v. Diamond Automation*, 325 F.3d 1306, 1322 (2003) (Rader, J., concurring).

15. This observation was one of the key themes that I developed in *Digital Phoenix: Why the Information Economy Collapsed and How It Will Rise Again* (Cambridge, MA: MIT Press, 2005).

16. John Stuart Mill, "On Conservative and Liberal Poets (1838)," in John M. Robson, ed., *John Stuart Mill: A Selection of His Works* (New York: St. Martin's Press, 1966), 429.

17. One interesting exception to this general rule emerges from the Federal Circuit's review of the Merit Systems Protection Board (MSPB), the arbiter of disputes involving federal employees. Under the Hatch Act, most government employees are prohibited from engaging in many partisan political activities. When the MSPB determines that an employee has violated the Hatch Act, First Amendment challenges arise almost as a matter of course. See, for example, *Briggs v. MSPB*, 331 F.3d 1307 (2003).

CHAPTER 3

1. See Patent Office (UK), *History of Patents*, http://www.patent.gov.uk/about-history-patent.htm.

2. Patent Office (UK), *History of Patents*.

3. 21 Jac. I, c. 3 (1623).

4. U.S. Const. Art. I § 8 cl. 8.

5. See Fritz Machlup and Edith Penrose, "The Patent Controversy in the Nineteenth Century," 10 *Journal of Economic History* 1 (1950); Dominique Ritter, "Switzerland's Patent Law History," 14 *Fordham Intell. Prop. Media & Ent. L. J.* 463 (2004).

6. See Shondeep Banerji, "The Indian IP Rights Regime and the TRIPs Agreement," in Clarisa Long, ed., *Intellectual Property Rights in Emerging Markets* (Washington, DC: AEI Press, 2000); and Bruce Abramson, *From Saraswati to Laxmi: India's Journey toward an Effective Patent System* (Washington, DC: World Bank, forthcoming).

7. Robert P. Merges, Peter S. Menell, Mark A. Lemley, and Thomas M. Jorde, *Intellectual Property in the New Technological Age* (New York: Aspen Law & Business, 1997), 126–27.

8. Suzanne Scotchmer, *Innovation and Incentives* (Cambridge, MA: MIT Press, 2004), 66.

9. The struggles between those trying to free digital content and those trying to preserve the rights of content holders are among the most exciting and most controversial in all of contemporary IP law. I discussed these struggles in detail in chapter 7 of *Digital Phoenix: Why the Information Economy Collapsed and How It Will Rise Again* (Cambridge, MA: MIT Press, 2005).

10. William M. Landes and Richard A. Posner, *The Economic Structure of Intellectual Property Law* (Cambridge, MA: Harvard University Press, 2003), 4.

11. Fred Warshofsky, *The Patent Wars: The Battle to Own the World's Technology* (New York: Wiley, 1994), book jacket, 270–71.

12. Thomas L. Friedman, *The World Is Flat: A Brief History of the Twenty-First Century* (New York: Farrar, Straus and Giroux, 2005), 8–9.

13. Friedman, *World Is Flat*, 30.

14. Friedman, *World Is Flat*, 246.

15. Scotchmer, *Innovation and Incentives*, ix.

CHAPTER 4

1. *Markman v. Westview Instruments, Inc.*, 52 F.3d 967, 972 (Fed. Cir. 1995) (en banc).

2. *Id.* at 973.

3. *Id.*

4. *Id.* at 977, 979.

5. *Marbury v. Madison*, 5 U.S. 137, 177–78 (1803).

6. *Markman*, 52 F.3d at 978–79.

7. *Id.*

8. *Id.* at 999 (Newman, J., dissenting).

9. "In Suits at common law, where the value in controversy shall exceed twenty dollars, the right of trial by jury shall be preserved, and no fact tried by a jury, shall be otherwise re-examined in any Court of the United States, than according to the rules of the common law." U.S. Const. Amend. VII.

10. *Markman*, 52 F.3d at 990–93 (Mayer, J., dissenting).

11. *Markman v. Westview Instruments*, 517 U.S. 370, 388–89 (1976).

12. Robert P. Merges, Peter S. Menell, Mark A. Lemley, and Thomas M. Jorde, *Intellectual Property in the New Technological Age* (New York: Aspen Law and Business, 1997), 254–55.

13. *Vitronics Corp. v. Conceptronic, Inc.*, 90 F.3d 1576, 1582–84 (Fed. Cir. 1996).

14. *Tex. Digital Sys. v. Telegenix, Inc.*, 308 F.3d 1193, 1202–05 (Fed. Cir. 2002).

15. Polk Wagner and Lee Petherbridge, "Is the Federal Circuit Succeeding? An Empirical Assessment of Judicial Performance," 152 *U. Penn. L. Rev.* 1105 (2004). As a technical matter, their study included every claim construction opinion that the Federal Circuit issued between April 23, 1996, and November 1, 2002.

16. Wagner and Petherbridge, "Is the Federal Circuit Succeeding?" 1133–34.

17. Wagner and Petherbridge, "Is the Federal Circuit Succeeding?" 1134.

18. From time to time, the court has changed its rules about precisely how far in advance of the oral arguments it told counsel which judges would hear their case. Under all such variations, however, attorneys for both sides have had to write their briefs and prepare most of their materials without any idea as to which of the Federal Circuit's judges they would address.

19. Wagner and Petherbridge, "Is the Federal Circuit Succeeding?" 1113.

20. *Novartis Pharm. Corp. v. Eon Labs Mfg.*, 363 F.3d 1306 (Fed. Cir. 2004).

21. *Id.* at 1313–16 (Clevenger, J., dissenting).

22. *Id.* at 1316.

23. *Phillips v. AWH Corp.*, 363 F.3d 1207 (Fed. Cir. 2004).

24. See *Phillips v. AWH Corp.*, 376 F.3d 1382 (Fed. Cir. 2004) (en banc).

25. *Id.* at 1382 (Rader, J., concurring).

26. *Id.* at 1382 (Mayer, C. J., dissenting).

27. *Phillips v. AWH Corp.*, 415 F.3d 1303, 1312 (Fed. Cir. 2005) (en banc).

28. *Id.* at 1324.

29. *Id.*

30. Harry Belafonte and Jack Rollins, "Man Piaba," 1954.

31. Polk Wagner, "Phillips Analysis, Part 1: The New Rule Is There Are No Rules," July 15, 2005, http://www.polkwagner.com.

32. *Phillips*, 415 F.3d at 1332–34 (Mayer, J., dissenting).

33. *Id.* at 1330n1 (Mayer, J., dissenting).

34. See *Amgen, Inc. v. Hoechst Marion Roussel, Inc.*, 457 F.3d 1293 (Fed. Cir. 2006).

35. *Amgen, Inc. v. Hoechst Marion Roussel, Inc.*, 469 F.3d 1040 (Fed. Cir. 2006) (Michel, C. J., dissenting).

36. *Id.* at 1041 (Newman, J., dissenting).

37. For one excellent example of this critique, see Glynn S. Lunney Jr., "Patent Law, the Federal Circuit, and the Supreme Court: A Quiet Revolution," 11 *S. Ct. Econ. Rev.* 1 (2004).

38. *In re Yamamoto*, 740 F.2d 1569, 1571 (Fed. Cir. 1984).

39. Ronald H. Coase, *The Firm, the Market, and the Law* (Chicago: University of Chicago Press, 1988), 178.

40. *Markman*, 52 F.3d at 989 (Mayer, J., dissenting).

41. See 35 U.S.C. §§ 101, 103, and 102, respectively.

42. *Diamond v. Chakrabarty*, 447 U.S. 303, 309 (1980).

43. *Id.*

44. See *Gottschalk v. Benson*, 409 U.S. 63 (1972).

45. See *Diamond v. Diehr*, 450 U.S. 175 (1981).

46. See *In re Alappat*, 33 F.3d 1526 (Fed. Cir. 1994) (en banc).

47. See *State Street Bank & Trust Co. v. Signature Financial Group, Inc.*, 149 F.3d 1368 (Fed. Cir. 1998).

48. See *Amazon.com, Inc. v. Barnesandnoble.com, Inc.*, 73 F.Supp.2d 1228 (W.D. Washington, 1999).

49. See *Amazon.com, Inc. v. Barnesandnoble.com, Inc.*, 239 F.3d 1343 (Fed. Cir. 2001).

50. For one excellent example of this critique, see Lunney, "Patent Law."

51. The exchange, which began when the Federal Circuit issued a bold *en banc* change to the doctrine in 1995—see *Hilton Davis Chem. Co. v. Warner-Jenkinson Co.*, 62 F.3d 1512 (Fed. Cir. 1995) (en banc)—finally ended with a new set of rules issued in 2003. See *Festo Corp. v. Shoketsu Kinzoku Kogyo Kabushiki Co.*, 344 F.3d 1359 (Fed. Cir. 2003) (en banc).

52. See *Graver Tank & Mfg. Co. v. Linde*, 339 U.S. 605 (1950).

53. See *Hilton Davis*, 62 F.3d at 1512.

54. See *Warner-Jenkinson Co. v. Hilton Davis Chem. Co.*, 520 U.S. 17 (1997).

55. See *Festo Corp. v. Shoketsu Kinzoku Kogyo Kabushiki Co.*, 234 F.3d 558 (Fed. Cir. 2000) (en banc).

56. See *Festo Corp. v. Shoketsu Kinzoku Kogyo Kabushiki Co.*, 535 U.S. 722 (2002).

57. See *Festo Corp. v. Shoketsu Kinzoku Kogyo Kabushiki Co.*, 344 F.3d 1359 (Fed. Cir. 2003) (en banc).

58. I discussed this issue in depth in Bruce Abramson, "A First Principles Approach to IP Reform," 8 *Boston University Journal of Science and Technology Law* 75 (2002).

59. This analysis applies equally well to patents and copyrights. In fact, my treatment in "A First Principles Approach" is set in a context closer to copyright law than patent law.

60. Most students of innovation agree that grants and prizes can play a useful role in motivating innovation, often in conjunction with patents. See generally Brett Frischmann, "Innovation and Institutions: Rethinking the Economics of U.S. Science and Technology Policy," 24 *Vt. L. Rev.* 347 (2000); Suzanne Scotchmer, *Innovation and Incentives* (Cambridge, MA: MIT Press, 2004).

61. This situation technically describes a *local* optimum, not necessarily a *global* optimum.

62. Stephen A. Merrill, Richard C. Levin, and Mark B. Myers, eds., *A Patent System for the 21st Century* (Washington, DC: National Academies Press, 2004).

63. Rochelle Cooper Dreyfuss, "The Federal Circuit: A Case Study in Specialized Courts," 64 *NYU L. Rev.* 1, 8, 24 (1989).

64. Rochelle Cooper Dreyfuss, "The Federal Circuit: A Continuing Experiment in Specialization," 54 *Case W. Res. L. Rev.* 769, 770–71 (2004).

65. *Id.* at 773–75 (2004).

66. Adam B. Jaffe and Josh Lerner, *Innovation and Its Discontents: How Our Broken Patent System Is Endangering Innovation and Progress, and What to Do about It* (Princeton, NJ: Princeton University Press, 2004), 125–26.

67. Lunney, "Patent Law," 1–2, 8, 16–17, 36.

68. See 35 U.S.C. § 282.

69. Kathleen M. O'Malley, Patti Saris, and Ronald H. Whyte, "A Panel Discussion: Claim Construction from the Perspective of the District Judge," 54 *Case W. Res. L. Rev.* 671, 671 (2004).

70. *Id.* at 675.

71. Paul Michel, "Judicial Constellations: Guiding Principles and Navigational Aids," 54 *Case W. Res. L. Rev.* 757, 760–61 (2004).

72. *Id.* at 767.

CHAPTER 5

1. Kurt Vonnegut Jr., *Cat's Cradle* (New York: Holt, Rinehart, and Winston, 1963).
2. Vonnegut, *Cat's Cradle*, chap. 4.
3. Vonnegut, *Cat's Cradle*, chap. 20.
4. Vonnegut, *Cat's Cradle*, chap. 22.
5. The district court provided an excellent discussion of this case's facts. See *SmithKline Beecham Corp. v. Apotex Corp.*, 247 F.Supp.2d 1011, 1013–25 (E.D. Ill. 2003).
6. Because the litigation over paroxetine started between SmithKline's acquisition of Beecham and GlaxoWellcome's acquisition of SmithKline Beecham, the courts refer to the patentee under its old acronym of SKB.
7. As a technical matter, the inclusion of a water molecule meant that the two were not identical and were thus pseudopolymorphs rather than true polymorphs.
8. See 21 U.S.C. § 355.
9. *SmithKline Beecham Corp. v. Apotex Corp.*, 365 F.3d 1306, 1330–31 (2004) (Gajarsa, J., concurring) (emphasis in original).
10. *SmithKline Beecham Corp. v. Apotex Corp.*, 286 F.Supp.2d 925, 932 (2001).
11. *Id.* at 938.
12. *SmithKline*, 247 F.Supp.2d at 1052.
13. *Id.* at 1026. Immediately following this caricature of GSK's argument is a parenthetical disclaimer: "(Actually this is wrong; the 'first sale' doctrine would allow the worker to do anything he wanted with Paxil tablets that he had bought. The example is saved by assuming that the source of the seeds is a [GSK] executive who picked them up while visiting a seeded [GSK] facility and later visited the chocolate factory.)"
14. *Id.* at 1028.
15. *Id.* at 1029–30.
16. *Johnson Worldwide Associates, Inc. v. Zebco Corp.*, 175 F.3d 985, 989 (Fed. Cir. 1999).
17. *SmithKline*, 247 F.Supp.2d at 1030.
18. *Id.* at 1046.
19. *Netscape Communications Corp. v. Konrad*, 295 F.3d 1315, 1321 (Fed. Cir. 2002).
20. Just to make things even more fun, patent law maintains two distinct, unrelated "experimental use" doctrines. The idea that experimentation doesn't count as a public use is one of them. The second exempts infringement among those who make or use patented inventions for reasons of pure experimentation or philosophical inquiry.
21. *Baxter Int'l, Inc. v. Cobe Labs., Inc.*, 88 F.3d 1054, 1059 (Fed. Cir. 1996).
22. *SmithKline*, 365 F.3d at 1317.
23. *Id.* at 1317.
24. *Id.* at 1318–20.
25. *Id.* at 1324–25 (Gajarsa, J., concurring).
26. *Id.* at 1333 (Gajarsa, J., concurring).
27. 35 U.S.C. § 101.
28. *Diamond v. Chakrabarty*, 447 U.S. 303, 308–9 (1980).

29. *PSC Computer Prods. v. Foxconn Int'l*, 355 F.3d 1353, 1359 (Fed. Cir. 2004).

30. *O'Reilly v. Morse*, 56 U.S. 62 (1853).

31. *Bates v. Coe*, 98 U.S. 31, 39 (1878).

32. *SmithKline*, 365 F.3d at 1328 (Gajarsa, J., concurring).

33. *Id.* at 1329 (Gajarsa, J., concurring).

34. See *Amgen, Inc. v. Hoechst Marion Roussel*, 314 F.3d 1313, 1329 (Fed. Cir. 2003).

35. *SmithKline*, 365 F.3d at 1331 (Gajarsa, J., concurring).

36. "Judge Gajarsa . . . in his concurring opinion under United States law under the heading of 'patentable subject matter,' . . . serves as an inspiration for the Court in respect of the present infringement issue." *SmithKline Beecham PLC v. Farmaceutisch Analytisch Laboratorium Duiven B.V.* (translation) at ¶¶ 4.25–26 (Dist. Ct. The Hague, March 22, 2006).

37. See, for example, Robert Schubert, "Federal Judge's Opinion Shows Understanding of Patented Gene Spread," *CropChoice*, May 17, 2004, http://www.cropchoice.com/leadstry1659.html?recid=2560.

38. *SmithKline Beecham Corp. v. Apotex Corp.*, 403 F.3d 1331 (Fed. Cir. 2005).

39. *SmithKline Beecham Corp. v. Apotex Corp.*, 403 F.3d 1328, 1331 (en banc) (Newman, J., dissenting).

40. *SmithKline*, 403 F.3d at 1351 (Gajarsa, J., concurring).

41. Vonnegut, *Cat's Cradle*, chap. 116.

42. Roger Parloff, "BlackBerry Held Hostage," *Fortune*, November 29, 2005.

43. David M. Ewalt, "BlackBerry Raspberries," *Forbes*, February 2, 2006.

44. "American Dream Series: Thomas Campana Profile," *America Daily*, http://america-daily.com/?page_id=201.

45. See *NTP, Inc. v. Research in Motion, Ltd.* 418 F.3d 1282 (Fed. Cir. 2005).

46. *NTP, Inc. v. Research in Motion, Ltd.*, 392 F.3d 1336, 1340 (Fed. Cir. 2004).

47. Barrie McKenna, "RIM Chairman Call for Overhaul of U.S. Patent Laws," *Globe and Mail* (Toronto), April 6, 2006, available at http://www.theglobeandmail.com/servlet/story/LAC.20060406.RRIM06/TPStory/Business.

48. Governmental actors often play by different rules in the patent world. One of the other nonvanilla issues that arose in the BlackBerry case was a long-standing but controversial rule limiting government liability in patent cases to *direct* infringement; though RIM infringed NTP's patent directly, BlackBerry users were only indirect infringers. Cf. *Zoltek Corp. v. United States*, 442 F.3d 1345, 1353 (Fed. Cir. 2006) (Gajarsa, J., concurring) ("I agree that we are bound by our panel decision in [*NTP v. RIM*], in which we held that direct infringement . . . is a necessary predicate for government liability. . . . However, the NTP proposition is, in my view, the result of an unchecked propagation of error in our case law, and its viability may eventually be challenged."), and *Zoltek*, 442 F.3d at 1367–68 (Dyk, J., concurring) ("I . . . write separately to express my view that the court correctly held in [*NTP v. RIM*], that the government can only be liable for infringement . . . if the same conduct would render a private party liable for [direct] infringement.").

49. George Wheeler, "NTP Patents are Strong," *National Law Journal*, March 13, 2006, available at http://www.law.com/jsp/nlj/PubArticleNLJ.jsp?id=1141985112556.

CHAPTER 6

1. Ecclesiastes 1:9.

2. See Fred Warshofsky, *The Patent Wars: The Battle to Own the World's Technology* (New York: Wiley, 1994), chap. 3.

3. Stephen A. Merrill, Richard C. Levin, and Mark B. Myers, eds., *A Patent System for the 21st Century* (Washington, DC: National Academies Press, 2004), 38.

4. Alan Murray, "War on 'Patent Trolls' May Be Wrong Battle," *Wall Street Journal*, March 22, 2006. Available at http://online.wsj.com/article/SB114298577458004598.html.

5. Murray, "War on 'Patent Trolls.'"

6. Federal Trade Commission, *To Promote Innovation: The Proper Balance of Competition and Patent Law and Policy* (Washington, DC: GPO, 2003). Available at http://www.ftc.gov/os/2003/10/innovationrpt.pdf.

7. Federal Trade Commission, *To Promote Innovation*, 7–17.

8. The term *patent bar* takes on different meanings in different settings. At times, it refers to the unofficial collection of all attorneys whose work includes some elements of patent law. In the official PTO sense, it refers to people authorized to practice in front of the PTO. In this sense, the Patent Bar is not your typical "bar." Membership in the Patent Bar qualifies people to work as patent examiners and to prepare patent applications. No formal legal training is required to take the Patent Bar, but a solid technical background is considered important. See http://www.uspto.gov/web/offices/dcom/olia/oed/grb15oct03.pdf.

9. See the discussion in chapter 4 in the section "The Main Tent."

10. Adam B. Jaffe and Josh Lerner, *Innovation and Its Discontents: How Our Broken Patent System Is Endangering Innovation and Progress, and What to Do about It* (Princeton, NJ: Princeton University Press, 2004), 110–15, 115, 119, 123.

11. A preliminary injunction is a judicial order granted early in litigation that prohibits defendants from continuing their allegedly inappropriate behavior. Preliminary injunctions invert the normal courses of both business and litigation. Under normal circumstances, defendants may continue the behavior of which plaintiffs complain unless and until the plaintiffs win their suits. If a judge determines that the plaintiff's victory is likely, and that the plaintiff is likely to suffer irreparable damage during the suit, he may enjoin the defendant's behavior "preliminarily." In a patent case, a preliminary injunction forces a defendant to change whatever (business) practice generated the alleged infringement.

12. *Atlas Powder Co. v. Ireco Chems.*, 773 F.2d 1230, 1232–33 (1985).

13. *MercExchange, LLC v. eBay, Inc.*, 401 F.3d 1323, 1338–39 (Fed. Cir. 2005).

14. See *eBay, Inc. v. MercExchange, LLC*, 126 S. Ct. 1837 (2006).

15. 35 U.S.C. § 101.

16. *State St. Bank & Trust Co. v. Signature Fin. Group*, 149 F.3d 1368, 1372–73 (Fed. Cir. 1998)

17. See Glynn S. Lunney Jr., "Patent Law, the Federal Circuit, and the Supreme Court: A Quiet Revolution," 11 *S. Ct. Econ. Rev.* 1 (2004).

18. Dan L. Burk and Mark A. Lemley, "Is Patent Law Technology-Specific?" 17 *Berkeley Tech. L. J.* 1155, 1155–57, 1205 (2002).

19. Dan L. Burk and Mark A. Lemley, "Policy Levers in Patent Law," 89 *Va. L. Rev.* 1575, 1577 (2003).

20. Burk and Lemley, "Policy Levers," 1638–39.

21. Burk and Lemley, "Policy Levers," 1639.

22. Burk and Lemley, "Policy Levers," 1637–38.

23. I have written in favor of industry-specific rights in a number of places and continue to support them. See, for example, *Digital Phoenix: Why the Information Economy Collapsed and How It Will Rise Again* (Cambridge, MA: MIT Press, 2005), chap. 8; and "A First Principles Approach to IP Reform," 8 *Boston University Journal of Science and Technology Law* 75 (2002).

24. Burk and Lemley, "Policy Levers," 1696, 1578–79.

25. R. Polk Wagner, "Of Patents and Path-Dependency: A Comment on Burk and Lemley," 18 *Berkeley Tech. L. J.* 1341, 1342–45 (2003).

26. See *KSR v. Teleflex*, 126 S. Ct. 2966 (2006). The Supreme Court issued its ruling as we were on the way to press. In an opinion whose full consequences may take some time to unfold, the Supreme Court agreed with the District Court that Teleflex's invention was obvious, and that the PTO should not have issued the patent. The Supreme Court chastised the Federal Circuit for applying its own "teaching, suggestion, or motivation" test too rigidly, but did not reject either the test itself or the conclusions that the Federal Circuit had reached in other cases, where it applied the test more flexibly. As a result, while KSR's victory is certainly complete, it is unclear whether the amici, including those from the software industry, successfully raised the threshold for proving obviousness—which was, after all, their goal. See *KSR Int'l v. Teleflex, Inc.* 127 S.Ct. 1727 (2007).

27. *Teleflex, Inc. v. KSR Int'l Co.*, 119 Fed. Appx. 282, 285 (Fed. Cir. 2005).

28. *KSR v. Teleflex*, transcript of oral argument at 53 (November 28, 2006).

29. *KSR v. Teleflex*, Brief of Twenty-Four Intellectual Property Law Professors as Amici Curiae in Support of Petitioner at 12.

30. See *KSR v. Teleflex*, Brief of Business and Law Professors as Amici Curiae in Support of the Respondents.

31. Lawrence B. Ebert, "Lemley Switches Sides in *KSR v. Teleflex*," IPBIZ, November 24, 2006, http://ipbiz.blogspot.com/2006/11/lemley-switches-sides-in-ksr-v.html.

32. See Abramson, *Digital Phoenix*, chap. 7, for my earlier thoughts on this issue.

33. The Act would have joined the rest of the world in awarding a patent to the first inventor to file a claim (something that is easy to determine) rather than the first to invent (a contentious point that often requires an expensive evidentiary hearing), eliminated a controversial requirement that a patent disclose the "best mode" of implementing the invention, amended the procedures for determining whether a patentee had met his duty of candor to the PTO when filing for the patent, and changed the rules for "continuation" applications. See H.R. 2795 (109th Cong.).

34. Dennis Crouch, "Patent Reform: Patent Act of 2005," June 9, 2005, http://patentlaw.typepad.com/patent/2005/06/patent_reform_p.html.

35. James V. DeLong, "Patent Reform Hits the Hill," *Tech Central Station*, June 21, 2005, http://www.tcsdaily.com/article.aspx?id=062105E.

36. Holman W. Jenkins Jr., "What's Good about Patent Wars," *Wall Street Journal*, April 19, 2006.

37. Jenkins, "What's Good."

38. *eBay*, 126 S. Ct. at 1840.

39. *Id.* at 1841 (Roberts, C. J., concurring) (emphasis in the original).

40. *Id.* at 1842 (Kennedy, J., concurring).

41. See William J. Baumol, *The Free Market Innovation Machine* (Princeton, NJ: Princeton University Press, 2002), 120–23.

CHAPTER 7

1. Adam Smith, *The Wealth of Nations* (1776; Indianapolis, IN: Bobbs-Merrill, 1961), 167–68.

2. David Ricardo, *Principles of Political Economy and Taxation* (1817; Amherst, NY: Prometheus, 1996), chap. 7.

3. Ricardo, *Principles of Political Economy*, chap. 7.

4. See, for example, World Trade Organization, *Comparative Advantage*, http://www.wto.org/english/res_e/reser_e/cadv_e.htm (citing P. A. Samuelson, "The Way of an Economist," in P. A. Samuelson, ed., *International Economic Relations: Proceedings of the Third Congress of the International Economic Association* [London: Macmillan, 1969], 1–11).

5. World Trade Organization, *Comparative Advantage*.

6. World Trade Organization, *Comparative Advantage*.

7. See Dan L. Burk and Mark A. Lemley, "Policy Levers in Patent Law," 89 *Va. L. Rev.* 1575, 1637–38 (2003).

8. James M. Buchanan and Gordon Tullock, *The Calculus of Consent* (Ann Arbor, MI: Ann Arbor Paperback, 1965), 304.

9. Joseph Stiglitz, *Making Globalization Work* (New York: Norton, 2006), 65.

10. http://www.eftafairtrade.org/definition.asp. The organizations comprising FINE are: Fairtrade Labelling Organizations International, the International Fair Trade Association, the Network of European Worldshops, and the European Fair Trade Association. I take no position on the work of any of these groups.

11. Stiglitz, *Making Globalization Work*, 73.

12. John H. Jackson, *The World Trading System*, 2nd ed. (Cambridge, MA: MIT Press, 1997), 12.

13. Jackson, *World Trading System*, 21–24.

14. J. Michael Finger and Julio J. Nogués, eds., *Safeguards and Antidumping in Latin American Trade Liberalization* (Washington, DC: World Bank, 2006), 25–26.

15. Seth T. Kaplan, book jacket to Finger and Nogués, *Safeguards and Antidumping*.

16. Ricardo, *Principles of Political Economy*, 94–95.

17. Historical examples abound. Consider, for example, the notorious Fordney-McCumber Tariff of 1922 and the Smoot-Hawley Tariff of 1930. Between them, they savaged the global trading system's recovery after World War I, created the conditions for the Great Depression, and then exacerbated the consequent economic decline both in the United States and abroad.

18. *Structural Indus. v. United States*, 240 F.Supp.2d 1327 (Ct. Intl. Tr. 2002).

19. *Structural Indus. v. United States*, 356 F.3d 1366 (Fed. Cir. 2004).

20. *Structural Indus. v. United States*, 360 F.Supp.2d (Ct. Intl. Tr. 2005).

21. See *Pomeroy Collection, Ltd. v. United States*, 336 F.3d 1370 (Fed. Cir. 2003).
22. See *Pillsbury Co. v. United States*, 431 F.3d 1377 (Fed. Cir. 2005).
23. See *Warner-Lambert Co. v. United States*, 407 F.3d 1207 (Fed. Cir. 2005).
24. See *Bauer Nike Hockey USA, Inc. v. United States*, 393 F.3d 1246 (Fed. Cir. 2004).
25. See *Russ Berrie & Co. v. United States*, 381 F.3d 1334 (Fed. Cir. 2004).
26. See *Rubie's Costume Co. v. United States*, 337 F.3d 1350 (Fed. Cir. 2003).
27. See *Nucor Corp. v. United States*, 414 F.3d 1331 (Fed. Cir. 2005).
28. See *Corus Staal BV v. DOC*, 395 F.3d 1343 (Fed. Cir. 2005).
29. See *Eurodif S.A. v. United States*, 423 F.3d 1275 (Fed. Cir. 2005).
30. See *Dupont Teijin Films USA, LP v. United States*, 407 F.3d 1211 (Fed. Cir. 2005).
31. See *Hynix Semiconductor, Inc. v. United States*, 424 F.3d 1363 (Fed. Cir. 2005).
32. See *NEC Solutions (Am.), Inc. v. United States*, 411 F.3d 1340 (Fed. Cir. 2005).
33. See *Int'l Trading Co. v. United States*, 412 F.3d 1303 (Fed. Cir. 2005).
34. See *Zhejiang Native Produce & Animal By-Products Imp. & Exp. Corp. v. United States*, 432 F.3d 1363 (Fed. Cir. 2005).
35. See *Cathedral Candle Co. v. United States ITC*, 400 F.3d 1352 (Fed. Cir. 2005).
36. See *Tak Fat Trading Co. v. United States*, 396 F.3d 1378 (Fed. Cir. 2005).
37. Finger and Nogués, *Safeguards and Antidumping*, 39.
38. See U.S. International Trade Commission, *The Economic Effects of Antidumping and Countervailing Duty Orders and Suspension Agreements*, Investigation no. 332–344 (Washington, DC: International Trade Commission, 1995), x.
39. "Commissioner Comments," in International Trade Commission, *Economic Effects*, VIII–IX, available at http://hotdocs.usitc.gov/docs/pubs/332/pub2900/views.pdf.
40. Morris Morkre and Kenneth Kelly, *Effects of Unfair Imports on Domestic Industries* (Washington, DC: Federal Trade Commission, 1994), 69–70.
41. *Bratsk Aluminium Smelter v. United States*, 444 F.3d 1369, 1372–73 (Fed. Cir. 2006).
42. Finger and Nogués, *Safeguards and Antidumping*, 40–41.
43. See Public Law 106-387 (2000).
44. There were technical loopholes that *might have* rendered such subsidies WTO compliant, but they would nevertheless have violated its spirit and complicated the jobs of American trade negotiations. Furthermore, they proved to be irrelevant because no one took the time to incorporate them into the law.
45. See Hale E. Sheppard, "The Continued Dumping and Subsidy Offset Act (Byrd Amendment): A Defeat before the WTO May Constitute an Overall Victory for U.S. Trade," 10 *Tul. J. Int'l & Comp. L.* 121 (2002).
46. See Delegation of the European Union to the United States, "US Congress Repeals Byrd Amendment but Allows for a Transition Period," No. 128/05, December 20, 2005, http://www.eurunion.org/News/press/2005/2005128.htm.
47. "Byrd Brained," *Economist*, September 2, 2004.
48. *Candle Corp. of Am. v. United States Int'l Trade Comm'n*, 374 F.3d 1087, 1094 (Fed. Cir. 2004).
49. See *id.* at 1096 (Gajarsa, J., dissenting).
50. See *Cathedral Candle*, 400 F.3d 1352 (Fed. Cir. 2005).
51. Greg Rosenberg, "Bye Bye Birdie," *Forbes*, March 23, 2005.

52. See Public Law 109-171 (2006).

53. Rosenberg, "Bye Bye Birdie."

54. *Nucor Corp. v. United States*, 414 F.3d 1331, 1334–35 (Fed. Cir. 2005).

55. *Id.*

56. Dan Ackman, "Bush Cuts Steel Tariffs, Declares Victory," *Forbes*, December 5, 2003.

57. See *Nucor*, 414 F.3d at 1331.

CHAPTER 8

1. "Neither slavery nor involuntary servitude, except as a punishment for crime whereof the party shall have been duly convicted, shall exist within the United States, or any place subject to their jurisdiction." U.S. Const. Amend. XIII.

2. The White House, "Expanding Opportunity," http://www.whitehouse .gov/infocus/internationaltrade/taapager.html.

3. The ITC's cost estimate of $1.59 billion for 1991 is now fifteen years old. Nevertheless, even given reasonable adjustments for inflation and $250 million per year growth for the Byrd Amendment, there is no reason to believe that the quantifiable societal costs of antidumping and countervailing duties have sky-rocketed. Their current total is likely in the neighborhood of a few billion dollars—money that would be better spent on expanded TAA programs.

4. Brad Brooks-Rubin, "The Certification Process for Trade Adjustment Assistance: Certifiably Broken," 7 *U. Pa. J. Lab. & Emp. L.* 797, 806–07 (2005).

5. *Id.* at 799–803 (2005).

6. *Former Emples. of Chevron Prods. Co. v. United States Secretary of Labor*, 298 F.Supp.2d 1338 (Ct. Int'l. Tr. 2003).

7. *Id.*

8. See *Former Emples. of Quality Fabricating, Inc. v. United States Secretary of Labor*, 448 F.3d 1351 (Fed. Cir. 2006).

9. See *Former Emples. of Marathon Ashland Pipeline, L.L.C. v. Chao*, 370 F.3d 1375 (Fed. Cir. 2004); *Former Emples. of Barry Callebaut v. Chao*, 357 F.3d 1377 (Fed. Cir. 2004).

10. See *Former Emples. of Sonoco Prods. Co. v. Chao*, 372 F.3d 1291 (Fed. Cir. 2004).

11. Michael Borrus and Judith Goldstein, "The Political Economy of International Trade Law and Policy: United States Trade Protectionism: Institutions, Norms, and Practices" 8 *NW. J. Int'l L. & Bus.* 328, 353–56 (1987).

12. Marcus Walker, "For the Danish, A Job Loss Can Be a Learning Experience" *The Wall Street Journal*, March 26, 2006.

13. Max Baucus, "A Democratic Trade Agenda," *Wall Street Journal*, January 4, 2007.

14. Baucus, "Democratic Trade Agenda."

15. See *NTP, Inc. v. Research in Motion, Ltd.*, 418 F.3d 1282 (Fed. Cir. 2005).

16. *Texas Instruments, Inc. v. Tessera, Inc.*, 231 F.3d 1325, 1330 (Fed. Cir. 2000).

17. See *eBay Inc. v. MercExchange, L.L.C.*, 126 S. Ct. 1837 (2006).

18. "Smoot Hawley's Revenge," *Wall Street Journal*, August 23, 2006.

19. See, for example, *Fuji Photo Film Co. v. Benun*, 463 F.3d 1252 (Fed. Cir. 2006).
20. *Texas Instruments*, 231 F.3d at 1330.
21. See Annex 1C to the WTO Treaty covering Trade Related Aspects of International Property.
22. See *Voda v. Cordis Corp.*, 2007 U.S. App. LEXIS 2134 (Fed. Cir. 2007).
23. *Id.*
24. *Id.* (Newman, J., dissenting).
25. The Federal Circuit's ruling in this case was less than a month old when we went to press.
26. *Roche Prods. v. Bolar Pharmaceutical Co.*, 733 F.2d 858, 861 (Fed. Cir. 1984).
27. See 21 U.S.C. § 355.
28. TRIPS Article 27.1
29. See World Trade Organization, *Canada—Patent Protection of Pharmaceutical Products:. Complaint by the European Communities and Their Member States*, WTO Panel Report WT/DS114/R, March 17, 2000, available at http://www.wto.org/english/tratop_e/dispu_e/7428d.pdf.
30. See Ryan Goldstein, "Specialized IP Trial Courts around the World," 16 *International Law* 1 (North Carolina Bar Association International Law Section, Sept. 2006); and Bruce Abramson, *From Saraswati to Laxmi: India's Journey toward an Effective Patent System* (Washington, DC: World Bank, forthcoming).
31. See Shondeep Banerji, "The Indian IP Rights Regime and the TRIPs Agreement," in Clarisa Long, ed., *Intellectual Property Rights in Emerging Markets* (Washington, DC: AEI Press, 2000), 62–69; and Abramson, *From Saraswati to Laxmi*.

CHAPTER 9

1. Declaration of Independence.
2. *Bank of United States v. Planters' Bank of Georgia*, 22 U.S. 904, 907 (1824).
3. See, for example, *Alfred Dunhill of London, Inc. v. Republic of Cuba*, 425 U.S. 682 (1976).
4. Abraham Lincoln, Gettysburg Address, November 19, 1863.
5. Erwin Chemerinsky, "Symposium: Shifting the Balance of Power? The Supreme Court, Federalism, and State Sovereign Immunity: Against Sovereign Immunity," 53 *Stan. L. Rev.* 1201, 1201–3 (2001).
6. *Id.*
7. *Kennecott Copper Corp. v. State Tax Commission*, 327 U.S. 573, 580–81 (1946) (Frankfurter, J., dissenting).
8. Abraham Lincoln, State of the Union Address, December 3, 1861.
9. *Kennecott Copper*, 327 U.S. at 582 (Frankfurter, J., dissenting).
10. 28 U.S.C. § 1491 in the current numbering of statutes. Congress has amended the Tucker Act numerous times since 1887, most recently in 1996.
11. ". . . nor shall private property be taken for public use, without just compensation." U.S. Const. Amend. V.
12. 28 U.S.C. § 1346.
13. *Keifer & Keifer v. R. F. C.*, 306 U.S. 381, 391 (1939).

14. 28 U.S.C. §§ 2671 et seq.

15. John T. Noonan, *Narrowing the Nation's Power* (Berkeley: University of California Press, 2002), 12.

16. Noonan, *Narrowing the Nation's Power*, 12.

17. *College Sav. Bank v. Florida Prepaid Postsecondary Educ. Expense Bd.*, 948 F.Supp. 400 (D.N.J. 1996).

18. *College Sav. Bank v. Florida Prepaid Postsecondary Educ. Expense Bd.*, 148 F.3d 1343 (Fed. Cir. 1998).

19. *Florida Prepaid Postsecondary Educ. Expense Bd. v. College Sav. Bank.* 527 U.S. 627 (1999).

20. See *Sandstrom v. Principi*, 16 Vet. App. 481 (2002) *aff'd* 358 F.3d 1376 (Fed. Cir. 2004).

21. U.S. Department of Veterans Affairs, "About VA Home," http://www.va .gov/about_va/.

22. See 38 U.S.C. § 5103A.

23. See 38 U.S.C. § 1114.

24. 38 U.S.C. § 1114(m).

25. 38 U.S.C. § 1114(n).

26. 38 U.S.C. § 5109A(b) (emphasis added).

27. *Sandstrom*, 358 F.3d at 1358.

28. See 38 U.S.C. § 7292(c); *Forshey v. Principi*, 284 F.3d 1335, 1338 (Fed. Cir. 2002) (en banc).

29. *Sandstrom*, 358 F.3d at 1380–81.

30. *Angarica v. Bayard*, 127 U.S. 251, 252 (1888).

31. *Id.* at 260.

32. *United States v. North Carolina*, 136 U.S. 211, 216 (1890).

33. *Library of Congress v. Shaw*, 478 U.S. 310, 316, 316n3, 317 (1986).

34. 42 U.S.C. § 2000e-5(k).

35. *United States v. N. Y. Rayon Importing Co.*, 329 U.S. 654, 658 (1947).

36. *Smith v. Principi*, 281 F.3d 1384, 1387–1388 (Fed. Cir. 2002).

37. 42 U.S.C. § 2000e-16(d).

38. *Landgraf v. Usi Film Prods.*, 511 U.S. 244 (1994).

39. Tax law similarly contains a fix incomprehensible to those who don't know its history. Taxpayers who prevail in suits against the Internal Revenue Service collect both principal and interest because the tax laws waive the no-interest rule explicitly: "Interest shall be allowed and paid upon any overpayment in respect of any internal revenue tax" (26 U.S.C. § 6611). That waiver, which has long been the law, however, waives the government's immunity from *simple* interest, or interest on "any overpayment." It says nothing about *compound* interest, or interest on the interest. Sovereign immunity precluded taxpayers from collecting compound interest until 1982, when a new statute redefined the waiver's terms: "In computing the amount of any interest required to be paid under this title . . . by the Secretary or by the taxpayer, or any other amount determined by reference to such amount of interest, such interest and such amount shall be compounded daily" (26 U.S.C. § 6622). See also, *Cohn v. United States*, 872 F.2d 533, 533 (2d. Cir. 1989).

40. Chief Judge Kramer of the CAVC challenged even that logic: "[C]ontrary to [Sandstrom's] argument, nowhere does [veterans' law] provide that the corrected

decision shall have the effect that the prior decision containing CUE had never been made; rather, the statute provides, in effect, that the erroneous decision, when made, was decided correctly." *Sandstrom*, 16 Vet. App. at 486 (Kramer, C. J., concurring).

41. *Sandstrom*, 358 F.3d at 1379.
42. Homer, *Iliad* 6.179–181, trans. Richmond Lattimore (Chicago: University of Chicago Press, 1961).
43. Woody Allen, *Without Feathers* (New York: Random House, 1972), 193.
44. See *AINS, Inc. v. United States*, 56 Fed. Cl. 522 (2003) *aff'd*, 365 F.3d 1333 (Fed. Cir. 2004).
45. 28 U.S.C. § 1491(a)(1).
46. *Alden v. Maine*, 527 U.S. 706, 768 (1999) (Souter, J., dissenting).
47. *AINS*, 56 Fed. Cl. at 527–28.
48. *Standard Oil Company of California v. Johnson*, 316 U.S. 481, 484–85 (1942).
49. *Id.*
50. *Borden v. United States*, 126 Ct. Cl. 902, 907–9 (1953).
51. *Id.* at 910–13 (Whitaker, J., dissenting).
52. *Pulaski Cab Co. v. United States*, 141 Ct. Cl. 160 (1958).
53. See *Borden*, 126 Ct. Cl. at 909; *Borden*, 126 Ct. Cl. at 910–14 (Whitaker, J., dissenting); *Pulaski*, 141 Ct. Cl. at 166 (Whitaker, J., concurring).
54. See *Kyer v. United States*, 369 F.2d 714, 717–19 (Ct. Cl. 1966).
55. *Id.* at 754.
56. 28 U.S.C. 1491(a)(1). See also, *McDonald's Corp. v. United States*, 926 F.2d 1126, 1129–33 (Fed. Cir. 1991).
57. See *United States v. Hopkins*, 427 U.S. 123, 125–26 (1976).
58. See *Atkins v. United States*, 214 Ct. Cl. 186, 266 (1977).
59. See *L'Enfant Plaza Props., Inc. v. United States*, 229 Ct. Cl. 278 (1982).
60. See *Denkler v. United States*, 782 F.2d 1003 (Fed. Cir. 1986).
61. See *Furash & Co. v. United States*, 252 F.3d 1336 (Fed. Cir. 2001).
62. See *Core Concepts of Fla., Inc. v. United States*, 327 F.3d 1331 (Fed. Cir. 2003).
63. *AINS*, 365 F.3d at 1342.
64. *AINS*, 56 Fed. Cl. at 543–44.
65. *AINS*, 365 F.3d at 1344.

CHAPTER 10

1. Public Law 101-647 (1990).
2. U.S. Const. Art. I § 8 Cl. 3.
3. *United States v. Lopez*, 514 U.S. 549, 551 (1995).
4. *Employment Div. v. Smith*, 494 U.S. 872, 874 (1990).
5. *City of Boerne v. Flores*, 521 U.S. 507, 511–512 (1997).
6. William Shakespeare, *Hamlet*, act I, scene 2.
7. *Marbury v. Madison*, 5 U.S. 137, 177–78 (1803).
8. Shakespeare, *Hamlet*, act I, scene 2.
9. *Boerne*, 521 U.S. at 536.

10. *Griswold v. Connecticut*, 381 U.S. 479 (1965).

11. *Roe v. Wade*, 410 U.S. 113 (1973).

12. John T. Noonan, *Narrowing the Nation's Power* (Berkeley: University of California Press, 2002), 11.

13. Noonan, *Narrowing the Nation's Power*, 42.

14. *Seminole Tribe v. Fla.*, 517 U.S. 44, 54, 68 (1996).

15. See Noonan, *Narrowing the Nation's Power*, 1–2.

16. Noonan, *Narrowing the Nation's Power*, 156.

17. *Fla. Prepaid Postsecondary Educ. Expense Bd. v. College Sav. Bank*, 527 U.S. 627 (1999).

18. *Chew v. California*, 893 F.2d 331 (Fed. Cir. 1990).

19. *Id.* at 334.

20. *Id.* at 335.

21. 35 U.S.C. § 271(h) (1994).

22. 35 U.S.C. § 296(h) (1994).

23. *College Sav. Bank*, 148 F.3d at 1346.

24. *Id.* at 1349–55.

25. *Fla. Prepaid*, 527 U.S. at 635.

26. *Id.* at 640–41, 643, 646–47, 647.

27. Noonan, *Narrowing the Nation's Power*, 94–95.

28. Derek Bok, *Universities in the Marketplace* (Princeton, NJ: Princeton University Press, 2003), 11–12.

29. See Bok, *Universities in the Marketplace.*

30. David C. Mowery, Richard R. Nelson, Bhaven N. Sampat, and Arvids A. Ziedonis, *Ivory Tower and Industrial Innovation: University–Industry Technology Transfer before and after the Bayh-Dole Act* (Stanford, CA: Stanford University Press, 2004), 1–3.

31. Mowery et al., *Ivory Tower*, 2, 191–92.

32. See *Regents of the Univ. of N.M. v. Knight*, 321 F.3d 1111 (Fed. Cir. 2003).

33. See *Competitive Techs., Inc. v. Fujitsu Ltd.*, 374 F.3d 1098 (Fed. Cir. 2004).

34. The doctrine at issue here is but one of two "experimental use" doctrines in patent law. The other, unrelated doctrine, was relevant to the court's consideration of GSK's claims in its fights about Paxil (see chapter 5). In that context, an inventor's experimental tests do not start the one-year clock before which he must file his patent application.

35. See *Madey v. Duke Univ.*, 307 F.3d 1351 (Fed. Cir. 2002).

36. AAAS Research Exemption Working Group, "Background," 2005, http://sippi.aaas.org/rschexemption.shtml.

37. *Kelo v. City of New London*, 125 S. Ct. 2655, 2667–68 (2005).

38. See *Toews v. United States*, 376 F.3d 1371 (Fed. Cir. 2004).

39. See *Tuthill Ranch, Inc. v. United States*, 381 F.3d 1132 (Fed. Cir. 2004).

40. 7 U.S.C. §§ 601 et seq.

41. *Lion Raisins, Inc. v. United States*, 416 F.3d 1356, 1367–68 (Fed. Cir. 2005).

42. The territoriality limitation loomed large when Voda tried to bring his foreign patent claims in Oklahoma, see *Voda v. Cordis Corp.*, 2007 U.S. App. LEXIS 2134 (Fed. Cir. 2007); when RIM attempted to avoid infringement liability because its relays were in Canada, see *NTP, Inc. v. Research in Motion, Ltd.* 418 F.3d 1282 (Fed. Cir. 2005); and in every 337 case that the ITC has ever heard.

43. 28 U.S.C. § 1498(a).
44. 28 U.S.C. § 1498(c).
45. See *id.*
46. *Zoltek Corp. v. United States*, 442 F.3d 1345, 1352 (Fed. Cir. 2006).
47. *Id.* at 1373–74 (Plager, J., dissenting).
48. *Id.* at 1367 (Gajarsa, J., concurring).
49. *Id.* at 1378 (Plager, J., dissenting).
50. *Id.*
51. *College Sav. Bank*, 148 F.3d at 1349–10.
52. The possibility that the limitation on government infringement is little more than a preservation of the general rule that patent rights—whether based in property or regulation—simply evaporate at the border is consistent with some important trends in patent law. As the Supreme Court recently reiterated, "The presumption that United States law governs domestically but does not rule the world applies with particular force in patent law. The traditional understanding that our patent law operates only domestically and does not extend to foreign activities is embedded in the Patent Act itself, which provides that a patent confers exclusive rights in an invention within the United States." *Microsoft Corp. v. AT&T Corp.*, 127 S.Ct. 17426, 1758 (2007).
53. *Oklahoma Tax Comm'n v. Citizen Band Potawatomi Indian Tribe*, 498 U.S. 505, 509 (1991).
54. See *Demontiney v. United States*, 255 F.3d 801 (9th Cir. 2001); *Demontiney v. United States*, 54 Fed. Cl. 780 (2002) *aff'd* 81 Fed. Appx. 356 (Fed. Cir. 2003).
55. *Alden v. Maine*, 527 U.S. 706, 715–16 (1999).
56. *Id.* at 803 (Souter, J., dissenting) (quoting William Blackstone, *Commentaries on the Laws of England*, 1:241).
57. *Id.* at 814 (Souter, J., dissenting) (quoting *Marbury*, 5 U.S. at 137).
58. Erwin Chemerinsky, "Symposium: Shifting the Balance of Power? The Supreme Court, Federalism, and State Sovereign Immunity: Against Sovereign Immunity," 53 *Stan. L. Rev.* 1201, 1204–10 (2001).
59. Attributed to Rabbi Mordecai Kaplan.
60. Frederic Bastiat, *The Law* (first published in French, 1850), trans. Dean Russell (Irvington-on-Hudson, NY: Foundation for Economic Education, 1998), 68.
61. Declaration of Independence.
62. Declaration of the Rights of Man and of the Citizen, August 26, 1789.
63. Declaration of Independence.
64. Bastiat, *The Law*, 68.
65. *Griswold*, 381 U.S. at 492–94 (1965) (Goldberg, J., concurring).
66. Abraham Lincoln, State of the Union Address, December 3, 1861.

CHAPTER 11

1. See Article 37 of the Anglican Church's Articles of Religion in the 1571 and 1662 versions of its Book of Common Prayer.
2. *Black's Law Dictionary*, abridged 6th ed. (St. Paul, MN: West Publishing, 1991).
3. 28 U.S.C. § 2502(a).

4. *Id.*

5. *Ferreiro v. United States,* 350 F.3d 1318, 1323 (Fed. Cir. 2003).

6. *Id.* at 1324.

7. *Id.* at 1322 (citing *Zalcmanis v. United States,* 173 F.Supp. 355, 357 [Ct. Cl. 1959]).

8. *Id.*

9. *El-Shifa Pharm. Indus. Co. v. United States,* 55 Fed. Cl. 751 (2003).

10. *El-Shifa Pharm. Indus. Co. v. United States,* 378 F.3d 1346, 1348 (Fed. Cir. 2004).

11. 28 U.S.C. § 1346.

12. *Doe v. United States,* 372 F.3d 1308, 1310 (Fed. Cir. 2004).

13. *Britell v. United States,* 372 F.3d 1370, 1384 (Fed. Cir. 2004).

14. See *Christopher Village, Ltd. Pshp. v. Retsinas,* 190 F.3d 310 (5th Cir. 1999).

15. *Id.* at 315.

16. *Id.* at 316.

17. *Id.* at 318.

18. *Warner v. Cox,* 487 F.2d 1301, 1306 (5th Cir. 1974).

19. *Christopher Vill., L.P. v. United States,* 360 F.3d 1319, 1333 (Fed. Cir. 2004).

20. *Christianson v. Colt Industries Operating Corp.,* 798 F.2d 1051, 1055–58 (7th Cir. 1986).

21. *Id.* at 1058n5.

22. *Christianson v. Colt Indus. Operating Corp.,* 822 F.2d 1544, 1546, 1550, 1559–60 (Fed. Cir. 1987).

23. See *Christianson v. Colt Industries Operating Corp.,* 486 U.S. 800 (1988).

24. *Holmes Group, Inc. v. Vornado Air Circulation Sys.,* 535 U.S. 826, 834 (2002).

25. See *Schinzing v. Mid-States Stainless, Inc.,* 415 F.3d 807, 811 (8th Cir. 2005).

CHAPTER 12

1. John Milton, *Areopagitica: A Speech for the Liberty of Unlicensed Printing* (1644). See http://www.gutenberg.org/etext/608.

2. 8 Anne, c. 19 (1710).

3. *Id.*

4. For an excellent review of this early history, see Paul Goldstein, *Copyright's Highway: From Gutenberg to the Celestial Jukebox* (Stanford, CA: Stanford University Press, 2003), chap. 2.

5. See discussion of zip, wip, and sip, in chapter 4 in the section "The Main Tent."

6. 17 U.S.C. § 107.

7. See *Sony Corp. of America v. Universal City Studios, Inc.,* 464 U.S. 417 (1984).

8. *Id.*

9. 17 U.S.C. § 1201.

10. *Id.*

11. Jane C. Ginsburg, "Copyright Legislation for the 'Digital Millennium,'" 23 *Colum—VLA Journal of Law & the Arts* 137 (1999).

12. David Nimmer, "A Riff on Fair Use in the Digital Millennium Copyright Act," 148 *U. Pa L. Rev.* 673 (2000).

13. *Id.*

14. *Id.*

15. *RealNetworks, Inc. v. Streambox, Inc.*, 2000 U.S. Dist. LEXIS 1889, at *23, No. 2:99CV02070 (W.D. Wash., Jan. 18, 2000).

16. *Universal City Studios, Inc. v. Reimerdes*, 111 F.Supp.2d 294, 319 (S.D.N.Y. 2000).

17. For a more detailed discussion of these debates, see Bruce Abramson, *Digital Phoenix: Why the Information Economy Collapsed and How It Will Rise Again* (Cambridge, MA: MIT Press, 2005), chap. 7.

18. *Chamberlain Group, Inc. v. Skylink Techs., Inc.*, 381 F.3d 1178 (Fed. Cir. 2004).

19. *Lexmark, Int'l, Inc. v. Static Control Components, Inc.*, 387 F.3d 522 (6th Cir. 2004).

20. Jane Ginsburg, testimony at Copyright Office Anti-Circumvention Rulemaking Hearing, May 9, 2003, p. 46, http://www.copyright.gov/1201/2003/hearings/transcript-may9.pdf

21. *In re Aimster Copyright Litigation*, 334 F.3d 643, 655 (7th Cir. 2003).

22. *Chamberlain*, 381 F.3d at 1192–93, 1193–94.

23. *Id.* at 1196–97.

24. *Id.* at 1197.

25. *Id.* at 1199–1200.

26. *Id.* at 1202.

27. *Lexmark*, 387 F.3d at 522.

28. Mike Madison, "Copyright in Everyday Things," *madisonian.net*, September 1, 2004, http://madisonian.net/archives/2004/09/01/copyright-in-everyday-things/#comments.

29. Jason Schultz, "Skylink Wins! Fed. Cir. Shoots Down Chamberlain's DMCA Claim," *Lawgeek*, August 31, 2004, http://lawgeek.typepad.com/lawgeek/2004/08/skylink_wins_fe.html.

30. Adam Thierer, "DMCA Will Not Keep You from Opening Your Garage Door," *Technology Liberation Front*, September 1, 2004, http://www.techliberation.com/archives/014121.php.

31. See, for example, Joseph J. Laferrera, "Court Limits Reach of DMCA—The *Chamberlain* Case," *GesmerUpdegrove*, http://www.gesmer.com/newsletter/chamberlain.php, and Jere Webb, "Federal Circuit Provides Potentially Controversial Relief from Stringent Digital Millennium Copyright Act Provisions," *StoelRives*, http://www.stoel.com/showarticle.aspx?Show=1880, both providing favorable reviews of the DMCA rulings.

32. Ed Felten, "Skylink, and the Reverse Sony Rule," *Freedom to Tinker*, September 2, 2004, http://www.freedom-to-tinker.com/?p=673.

33. Seth Finkelstein, "*Chamberlain v. Skylink* (Garage Door Openers), DMCA, and Fair Use," *Infothought*, August 31, 2004, http://sethf.com/infothought/blog/archives/000688.html.

34. *Storage Tech. Corp. v. Custom Hardware Eng'g & Consulting, Inc.*, 421 F.3d 1307, 1318 (Fed. Cir. 2005).

35. SIIA Government Affairs, amicus brief urging the Federal Circuit to grant a rehearing of the StorageTek Decision, October 11, 2005, http://www.siia.net/govt/issue.asp?issue=IP.

36. *Storage Tech. Corp. v. Custom Hardware Eng'g & Consulting, Inc.*, 431 F.3d 1374 (Fed. Cir. 2005).

37. Ernest Miller, "Judge Asserts Pseudo Distinction to Preserve DMCA," *LawMeme*, September 3, 2004, http://research.yale.edu/lawmeme/modules .php?name=News&file=article&sid=1187.

38. Zohar Efroni, "A Momentary Lapse of Reason: Digital Copyright, the DMCA and a Dose of Common Sense," 28 *Colum. J.L. & Arts* 249, 311 (2005).

39. *Id.* at 312–13.

40. *Id.*

41. *Id.*

42. William W. Fisher III, *Promises to Keep* (Stanford, CA: Stanford University Press, 2004), 201–3.

43. See generally, Abramson, *Digital Phoenix*, where I developed this pattern as one of the dominant themes of the information age.

44. See Abramson, *Digital Phoenix*.

CHAPTER 13

1. 15 U.S.C. §§ 1–7.

2. Adam Smith, *The Wealth of Nations* (1776), book 1, chap. 10.

3. W. J. Baumol and J. A. Ordover, "Use of Antitrust to Subvert Competition," 28 *Journal of Law and Economics* 247 (1985).

4. Alan Greenspan, "Antitrust," presentation to the Antitrust Seminar of the National Association of Business Economists, September 25, 1961.

5. I presented a specific instance of this argument in chapter 5 of *Digital Phoenix: Why the Information Economy Collapsed and How It Will Rise Again* (Cambridge, MA: MIT Press, 2005), where I argued that the government's case against Microsoft in the late 1990s was necessary only because bad IP policies enabled Microsoft to deter innovation in software.

6. Richard Hofstadter, "What Happened to the Antitrust Movement?" in *The Paranoid Style in American Politics, and Other Essays* (1965; Cambridge, MA: Harvard University Press, 1996), 192–93.

7. Hofstadter, "What Happened," 234–35.

8. The few vestiges of commercial regulation that favor interests other than consumers, such as trade law, are widely recognized as elevations of interest group politics over sound economics.

9. Louis Kaplow, "The Patent-Antitrust Intersection: A Reappraisal," 97 *Harv. L. Rev.* 1813 (1984).

10. Robert H. Bork, *The Antitrust Paradox: A Policy at War with Itself* (New York: Basic Books, 1978), 10–11.

11. The Supreme Court may even have started its realignment a few years earlier. Its first hints came in a 1977 declaration that "departure[s] from the rule-of-reason standard must be based upon demonstrable economic effect rather than . . . upon formalistic line drawing." *Continental T. V. v. GTE Sylvania*, 433 U.S. 36 (1977) overruling *United States v. Arnold, Schwinn & Co.*, 388 U.S. 365 (1967).

12. See discussion in chapter 1.

13. See Bruce B. Wilson, "Remarks before the Fourth New England Antitrust Conference, Patent and Know-How License Agreements: Field of Use, Territorial, Price and Quantity Restrictions," November 6, 1970.

14. Abbott B. Lipsky, "Current Antitrust Division Views on Patent Licensing Practices," 50 *Antitrust L. J.* 515–24 (1981).

15. *Schenck v. Nortron Corp.*, 713 F.2d 782, 784, 786n3 (Fed. Cir. 1983).

16. Closer scrutiny of his comments also revealed two other interesting beliefs: Markey took particular offense at the term "patent monopoly." His offense on this point is probably well taken, for though patents do confer monopolies in the strictest sense of the term (i.e., the patentee retains exclusive control over the patent), antitrust law uses the word *monopoly* in a very specific technical sense; injections of colloquial monopolies into legal discussions are more likely to confuse than to inform. Markey recognized that, although King James saw patents as exceptions to the general rule against monopolies, this point of historical interest has no bearing on contemporary American law. See *id.*

17. See *Walker Process Equipment, Inc. v. Food Machinery & Chemical Corp.*, 382 U.S. 172 (1965).

18. See *American Hoist & Derrick Co. v. Sowa & Sons, Inc.*, 725 F.2d 1350 (Fed. Cir. 1984).

19. See *Nobelpharma AB v. Implant Innovations*, 141 F.3d 1059, 1061–63 (Fed. Cir. 1998).

20. *Id.* at 1068n5.

21. *Id.* at 1067–68.

22. James B. Gambrell, "The Evolving Interplay of Patent Rights and Antitrust Restraints in the Federal Circuit," 9 *Tex. Intell. Prop. L. J.* 137 (2001).

23. *Id.*

24. *Unitherm Food Sys. v. Swift-Eckrich, Inc.*, 375 F.3d 1341, 1355–57 (Fed. Cir. 2004).

25. *Unitherm Food Sys. v. Swift-Eckrich, Inc.*, 126 S. Ct. 980 (2006).

26. *Intergraph Corp. v. Intel Corp.*, 195 F.3d 1346, 1351 (Fed. Cir. 1999).

27. *Id.*

28. *Brown Shoe Co. v. United States*, 370 U.S. 294, 320 (1962).

29. *Intergraph*, 195 F.3d at 1354, 1358, 1362.

30. *Id.* at 1367.

31. *Id.*

32. See Albert Foer and Robert Lande, "Envisioning a Post-Chicago Antitrust," November 2, 1998, http://www.antitrustinstitute.org/archives/10.ashx.

33. Robert Pitofsky, "Challenges of the New Economy: Issues at the Intersection of Antitrust and IP," remarks at the American Antitrust Institute's conference "An Agenda for Antitrust in the 21st Century," June 15, 2000, http://www.ftc.gov/speeches/pitofsky/000615speech.htm.

34. *Id.*

35. See *CSU, L.L.C. v. Xerox Corp. (In re Independent Serv. Orgs. Antitrust Litigation)*, 203 F.3d 1322, 1327–28 (Fed. Cir. 2000).

36. See *Eastman Kodak Co. v. Image Tech. Servs.*, 504 U.S. 451 (1992).

37. See *Image Tech. Servs. v. Eastman Kodak Co.*, 125 F.3d 1195, 1201 (9th Cir., 1997).

38. *Eastman Kodak*, 504 U.S. at 495, 503 (Scalia, J., dissenting).

39. *Id.* at 479, 486.

40. See Greenspan, "Antitrust."

41. I expanded my comments in a special issue of the *Rutgers Law Journal* dedicated to papers of the 2006 AAI conference. See Bruce Abramson, "Intellectual Property and the Alleged Collapsing of Aftermarkets," *Rutgers L. J.* (forthcoming).

42. Joseph A. Schumpeter, *Capitalism, Socialism and Democracy* (1942; New York: Harper & Row, 1975), 82–86.

43. Schumpeter, *Capitalism*, 86.

44. See Abramson, "Intellectual Property."

45. I discussed these cases in considerable detail in Bruce Abramson, "Analyzing Antitrust Analysis: The Roles of Fact and Economic Theory in Summary Judgment Adjudication," 69 *Antitrust L. J.* 303 (2001).

46. *Image Tech. Servs*, 125 F.3d at 1217–18 (citations omitted).

47. Although no one challenged this appellate path at the time, the Supreme Court subsequently ruled that a trial's appellate path rests entirely upon the plaintiff's claim, not the defense. Appeals from antitrust claims raising no patent issues brought today would go to the regional circuits even if the defendant subsequently implicated matters of patent law. See *Holmes Group, Inc. v. Vornado Air Circulation Sys.*, 535 U.S. 826 (2002).

48. *CSU*, 203 F.3d at 1327–28.

49. Patrick H. Moran, "The Federal and Ninth Circuits Square Off: Refusals to Deal and the Precarious Intersection between Antitrust and Patent Law," 87 *Marq. L. Rev.* 387, 411 (2003).

50. Following fact-specific analyses to different conclusions is *precisely* the Post-Chicago approach. Justice Blackmun, for example, had noted that Kodak might be able to prove its case—but that it would have to do so by showing that the facts were consistent with its economic theories. See *Eastman Kodak*, 504 U.S. at 486. When the Ninth Circuit found that Kodak had failed to prove its case given the facts, it said nothing at all about Xerox's case given potentially different evidence. No good Post-Chicagoan would argue that case-specific facts are irrelevant to a case's outcome. Xerox may thus say less about the Federal Circuit's refusal to evolve into a Post-Chicago world than many might believe.

CHAPTER 14

1. Paul Michel, "Judicial Constellations: Guiding Principles and Navigational Aids," 54 *Case W. Res. L. Rev.* 757, 767 (2004).

2. *C.R. Bard, Inc. v. M3 Sys., Inc.*, 157 F.3d 1340, 1372 (1998).

3. *Id.* at 1373.

4. *USM Corp. v. SPS Technologies, Inc.*, 694 F.2d 505, 512 (7th Cir. 1982).

5. See discussion in chapter 5.

6. See 35 U.S.C. § 271 (d).

7. See *Indep. Ink, Inc. v. Ill. Tool Works, Inc.*, 396 F.3d 1342 (Fed. Cir. 2005).

8. See *id.*

9. *United States v. Microsoft Corp.*, 253 F.3d 34, 84 (D.C. Cir. 2001) (en banc).

10. See *Senza-Gel Corp. v. Seiffhart*, 803 F.2d 661, 662 (Fed. Cir. 1986).

11. Dan L. Burk and Mark A. Lemley, "Policy Levers in Patent Law," 89 *Va. L. Rev.* 1575, 1664 (2003).

12. "Is the Patent Misuse Doctrine Obsolete?" 110 *Harvard L. Rev.* 1922 (1997). The *Harvard Law Review*, like many but not all law journals, refuses to give law

students full credit for the work they put into preparing case notes. Rather than naming the author and describing his or her credentials, as any reputable publication should, these journals apparently feel that student contributions are necessarily less worthy than those they receive from members of the various legal faculties. This practice is unconscionable. As a reader and an author, I feel deprived by my inability to attach a name to an article and its ideas—particularly given that many Harvard Law students have become prominent scholars, attorneys, and jurists. (For the record, I have no personal beef here—I have never published an anonymous journal article.) The decision to withhold authorship information degrades the integrity of the journal—which is the business of its editorial staff—and of those who cite it—which has now become my business.

13. Other conservatives may disagree. Judge Noonan, for example, described *Lochner* as having "had a negative effect on the conditions of employment for over a quarter of a century," hardly a ringing endorsement of the ruling. John T. Noonan, *Narrowing the Nation's Power* (Berkeley: University of California Press, 2002), 13.

14. *Henry v. A. B. Dick Co.*, 224 U.S. 1, 18 (1912).

15. 15 U.S.C. § 14.

16. *Motion Picture Patents Co. v. Universal Film Mfg. Co.*, 243 U.S. 502, 519 (1917).

17. *United States v. United Shoe Machinery Co.*, 247 U.S. 32, 63–65 (1918).

18. See *Morton Salt Co. v. G. S. Suppiger Co.*, 314 U.S. 488 (1942).

19. *United States Gypsum Co. v. National Gypsum Co.*, 352 U.S. 457, 465 (1957).

20. *Mallinckrodt, Inc. v. Medipart, Inc.*, 976 F.2d 700, 703–04 (Fed. Cir. 1992) (citing *E. Bement & Sons v. National Harrow Co.*, 186 U.S. 70, 91 [1902]).

21. *Id.* at 703.

22. *Id.* at 706.

23. Robert J. Hoerner, "The Decline (and Fall) of the Patent Misuse Doctrine in the Federal Circuit," 69 *Antitrust L. J.* 669 (2002).

24. See *United States v. Glaxo Group, Ltd.*, 410 U.S. 52 (1973)

25. I presented this argument in detail in chapter 5 of *Digital Phoenix: Why the Information Economy Collapsed and How It Will Rise Again* (Cambridge, MA: MIT Press, 2005).

26. Joe Potenza, Phillip Bennett, and Christopher Roth, "Patent Misuse—The Critical Balance: A Patent Lawyer's View," 15 *Fed. Cir. B.J.* 69 (2005/06).

27. See International Trade Commission, *In re Certain Recordable Compact Discs & Rewritable Compact Discs*, Inv. no. 337-TA-474, March 25, 2004.

28. *U.S. Philips Corp. v. ITC*, 424 F.3d 1179, 1190–92 (Fed. Cir. 2005).

29. *Id.*

30. See *Rambus, Inc. v. Infineon Techs. AG*, 164 F.Supp.2d 743 (E.D. Va. 2001).

31. *Rambus, Inc. v. Infineon Techs. AG*, 318 F.3d 1081, 1098–1102 (Fed. Cir. 2003).

32. *Id.*

33. *Id.* at 1107 (Prost, J., dissenting).

34. *Id.* at 1118 (Prost, J., dissenting).

35. *In the Matter of Rambus, Inc.*, Federal Trade Commission Docket No. 9302, opinion of the Commission, public record version, August 3, 2006, at 3–5.

36. Don Clark, "FTC Rules against Rambus in Memory-Chip Patent Case," *Wall Street Journal*, August 3, 2006.

CHAPTER 15

1. See, for example, *Allergan, Inc. v. Alcon Labs.*, 324 F.3d 1322 (Fed. Cir. 2003); *Merck KGaA v. Integra Lifesciences I, Ltd.*, 545 U.S. 193 (2005).

2. 28 U.S.C. § 1295(a)(4)(B).

3. See, for example, *Fannie Mae v. United States*, 2006 U.S. App. LEXIS 28057 (Fed. Cir. 2006); *Coltec Indus. v. United States*, 454 F.3d 1340 (Fed. Cir. 2006).

4. See, for example, *Empire Energy Mgmt. Sys. v. Roche*, 362 F.3d 1343 (Fed. Cir. 2004); *West v. All State Boiler*, 146 F.3d 1368 (Fed. Cir. 1998); *Night Vision Corp. v. United States*, 2006 U.S. App. LEXIS 28958 (Fed. Cir. 2006).

5. See, for example, *Barron Bancshares, Inc. v. United States*, 366 F.3d 1360 (Fed. Cir. 2004); *United States v. Winstar Corp.*, 518 U.S. 839 (1996).

6. See, for example, *Navajo Nation v. United States*, 347 F.3d 1327 (Fed. Cir. 2003).

7. H. Robert Mayer, foreword to Kristin L. Yohannon, ed., *The United States Court of Appeals for the Federal Circuit: A History, 1990–2002* (Washington, DC: Court of Appeals for the Federal Circuit, 2004), xxi–xxii.

8. Karl Marx and Friedrich Engels, *Manifesto of the Communist Party* (1848; English ed., 1888), chap. 1; reprinted in *The Marx-Engels Reader*, ed. Robert Tucker (New York: W. W. Norton, 1978), 475–78.

9. Some might argue that rampant speculation producing "bubbles" in markets represent the same sort of viral phenomenon. See, for example, Robert Shiller, *Irrational Exuberance* (Princeton, NJ: Princeton University Press, 2000).

10. See Joseph A. Schumpeter, *Capitalism, Socialism and Democracy* (1942; reprint, New York: Harper & Row, 1975).

11. See William J. Baumol, *The Free Market Innovation Machine* (Princeton, NJ: Princeton University Press, 2002).

12. See *Unitherm Food Sys. v. Swift-Eckrich, Inc.*, 375 F.3d 1341, 1355–57 (Fed. Cir. 2004).

13. See *Indep. Ink, Inc. v. Ill. Tool Works, Inc.*, 396 F.3d 1342 (Fed. Cir. 2005).

14. See *State Street Bank & Trust Co. v. Signature Financial Group, Inc.*, 149 F.3d 1368 (Fed. Cir. 1998).

15. *Zoltek Corp. v. United States*, 442 F.3d 1345, 1352 (Fed. Cir. 2006).

16. See Dan L. Burk and Mark A. Lemley, "Policy Levers in Patent Law," 89 *Va. L. Rev.* 1575, 1577 (2003).

17. See Adam B. Jaffe and Josh Lerner, *Innovation and Its Discontents: How Our Broken Patent System Is Endangering Innovation and Progress, and What to Do about It* (Princeton, NJ: Princeton University Press, 2004).

18. See Rochelle Cooper Dreyfuss, "The Federal Circuit: A Continuing Experiment in Specialization," 54 *Case W. Res. L. Rev.* 769, 770–71 (2004).

19. See J. Michael Finger and Julio J. Nogués, eds., *Safeguards and Antidumping in Latin American Trade Liberalization* (Washington, DC: World Bank, 2006), 25–26.

20. See Dan L. Burk and Mark A. Lemley, "Is Patent Law Technology-Specific?" 17 *Berkeley Tech. L. J.* 1155, 1155–57 (2002).

21. See R. Polk Wagner, "Of Patents and Path-Dependency: A Comment on Burk and Lemley," 18 *Berkeley Tech. L. J.* 1341, 1342–45 (2003).

Index

patents and, 5–8, 11–13, 18, 34, 45,
46–49, 119, 139–40, 225–26, 291–92,
313–14, 339, 344; policies and, 6–13,
24, 32–36, 122; Reagan and, 8–13,
290–92, 301, 305, 311–12, 325, 327,
333, 343, 344; technology and,
265–68, 275, 283–85, 348; trade and,
6, 32, 34–36, 39–40, 46–47, 143–70,
343, 349, 366n17; trade, policies
and, 32, 35–36, 146–54, 162–64,
172–73, 350–54. *See also* Chicago
School economics; free markets;
information economy
Edward I, King (of England), 189–91,
193
Efroni, Zohar, 280–83
EIA. *See* Electronic Industries
Association
Electronic Industries Association
(EIA), 329–30
Eleventh Amendment, 219–25, 228–29,
238, 240, 245
Elizabeth II, Queen (of England), 190
Elizabeth I, Queen (of England), 40,
264
*El-Shifa Pharm. Indus Co. v. United
States*, 251, 253–54
Emergency Petroleum Allocation Act
of 1973, 30
eminent domain, 134, 229–30, 235–36,
242
employment, 4; *Lochner v. New York*
and, 319–20, 378n13; trade and, 149,
151. *See also* unemployment;
workers, displaced
Employment Div. v. Smith, 216–17
en banc sessions, 27–28, 53, 105; for
Amgen, 71; for doctrine of
equivalents, 361m51; in *Markman*,
57; for *Nobelpharma*, 295–96; for
NTP v. Research in Motion, 113;
Phillips and., 68; for StorageTek, 279
Energy Policy and Conservation Act,
30
England: manufacturing in, 143–45;
patents in, 40–41, 49; sovereign
immunity in, 189–91, 207, 238–39;

Statute of Anne and, 263–65, 283;
Statute of Monopolies and, 40–41,
143, 264; wine and, 145, 147, 161
Enlightenment, 264, 265
entrepreneurs, 10, 39, 40, 144, 343–44,
354
environmental standards, labor, trade
and, 148–49
Eon Labs, 65–67
equity: injunctions and, 124;
SmithKline Beecham and, 97–100, 103
equivalents, doctrine of, 80–81, 86–87,
89, 361n51
ethanol, Brazilian sugar *v.* domestic
corn, 146–47
Euro Clips, 155–56
evidence: ambiguity and, 62–63;
changing, position flipped in light
of, 132; extrinsic, 62–64;
inconsistence with facts,
overturning and, 26, 51–52;
intrinsic, 62–65, 67–69; patent
lawsuits and, 58–59, 62–64
evidentiary hearing, 156, 365n33
exclusivity: copyrights and, 264, 267,
269; patents and, 7, 41, 47, 49, 72,
93–94, 103–4, 109, 120, 138, 183–84,
186, 262, 289–90, 294–95, 314
experimental use: infringement and,
362n20; inherent anticipation and,
105–6; patent law and, 100–102,
105–6, 228, 362n20, 372n34; public
use *v.*, 100–102, 362n20
exports, imports and, 4, 143–47, 150,
157–65, 167–68, 170, 351, 368n3. *See
also* countervailing

facts: evidence inconsistence with,
overturning and, 26, 51–52; law
and, 20–21, 24, 56–62, 66, 358n10;
specific analysis, 310–11, 317,
378n50. *See also* trier of fact
fairness, 148, 171, 188
fair trade, 148–51, 366n10
fair traders, 148
fair use, copyrights and, 265, 268–69,
272, 275–78, 281

banc session for, 113; government and, 114, 363n48; injunction with, 110, 112, 114; royalties with, 110, 111, 114; summary judgment with, 110; territoriality and, 108, 110, 113, 114, 179, 372n42

Nuzum, Janet, 161

obviousness, 78, 79–80; commercial value of patents and, 126; FTC on, 119; policy levers and, 126–33; prior art and, 121, 131. *See also* nonobviousness

O'Connor, Sandra Day, 238

OEMs. *See* original equipment manufacturers

Office for Improvements in the Administration of Justice (OIAJ), 15–17

OIAJ. *See* Office for Improvements in the Administration of Justice

O'Malley, Kathleen, 87–88

one-click shopping, 79

opinions: appellate judges', 25, 36; nonprecedential/unpublished, 131, 337; study of, on claim construction, 64, 360n15. *See also* *specific judges*

optimality, 82–84, 361n61

Ordover, Janusz, 288–89

original equipment manufacturers (OEMs), 302–3, 308, 316

originalism, 60, 242–43, 320

paroxetine, 92–107, 130, 315, 362n6

"Paroxetine Polymorphism" (Curzons), 93

patent(s): on algorithms, 12, 79, 124–25; annual maintenance fee on, 138; antitrust laws and, 125, 133, 259, 287–312, 314–19, 321, 323–27, 333, 344–45, 348, 353, 377n47; applications, 119, 330, 365n33; canceled/invalidated, 73, 78, 96, 98, 101–2, 112, 119, 326; Congress on, 41, 42, 45–46, 49, 53, 86–89, 119, 124–26, 128–30, 132, 182–84, 221–24,

260, 316; consumers and, 31, 35, 40, 94, 110–11; contestation of, 134, 138; as contracts, 58, 323; copyrights and, 134, 180, 183, 186, 247, 262, 270, 274, 283–85, 333, 361n59; deadweight, 138; deeds and titles compared to, 44, 45; definition/ meaning of, 42, 51, 58, 72; denial of, 119; Domestic Policy Review and, 7–8, 11–13, 14–15, 17; economy and, 5–8, 11–13, 18, 34, 45, 46–49, 119, 139–40, 225–26, 291–92, 313–14, 339, 344; examiners, 49–50, 72–74, 77, 81, 112, 364n8; exclusivity and, 7, 41, 47, 49, 72, 93–94, 103–4, 109, 120, 138, 183–84, 186, 262, 289–90, 294–95, 314; FDA and, 12, 183–84, 336; foreign *v.* U.S., 78, 93, 108, 182–86, 233–34, 372n42; forum shopping and, 8, 14–15, 84; government and, 114, 363n48; ineligibility of, 78; innovation and, 5–8, 12, 18, 19, 31, 36, 37, 39–41, 43, 49, 52, 72, 313, 343, 349, 354; IP and, 42–43, 49; jurisdiction and, 30–31, 247, 259–62; as legal documents, 51–52, 57–59, 61, 72, 75; licenses, 92–93, 113, 291–92; life of, 55, 183–84, 186, 293, 314; missing filing deadlines for, 81, 96, 99–100; misuse, 313–34, 345, 353; monopolies and, 40–41, 94, 179, 184, 287, 289–95, 299, 309, 315–19, 321–22, 345, 376n16; 196, 92, 93–94; Pierce, of 1621, 39; pooling, 326–28; preliminary rejections of, 112; pro- patent *v.* "bad patent," 119–20; as property, 35, 44–46, 122–24, 133–39, 179, 223–24, 230, 233–37, 293, 298, 305, 350, 352; prosecution, 49–50, 117–18, 126; public opinion on, 41–42; reexamination of, 72–74, 111, 112–14; as regulation, 122–24, 133–34, 136, 138–39, 293, 298, 305, 320; reissue of, 72, 73, 111; 723, 93–94, 96, 99–104; single use of, 322–23; sovereign immunity and,

About the Author

Bruce D. Abramson received his Ph.D. from Columbia and his J.D. from Georgetown. He is the President of Informationism, Inc., a San Francisco-based consultancy that helps an international clientele understand the law, the policies, the economics, and the strategic uses of intellectual property. He has served as a member of the Computer Science faculty at the University of Southern California and as a law clerk at the Court of Appeals for the Federal Circuit. He is the author of *Digital Phoenix: Why the Information Economy Collapsed and How It Will Rise Again* (MIT Press, 2005). His blog, *The Informationist*, (www.theinformationist.com), contains his musings on IP, tech policy, and numerous other issues.